Howard Risher
Charles Fay
Editors

The Performance Imperative

The Performance Imperative

Strategies for Enhancing Workforce Effectiveness

Jossey-Bass Publishers • San Francisco

Substantial discounts on bulk quantities of Jossey-Bass books are available to corporations, professional associations, and other organizations. For details and discount information, contact the special sales department at Jossey-Bass Inc., Publishers. (415) 433–1740; Fax (800) 605–2665.

For sales outside the United States, please contact your local Paramount Publishing International Office.

TCF Manufactured in the United States of America on Lyons Falls Pathfinder Tradebook. This paper is acid-free and 100 percent totally chlorine-free.

Library of Congress Cataloging-in-Publication Data

The performance imperative : strategies for enhancing workforce effectiveness / Howard Risher, Charles Fay, editors. — 1st ed.
    p. cm. — (The Jossey-Bass management series)
    Includes index.
    ISBN 0-7879-0085-0
    1. Industrial productivity. 2. Industrial management. 3. Labor productivity. I. Risher, Howard II. Fay, Charles
III. Series.
HD56.P455   1995
658.3'14—dc20   95-8242

FIRST EDITION
HB Printing   10 9 8 7 6 5 4 3 2 1

The Jossey-Bass Management Series

Contents

*To my wife, Mary, who has
had to put up with all too
many evenings when
I was busy writing.*
H. R.

To J., who knows why.
C. F.

Preface

The Performance Imperative was developed to bring together expertise from the several professional fields interested in workforce performance. Workforce productivity, interpreted in the broadest sense, has become a survival issue for many organizations. Moreover, there is increasing recognition that individuals who have contact with customers, suppliers, and other outside organizations can have a significant impact on financial results and on their organization's image in the marketplace. This fact transcends industry boundaries and is equally important to health care providers confronted by the austerity of proposed reform and to government officials as voters demand improved performance along with reduced spending.

From a different perspective, the importance of increased productivity is often cited as the key to gaining competitive advantage in world markets. Both technology and financial resources are available to competitors, making employees and their performance the only sustainable source of competitive advantage. It has been popular for a decade or more to cite employees as a valuable asset, but for the first time this theme is influencing the policies and practices that govern both the organization and management of work and worker performance.

Realistically, no single field has the know-how to generate the dramatic increases in productivity realized by a mushrooming number of companies. The primary impetus for change came with quality management initiatives, starting in the late 1980s. Quality advocates highlighted the importance of empowerment and the employee's need to be responsive to customers, both internal and external. Productivity increases were also espoused by the organizations and people who migrated to reengineering. New concepts, such as the virtual corporation, were introduced by organizational theorists. Supporting all these changes was a revolution in the field of human resource management.

A key issue is the replacement of the traditional "command and control" model that has dominated organization thinking since the turn of the twentieth century. During that era, Frederick W. Taylor developed his principles of scientific management, principles that evolved into the field of industrial engineering and also became the foundation of organizational theory. These principles served organizations well for decades, but today's workers are different from the immigrants from the American farm or from Europe who made up the labor force of the late nineteenth century. Scientific management no longer "works"; it has become necessary to develop principles for managing work that fit current organizations and the contemporary labor force.

Overview of the Contents

Our objective as editors was to bring together experts whose contributions have been recognized in their individual fields. The chapters are not intended to provide comprehensive coverage of the subjects. Each chapter could effectively be developed into a separate book. In fact, a number of the contributors have offered more extensive coverage of their subjects in works of their own.

The introductory chapter, by Howard Risher and Charles Fay, discusses the problems that organizations face and the various responses offered by the book's contributors.

Part One provides an overview of the changes affecting organizations and work management practices. Chapter Two, by Charles Fay, focuses on key environmental changes facing U.S. corporations. The diverse fields from which his study is drawn serves to clarify why organizations have trouble being fully responsive to their external environments. Edward E. Lawler III, the author of Chapter Three, shifts to the emerging ideas that affect the way workers are managed. One of the primary alternatives is the design of organizational systems based on the capabilities of individual workers. In Chapter Four, Jennifer Jarratt and Joseph F. Coates discuss the evolving role of the human resource function in the world of work. They cite four people-centered management initiatives that carve out a larger and more prominent role for the human resource function (although not necessarily for the traditional human resource department).

Part Two surveys emerging approaches to organization design. In Chapter Five, N. Fredric Crandall and Marc J. Wallace, Jr., compare the traditional organizational model with the high-performance or team-based approach to organizing, as well as with the newer virtual organization concept. Each of these three concepts has significantly different implications for staffing and managing the workplace. Alfred J. Walker focuses in Chapter Six on the potential of reengineering to improve business processes. Reengineering typically results in the introduction of work organizations and procedures that trigger dramatic changes in the way work is organized. Chapter Seven, by Stuart S. Winby, looks at the kinds of organizations that are beginning to emerge and that we can expect to see in the future. Winby introduced the concept of the "value chain process," which shifts the focus of organization planning from the vertical to the horizontal.

Part Three examines the importance of top management's leadership to enhanced organization performance. Irvine O. Hockaday, Jr., CEO of Hallmark Cards and author of Chapter Eight, describes his thinking in developing a new vision for his company. He argues that one of the overriding considerations in planning a work management strategy is the importance of leadership and the commitment by senior executives to the initiative and to its underlying philosophy. In Chapter Nine, Richard Whiteley summarizes research on the behaviors that characterize leaders in companies that are customer-driven. To transform an organization, its leaders have to articulate and reinforce their vision of the future. Chapter Ten, by Philip B. Crosby, discusses the role of leaders in creating corporate culture and in establishing the priority commitments that drive performance. He argues that true quality is not a series of techniques and procedures but rather a way of managing that depends on top management leadership.

Part Four develops three themes that are central to the creation of what are often referred to as high-performance organizations. In Chapter Eleven, Craig Eric Schneier summarizes his research findings on the way performance measurement, management, and appraisal practices in high-performing organizations differ from those in more traditional, less successful organizations. High-performing firms view performance management as a key business tool for use by all managers and supervisors. Chapter Twelve, by Susan Albers Mohrman, discusses the issues relevant to taking full advantage of the team concept. Experience with teams has shown repeatedly that it is possible to achieve surprisingly high levels of performance. Then, in Chapter Thirteen, Carl G. Thor covers the key issues involved in developing and using performance measurement data. There is an old saying, "What gets measured gets done." Thor sets forth a framework for developing a performance measurement strategy.

Part Five covers the new philosophies and practices governing employee rewards. In Chapter Fourteen, Howard Risher discusses the new model for salary management. After operating on basically the same program concepts since the end of World War II, organizations are reconsidering the fundamental propositions of their base-pay programs, with a new emphasis on the responsibility of managers and supervisors for managing the pay of their subordinates. In Chapter Fifteen, Richard W. Beatty, B. Nicholas Dimitroff, and Dennis J. O'Neill examine a new rationale for salary increases. The new premise is that workers should be paid for what they can do, their skills and competencies, rather than last year's performance. Chapter Sixteen, by John G. Belcher, Jr., provides an overview of the thinking involved in designing gain-sharing and related group incentive programs. These plans have been shown to be powerful incentives for improved performance. In Chapter Seventeen, Jerry L. McAdams completes the coverage of reward systems with a discussion of low-cost, high-impact awards. These rewards can include almost anything that has value to an employee or that serves as a basis for public recognition of an employee's contribution. When effectively linked to employee accomplishments, low-cost, high-impact rewards can be an important tool to improve employee performance.

Part Six summarizes federal law governing the involvement of workers in operational decisions. Chapter Eighteen, by James R. Redeker and Daniel P. O'Meara, discusses the implications of the recent National Labor Relations Board decision involving Electromation, Inc., that effectively limits employee participation. In Chapter Nineteen, Lynn R. Williams, recently retired president of the United Steelworkers Union, sets forth his view of worker participation and describes recently negotiated changes in labor contracts that provide for increased participation.

Part Seven synthesizes what organizations must do if they are to remain competitive. Chapter Twenty, by Howard Risher and Charles Fay, summarizes the findings presented in *The Performance Imperative* and offers a blueprint for maintaining competitive advantage through appropriate management of employees.

April 1995

Howard Risher
Conshohocken, Pennsylvania

Charles Fay
New Brunswick, New Jersey

The Editors

Howard Risher is a principal in the consulting firm of Godwins Booke & Dickenson in Conshohocken (near Philadelphia). He received his B.A. degree (1965) in psychology from the Pennsylvania State University and both his M.B.A. degree (1968) in human resource management and his Ph.D. degree (1972) in labor relations and economics from the Wharton School, University of Pennsylvania.

Risher has twenty-five years of experience in the areas of workforce management, reward system design, and employee research. Before joining his current firm, he managed consulting practices for two other international consulting firms. He has served as a consultant to many major corporations and hospitals, to federal and state government agencies, and to colleges and universities.

Risher is a member of several professional associations and serves as an instructor for certification in human resource management. He has authored or coauthored more than twenty articles and book chapters on human resource topics.

Charles Fay is associate professor of human resource management at the School of Management and Labor Relations, Rutgers University. He received his B.A. degree (1961) in English and history from New York University, his M.B.A. degree (1963) from Columbia Graduate School of Business, and his Ph.D. degree (1979) in organization and management theory from the University of Washington.

Fay conducts research focused on compensation, performance

appraisal, and the use of expert systems and other human resource decision support systems. His research results have been presented in many journals. He is the coauthor of several books, including *Compensation Theory and Practice, The Compensation Sourcebook,* and *Research-Based Decisions.* He is editor of *Human Resource Planning* and serves on the board of directors and the research committee of the Human Resource Planning Society.

Fay is a certified compensation professional and teaches in the American Compensation Association Certification Program. He was previously chair of the association's research committee. He is also a member of the Federal Salary Council, a presidential council that advises the federal pay agent on salary issues concerning General Schedule employees. He consults with a variety of organizations in the area of performance management, compensation systems, and human resource information systems.

The Contributors

Richard W. Beatty is professor of human resource management in the School of Management and Labor Relations, Rutgers University. He received his Ph.D. degree in human resources and organization behavior from Washington University. Beatty has consulted to a variety of organizations, including A&P, ARCO, Bell Laboratories, Du Pont, Honda, IBM, NutraSweet, Pacific Telesis, and Whirlpool. He is past chair of the Personnel/Human Resource Division of the Academy of Management and president of the SHRM Foundation. His research has been published in many journals, including the *Academy of Management Journal*, the *Journal of Applied Psychology*, and the *Sloan Management Review*. His books include *Personnel Administration: An Experiential Skill-Building Approach*, *Performance Appraisal*, and *The Compensation Sourcebook*.

John G. Belcher, Jr., is the founder of J. G. Belcher Associates, a management consulting firm specializing in alternative compensation systems and organizational change initiatives. He has served over two hundred clients in a wide variety of manufacturing and service industries in the United States, Canada, Venezuela, Colombia, Italy, Singapore, and Saudi Arabia. He previously served as a vice president of the American Productivity and Quality Center and is currently an adjunct consultant to the center. He has also been operations manager for a steel-fabricating subsidiary of Ogden Corporation and director of operations analysis for Ogden's Metals Group. Belcher's background also includes financial management experience with United Technologies Corporation and the Ford

Motor Company. He received his M.B.A. degree from the University of Michigan and is the author of *Gain Sharing* and *Productivity Plus*.

Joseph F. Coates is president of J. F. Coates, Inc., and adjunct professor at George Washington University, where he teaches graduate courses on technology and on the future. He received his M.S. degree (1953) in organic chemistry from the Pennsylvania State University in organic chemistry and holds an honorary degree from Claremont Graduate School. His principal current work is the study of the future. He has produced more than seventy studies, including several on the future of the workforce. His other areas of interest are technology assessment, scientific and technological innovation, strategic planning, and issues management. In 1985, Coates and his associates received the Rose-Hulman Award from the International Association for Impact Assessment. Coates is coauthor of *What Futurists Believe* and *Issues Management: How You Can Plan, Organize, and Manage for the Future*.

N. Fredric Crandall is a founding partner of the Center for Workforce Effectiveness, Inc. He serves as a management consultant specializing in reward systems and organizational change management. He has extensive consulting experience in strategic planning, executive and general compensation, job evaluation, salary administration, incentive plans, and human resource and organization effectiveness. He received his Ph.D. degree from the University of Minnesota. He has served as associate professor of organizational behavior and administration at the Cox School of Business, Southern Methodist University, and is past president of the ASPA Foundation's board of directors. He has also been an instructor and course developer for the American Compensation Association. Crandall is coauthor of *Administering Human Resources*, as well as numerous articles on human resource planning and management.

Philip B. Crosby's first career began with the U.S. Navy during World War II. He moved on to college and was then called back to the Navy for the Korean Conflict. His second career spanned twenty-seven years as a quality management professional. He started on an assembly line and progressed to being corporate vice president of ITT. He was also quality manager for Martin Marietta for eight years. It was at Martin, in 1961, that he came up with the concept of zero defects and wrote his first book, *Cutting the Cost of Quality*. In 1979, a third career began when he published *Quality Is Free*, which became an instant best-seller. He founded Philip Crosby Associates, Inc., now the largest quality management consulting firm in the world. While running that company, he also found time to write seven books and dozens of articles expressing his philosophy of business management. In 1991, he retired from Philip Crosby Associates and, with his daughter Phylis as CEO, founded Career IV, Inc. He concentrates now on writing and speaking. In addition, he is featured in a weekly commentary, "On Improvement," on USA News's *First Business* television program. His newest book, *Completeness: Quality for the 21st Century*, reflects his concern to help management learn how to make employees, suppliers, and customers successful.

B. Nicholas Dimitroff has been designing and implementing performance management, organizational development, total quality management, integrated human resource, and change management systems for more than two decades. He has held senior human resource and TQM executive positions with Nissan, Philips, Unisys, and Gould, where he has acted as a change agent in senior management teams devoted to market-driven organizational and culture transformation. As a consultant, Dimitroff has worked extensively with clients to improve marketing focus, sales capability, leadership, and strategic planning. He has also designed and delivered numerous cross-cultural sensitivity programs internationally.

Irvine O. Hockaday, Jr., is president and CEO of Hallmark Cards, Inc., the world's largest publisher of greeting cards and related products. He also serves as chairman and chief executive officer of Hallmark's Personal Communications Group, the company's principal business. Prior to joining the corporation in 1983, Hockaday served as president and CEO of Kansas City Southern Industries, Inc., a diversified New York Stock Exchange company. He is currently a director of the Ford Motor Company; Dow Jones, Inc.; and the Continental Corporation. Hockaday has served as chairman of the board of the Tenth District Federal Reserve Bank, the Civic Council of Greater Kansas City, and the Midwest Research Institute. He received his J.D. degree (1961) from the University of Michigan Law School. Prior to joining Kansas City Southern Industries in 1968, he practiced law in Kansas City with the firm of Lathrop, Koontz, Righter, Clagett & Norquist.

Jennifer Jarratt is vice president of Coates & Jarratt, Inc., a consulting firm that studies aspects of long-range planning and social and technological change for a variety of organizations. With Joseph F. Coates, she is coauthor of *The Future at Work* (a newsletter on emerging management issues in human resources) and *Future Work* (1990, also with J. B. Mahaffie), as well as *Managing Your Future as an Association* (1994), published with the ASAE Foundation. She received her M.A. degree in studies of the future from the University of Clear Lake and was a visiting faculty member there in 1990–91. She has participated in or been responsible for more than twenty-seven futures projects with Coates & Jarratt, several of them on the future of human resource management and the future of work.

Edward E. Lawler III is professor of management and organization in the business school at the University of Southern California and founding director of the Center for Effective Organizations. He received his Ph.D. degree (1964) in psychology from the

University of California, Berkeley. He has consulted with more than one hundred organizations and four national governments on employee involvement, organizational change, and compensation and has been honored as a top contributor to the fields of organization development, organizational behavior, and compensation. He is the author of more than two hundred articles and twenty-two books, and his works have been translated into seven languages. His books include *High-Involvement Management* (1986), *Strategic Pay* (1990), and *The Ultimate Advantage* (1992). He is coauthor of *Employee Involvement and Total Quality Management: Practices and Results in Fortune 1000 Companies* (1992) and *Organizing for the Future: The New Logic for Managing Complex Organizations* (1993).

Jerry L. McAdams is vice president for performance improvement resources at Maritz, Inc., where he has worked with many organizations to design and install performance-based reward systems such as gain-sharing, objective-based, cost reduction, and sales incentive plans for sales and marketing, manufacturing, health care, and service groups. Prior to joining Maritz in 1973, he was with General Electric for eleven years, working in the United States and Europe. He has partnered with the American Productivity and Quality Center since 1981 on reward systems and their impact on productivity, quality, and human performance. He also served as a member of the Reward Systems Committee of the White House Conference on Productivity. In 1991, he became director of the Consortium for Alternative Rewards Strategies Research (CARS), a national database for the study of alternative reward plans and their supportive human resource practices. He is coauthor of three studies on alternative reward systems: *People, Productivity and Pay*; *Capitalizing on Human Assets*; and *Organizational Performance and Rewards*.

Susan Albers Mohrman is senior research scientist at the Center for Effective Organizations. She received her Ph.D. degree (1978) in organizational behavior from Northwestern University. Mohrman has served on the faculty of the organizational behavior department of the business school of the University of Southern California. Her research focuses on innovations in human resource management, organizational change, and organizational design processes. She has consulted with a variety of organizations introducing employee involvement programs and labor-management cooperative projects, as well as with organizations that are redesigning structures and systems. Her publications deal with employee participation, quality of work life, self-designing processes in organizations, high-technology management, and the production of research useful to organizations. Mohrman is coauthor of *Self-Designing Organizations: Learning How to Create High Performance* (1989) and *Large-Scale Organizational Change* (1989, with A. M. Mohrman, Jr., G. E. Ledford, Jr., T. G. Cummings, and E. E. Lawler III).

Daniel P. O'Meara is an attorney in Wolf, Block, Schorr and Solis-Cohen's Labor and Employee Relations Department. He is author of *Protecting the Growing Number of Older Workers: The Age Discrimination in Employment Act* (1989) and has been featured as a legal expert on several television shows.

Dennis J. O'Neill is corporate vice president of human resources at New York Life. He received his Ed.D degree from Columbia University. O'Neill's background includes human resource consulting, domestically and internationally. He currently works with external consultants on work and family issues, assessment, feedback, executive competencies, research, and WorkOut!

James R. Redeker is chairman of Wolf, Block, Schoor and Solis-Cohen's Labor Law and Employee Relations Department. He received his J.D. degree from the University of Pennsylvania School of Law. He represents both unionized and nonunionized companies in their personnel and labor relations, representing them before enforcement agencies as well as the courts. He has served as special council to General Electric, AT&T, Northwest Airlines, Exxon, Georgia Power, Amoco Oil, Shell Oil, and other national companies to assist in implementing unusual personnel systems and resolving complex culture change issues. In addition, he has appeared on radio and television as a guest commentator and since 1986 has been a regular guest lecturer at the Wharton School. He is the creator of Workplace Due Process, an employer self-development program for the creation of personnel programs designed to insulate employers from union organization, wrongful discharge liability, and equal employment claims while building employee responsibility and commitment to the enterprise. He is the author of four books: *Strategies for Bargaining Fringe Benefits*, *How to Draft Contracts to Avoid Disputes*, *Discipline: Policies and Procedures*, and *Employee Discipline: Policies and Practices*.

Craig Eric Schneier heads his own management consulting firm in Princeton, New Jersey, and is adjunct professor in the School of Business at Columbia University. He was managing principal and national director for human resource and organization effectiveness practice for Sibson & Company, Inc., an international consulting firm, and was vice president of consulting services at Organizational Dynamics, Inc., a consulting and training company. Schneier works with clients in the areas of performance measurement and management, culture change, work process improvement, and human resource management.

Carl G. Thor is president of JarrettThor International, a consulting firm specializing in quality and productivity improvement. He concentrates on developing performance measurement, benchmarking, and gain-sharing programs around the world. Thor spent fifteen years with the American Productivity and Quality Center in Houston, where he was president and vice chairman. While there, he led the development of popular seminars, gave many speeches, and was a consultant to dozens of private and public organizations. Earlier in his career, he held positions with Anderson, Clayton & Co. and with Exxon. He is the author of *Measures of Success* (1994) and coauthor of *Handbook for Productivity Measurement and Improvement* (1993).

Alfred J. Walker is a principal with Towers Perrin, serving as national practice leader for human resources information management, which includes the human resource systems and human resource reengineering areas. Before joining Towers Perrin in 1984, he directed the human resource systems work at AT&T for more than seventeen years. Walker is a founder and former board member of the Human Resource Systems Professionals and the Human Resource Planning Society and was the 1994 winner of the Summit Award, given by the former society for lifetime achievement in the human resource systems field. He is the author of *HRIS Development* (1982) and *Handbook of HRIS: Reshaping the HR Function with Technology* (1994). Walker received his M.B.A. degree in economics and has done postgraduate work in operations research.

Marc J. Wallace, Jr., is a partner of the Center for Workforce Effectiveness, Inc. Prior to founding the center in 1992, he was professor and Ashland Oil Fellow in the Department of Management, University of Kentucky. He received his Ph.D. degree in industrial relations from the University of Minnesota. His research findings have been published in more than sixty articles and papers in such periodicals as the *Journal of Applied Psychology, Industrial Relations, Compensation and Benefits Review, Decision Sciences,* and the *Journal of Vocational Behavior.* He has coauthored nine books on management and human resources and has served as an expert witness before the federal judiciary and as a special consultant to the U.S. Equal Employment Opportunity Commission on matters regarding fair employment practices. He has served on the board of the ASPA Foundation and was the 1985–86 chair of the Personnel and

Human Resources Division of the Academy of Management. Wallace has been an instructor and course developer for the American Compensation Association.

Richard Whiteley is vice chairman and founder of the Forum Corporation, an international training and consulting firm based in Boston. Forum helps companies become customer-driven and specializes in the areas of quality and service, management and leadership, and sales productivity. Whiteley is the author of *The Customer-Driven Company*, which was named one of the four best business books of the year by *Fortune* magazine. He has worked with such organizations as General Electric, Xerox, Motorola, 3M, Harris Bank, Thomas Cook, and Citibank. He has taught in the M.B.A. program at Northeastern University and has been a guest lecturer at the Massachusetts Institute of Technology, the University of Southern California, and other universities. Whiteley's appearances on television and radio keep him very busy as a public speaker.

Lynn R. Williams recently retired as international president of the United Steelworkers of America. A Canadian, he was educated at McMaster University. He joined the Steelworkers in Toronto in 1947, served as staff representative from 1956 to 1957, and was assistant director of District Six from 1963 to 1973 and director from 1973 to 1977. He became international secretary in 1977 and served in that position until he became international president in 1983. He has also served on the executive committee of the AFL-CIO, as a director of the American Arbitration Association, and as a member of the board of directors of the African-American Labor Center, the Committee for National Health Insurance, and the Work in America Institute.

Stuart S. Winby is director of product process change management at Hewlett-Packard Company, where his responsibilities include strategic planning and modeling, organization and business process design, and systems analysis and modeling programs. He was vice president for advisory services and research at the American Productivity and Quality Center, where he was responsible for organizational design and management, productivity management, and work innovations research and application. Winby has consulted in a wide variety of manufacturing and service industries in the United States, Canada, Mexico, Iceland, England, Germany, Italy, Singapore, and Australia. His consulting assignments have included companies in the oil, gas, steel, automotive, aluminum, chemicals, airline, financial, aerospace, and electronics industries. Winby received his M.S. degree from San Jose State University in California. His current interests are the integration of people, work, and technology in the redesign of value chain processes to improve business performance.

The Performance Imperative

Chapter One

Raising the Bar: Strategies for Achieving High Performance

Howard Risher, Charles Fay

American industry is on the verge of a second revolution. After relying on the principles of scientific management for almost a century, a rapidly increasing number of employers are searching for and experimenting with new approaches for the organization and management of work. Their primary objective is simple: to enhance productivity (Case, 1993; Kiechel, 1993).

The results of this early experience have not been consistent; in some organizations, the changes have been disruptive to the employer-employee relationship. However, there is a growing body of evidence that significant productivity increases—as much as 30 to 40 percent—are possible. The work management changes that precede what can only be described as awesome productivity increases are best viewed as the reengineering of the management concepts that have been almost universal in their acceptance for decades.

The concern with productivity is long-standing but has mushroomed in the past few years as world competition and recession have forced companies to find ways to cut costs. There are only two work management strategies to accomplish this: to reduce staff and compel the remaining workers to increase their workload or to encourage employees to find or develop innovative ways to improve the quality or quantity of their output. To be sure, the former is a quicker way to generate needed savings, but it can also trigger employee animosity and have adverse long-term consequences. The development of strategies to generate innovative and more productive ways of working is the theme of this book. Although that is not as easy as cutting staff, it is a more positive approach that represents a "win-win" deal for the company and employees alike.

Employee productivity has traditionally been defined as a quantity issue, essentially limited to blue-collar operations, where it has always been a concern. With the shift from manufacturing to services, thinking also began to shift but still concentrated on ways to increase the volume and level of work handled by each worker.

In the late 1970s, the American Productivity Center (later to become the American Productivity and Quality Center, or APQC) was founded to raise the prominence of the problem, stimulate research, and provide a forum for exchanging information. An ongoing APQC theme has been that people, rather that technology, are the keys to productivity improvement. The emissaries of the center spread the gospel and over time have established prominent roles as consultants and line managers. Several of the contributors to this book were at one time associated with the APQC.

A more recent trend has been the growing interest in the total quality management (TQM) philosophy. This approach to management has been quietly instrumental in redefining the role of employees, giving considerably more emphasis to empowerment and to employee accountability. TQM programs sensitize employees to customer expectations and to the quality issues that affect customer satisfaction. This in turn makes employees more sensitive to other ways in which the company can improve its operations. The TQM philosophy highlights the role of employees in improving performance and thereby raises performance expectations. Concomitant with this is the recognition that employees are expected to be forthcoming with their ideas and suggestions. This is a radical departure from traditional management thinking.

The decade of the 1980s saw significant investments in high technology and automated equipment. This economic phenomenon was described in a lead *Business Week* article, "The Technology Payoff" (Gleckman, 1993). As the writer found, however,

> The great surprise behind the [productivity] statistics is in why productivity is improving. It isn't simply cost-cutting or because corporations have thrown huge sums of money at technology. The productivity lesson of the 1990s is that technology is necessary but not sufficient for productivity growth. *The big gains come about through the reorganization of work.*
>
> The reengineering of organizational structures is vital. Decentralizing old corporate hierarchies and empowering employees making and selling products are the first steps to improving productivity. *Providing them with the right kinds of technology is the critical next step* [p. 57; emphasis added].

From a different perspective, another *Business Week* article, "Management's New Gurus" (Byrne, 1992), provides confirmation of the current importance of work management issues. Of the four experts that were the focus of the article, three concentrate on the organization and management of corporations. Michael Hammer is the father of reengineering. David Nadler is recognized for his work in "organizational architecture." Peter Senge developed the notion of the "learning organization." The fourth expert, George Stalk, is heavily involved in strategic planning but has also gained prominence for his work in corporate capabilities. The overriding theme running through the writings of these management gurus is that the key to improved organization performance is the workforce and the management of work.

Significantly, none of the individuals mentioned in the article works in a core business function such as finance or marketing. If we were to go back less than a decade, these functions would have accounted for most of the space in the business press. Employee capabilities would have only rarely been the subject of an article.

The End of the Scientific Management Era

These disparate trends and thinking come together now to prompt the realization in a surprisingly diverse group of corporations and other types of organizations that there must be a better way. The organization and management of work have been based on the ideas espoused by Frederick W. Taylor at the turn of the twentieth century. His principles of scientific management have been the accepted foundation for managing large-scale operations ever since.

Taylor's thinking gained acceptance at a time when manufacturing was in a rudimentary stage of development and contributed to the growth of the U.S. economy for the next several decades. His principles were also instrumental in creating the "us versus them" mind-set that governed the manager-worker relationship during those turbulent decades of industrial growth.

The workforce in the late 1890s was composed of recent immigrants and farmworkers with little or no education and no prior experience in a regimented industrial setting. The work was demanding, and working conditions were both dangerous and harsh. The reluctance among workers to tolerate these conditions led to what by today's standards were extremely high rates of turnover and absenteeism. This, together with rapid economic expansion, meant that most factories were adding or replacing workers all the time. This made it essential to define jobs as narrowly as possible so that workers could be replaced readily and could function with little or no training or prior experience. The first-level supervisor ran the show, wielding almost complete authority to hire, fire, and discipline, and it was a supervisor's responsibility to meet production quotas at any cost.

Taylor's principles of scientific management represented a breakthrough in the organization of work. Taylor's objective was to rationalize the production process by breaking it down into its smallest components. He emphasized specialization and standardized production methods designed to minimize inefficiencies.

Employees were not expected to think and were treated as "cogs in the wheel."

Significantly, the management concepts developed for these primitive production operations were extended to clerical, technical, service, and even professional occupations. If we cannot trust manual workers to make intelligent decisions or to work in the interest of the company, we have the same possible problem with virtually everybody who isn't an owner! In keeping with scientific management thinking, the early "experts" in organization design made it important for managers to limit their span of control to six or seven subordinates—with the emphasis on control—and to break every operation and job down into small tasks so that the work could be planned and carried out efficiently. The traditional craft orientation, with the worker wholly responsible for making the final product—and gaining the pride and satisfaction that can generate—has been displaced in most occupations by the drive for maximum efficiency.

The obvious fact is, however, that our organizations have very different needs than they did a century ago. The book jacket of Tom Peters's 1992 best-seller *Liberation Management* refers to "nanosecond management," a concept that would have been incomprehensible more than a few years ago. Technological or knowledge breakthroughs in some sectors of our economy have become a part of daily organizational life. It is difficult in the 1990s, with the emphasis on continuing change and intense global competition, to imagine relying on concepts and practices that are now a century old.

In the early years, when scientific management principles represented a better answer, it may be that workers did not have much to contribute. Even then, however, management would certainly have benefited from workers' hands-on experience and their informal, often secretive attempts to try untested approaches. The tedium of many assembly-line jobs had to have spawned an interest in trying new ways of handling materials or using tools.

It is useful to recognize that the earliest management thinking evolved from a military model, where strict obedience is important to battlefield success. This thinking carried over into the railroads, where direct supervision was often impossible and rules were needed to ensure that workers reacted correctly to signals and written orders. Some version of this model has prevailed in virtually every U.S. organization until very recently.

A Win-Win Strategy

The potential business value of a work redesign initiative is a clear and definitive bottom-line improvement. In addition to this, however, there is an improved work ethic that is almost palpable when one enters a plant or other work facility with a successful work management initiative. Employees often exhibit a sense of commitment and levels of work activity that are unusual in a work setting.

This proposition is not a new idea. Management theorists over the past three decades have been using somewhat different arguments to convince corporate leaders that workers could make a greater contribution if their work were structured and managed differently. Douglas McGregor, with his Theory X and Theory Y management styles, was one of the earliest. Abraham Maslow was another well-known theorist who argued that a worker whose basic needs were met would be motivated by higher-order self-satisfaction needs. Another less well known but equally important researcher in term of his practical contribution is David McClelland, whose studies showed that many workers are motivated by a need for achievement. Many other writers and researchers have espoused the same basic theme: the traditional, scientific management practices are not effective at tapping the reservoir of talent in our workforce.

The challenge now is to develop strategies that will enable employers to make fullest use of the capabilities of their employees. That is a focus of work redesign efforts and an ongoing theme throughout this book. For many workers, experience in traditional work settings has been sufficiently negative to make this difficult. They do not trust management's intentions and are angry about their treatment by managers and supervisors. It may prove to be impossible to transform these workers to full productivity. The same can be said for many professionals and managers who would be uncomfortable with greater decision-making authority.

There is reason to believe, however, that many managers and workers will be able to make the transition. Our knowledge of human motivation and the factors that affect worker performance strongly support the potential value of the new approaches to the organization and management of work. People like to be challenged; they appreciate and respond strongly to the sense of achievement they get when they meet or exceed high goals; they want to feel that they have made a contribution and that their efforts are appreciated.

When this occurs, workers will often achieve levels of performance that surprise even the theorists. This is not to suggest that every worker will become a superstar. Everyone's performance is limited in some respect. Moreover, there is no reason to think that every job can be converted to a challenging, enjoyable experience. Every organization has and will continue to have many jobs that for at least a portion of the day are mundane and less than stimulating. However, there are too many examples in everyday life of workers in what appear to be the worst jobs who consistently demonstrate a commitment to customer satisfaction, quick response, and impressive work effort.

One of Maslow's concepts was self-actualization, which refers to the need to realize and use one's innate capabilities. With the rise of knowledge workers and new technologies, opportunities will increase, along with the need for workers at all levels to expand their competency. Employers will have to invest in and otherwise support their individual development efforts. Corporations in the United States have not spent as much on employee training as their competitors in other countries. This problem was the subject of *Thinking for a Living,* by Ray Marshall, former U.S. secretary of labor, and Marc Tucker (1992).

For employees that make the transition, the future should be a win-win situation. Employers will benefit from higher productivity or enhanced performance, and workers will have jobs that are more satisfying than those typically found in more traditional organizations. These are jobs that workers will take pride in and look forward to, day after day. A successful work redesign initiative can energize an organization, generating excitement and building confidence that can lead to improved profitability. Workers want to be associated with a winner and to feel that they have contributed to the success. That's a good situation for everyone.

Work Redesign "Action Levers"

Unfortunately, few meaningful research studies of company experience with work redesign initiatives have been conducted. The most extensive studies were completed by Barry Macy, director of the Texas Center for Productivity and Quality of Work Life at Texas Tech University. His analyses summarize the results reported in 131 field studies conducted between 1961 and 1991 (Macy and Izumi, 1993). They confirm a possible 30 to 40 percent increase in organizational results.

Stu Winby, author of Chapter Seven and director of Hewlett-Packard's Product Generation Change Management Team, feels that companies should be able to expect "this and possibly more." That possibility is what has prompted a mushrooming number of companies to begin work redesign initiatives.

The outcomes or results reported in the field studies include a broad range of measures that are listed in Chapter Twenty. Success depends on showing improvement in one or more outcomes over time. As with TQM initiatives, measurement is a key issue, and it is important to identify measures that are relevant and credible and then to monitor progress.

Macy has also categorized the "action levers," or possible changes, into four broad groups: organization structure, human resource policies and practices, technology, and quality management. The action levers are listed in Exhibit 1.1. By his count, forty different types of changes can be implemented, all intended to

Exhibit 1.1. Work Redesign Action Levers.

Organization Structure
Multiskill or generic job classifications
Job rotation and cross-training
Employee involvement groups
Nontraditional work schedules
Reengineering
Self-directed work teams
Human factors design
Behavior modification and
  reinforcement systems
All-salaried workforce
Status equality
360-degree appraisal feedback

Technology
CAD/CAM
Robotics
Flexible manufacturing systems
Just-in-time systems
Statistical process control systems
Automated control and
  measurement systems
MIS and decision support systems
Computer network or electronic
  mail
Office automation or paperless
  office
Capital investment in plant and
  equipment

Total Quality Management
TQM core values and charter
  development
Continuous improvement philosophy
Cost of quality training
Focus on external customer
Focus on internal customer
Customer-supplier-vendor partnership
Line employee inspection
SPC-SQC-TQC training
Just-in-time delivery
Customer complaints to employee

Human Resources
Employee recognition systems
Alternative reward systems
Multiskill training
Job enrichment and task variety
  systems
Team building and group process
  training
Culture assessment
Peer review
"Open" communications
Employee forums

improve the organization's performance. Each of these action levers can be implemented in multiple permutations. The range of possibilities makes it important to plan an initiative carefully.

These changes can be implemented in isolation or in combination. Macy's research shows clearly that an integrated or "holistic" strategy can be expected to generate significantly better results. This is a key finding and an important issue in planning a work redesign initiative. It is consistent with the approach to reengineering efforts. Starting with a clean slate and developing what would in a different era have been perceived as a radically different approach is likely to produce more impressive results than the traditional fine-tuning or conservative approach.

Managing the Workforce to Gain Competitive Advantage

A theme of this book is the need to integrate the knowledge and experience from what have been disparate and all too often isolated fields of management thinking. The chances for realizing the full potential from a work redesign initiative are significantly higher when we take advantage of all of our collective knowledge. Human resource specialists must collaborate with information system specialists. Industrial engineers must work with TQM advocates.

Figure 1.1 illustrates the basic drivers of employee performance. Each of the outer circles on the illustration has been discussed in numerous business publications over the years. Each circle represents a separate professional discipline, with its own theories and accepted practices. Strategies to improve employee performance that are too narrowly focused cannot be expected to realize the full potential of untapped capabilities.

As is common in any field, the "wisdom" of the experienced practitioners involved in the organization and management of work has been documented and passed along over time. Most of the professional groups involved in this area support education and

Figure 1.1. Basic Drivers of Employee Performance.

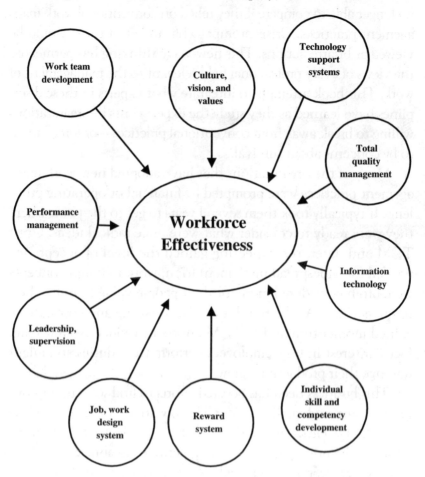

training that serve to disseminate the established body of knowledge. The professional wisdom changes slowly, but there is strong resistance to any beliefs that contradict accepted practice. It is often easier to introduce change from outside of a professional field. Despite the changes in our labor force and in our organizations, there has been a reluctance, in some cases to the point of adamant refusal, to consider new work management practices.

The impetus for change was the realization that companies were no longer able to compete if they relied on conventional work management practices. Crisis prompts what in better times would be viewed as bizarre actions. This new-wave thinking has permeated the views of every professional field relevant to the management of work. This book attempts to integrate what experts in these disciplines have learned as they study the experiments in organizations willing to break away from conventional practices—or forced to do so by concerns about survival.

Many of the organizations that have adopted new work management practices were prompted by financial or operating problems. It typically took them several years to get to the point where they were ready to consider what were once radical ideas. Until TQM and, later, reengineering gained the level of acceptance needed for widespread implementation, work redesign concepts were often considered more for their people value than for their business value. As the trend toward downsizing and cost-cutting gained momentum and as TQM efforts introduced a new team focus, interest in how employees perform their duties and might improve their productivity grew.

This business need has boosted efforts to find ways to improve productivity and quality. Lester Thurow, in his 1992 best-selling book *Head to Head*, argues that workforce productivity will in the future be the principal source of competitive advantage—the "key competitive weapon." Financial resources have provided a competitive advantage in the past, but today, investment funds are available to any company with a sound business plan. From a different perspective, technological resources can provide a short-term advantage, but it has become almost impossible to protect and rely on new products or scientific developments. It is too easy for companies to clone technology or products. If Thurow is correct, organizations that get the best from their people will prove to be the winners. This makes an organization's people, their skills, and their level of effort the only sustainable sources of competitive advantage.

The research results on new work management concepts are

inconclusive. The studies that make it into business and professional periodicals take several years to get into print and obviously represent a small and far from representative sample of the experience across the United States. We are only beginning to see the results from organizations that have been able to take advantage of the creative approaches developed and tested over the past couple of years. In contrast to the often simplistic principles of organization that prevailed until recently, the new concepts are still evolving and will require considerably more testing before anyone can claim to have developed a new set of principles.

We also have significant hurdles to overcome. Years of acrimonious labor-management relations have created a work environment that is too often characterized by hostility and lack of trust. In many companies, experienced workers may never believe that it is to their benefit to become more productive. There is also the problem of getting workers to change their work practices. This is a problem for workers at every level; we all develop work habits and attitudes—"This is the way I do my job"—that prompt us to resist change. In this context, managers and senior professionals, who have worked to achieve status and respect in their organization, have something to lose—the power and authority to control. This gives them a reason to resist. Change is never easy to accept, particularly when the future is uncertain.

Despite the problems, work redesign initiatives have the potential to transform our organizations. The answers that made sense in 1890 and served us well for decades are simply incompatible with the demands on organizations in the 1990s. There is broad and growing recognition that we need new answers to make our organizations more responsive and vital. The key is tapping—unleashing—the unused capabilities of our workers.

The need to improve workforce productivity is currently a driving force in all sectors of our society, including health care and government. In fact, *Reinventing Government* (Osborne and Gaebler, 1992) was an early stimulus for this book. There is probably no better model of an unresponsive, slow-moving bureaucracy than government, at all levels. Our experience as consultants to government has convinced us that public employees are generally as talented as those in the private sector, but the work management practices in government have inadvertently suppressed the normal reasons employees strive for outstanding performance. We cannot afford to allow that to continue.

An unfortunate point is that most managers know that the lower-level staff has more to contribute than the managers have been willing to acknowledge publicly. The culture in the typical organization makes it too easy to suppress creative ideas that might be interpreted as criticism or lead to changes in the established work pattern. Where supervisor-subordinate relationships are not open to easy communication, it is common for the workers to have side discussions of "management's stupidity" in handling operating concerns. After only a few days on a new job, workers have a habit of seeing things that could be done better; the traditional, scientific management philosophy, however, has never recognized that workers have the ability to think.

Developing and carrying out strategies to overcome the impediments will require an extended senior management commitment. It took us a hundred years to get to this point; we now have deeply entrenched attitudes that cannot be altered quickly or without turmoil. Workforce problems have traditionally been delegated to the human resource function, and these specialists clearly need to play a prominent role in changing the way work is organized and managed. But that will not be an adequate response. There is a need for a broader, multidisciplinary strategy—a holistic strategy. The goal is the transformation of our traditional organizations. The potential payoff warrants the commitment.

References

Byrne, J. A. (1992, Aug. 31). Management's new gurus. *Business Week*, pp. 42–52.
Case, J. (1993, April). A company of business people. *Inc.*, pp. 79–93.

Gleckman, H. (1993, June 14). The technology payoff. *Business Week*, pp. 56–68.

Kiechel, W., III. (1993, May 17). How will we work in the year 2000? *Fortune*, pp. 38–52.

Macy, B. A., and Izumi, H. (1993). Organizational change, design, and work innovation: A metanalysis of 131 North American field studies, 1961–1991. In R. Woodman and W. Pasmore (Eds.), *Research in Organizational Change and Development* (Vol. 7, pp. 235–311). Greenwich, Conn.: JAI Press.

Marshall, R., and Tucker, M. (1992). *Thinking for a Living: Education and the Wealth of Nations*. New York: Basic Books.

Osborne, D., and Gaebler, T. (1992). *Reinventing Government*. Reading, Mass: Addison-Wesley.

Peters, T. (1992). *Liberation Management*. New York: Knopf.

Thurow, L. C. (1992). *Head to Head: The Coming Economic Battle Among Japan, Europe, and America*. New York: Morrow.

Part One

Understanding the Emerging World of Work

Change may be the only constant. In business periodicals such as *Fortune* and *Business Week*, virtually every issue has at least one article on the trends affecting U.S. corporations. The environmental changes—changes that are external to the company—prompt internal organizational changes. Companies have come to realize that their success rides on quick and effective responses to what at times seems to be an overwhelming array of external trends and developments.

What differentiates the present situation from the past are the speed and complexity of change. The rate of change seems to increase weekly. Today, with the technology available for the instantaneous exchange of information, the biggest obstacle to good decisions is the human factor—the time needed to comprehend, synthesize, and interpret an array of information, to evaluate alternatives, to reach a decision, and then to trigger the organizational actions necessary to respond to an external development. The pressure to respond quickly is one of the primary reasons that companies have started to delegate decision-making responsibility to the lowest possible level in the organization.

Chapter Two, by Charles Fay, provides an overview of the environmental changes that are affecting U.S. corporations. The chapter pulls together the disparate trends and developments that prompted the organizational revolution. The diversity of fields from which this information has been drawn serves to clarify why organizations have trouble being fully responsive to their environment.

The impact of international competition and the need for cost-cutting have been of concern for at least a decade, although they have become widely shared survival issues only in the past few years. New technology, particularly technology that affects communications and the exchange of information, has only recently been recognized as a major force, and its impact on organizations is still a subject for conjecture in the business literature. Only recently has the so-called virtual corporation become technically feasible; it will be a few years before we see whether large-scale operations based on this concept provide a competitive advantage. Less widely appreciated is the importance of demographic and occupational trends that affect workforce availability.

These trends are affecting career patterns and every facet of corporate human resource policies and practices. The changes are transforming the way companies handle staffing, training, development, compensation, and benefits. The impact on employer-employee relationships has been profound; the traditional paternalistic culture is rapidly being replaced by a new philosophy: "What have you done for me lately?" The new organization is characterized by reduced loyalty and commitment on both sides of the employer-employee equation.

Organizations have responded to the changing environment with a number of popular initiatives such as reengineering, total quality management, and empowerment. They have also worked to introduce fundamental changes in the way work is organized and managed. Chapter Three, by Edward E. Lawler III, discusses some of these organizational changes.

One of the emerging concepts is competency-based organizing. The traditional strategy for organizing focused on jobs as the basic building blocks of an organization. The idea that each worker has a well-defined set of duties and accountabilities has been central to organizational planning since the beginning of the era of scientific management. The concept has served as the underpinning of employee selection, training, performance management, and compensation. Organizing work and workers around a fixed set of job duties is now coming to be viewed as an impediment to organizational change and flexibility.

The new thinking views employees as human resources that support organizational strategies through their activities. This changes the focus from the job to the individual employee's competencies—what he or she is capable of doing—and to the aggregate capabilities of the organization. Instead of the employee being an interchangeable cog in the machinery of the bureaucratic organization, he or she is viewed as an asset that can play a vital role in the organization's efforts to compete and its ability to learn about and respond to customers. This new view recognizes that hiring and paying workers "to do a job" runs the risk of underutilizing employees by confining them to narrowly defined roles and that the expectations driving their performance will fail to make full use of a valuable asset.

The emerging alternative is to design organizational systems around the capabilities of individual workers. The objective is to support the development of individual capabilities or competencies and then to organize and manage the workforce so that those competencies can be utilized effectively. When organizations were operating in essentially static environments, it made sense to have workers perform the same tasks over and over and to organize around the concept of the job. As we have moved toward change and turbulence in the environment, the traditional job concept has become a constraint to effective workforce management.

This new logic has been referred to as the "learning organization." The underlying assumptions emphasize the need for organizations to change in response to the external environment and to learn ways to perform better and interface more effectively with the environment. It is becoming apparent that organizations that are best at adapting and at finding new approaches will have a competitive advantage. The successful organizations are willing to experiment, assess their experience with new approaches, and then move forward with this knowledge.

The trends and developments in organizing and managing work are transforming organizations. If the lessons learned over the past few years are meaningful, the key to success in the future will lie in the ability of the organization to align its organization design and management strategy with its business strategy. This ability has the potential to be a key in achieving and sustaining competitive advantage, for it normally takes time to develop a successful answer, and it is unrealistic simply to clone the strategy of other successful companies. In fact, no company has long succeeded with a copycat strategy.

The competitive world has simply bypassed many of the traditional practices that were once viewed as foolproof paths to effectiveness (and are in fact still enshrined in many management textbooks). This is one of the reasons why many formerly prominent and successful companies have become corporate dinosaurs in today's environment. They are still concentrating on doing the old ways better.

Making effective use of the organization's human resources requires a different attitude toward human resource management. That is the subject of Chapter Four, by Jennifer Jarratt and Joseph Coates. These futurists discuss the emerging role of the human resource function as a powerful force in achieving organizational success through the best use of people.

Human resource specialists have often found themselves between two organizational poles. On the one hand, they are often viewed as the advocates of workers, representing their needs and presenting their viewpoint to senior management. On the other hand, they are expected to serve as agents of senior management and to work to gain acceptance of management's goals and action plans by the workforce. In their new role, they will have to work productively to understand the organization's people management needs, develop effective solutions, and drum up needed support for new policies and practices. The human resource function does not have the organizational credibility or power to impose new work management practices, but it is apparent that if it is to survive as a separate function, it must play a leading role in the change process.

Four people-centered management initiatives will affect the role of human resource specialists. First, the quality management movement seeks a significant shift in the way workers approach their jobs—a shift that requires both new behavior and new beliefs. As many organizations have learned the hard way, the success or failure of a quality initiative rides on people management considerations. Second, the just-in-time approach to the delivery of products and services has carried over to internal corporate services such as human resource management. Human resource specialists will be expected to deliver the right service at the right time. Third, focusing on the customer requires a different staffing, training, and reward strategy, and the human resource function must take the lead in creating and driving this new culture. Finally, the new empowered, high-involvement culture intensifies the importance of finding the right people and training them so that they are ready to assume this expanded role. In an empowered organization, the people make the culture, and that makes expertise in handling workforce problems a front-burner concern.

As we move toward the new organization, new managerial styles will be required. There is a need for managers to learn to operate effectively in a more open-ended, ambiguous environment that is subjected to continuous external change, where flexibility and innovation are highly valued. The human resource function will have a central role in helping managers and supervisors prepare for this new world and for dealing with the highly educated, assertive workers that will be needed for success in the future.

Finally, the human resource function must help managers understand, evaluate, and make people management decisions. When performance information was limited to last month's bottom-line numbers and distributed to a selected shortlist of executives, not only did human resource specialists not play a role in using the data, but they often did not even see it. Now human resource specialists will have to help nonexecutives understand performance data. They will also have to help even seasoned executives deal with the softer, more subjective information that affects workforce decisions.

When Frederick W. Taylor conceived his approach to management in the late 1890s, the world of work was simple and more or less stagnant. The same products were manufactured every day for months without any change in the production process. Taylor's legacy and that of other industrial leaders who followed could be based on doing the same old thing better and better. They did not have to worry about the myriad environmental changes that have mushroomed over the past two decades. These old leaders would have labeled the subjects discussed in this book science fiction, not required reading for understanding current problems. The doors to this past era are swinging shut, and every corporation will need to worry about survival in the new world of work.

Chapter Two

The Changing Nature of Work

Charles Fay

In the past several years, fundamental environmental changes have had a major impact on the way American organizations are structured, how they do work, and the labor forces they have at their disposal. These changes in turn affect prototypical human resource policies and programs. Bellwether organizations have already begun to indicate the way the typical organization is likely to respond to key environmental changes.

Areas of Change

The changes that are affecting organizations and work design include the increasing intensity and scope of international competition, a drive by American organizations to cut costs (in part to meet foreign competition relying on lower labor costs), a continued move toward automation of production processes, a reliance on more sophisticated information processing technologies, and greater use of communication technology in place of face-to-face interactions. The results have been an entirely different approach to the way work is done and a very different kind of organization to manage that new work.

International Competition

Postwar America was largely free from international competition. As the only major industrial power to escape large-scale destruction of its manufacturing base, the United States enjoyed a period of world dominance in most industries. Domestic demand was high, and few organizations were concerned about the threat of foreign competition. Now, with Japanese and European economic power rivaling that of the United States, American dependence on a global economy is a fact of life for most organizations.

Although the postwar United States had higher labor costs than its principal trading partners, a combination of higher productivity, greater access to capital, and better design allowed it to be dominant in its domestic market and competitive in world markets. As Europe and Asia recovered from World War II, they gained on the United States in technology and design and developed adequate capital but maintained lower labor costs. In much of the manufacturing sector, foreign competitors can deliver equivalent or better products than U.S. manufacturers can, and at lower cost. Initial effects were seen in low-technology, labor-intensive industries such as clothing and apparel. As foreign industry has increased in technological sophistication, much of American manufacturing, particularly in high-value industries such as automobiles and consumer electronics, has been partly or completely supplanted by overseas corporations. Many of these overseas corporations have been able to set up manufacturing units in the United States and, applying their own work technology and management style, produce high-quality lower-cost products with an American workforce (but not American management).

International competition has expanded from the manufacturing sector to the service sector. Banking and financial service organizations are feeling domestic pressure from foreign competition, and overseas retailing, grocery, and restaurant chains have become fixtures in American cities and shopping malls. Foreign construction conglomerates compete for major American private, state, and local government contracts.

This global competition has had three major effects on American organizations. First, there has been a major restructuring of organizations, primarily downsizing, to reduce labor costs and become more competitive. This restructuring has resulted in massive job losses, which differ from job losses experienced by the U.S. labor force in previous bad economic times in that there is almost no chance that laid-off employees will be rehired as the organization grows. Second, the classes of workers whose jobs have been cut also differ from previous reductions in force. Many of the jobs that have disappeared are middle-management and senior administrative staff jobs. More tasks previously carried out by staff units, including human resource functions, are being reassigned to line managers.

Third, American organizations have themselves become more global, exporting jobs to low-wage areas. Back-office operations have been moved to lower-wage areas in the United States or off-shore. Manufacturing units have been moved to areas that offer a trained workforce, cooperative or no unions, and lower wages. Some large organizations, such as General Electric and IBM, have even moved business unit headquarters overseas. Du Pont is typical of the global corporation that has shifted control of some operations abroad: its Lycra business is headquartered in Geneva; its automotive business is centered in Troy, Michigan; and its electronics business has recently been relocated to Tokyo. "The move is in line with the chemical company's evolving strategy of reducing central headquarters' direct oversight, by granting control to operations geographically closer to [major] customers" (Miller, 1992).

Cost-Cutting

The emphasis on cost-cutting—the need to be more efficient and effective—has affected human resource practice to a greater degree than most other functional areas. This is because of a recognition that the contribution of improved human resource practice offers the potential of greater improvements in profit margins than is likely in any other area. There are several reasons for this.

Technologies in production, marketing, and financing are well developed, and for the most part, improvements are likely to occur in small increments. The return on investment in these areas is limited. Further, knowledge in these technologies is widely dispersed; a technology developed in one country can be transferred to another country fairly quickly. Thus the competitive advantage gained from investment in these technologies may be short-lived.

Human resource technology is not as well developed, and the opportunity for improvements is great, at least theoretically. Labor costs are a major expenditure for most large organizations. Making this type of spending more efficient and the resource more effective promises a large return on investment.

Examples of greater productivity accompanied by higher-quality products and services developed and produced over shorter lead times in Asian and European organizations (and even units of those organizations located in the United States and employing Americans) suggest that such returns are possible. The transfer of human resource technologies, however, seems to be much more difficult. Organizations have tended to keep their human resource practices confidential, sometimes from their own employees. Less of human resource practice is grounded in empirical research than is the case with other functional technologies. Cultural change in organizations is a slow process and, owing to the subjective base of much of the technology, resistance to change in human resource practices—particularly if it threatens managerial authority—is strong.

As a result, much of the emphasis on changes in human resource technology focuses on cost reduction, particularly in organizations that remain job-focused and bureaucratic. These organizations seek to cut the number of employees where possible, reduce (or maintain level) the costs of employee benefits, and find systems that allow flexibility in wage levels.

New Technologies

Developments in technology have altered organizational human resource practices in a number of important ways and promise even greater change in the future. The three technologies that have had the greatest impact are automation, information processing, and communications. The result is a new technology of work and the possibility of a new form of organization. Both the new work and the new organization require different human resource practices.

Automation. Developments in automation have had two consequences. Jobs that once required multiple employees now require fewer employees or none at all. Other jobs have been "deskilled," meaning that a lower level of judgment or technical skill is required for satisfactory performance. The effects of automation were felt first at the lowest levels: elevator operators were replaced by control panels, welding on assembly lines is now done by robots, and equipment repairers plug in new components instead of repairing broken ones.

Developments in automation (combined with advances in information processing) have resulted in expert systems, which can substitute for or deskill higher-level employees. Prototype benefit-counseling systems, for example, can provide employees with expert advice on appropriate choices from options available under a flexible benefit plan, taking specific employee circumstances into account.

Information Processing. Information processing has had several important consequences for work. Many clerical and secretarial functions have been redistributed to employees who were formerly supported by these functions. Many managers do much of their own word processing now, and in the electronic office, filing is fast becoming an obsolete task. Employees in the field can enter sales orders, service call records, and similar information directly into analytical databases. Doing one's own word processing alters one's work style significantly. As multiprocessing operating systems become more widespread, equally significant changes will occur in the way people think about work, moving from a linear "one task at a time" approach to a more ambiguous, interconnected, multitask style. Other changes in the way employees think about work come about from the use of spreadsheets (especially "what if" capabilities), databases, and analytical software.

Software allows on-line interactive joint efforts in document development, decision making, and goal setting. This allows for self-directed work team activity in areas that were previously resistant to such efforts. Related information-sharing capacity fosters team efforts in a variety of settings, including the formation of teams at geographically dispersed sites.

Communication.   New communication technologies may transform the workplace more than any other single factor. Networking makes information processing a joint activity. Other communications technologies remove the necessity for physical proximity, enabling several innovations: organizations can move some activities to low-wage areas yet still have those activities integrated with other organizational functions. Many organizations have already done this with back-office operations.

The greatest work transformation that may result from new communications technology is telecommuting. Employees may enjoy the same degree of integration they currently have with the organization yet rarely set foot on company premises. Organizations are already experimenting with telecommuting on a limited scale, mostly with professional employees. Employees whose jobs involve considerable use of the computer are candidates for telecommuting; even some secretaries telecommute one or two days a week.

The New Work.   These new technologies have prompted a change in the metaphor for work in some organizations—a change that is likely to spread. Instead of an assembly line, with a consequent focus on jobs, the new metaphor is the purposeful organism or system centered on workers or autonomous work groups that change in response to organizational needs (Dobbins, Cardy, and Carson, 1991, pp. 11–13). Jobs are broad in scope, amorphous in form, and subject to change, defined in the context of groups of employees (Lawler, 1986, pp. 101–118). Tasks are functions of groups, not jobs (Safizadeh, 1991). The change of metaphor has great consequences for human resource practices (Sundstrom, De Meuse, and Futrell, 1990).

The New Organization. The new work metaphor changes the nature of organizations that adopt it. As employees and groups become more self-managing, the old types of supervision are no longer necessary and in fact become a hindrance. Organizations can become flatter, with fewer layers of hierarchy. Work teams substitute for hierarchy (Miles and Snow, 1992). Such organizations are likely to be more egalitarian. Because there are fewer layers of management, employees tend to have a better understanding of organizational needs and goals. Even lower-level employees can grasp the organization's strategy, and a performance culture is more likely to exist (Lawler, 1986). Likewise, the "us versus them" attitude tends to diminish, and more employees are seen as capable of participating in the decision-making process. Human resource processes, like other staff functions, are regarded less as the province of specialists who control supervisory decisions and more as integral parts of line managers' jobs or of work groups themselves. Staff specialists, where they exist at all, are likely to become internal consultants.

Large corporations experimented with the new organization in the early 1980s and have expanded use of the concepts since the latter part of that decade. Motorola, Cummins Engine, Ford, and LTV are examples of corporations that have reorganized around the team concept. The team approach has increased both productivity and quality, and the new organization is seen as a source of competitive advantage.

Demographics

The makeup of the United States population has changed significantly in the past twenty years in terms of size, age distribution, mortality and morbidity patterns, family structure, the role of minorities in society, immigration, and geographical shifts (Bezold, Carlson, and Peck, 1986). The population of the United States was approximately 237 million in 1984; projections are 260 million by 1995, 270 million by 2000, and 280 million by 2005 (U.S. Bureau of Labor Statistics, 1986; Saunders, 1992, p. 13).

The median age in 1982 was 30.6; by 2000 it is estimated to rise to 36.3 (Cetron, Soriano, and Gayle, 1985, p. 37). Not only is the population aging, but the age distribution is changing as well (Bollick and Neselroth, 1989, p. 5). Morbidity and ill health of the sort that prevents labor force participation may increasingly be postponed until the last few years of life; not only may people live longer, but they may remain able to participate in the labor force for a longer part of their increased life span.

The traditional postwar American family, with working father, homemaker mother, and children, is increasingly being supplanted by single-parent families, unmarried individuals living under various sharing arrangements, and dual-career couples. The racial and ethnic mix of the population will continue to move toward greater diversity; minorities may account for as much as 29 percent of the U.S. population by 2000. In fact, if immigration patterns and differential birthrates persist, whites may be in the minority by the end of the twenty-first century (Bezold, Carlson, and Peck, 1986, p. 24; Cetron, Soriano, and Gayle, 1985, p. 167). An increasingly large portion of the population entering the workforce may speak English only as a second language. Already today, significant numbers of new employees, though in possession of a high school diploma, require remedial help in reading to be able to function. Significant numbers of labor market entrants for whom English is a second language will both complicate and intensify the remedial-training need.

The labor supply is a subset of the total population, but the same trends are expected. In 1985, the labor force participation rate was 65.9 percent, with a total labor force of 118.6 million (Bezold, Carlson, and Peck, 1986, p. 27); a rate of 69 percent is projected for 2005, with a total labor force of 150.7 million (Fullerton, 1992, p. 29).

Major changes in the labor supply are caused by the increased participation of subsets of the population (Fullerton, 1992, p. 32). So even though the participation of older male workers is expected to remain below 1975 levels, older workers will still be abundant in the workforce because of increased participation by older women. Participation rates are not expected to change substantially for minorities in the aggregate, but the distribution of minorities across occupational categories is expected to become more even. The labor supply will more nearly reflect the general population in terms of gender and race. It will be an older workforce, capable of continuing work well into what are currently considered the retirement years. New family patterns may well make continued work a necessity for most employees.

Though nominal levels of education will increase, much of the new workforce will be sorely lacking in even the most basic skills. Functional illiteracy is already a major problem for most organizations. Lack of numerical skills is more widespread, and proficiency at analytical skills is even harder to come by. The failure of the public education system is of major concern for organizations seeking competitive advantage through the productivity of its employees.

Although much of the workforce lack fundamental skills, projected occupational openings show an increase in skill demand in the new workplace (see Table 2.1). Most job growth will occur in sectors requiring higher skill levels. In fact, at the narrower occupational level, many of the occupations projected to grow most rapidly by 2005 are those demanding higher levels of education and yielding higher earnings (Silvestri and Lukasiewicz, 1992).

Forecast of Future Changes

The pressures for change are likely to continue and even intensify. As the economy becomes more fully globalized, every organization

Table 2.1. Employment Change by Job Category, 1990–2005.

Category	Anticipated Change (percent)
Technicians and related support occupations	+36.9
Professional specialty occupations	+32.3
Service occupations	+29.3
Executive, administrative, and managerial occupations	+27.4
Marketing and sales occupations	+24.1
Total, all occupations	**+20.1**
Administrative support occupations, including clerical	+13.1
Precision production, craft, and repair occupations	+12.6
Agriculture, forestry, fishing, and related occupations	+ 4.5
Operators, fabricators, and laborers	+ 4.1

Source: U.S. Bureau of Labor Statistics, 1992, tab. 6.

is likely to feel the impact of foreign competition. In some industries, it is beginning to be difficult to determine what is an American product and what is a foreign one—Japanese automobile models may be built in this country and contain more parts of North American origin than some American models that are assembled overseas with little North American content. American companies will become even more global, shifting operations to areas that meet corporate requirements.

Cost control will continue to be a major concern of organizations competing in global markets. With the international homogenization of manufacturing technology and finance, sustained competitive advantage will come from human resources, through some combination of controlling the costs of human resources and increasing their effectiveness.

Change in technology is likely to accelerate. As we move further toward the information society, organizations that can develop and exploit automation, information processing, and communications will have more options for defining work and for designing and setting up organizations that can make best use of human resources to achieve corporate goals. Labor force characteristics for the next decade or two are already determined (barring major catastrophes or unexpected social change)—a more diverse, older workforce with increasing expectations for meaningful work and more control of their work life.

Major Implications of a Changing Workplace for Compensation and Related Human Resource Systems

Changing environmental pressures and new approaches toward work design are having a fundamental impact on all aspects of the workplace. Because workers no longer interact with employers through the focus of the job, old human resource management systems are no longer applicable. Environmental pressures are forcing employers to rethink the role of labor in the production of goods and services.

Career Patterns

Career patterns are likely to become unstable and unpredictable. As the focus in organizing work shifts from the job to employee skills, from individuals to groups, and from fixed task sets to changing, flexible, and ambiguous work activities, it will become impossible to chart a fixed career course. Multiple and varied career patterns are likely to emerge. One pattern that may become common is the multioccupation career punctuated by periods of intensive retraining or formal education. (Surveys of dislocated workers indicate that many workers who lose jobs—63 percent of those surveyed—end up in other industries; Doeringer and others, 1991, p. 85.) This pattern will be further driven by technological or economic change leading to skill obsolescence.

For example, Eastman Kodak shifted large numbers of employees to new jobs and different divisions after losing 6,700 employees in a downsizing early-retirement program. Although some previously acquired skills are used in new jobs, many employees required extensive retraining (Rigdon, 1992). Some organizations make this career instability a recruitment tool: Corning notes that employees can change careers without changing employers (Rigdon, 1992).

A second pattern, typical of the marginally employed today, that may increase in prevalence is a series of low-wage jobs for various employers (barely deserving to be called a career) punctuated by periods of unemployment (Lohr, 1992). This pattern will be driven by economic cycles leading to changing labor demand in industries. It is unlikely that any set of acquired skills or any degree will guarantee a traditional career pattern. Rapid obsolescence of specific work skills means that the most useful skills in the new workplace will be learning skills.

Employment will become sporadic for many workers, and increasing numbers will become part-time or temporary employees. There is considerable evidence that many of the jobs cut in the past decade through downsizing of major American corporations will not reappear when organizations become more successful: a lean workforce is seen as a key source of competitive advantage for global companies (O'Reilly, 1992). Smaller companies, traditionally the creators of most new jobs, are also traditionally more vulnerable to economic downturns and thus to variable employment levels. Many organizations, seeking flexible labor costs, will make greater use of temporary, part-time, and contract employees, all of whom may be let go when not needed and who do not pose the same benefits obligations as full-time employees.

There will be fewer long-term employment relationships and few expectations of a single-organization career. Employees who change occupations will have a better chance of staying with an employer for a longer period. Stability—and consequently the expectation of stability—will largely disappear. Workers may expect to change both employers and occupations more frequently, often with little warning.

Retirement

All the current data suggest that the trend toward earlier retirement will continue, although at a diminishing rate (Gendell and Siegel,

1992). The drop in median age has flattened out in the past decade, and this flatness is expected to continue over the next ten to fifteen years. ·

However, the validity of these estimates for future years is subject to question, given the change in organizational environments. Retirement may come at a later age and become largely involuntary. This could occur for many reasons. The main one is that employers have found that voluntary retirement programs are effective ways of reducing head count and payroll costs. One survey found that about 40 percent of the fifty largest American companies offered early-retirement programs in 1990 or 1991. In the preceding decade, fully 76 percent of the companies offered early-retirement opportunities (Bogan, 1992). A broader survey including private sector, nonprofit, and public sector employers found that 16 percent of them offered early-retirement incentives in 1991 (La Rock, 1992, p. 18). In some cases, voluntary retirement is a preferred alternative to being laid off or let go for poor performance.

Compensation

Compensation programs in the new organization will become less focused on the job and more focused on the employee or work group. At the same time, there will be increasing emphasis on flexibility and control, whether in matters of compensation level, form of delivery, or basis for increases. Compensation programs will become increasingly tied to the performance of the individual, the work group, and the organization (Manicatide and Pennell, 1992).

Organizations will accomplish this by decreasing the importance of base pay and putting a larger portion of an employee's pay "at risk." As jobs become less stable and more ambiguous, base pay itself is likely to depend less on the position held by the individual and more on the skill sets required, with additional skills acquired by the employee rewarded by increases in pay (Jenkins, Ledford, Gupta, and Doty, 1992). Base pay levels will also become tied more closely to organizational strategy (Lawler, 1990). Similar jobs in various parts of the organization may have differing pay levels to reflect differences in strategic importance. Organizations will pay more attention to wage levels in product market competitor organizations when setting base pay levels than they do now, whether those competitors are domestic or international. The combination of flattened organizations and emphasis on incentive pay to create pay differentials will result in smaller differences in base pay among employees.

More emphasis will be placed on incentive pay, over the short or long term. The typical employee's pay program will come to resemble a salesperson's pay package, with some base pay and a series of earnings opportunities based on individual, work group, and organizational performance. Such incentive programs are already in place at many organizations; they include lump-sum bonuses, suggestion awards, and key performer awards at the individual level; performance bonuses, gain sharing, and goal sharing at the group level; and gain sharing, goal sharing, and profit sharing at the organizational level (McAdams and Hawk, 1992). These incentive programs are not merely funding devices; they result in onetime cash payments to employees. Thus the typical pay program will become more like that currently used for sales staff: a relatively small base pay (perhaps 40 percent of target compensation) accompanied by a variety of earnings opportunities based on current organizational needs.

This emphasis on incentive pay has a number of consequences for the organization and for employees. Organizations can gain control of total compensation costs by varying incentive payouts. In addition, these payouts are likely to vary with organizational successes (Coates, 1991) and go to employees who contribute the most to organizational achievement. For employees, compensation levels are likely to be erratic during a career rather than progressing with career stage. This is because incentive pay must be re-earned every year, and longevity with an organization alone will not increase salary levels because previous performance rewards do not become entitlements. This will be reinforced in the flatter organization, where an employee may stay in one or two pay grades for an entire career. The midpoints for those grades may respond to labor market changes, but there will be much less likelihood of movement to a new salary grade with a higher midpoint. Erratic performance will be accompanied by erratic total pay, even when organizational earnings are stable.

Employee Benefits

Employee benefits will become much more integrated with compensation costs, and with much the same purpose: flexibility and cost control. The goal of this integration is ensuring that total compensation costs provide a competitive advantage where possible and are not entitlement payments entirely unrelated to employee and organizational performance.

Employers will control costs of benefit programs through coinsurance and copayment, reduction of coverage, and cost-cutting administrative techniques such as second opinions, lifestyle rewards, and selected provider options. While legislation such as the Americans with Disabilities Act limits employer action with respect to uses of lifestyle rewards and some other administrative techniques, benefit-cost reduction is a major goal for most employers.

In the past, most workers were covered by defined-benefit pension programs. Pension level under such a program is based on a formula related to years of employee service and employee earnings over, typically, the last five years of employment. The organization bears all responsibility for managing its contributions to the pension fund in such fashion as to ensure that money will be available to meet defined-benefit obligations.

Health care costs are the most rapidly rising employer costs, and some employer responses have been the reduction or abolition of postretirement health care benefits and the introduction of cost containment programs, coinsurance and copayment requirements for current employees, and flexible-benefit plans. The U.S. Supreme Court, in *Greenberg* v. *H&H Music Co.* (1992), upheld the rights of self-insured companies to reduce or cut coverage for specific diseases, provided that cost reduction is the goal. More than half of all American workers are employed by self-insured companies, and thus many organizations have an additional means of controlling health benefit costs (Barrett, 1992).

U.S. Bureau of Labor Statistics studies indicate that large numbers of organizations have such cost containment programs as preadmission certification and utilization review (Hyland, 1992). Wellness programs (such as smoking cessation and weight reduction) are also becoming more prevalent as organizations seek to reduce claims.

Staffing

In the new organization, staffing activities are typically focused on finding and hiring the person who is a good fit with a group and is perceived to have the potential to grow (Price, Lupton, and Henry, 1990, pp. 159–170). There is little concern about comparing the individual's formal achievements, knowledge, skills, or abilities with a specific, narrowly defined job, for the simple reason that the great majority of employees will never have such a job. Aptitudes (what the employee could do, with proper training) are of much more interest than abilities (what the applicant can do). Interpersonal skills, decision-making skills, communication skills, and the ability to work as part of a group take precedence; these are the techniques that successful employees must master (Bowen, Ledford, and Nathan, 1991). Salomon Brothers, a securities brokerage firm, has redefined many of its back-office jobs in this way: "Employees will no longer specialize in areas like accounting or data management. Instead, they are organized into about a dozen product teams, like foreign exchange or corporate bonds." Salomon's hiring strategy reflects this change. While some seasoned employees will be transferred into the new operation, most will be new: "former lifeguards, air traffic controllers and M.B.A.'s—most with no brokerage experience—who have a different way of thinking about themselves, their careers and how they get paid" (Gabor, 1992, p. F5).

The shift in focus from a specialized job with minimal task sets from which a rigid set of job specifications can be derived to a more generalized job with ambiguous and changing tasks and fluid job specifications creates major problems for selection technology. To the extent that new selection methods adversely affect applicants from protected groups, the courts will have to be persuaded that new definitions of work are appropriate. (There is no reason to believe that older employees—or members of any protected group—should be disadvantaged by new selection criteria. In fact, studies suggest that groups with divergent backgrounds, skills, abilities, and aptitudes are more productive than more homogeneous groups, provided that they can operate effectively as a team; Rix, 1990, pp. 61–63.)

A more difficult problem for staffing is a better understanding of what sets or patterns of characteristics are predictive of a high-performing team member and how these characteristics are related to more traditional knowledge, skills, abilities, and aptitudes. Because some of these characteristics are likely to be attitudinal, selection will not be easy. Staffing specialists will also have to develop a better understanding of the relationship between individual and team effectiveness—for example, a group of high-performing team members may not constitute the most effective team in a given instance.

In the flatter organization, promotion is no longer the way to get ahead (Walker, 1992, pp. 51–52). In some respects, this makes it easier for the staffing function. Fewer upper-level jobs will have to be filled, and more qualified internal candidates will be available to fill them. Lateral transfers will become more common, and team flexibility allows some senior workers to pass on some responsibilities as a prelude to retirement (Quinn, Burkhauser, and Myers,

1990, pp. 157–189). However, it may be more difficult to fill some openings with external candidates, as team cohesiveness may work against the effectiveness of an outsider.

Training and Development

Training and development will be critical issues for the new organization. For example, flexible manufacturing requires workers who are more akin to white-collar workers in terms of educational and skill requirements than to traditional blue-collar high school graduates. Unless the public education system increases its effectiveness, many organizations will be forced to provide remedial training to a large number of new employees. Such training will include basic reading, numerical, and analytical skills. If employees are to function well in autonomous work groups with changing task sets, they will have to possess not only reading and computational skills but also interpersonal skills.

Careerlong training will be required if the new work and the new organization are to remain successful. To be effective team members, employees will have to master not a few specific tasks but rather a wide range of frequently changing tasks *and* a set of interpersonal skills. Salomon Brothers has structured its pay system to complement this approach: "What we want is to pay for a set of social skills and the ability to learn" (Gabor, 1992, p. F5). Training will to some extent be replaced by self-learning. For example, the U.S. General Services Administration has set up thirteen Self-Learning Instructional Centers that offer more than 150 video and computer-assisted training programs ranging from basic typing skills to management counseling and coaching. Employees of the U.S. government go to the centers at nonpeak work times, and instruction is self-paced (U.S. Office of Personnel Management, 1991).

Cost control will reduce the role of training as an employee benefit. For training to be considered, it will have to meet specific perceived needs, and the degree to which it meets those needs will be evaluated. Autonomous work groups will take a much greater role in assessing their own training needs. More training is likely to be specialized to meet the particular needs of groups within an organization, and fewer off-the-shelf packages are likely to be used. Access to external training is likely to continue as a means of bringing new ideas into the group. The value of this training will also be evaluated by the group, and programs not providing value will not be repeated. The focus of current evaluation technology is on the individual; a technology for evaluating training as it affects a work group (whether all or only a few members participate in the training) has yet to be developed.

Employer-Employee Relationship: The Employer's View

The new organization may be characterized as continuously asking each employee (and each employee group), "What have you done for me lately, and what are you going to be doing for me now? How do you add value?" This is a major shift from the paternalistic organization, in which loyalty was a sufficient contribution. Organizations that adopt this view describe it as promotion of a "performance culture."

The performance culture goes beyond mere outputs; it also involves a commitment to fostering other aspects of organizational culture. General Electric's chief executive officer, Jack Welch, notes that a GE manager's job has two goals: making the numbers and supporting the GE culture. If a manager succeeds in both areas or fails in both, the consequences are clear. If a manager supports the culture but fails to make the numbers, some time will be allowed to bring the numbers into line. If a manager makes the numbers but fails to support the culture, the manager is likely to be terminated: getting to the right numbers in the wrong way is unacceptable (Hyatt, 1992).

With this perspective goes a recognition that the organization must be willing to share the outcomes of performance with the people who produce them. If the new organization has ended its loyalty to employees, it also recognizes that employees have little reason to stay with it if better opportunities exist elsewhere or if performance is not rewarded.

Although employers see the downside in the lack of loyalty because of a decrease in corporate memory, experience, and continuity, they recognize the advantage of having the flexibility to adjust workforce makeup to the skill base required in a changing marketplace (Solomon, 1992, p. 60). Employee complacency may also be lessened: an employee who recognizes that performance makes the difference between work and the unemployment line is less likely to shirk.

Employer-Employee Relationship: The Employee's View

Employees ended the paternalistic relationship with employers on a large scale before organizations shifted to performance cultures. The genesis of the reduction in loyalty can be traced back at least to the 1960s, when the demand for M.B.A.'s outran the supply. Young management professionals found that switching organizations provided a much larger increase in salary and responsibilities than internal growth opportunities did. The same held true for engineers and other employees in the defense industry and professional employees (such as financial analysts) in financial service industries. It can be argued, in fact, that a major contributing factor to the end of the paternalistic organization was the accession of these professionals and managers to senior executive positions in the late 1970s and early 1980s. Having felt no commitment to a single organization, these executives saw little reason for the organization to maintain a commitment to employees when it was not in the organization's economic interest to do so.

As employers have downsized and reduced their commitment

to employees, employees have responded with reduced trust in their employers and reduced commitment (Cumming, 1992). A comparison of the "psychological contract" between employers and employees in the 1950s and 1960s with the emerging contract reveals not only the change in commitment of both parties but also the change in focus (see Table 2.2).

Few employees today expect organizations to maintain nonproductive employees, and the expectation is that economic self-interest is the sole motivator for the organization. Jobs that can be exported to low-wage areas will be. Although employees are opposed to this, few have turned to collective bargaining as a solution. Union representation has dropped to approximately 16 percent of the workforce, a postwar low (Stelluto and Klein, 1990, p. 39). Were it not for the ready acceptance of unions by public sector administrators and legislatures in the 1970s and 1980s, this figure would be even lower.

Unions have also opposed the emergence of work teams and other nonunion employee empowerment approaches. A complaint

Table 2.2. The Psychological Contract of Yesterday and Today.

Employee's Responsibility	Employer's Responsibility
Yesterday	
Fair day's work	Fair day's pay
Sustained good work	Continued employment
Sustained good work	Merit pay increases
Extrahard work	Advancement
Quality work	Recognition and acknowledgment
Loyalty	Job security
Today	
Focus on personal needs	Focus on corporate goals
Career development, self-development	Corporate growth
Legal protection	Legal protection
Self-reliance	Self-reliance

Source: De Meuse and Tornow, 1990, p. 205. Used by permission.

filed by the Teamsters with the National Labor Relations Board argued that worker-management committees are in violation of the National Labor Relations Act unless they are created in unionized organizations with the participation of the union (Bernstein, 1992, p. 60). No final determination in the case has yet been reached, but an adverse ruling, if upheld on appeal, could halt some aspects of organizational restructuring.

The changing design of the organization reinforces the lack of expectation of a long-term relationship. As organizations flatten, promotional opportunities will become ever scarcer. Employees who seek advancement will increasingly have to look outside their current organization or view advancement as a series of lateral moves (Rigdon, 1992). External opportunities will be limited to the more able (that is, marketable) employees, and organizations may expect increased turnover among the employees they most want to retain.

Employer-Employee Relationship: Society's View

It is not clear at this point what society will do about the new work and the new organization. As with any fundamental change, there is strong opposition from the people who stand to lose the most. Politicians and unions advocate legislation barring transfer of jobs to low-wage areas. Unions argue that worker-management teams violate current labor laws. Similar efforts have been made to give the old relationship the force of law by the erosion of employment-at-will rights. Employment rights of various groups are being further protected by law—the Americans with Disabilities Act is the latest example of the creation of a new "protected" class of citizens (Lublin, 1992). However, it is unlikely that resistance will overcome the pressures exerted by the economic, technological, and demographic changes that are transforming the American organization.

Other major policy changes have been raised as possibilities. In the search for greater revenues, the federal government may seek to change tax policy with respect to employee benefits. The General Accounting Office notes that not taxing employee benefits as income results in $91 billion per year in forgone revenue and that a greater percentage of high-income employees than lower-income workers are covered (Noble, 1992). If such a policy change were to occur, much of the rationale for employee benefits (in lieu of wages) would disappear. Employers could well prefer to avoid the inflexibility of benefit payments, the lack of connection between benefits and organizational performance, and the administrative costs of benefit programs by getting out of the benefit business altogether.

Conclusion

Any forecast is subject to uncertainty. In predicting anything as complex as the future of the American workplace, the uncertainty is compounded. It seems clear, nevertheless, that the American workplace has been transformed by fundamental change in the past several years and that this change is almost certain to continue. Although it seems unlikely, unforeseen changes, whether technical, economic, or political, may cause the American workplace to become less driven by cost and flexibility or to focus on other areas than employees for savings or competitive advantage.

Any change as fundamental as the one now occurring is stressful to many people. Organizational dislocations have spurred public opposition. Much of the political rhetoric of the 1992 presidential election campaign centered on the need for more jobs—jobs of the sort that major employers have been eliminating and will continue to eliminate. Legislation has been proposed that in many cases treats the symptoms rather than the underlying causes of this dislocation. Legislation will not change the sources of competitive advantage for employers, although it could well restrict American employers in their search to compete in global markets. The attempt to legislate all or part of the old implicit contract may succeed, but it cannot make that contract a viable form of doing business.

Organizations, employees, and public policy makers need to understand what is likely to occur in the workplace over the next several years so that they can accommodate expected changes or work to channel change along different paths. Two major areas of concern exist in which action now may assist both the transformation of the workplace and the needs of the typical worker in accommodating to that transformation. The first of these is education and training, and the second is meeting the health and security needs of all Americans.

It is clear that the key to survival in the new workplace is a sound basic education and the ability to learn. Too many Americans enter the workforce with neither. Older workers with obsolete skills are no longer carried by their employers and reenter the labor market with little to offer prospective employers. The Office of Technology Assessment of the U.S. Congress (1990) has noted four general policy areas related to dealing with the training problem:

1. Reducing barriers to firm-based training (including a payroll tax or "training levy")
2. Retraining individual workers for career advancement
3. Linking training and technology assistance
4. Improving the quality and effectiveness of training

Successful solutions to the training problem would enable employees to contribute to organizations' competitive advantage and would thus replace the old implicit contract with a new contract based on self-reliance and value added. Such a contract is more likely to survive in an uncertain world.

References

Barrett, P. M. (1992, Nov. 10). Supreme Court refuses to hear appeal of benefit cut for workers with AIDS. *Wall Street Journal*, p. A4.

Bernstein, A. (1992, May 4). Putting a damper on that old team spirit. *Business Week*, p. 60.

Bezold, C., Carlson, R. J., and Peck, J. C. (1986). *The Future of Work and Health*. Dover, Mass.: Auburn House.

Bogan, P. (1992, Oct.). More early retirement windows opened during the past two years. *HR Focus*, p. 5.

Bollick, C., and Neselroth, S. (1989). *Opportunity 2000: Creating Affirmative Action Strategies for a Changing Workforce*. Washington, D.C.: U.S. Department of Labor.

Bowen, D. E., Ledford, G. E., and Nathan, B. R. (1991). Hiring for the organization, not the job. *Executive*, 5(4), 35–51.

Cetron, M. J., Soriano, B., and Gayle, B. (1985). *Schools of the Future: How American Business and Education Can Cooperate to Save Our Schools*. New York: McGraw-Hill.

Coates, E. M. (1991). Profit sharing today: Plans and provisions. *Monthly Labor Review*, 114(4), 19–25.

Cumming, C. M. (1992, Fall). Team players vs. hired guns: Leveraging a competitive advantage. *Compensation & Benefits Management*, pp. 28–33.

De Meuse, K. P., and Tornow, W. W. (1990). The tie that binds has become very, very frayed! *Human Resource Planning*, 13(3), 203–213.

Dobbins, G. H., Cardy, R. L., and Carson, K. P. (1991). Examining fundamental assumptions: A contrast of person and system approaches to human resource management. *Research in Personnel and Human Resources Management*, 9, 1–38.

Doeringer, P. B., and others. (1991). *Turbulence in the American Workplace*. New York: Oxford University Press.

Fullerton, H. N., Jr. (1992). Labor force projections: The baby boom moves on. In U.S. Bureau of Labor Statistics, *Outlook: 1990–2005* (Bulletin No. 2402, pp. 29–42). Washington, D.C.: U.S. Government Printing Office.

Gabor, A. (1992, May 17). After the pay revolution, job titles won't matter. *New York Times*, p. F5.

Gendell, M., and Siegel, J. S. (1992). Trends in retirement age by sex, 1950–2005. *Monthly Labor Review*, 115(7), 22–29.

Hyatt, J. C. (1992, Mar. 3). GE is no place for autocrats, Welch decrees. *Wall Street Journal*, pp. B1, B6.

Hyland, S. L. (1992). Health care benefits show cost-containment strategies. *Monthly Labor Review*, 115(2), 42–43.

Jenkins, G. D., Ledford, G. E., Gupta, N., and Doty, D. H. (1992). *Skill-Based Pay: Practices, Payoffs, Pitfalls, and Prescriptions*. Scottsdale, Ariz.: American Compensation Association.

La Rock, S. (1992). Both private and public sector employers use early retirement sweeteners. *Employee Benefit Plan Review*, 47(2), 14–19.

Lawler, E. E., III. (1986). *High-Involvement Management: Participative Strategies for Improving Organizational Performance*. San Francisco: Jossey-Bass.

Lawler, E. E., III. (1990). *Strategic Pay: Aligning Organizational Strategies and Pay Systems*. San Francisco: Jossey Bass.

Lohr, S. (1992, Aug. 14). More workers in the U.S. are becoming hired guns. *New York Times*, pp. A1, D2.

Lublin, J. S. (1992, July 7). Disabilities act will compel businesses to change many employment practices. *Wall Street Journal*, pp. B1, B4.

Manicatide, M., and Pennell, V. (1992, Oct.). Key developments in compensation management. *HR Focus*, pp. 3–4.

McAdams, J. L., and Hawk, E. J. (1992). *Capitalizing on Human Assets: The Benchmark Study*. Scottsdale, Ariz.: American Compensation Association.

Miles, R. E., and Snow, C. C. (1992). Causes of failure in network organizations. *California Management Review*, 34(4), 53–72.

Miller, J. P. (1992, Aug. 3). Du Pont shifts certain duties to Japan office. *Wall Street Journal*, p. B3A.

Noble, B. P. (1992, May 31). Should fringe benefits be taxed? *New York Times*, p. F23.

O'Reilly, B. (1992, Aug. 24). The job drought. *Fortune*, pp. 62–74.

Price, K. F., Lupton, D. E., and Henry, S. E. (1990). Selecting employees to "fit" the corporate culture. In R. J. Niehaus and K. F. Price, *Human Resource Strategies for Organizations in Transition*. New York: Plenum Press.

Quinn, J. F., Burkhauser, R. V., and Myers, D. A. (1990). *Passing the Torch: The Influence of Economic Incentives on Work and Retirement*. Kalamazoo, Mich.: Upjohn Institute for Employment Research.

Rigdon, J. E. (1992, May 26). Using lateral moves to spur employees. *Wall Street Journal*, pp. B1, B9.

Rix, S. E. (1990). *Older Workers*. Santa Barbara, Calif.: ABC-Clio.

Safizadeh, M. H. (1991). The case of workgroups in manufacturing operations. *California Management Review*, 33(4), 61–82.

Saunders, N. C. (1992). The U.S. economy into the 21st century. In U.S. Bureau of Labor Statistics, *Outlook: 1990–2005* (Bulletin No. 2402, pp. 11–28). Washington, D.C.: U.S. Government Printing Office.

Silvestri, G., and Lukasiewicz, J. (1992). Occupational employment projections. In U.S. Bureau of Labor Statistics, *Outlook: 1990–2005* (Bulletin No. 2402, pp. 62–92). Washington, D.C.: U.S. Government Printing Office.

Solomon, C. M. (1992). The loyalty factor. *Personnel Journal*, 71(9), 52–62.

Stelluto, G. L., and Klein, D. P. (1990). Compensation trends into the 21st century. *Monthly Labor Review*, 113(2), 38–45.

Sundstrom, E., De Meuse, K. P., and Futrell, D. (1990). Work teams: Applications and effectiveness. *American Psychologist*, 45(2), 120–133.

U.S. Bureau of Labor Statistics. (1986). *Occupational Projections and Training Data* (Bulletin No. 2251). Washington, D.C.: U.S. Government Printing Office.

U.S. Bureau of Labor Statistics. (1992). *Occupational Projections and Training Data* (Bulletin No. 2401). Washington, D.C.: U.S. Government Printing Office.

U.S. Congress, Office of Technology Assessment. (1990). *Worker Training: Competing in the New International Economy.* Washington, D.C.: U.S. Government Printing Office.

U.S. Office of Personnel Management. (1991). *Digest of Exemplary Personnel Practices.* Washington, D.C.: U.S. Government Printing Office.

Walker, J. W. (1992). *Human Resource Strategy.* New York: McGraw-Hill.

Chapter Three

Organizational Effectiveness: New Realities and Challenges

Edward E. Lawler III

The corporate landscape around the world has changed dramatically during the past decade. Major corporations, particularly in the United States, have gone through an unprecedented period of change. Particularly visible are the changes that have occurred in the largest U.S. corporations. Some of the most revered and respected corporations have fallen on hard times and have had to restructure dramatically. IBM, Sears, and General Motors have decreased in size and lost considerable market share. While the stock market went up over 200 percent between 1972 and 1992, the market value of IBM decreased by more than $17 billion. The problems with these three companies are particularly noticeable because historically they have been identified as being among the best-managed corporations in the United States; IBM in particular has been identified as a leader in modern human resource management.

One possibility is that the problems of IBM, Sears, and GM are simply aberrations brought about by poor management, bad luck, or extraneous events that could not be anticipated and therefore do not indicate anything significant about how corporations should be managed. The alternative interpretation is that their problems, along with those of many other large U.S. corporations, indicate that to be effective in today's environment, fundamental changes are needed in the way large firms are organized and managed. Evidence is growing that the latter alternative is true. It seems quite likely that because so many changes have occurred in the world in recent decades, it is simply no longer possible to be effective in many businesses with traditional organizational structures and management approaches (Peters, 1992). Indeed, the corporations that have been so good at the old management are often the ones that have the most trouble performing successfully in the new competitive environment that businesses face today (Lawler and Galbraith, 1994). Their past success often makes it difficult for them to adapt and change in ways that will make them successful in a very different environment (Galbraith, Lawler, and Associates, 1993).

New Business Environment

What is different about the environment in the 1990s? Perhaps the most significant difference is the nature of competition. Many businesses have become global, and as a result, success requires much higher levels of performance in three areas: the quality of goods and services produced, the cost at which they are produced, and the speed with which the producers innovate and get new products and services to the market (Lawler, 1992). In situation after situation, organizations have been able to improve their products and services dramatically, not just in one of these performance areas but in two and sometimes all three. For example, automobiles are much more technologically advanced, come to market much more quickly (in about three years), and have fewer defects (less than one per car for the best) than just a few years ago when U.S. companies dominated the North American market. The computer industry has undergone a similar performance improvement. Computers come to the market in record time (less than a year for personal computers), are virtually defect-free, and have a price-performance ratio that tends to improve by 20 to 30 percent annually. As a result, IBM, which once was threatened with breakup by the government for antitrust reasons, is struggling. It was simply unprepared for the dramatic changes in technology and the marketplace that it faced during the 1980s and early 1990s.

Much of the reason for increased performance standards in business after business has to do with the globalization of the economy. Organizations that operate in different countries have different competitive advantages and as a result are often able to enter the marketplace with products that are superior in a number of ways (Porter, 1990). Foreign competitors may also enter the marketplace with different management styles, and some of the success of these competitors is undoubtedly due to their use of these management approaches (Galbraith, Lawler, and Associates, 1993). Simply stated, they organize work differently, deal with people differently, and in some cases seem to perform better as a result. As long as U.S. companies competed only with companies that used a similar management style, the importance of management and organization was not evident and did not provide a competitive advantage unless someone (such as IBM) was particularly good at executing it.

Information Technology

Recent developments in information technology have important implications for the design and management of organizations. Expert systems, networks, personal computers, and a host of new voice communication devices create the possibility of moving information around complex organizations in new and revolutionary ways. Hierarchy has been the natural form of organization structure for decades, and a major reason is its ability to handle the movement of information efficiently. The information processing task involved in managing all the interfaces in a nonhierarchical organization is enormous. Hierarchy has the capability of reducing the number of interfaces by using fewer at each level, and it allows for centralized decision making, an important advantage in a world in which moving information is expensive and difficult. The difficulties of moving information have also led to organizations that are functionally specialized so a group or organizational unit typically performs but one step in a production or service process. With the new information technology, not only can information be moved laterally much more easily in organizations, but single individuals or groups of individuals can also easily gain access to large databases concerning particular products, processes, and customers. "Groupware" and "organizationware" can aid in the formation of a consensus for action and produce whole new decision models in organizations (Morton, 1991). Finally, expert systems can be used to aid decision makers at the lowest level of organizations and can also dramatically reduce the amount of time it takes to respond to customer requests.

Information technology may well tip the balance in favor of markets in the trade-off between using markets or using hierarchies to coordinate economic decisions (Williamson, 1975). More and more markets, including those in stocks, cattle, and used cars, are going electronic. Location-independent and network organizations that are facilitated by communications may make cottage industries competitive again. They can be particularly effective when they are coordinated by market forces rather than by superiors wielding authority.

Information technology has the possibility of revolutionizing the way human resources are managed in organizations. It allows for the easy storage of much greater amounts of information about individuals and their skills, and it potentially allows this information to be distributed widely throughout the organization. At the extreme, we can potentially find out what every individual in an organization can do and is planning to do—by looking not at an organization chart but at electronically stored profiles of individuals that include their work plans for the next year as well as their past accomplishments and present capabilities. Because this information is stored electronically, it can be made immediately and easily accessible to individuals throughout the organization.

The New Workforce

Much has been written about the changing nature of the workforce in the United States. It is becoming more diverse and in many respects more skilled. However, the critical workforce change in many businesses concerns the globalization of corporations and their capability of drawing on a global workforce. Countries differ in the kinds of skills their workforces possess and in the cost of employing individuals with particular skills (Johnson, 1991; Porter, 1990). This reality, as well as the continued development of information technology and information highways, is leading to location-free organization structures and work environments. Work is moving to wherever the skills exist at the best price. Electrical engineering work is increasingly being done in Israel, and software design is increasingly being done in India and Russia. This is happening because of the ability to move information, and in some cases products, around the world in a continuing search for competitive advantage.

Particularly in the more developed countries, the work that remains to be done requires relatively high levels of skills. This potentially has the effect of shifting power from the boardroom to the workplace (Doyle, 1990). The competitive advantage of organizations becomes the skills that employees have, not the skills of the senior executives and their ability to coordinate hierarchical structures.

Taken together, the changing nature of the competitive environment, the new information technology, and the changes in the workforce strongly suggest that new approaches to organizing and managing human resources are appropriate. Corporation after corporation has looked at the issue of organizational change, and many have launched major initiatives. Reengineering, total quality management, employee involvement, and a host of other strategic change efforts have been popularized to help organizations cope with the new environment that they face. The evidence of the success of these changes is mixed at best. There are some notable positive examples, including Xerox, Harley-Davidson, and Motorola, but there are also many others that have failed to change. It is beyond the scope of this chapter to discuss in detail the various change models that have been used and the reasons for the success of some and the failure of others. It is appropriate, however, to look at some of the new principles of organizing that are gradually emerging from these change efforts and to elaborate on them. They provide an important understanding about how organizations are likely to be able to gain competitive advantage in the future through the way they organize and manage their human resources.

Competency-Based Organizing

Research and theory in the fields of organizational behavior and human resource management have been focused for decades by the view that jobs are the basic building blocks of complex organizations. The idea that each individual has a job that involves specific accountabilities, responsibilities, and activities is well established and fundamental to the human resource management systems in most organizations, as well as in most management textbooks. The popularity of jobs can be traced back to the era of scientific management when the work of Frederick Winslow Taylor did much to develop the idea that jobs can be studied and specified and that work methods for doing them can be improved and rationalized if they are studied by experts. The evolution of the bureaucratic approach to organizing carried the idea of jobs further into an overall approach to organizing and managing large numbers of people to accomplish particular goals and objectives. It led to the rationalization and development of hierarchies, line and staff job differences, and a host of organizational design approaches that rest on the idea of individuals holding jobs.

Much of the technology in the area of human resource management is grounded in the idea of individuals holding jobs. Ash, Levine, and Sistrunk (1983) argue that the job paradigm is the unifying concept in employee selection, training, performance management, and compensation. Indeed, most organizations begin their concept of organizing with a job description that typically specifies an individual's duties and activities. Job descriptions are then used for training, selection, career development, and pay determination. These human resource management systems are all designed to ensure that individuals will be motivated and capable of performing jobs. They are selected to fit the jobs, trained to perform them, and rewarded according to how well they perform them. Job descriptions are also used as a basis for grouping individuals into organizational units and for rationalizing the overall structure of the organization.

Despite its historical utility, there are reasons to believe it is time to move away from the focus on jobs and toward a focus on individuals and their competencies (Lawler and Ledford, 1992; Lawler, 1994). Instead of thinking of people as having a job with a particular set of activities that can be captured in a relatively permanent and fixed job description, it may be more appropriate and more effective to think of them as human resources that work for an organization. The change from a job-based to a competency-based approach to organizing and managing individuals is a fundamental one that requires a change in virtually every management system in an organization.

Scientific management and the bureaucratic approach to organizing try to standardize the contributions of individuals to organizational effectiveness. Inherent in bureaucratic theory is the assumption that individuals add value to the degree that they can fit the work structure of an organization. Hence selection tests are designed to identify individuals who can fit an existing job opening, and training programs are used to develop the skills of individuals so that they can do the jobs that have been created. In a sense, effective organization in this approach usually means doing the basics of selection, job design, and organization design better than competing organizations. The implicit assumption is that the best way to optimize organizational performance is to fill jobs with appropriately skilled individuals and motivate them to perform effectively through pay and other rewards. The work on job enrichment and self-managing teams has taken this one step further by pointing out how job design can influence motivation (Hackman and Oldham, 1980). The hierarchy of responsibilities, duties, and accountabilities that is part of the bureaucratic approach leads to a command and control structure that has as its foundation the accountability of individuals for their own job performance and a supervisor or manager who assesses how well an individual performs his or her job duties.

The job-based approach to organizing fit the mass-production economy that dominated Europe and the United States during most of the twentieth century. A number of factors have combined, however, to call the future effectiveness of this approach into question. Work in the area of organization strategy suggests that organizations cannot be successful in many businesses simply by adopting a mass-production approach to the market (Porter, 1990; Galbraith, Lawler, and Associates, 1993). Rapid developments in computing, information technology, and the movement toward a global economy have combined to change business competition (Stalk, Evans, and Shulman, 1992). The consensus is that organizations need to be much more adaptable and to compete on the basis of their core competencies and skills (Hamel and Prahalad, 1989; Prahalad and Hamel, 1990). Indeed, it appears that competitive advantage often resides in the ability to develop particular organizational competencies, not in size, financial resources, or even technological resources (Lawler, 1992).

The emphasis on organizational capabilities directly affects the kind and amount of value that employees are expected to add. Instead of their simply being parts of a large, bureaucratic organization where they may do the same job as hundreds of other individuals, each of them becomes a key competitive asset (Doyle, 1990). Their knowledge and skills become crucial to the organization's ability to perform. Unlike individuals who are simply holding jobs that are designed to be easily filled through selection and training processes, they become key organizational resources. In essence, their skills, capabilities, and learning become an important part of the organization's ability to compete and are at the heart of its adaptability and ability to learn (Senge, 1990).

The trend for organizations needing to be more adaptable, to add more value to their products and services, and to rely on organizational capabilities as a source of competitive advantage combine to challenge fundamentally the idea of using jobs as a basis for managing individual and organizational behavior. When work is routine and focused on mass production, it is reasonable to assume that individuals can be managed through the use of job descriptions and systems related to them. Most individuals are not expected to make unique contributions or add significantly to the value of the products or services they deal with, nor are they expected to learn and change their behavior on a continual basis. Hence training them and paying them to do a particular job well is appropriate. However, that approach runs the risk of creating organizations that underutilize employees and do not develop the kinds of capabilities that are necessary to provide competitive advantage. In essence, the system fails to focus on the capabilities and motivation of individuals, a dangerous trend in situations where individuals have moved front and center as the key resource of organizations. The basic problem is that the development and management of individuals is a second-order effect of the management system that takes as its major focus filling jobs with individuals who can perform them.

The alternative to job-based organizing is to design systems in which the capabilities of individuals are the primary focus and are managed in a way that provides a competitive advantage. Such an organization, created to maximize individual and organizational capabilities, calls for different approaches to organization design, work design, and human resource management in the areas of selection, career development, pay, and overall competency management (Lawler and Ledford, 1992).

Dynamic Learning Organization

The traditional organizational chart, with its boxes, hierarchy, and commitment to fixed positions and job descriptions, in many ways symbolizes the stability that organizations have sought as a key to effectiveness. Indeed, major organizational changes rarely occur in a traditional organization because they are seen as tremendously complicated and difficult. They often involve a major dislocation of people and the rewriting and reanalysis of most of the jobs and relationships in an organization. Learning new working relationships and new jobs takes time, resulting in a temporary loss of efficiency. This has led organizations not to make major structural changes very frequently.

The new logic of organizing is perhaps best captured by the term *learning organization* (Senge, 1990). The assumptions here are very different from those of traditional organizing. They involve emphasis on the need for organizations to change not only as the external environment changes but also as they learn how to do things better and how to interface with the external environment more effectively (Mohrman and Cummings, 1989). In addition, it is important that they change as new technology becomes available and that they learn how to use it.

Effective organizational models and principles are becoming an increasingly important commodity (Lawler, 1992). Because organizations today often face new environments and have access to tools that have never existed before, the best way to organize often cannot be found in a textbook or in the history of the organization. It must evolve through experience and learning. Indeed, organizations that are the best at finding new approaches often end up with a competitive advantage over those that cannot. How organizations learn and how well they learn are of course critical to the effectiveness of any change that is attempted. Companies such as Toyota and 3M have maintained their competitive advantage largely because they have developed highly effective approaches to learning and improving their effectiveness as organizations (Pinchot, 1985; Womack, Jones, and Roos, 1990).

One way for organizations to learn is to adopt a scientific model with respect to learning: experiment with new approaches, assess those experiments, and move forward with a dynamic learning approach to organizing. In the social science literature, this "action research" approach has been discussed for a long time (Lawler and others, 1985). It has become increasing popular with major organizations. They are realizing that they can in fact experiment with new ways of organizing, learn from them, and move ahead to gain a competitive advantage. Through such learning processes, many organizations are gradually redesigning themselves in fundamental ways.

The Global Organization

U.S. corporations have been slower to adapt to global markets than firms in many smaller countries. For decades, American companies have tended to focus on the domestic market and to design products and services for that market (Porter, 1990). One explanation is the size of the U.S. domestic market: it was large enough to support such major corporations as AT&T, IBM, and GM, giving little impetus to enter global markets or produce global products. This thinking has changed dramatically in the past decade for a variety of reasons, including the increasing costs of developing products, greater competitiveness in domestic markets, and the need to compete with foreign competitors in their own markets so that they cannot cross-subsidize their products and gain a competitive advantage in the United States (Galbraith, Lawler, and Associates, 1993).

The drive to create more global organizations has had a number of interesting effects on the structure of organizations. Large corporations such as IBM and Hewlett-Packard have moved their headquarters for certain businesses overseas. They have located not just production facilities but also product development centers in other countries. A few companies, such as Shell, DHL, and ABB, have essentially become stateless corporations that can operate easily and comfortably without a strong national identity. This gives them the ability to avoid the image and entanglements that are associated with being primarily, say, American, French, or Japanese.

Overall, moving to a global footing requires a fundamental rethinking of most of a corporation's organization and human resource management practices. Suddenly, skills are needed for managing multiethnic workforces, and pay systems must reward different kinds of management behavior and the geographical mobility of employees. Finally, skills are needed for coordinating work that is done in different parts of the world by employees of different nationalities. In many cases, being successful with a global model requires that corporations understand local market environments and local preferences well enough to design products for them or create customized products that can be flexibly mass-produced for sale around the globe. Overall, globalization requires a dramatic change in the hiring, development, and human resource management principles that have so long dominated large corporations in the United States and Europe.

Rethinking Size

The most admired corporations in the United States have been among the largest. IBM, Sears, GM, AT&T, Kodak, and Exxon are among the largest corporations in the world. Such concepts as "economies of scale" have often led to the conclusion not only that bigness is desirable but also that it provides a strong competitive advantage. Size often does allow for better access to capital, the support of extensive research and development labs, the ability to purchase products and services at favorable prices, and entrée to global markets. It is becoming increasingly apparent, however, that the advantages of size have been overstated in many businesses. Many of the biggest corporations are experiencing the most severe performance problems. In some cases, size has become more a liability than an asset because it has made corporations inflexible and difficult to change and has created workforces that are not involved in the business and hence tend not to care much about it (Lawler, 1992). A great deal of research has revealed that size is disadvantageous in terms of involvement, satisfaction, and motivation. Historically, these were thought of as solvable or at least tolerable problems, not severe handicaps, particularly when compared to the advantages of large size. However, this thinking is changing.

To improve their effectiveness, such organizations as GE, AT&T, and IBM have had to downsize and dramatically change their approach to being large. This is particularly ironic in the case of IBM and AT&T because both of them were once regarded by the U.S. government as so big as to preclude effective competition. Today, we find them downsizing and restructuring so that they can be competitive with smaller organizations. In essence, IBM is doing to itself for reasons of effectiveness what the U.S. Justice Department tried to do to it several decades ago to make it *less* effective! What is going on here?

To put it simply, the world has changed. What used to lead to effectiveness does not necessarily do so in today's environment. Being big—particularly being big and poorly organized—is nowadays a distinct disadvantage. In many industries, the answer seems to be to find a way to be both large and small at the same time. In certain businesses, many advantages remain associated with size. It pays to be big when dealing in a global market, when raising capital, when supporting a research and development lab, and when developing an expensive new product. It does not pay to be big when it comes to exercising control, coordinating performance, motivating employees, getting individuals involved in the business, and making customers feel important. There is no easy way for organizations and companies to be simultaneously small and large; it requires breaking companies down into small, relatively decentralized units that deal with particular customers or deliver particular products. These units, to be effective, must have their own financial accountability, financial information systems, and reward systems (Mills, 1991).

Product and Customer Focus

The traditional logic calls for creating organizations that are divided into functional specialties. Sales, marketing, production, accounting, and personnel are among the many staff and line departments that typically exist. These units carry out various steps in the process of creating a product or providing service to a customer. They are typically controlled in part through a budget that is hierarchically negotiated. The advantages of a functional organization are many and particularly include the ability to have high levels of expertise in each of the functions. Specialists in sales, marketing, manufacturing, and other areas are developed, and the expectation is that corporations will excel because they are strong in the various functions that are needed to do business.

The problems with this approach to organizing have become increasingly apparent as competitive advantage depends more and more on speed and quality. Speed in particular tends to suffer with a functional organization form because products and services have to be passed from one function to another for development, and this always takes time (Stalk and Hout, 1990). In addition, customers and products may be dealt with poorly in the handoff process between one function and another (Hammer and Champy, 1993). Finally, functional organizations require an elaborate hierarchy to coordinate their actions. This often raises costs because hierarchical controls and individuals are expensive to develop and manage; it also slows down performance because decisions that involve multiple functions are often made high in the hierarchy after going through multiple levels of the organization.

A number of large organizations are moving away from the functional approach to organizational structures that are much more product- or customer-focused. This is one of the ways in which they operate simultaneously as small and large organizations. When it comes to developing a product or servicing a customer, they are small because a small group of cross-functionally trained and skilled employees deals with the customer or develops a product or service that is to be delivered. Among the companies that have moved to smaller, relatively autonomous units that are highly focused on one particular product or market segment are Xerox, Motorola, and Hewlett-Packard.

Meeting Customer Requirements

The logic of traditional bureaucracy calls for job descriptions and the evaluation of individuals against the details of the job description. In the stable world of the bureaucratic organization, with good top-down coordination of effort, this model makes sense. Indeed, if the organization is well designed and all employees perform their jobs well, it is likely that the organization will be effective. Problems occur when the environment is dynamic and the organization must respond to the changing needs of the customer. These conditions require that organizations focus their performance on meeting customer requirements or expectations. Undoubtedly, the strongest influence in moving organizations toward this approach has been the total quality management (TQM) movement (Deming, 1986; Juran, 1989). It has correctly pointed out that the key issue is not meeting job requirements but meeting customer requirements because it is the customers who provide the revenue and the customers who need to be satisfied by the services and products.

The TQM movement goes even further, emphasizing that there are both internal and external customers. Not every employee or group of employees has external customers, but most can and should have internal customers. This has led corporations such as Xerox, Motorola, and Federal Express to do extensive evaluation of internal and external customer satisfaction and to hold employees accountable for the results (Schmidt and Finnigan, 1992). This has the obvious advantage of focusing employees on results that are directly related to their activities and are often more meaningful than simply meeting the objectives in the job description.

Doing Only What You Can Do Best

The traditional approach to organizing has been to create organizations that are vertically, and in some cases horizontally, integrated. The U.S. automobile industry has been a classic example of this logic. Historically, some auto manufacturers made their own steel and glass. They transformed these raw materials into a finished product and sold the product through their own dealer network. In other words, they were vertically integrated, handling all aspects of manufacturing a product. They were also horizontally integrated in the sense that they had within their organization all the necessary staff functions and support services that were needed to create an effective organization. The logic supporting this approach is straightforward and has led to the bureaucratic organizations that exist today. In essence, the assumption has been that a large, well-run organization like IBM, Ford, or GM can do virtually anything better than anyone else, so why trust others to do it? In addition, it was reasoned that if there is a profit to be made by producing a particular part or providing a particular service, why shouldn't the large organization make that profit? Contracting with someone else to do it means that the other organization will gain a profit that should have been retained.

The problems with trying to do everything are becoming increasingly apparent to most corporations. The simple fact is that in a complex environment, performance demands in all areas are constantly going up, and the expertise needed to do things well is constantly increasing. Thus it is hard for any corporation, regardless of its resources, to be good at a variety of things. At the extreme, this has led to networked organizations in which a variety of smaller units are each responsible for just one aspect of what it takes to develop a product or deliver a service (Miles and Snow, 1986). They form a network with other organizations that excel at other activities. The network is generally held together by an organization that performs the key integration function that differentiates the product or service in its market environment.

A good example of a network organization is Nike. It does no shoe manufacturing because it does not feel that it can do as good a job as someone who is specialized in manufacturing. It specializes in designing, advertising, and marketing products. This has allowed Nike to become an extremely successful corporation with an enormous amount of revenue despite a relatively small employee population. Nike's success depends on being able to orchestrate a network of suppliers and distribution channels in a way that ensures the success of network members.

Similar thinking has caused many organizations to outsource some traditional support services. For example, organizations are increasingly outsourcing data processing and legal services. The decision to outsource is generally made after an analysis that attributes costs to particular activities involved in producing the product or service and adopting a customer orientation that emphasizes how well different pieces of the organization are serving other parts of the organization. This approach to accountability opens the possibility for external competitors to bid on things like information processing, equipment maintenance, personnel services, and other staff support services and for the organization to use cost and service quality as criteria for the "make or buy" decision.

Control Through Involvement

The traditional hierarchical approach to organizing assumes that control comes largely from hierarchical authority. This is played out through supervisor-subordinate reporting relationships, job descriptions, and reward systems that are tied to the effectiveness of individuals as measured against their job descriptions. Clearly, this approach has a number of advantages and is still appropriate in some environments. It tends to have significant problems, however, when performance must simultaneously emphasize low cost, high quality, and speed. It also has difficulties when teamwork is required. Decision-making processes tend to be slow because of the need for hierarchical clearances, costs tend to be high because control systems are expensive, and quality is often lost because the individuals actually doing the work or delivering the service are disassociated from the customer or not involved in the production of the total product (Lawler, 1992).

An alternative to command-and-control tactics is the high-involvement approach (Lawler, 1992). There is considerable evidence that corporations are switching to this approach in greater numbers (Lawler, Mohrman, and Ledford, 1992). Basically, it emphasizes moving substantial amounts of information, knowledge, power, and rewards to the lowest level of the organization. In the typical example, small groups, teams, or business units are given the financial resources, the information, the knowledge, and the power to make a particular product or serve a particular customer group. They are then rewarded on the basis of how well they satisfy their customer group or produce their product. Companies at the forefront of adopting this approach include Union Pacific, Xerox, ABB, and a host of others that need to increase their performance in difficult competitive environments. The details of how a more involvement-oriented approach to management can be implemented and where it works particularly well are beyond the scope of this chapter, but it is important to note that in many respects it is consistent with the new organizational approaches that have already been discussed (Lawler, 1992). For example, it requires creating small units focusing on products or services to meet customer requirements and adopting a dynamic or learning approach to organizing. It is also quite consistent with the idea of outsourcing many products and services and creating a world in which internal providers of services have to compete with external providers of the same services.

The New Competitive Advantage

The trends and developments reviewed so far suggest an important conclusion about where competitive advantage will be found in the future. It is not likely to be found simply in the quality of an organization's financing, its access to natural resources, or its country of origin. It also is not likely to be found simply in the quality of its workforce. Workforce quality is best seen as a necessary condition for effectiveness rather than as a key to effectiveness and competitive advantage. The key to effectiveness is likely to be the ability of an organization to match its organization design and management strategy to its business strategy. Organizational effectiveness increasingly depends on organizations' being able to develop their own particular approach to organizing and managing and to continue to evolve it in a continuous improvement mode. In short, organization is increasingly becoming the key source of competitive advantage in today's global businesses. Not only is it the most important source of competitive advantage, but it also has the potential to be sustainable.

Organizations that simply follow the traditional approaches to organizing and managing people appear to be destined to perform at a mediocre level or worse. The competitive world has simply passed by many of the traditional practices that in the past have been regarded as leading to effectiveness. This, more than anything else, is why many traditionally successful companies have become corporate dinosaurs in today's environment. They are still concentrating on doing the old things better, rather than concentrating on how to redesign themselves and create new management and human resource development systems that fit today's social, economic, and business realities. Clearly, it is not an easy task to change a traditional organization into one that is more learning-oriented, competency-focused, and controlled by involvement and customer satisfaction.

Because change is so difficult, it is not unreasonable to expect that many existing organizations will fail to adapt and therefore experience long periods of decline. They are likely to be replaced by organizations that start in today's new environment and hence do not have to be "reinvented." In many cases, it is easier to start new organizations designed to compete in today's environment than to adapt old ones to the new challenges (Lawler, 1992). The reasons for this include the commitment that the existing organizations often have to their in-place human resource management systems and their current structures, hierarchies, and reporting relationships. These often prove to be so critical an obstacle that they prevent change even in the face of significant threats to the continued existence of the organization. Mobilizing and engineering change in large, complex organizations remains a difficult and challenging activity. It is one thing to know how an organization should change and quite another to produce the change. Given the current rate of change in the business environment, the future success of most large organizations is likely to depend on their ability to master the change process. In essence, the ultimate core competency for an organization may be the ability to reinvent itself constantly and move on to the next generation of strategic competency.

References

Ash, R. A., Levine, E. L., and Sistrunk, F. (1983). The role of jobs and job-based methods in personnel and human resources management. In K. Rowland and G. Ferris (Eds.), *Research in Personnel and Human Resources Management* (pp. 45–84). Greenwich, Conn.: JAI Press.

Deming, W. E. (1986). *Out of the Crisis.* Cambridge, Mass.: Addison-Wesley.

Doyle, F. P. (1990). People-power: The global human resource challenge for the '90s. *Columbia World Business, 25*(1), 36–45.

Galbraith, J. R., Lawler, E. E., III, and Associates. (1993). *Organizing for the Future: The New Logic for Managing Complex Organizations.* San Francisco: Jossey-Bass.

Hackman, J. R., and Oldham, G. R. (1980). *Work Redesign.* Reading, Mass: Addison-Wesley.

Hamel, G., and Prahalad, C. K. (1989). Strategic intent. *Harvard Business Review, 67*(3), 63–76.

Hammer, M., and Champy, J. (1993). *Reengineering the Corporation*. New York: HarperCollins.

Johnson, W. B. (1991). Global workforce 2000: The new world labor market. *Harvard Business Review, 69*(2), 115–127.

Juran, J. M. (1989). *Juran on Leadership for Quality*. New York: Free Press.

Lawler, E. E., III. (1992). *The Ultimate Advantage: Creating the High-Involvement Organization*. San Francisco: Jossey-Bass.

Lawler, E. E., III. (1994). From job-based to competency-based organizations. *Journal of Organizational Behavior, 15*(1), 3–15.

Lawler, E. E., III, and Galbraith, J. R. (1994). Avoiding the corporate dinosaur syndrome. *Organizational Dynamics, 23*(2), 5–17.

Lawler, E. E., III, and Ledford, G. E., Jr. (1992). A skill-based approach to human resource management. *European Management Journal, 10*, 383–391.

Lawler, E. E., III, Mohrman, S. A., and Ledford, G. E., Jr. (1992). *Employee Involvement and Total Quality Management: Practices and Results in Fortune 1000 Companies*. San Francisco: Jossey-Bass.

Lawler, E. E., III, and others. *Doing Research That Is Useful for Theory and Practice*. San Francisco: Jossey-Bass, 1985.

Miles, R. E., and Snow, C. C. (1986). Organizations: New concepts for new forms. *California Management Review, 28*(3), 62–73.

Mills, D. Q. (1991). *Rebirth of the Corporation*. New York: Wiley.

Mohrman, S. A., and Cummings, T. G. (1989) *Self-Designing Organizations*. Reading, Mass.: Addison-Wesley.

Morton, M. (1991). *The Corporation of the 1990s*. New York: Oxford University Press.

Peters, T. (1992). *Liberation Management*. New York: Knopf.

Pinchot, G. (1985). *Intrapreneuring*. New York: HarperCollins.

Porter, M. E. (1990). *The Competitive Advantage of Nations*. New York: Free Press.

Prahalad, C. K., and Hamel, G. (1990). The core competence of the corporation. *Harvard Business Review, 68*(3), 79–93.

Schmidt, W. H., and Finnigan, J. P. (1992). *The Race Without a Finish Line: America's Quest for Total Quality*. San Francisco: Jossey-Bass.

Senge, P. M. (1990). *The Fifth Discipline*. New York: Doubleday.

Stalk, G., Evans, P. E., and Shulman, L. E. (1992). Competing on capabilities: The new rules of corporate strategy. *Harvard Business Review, 70*(2), 57–69.

Stalk, G., and Hout, T. M. (1990). *Competing Against Time*. New York: Free Press.

Williamson, O. E. (1975). *Markets and Hierarchies*. New York: Free Press.

Womack, J. P., Jones, D. T., and Roos, D. (1990). *The Machine That Changed the World*. New York: Rawson Associates.

Chapter Four

Supporting the Transition:
A Redefined Role for Human Resources

Jennifer Jarratt, Joseph F. Coates

A harsher environment in which to innovate is emerging. Recession, layoffs, rapid technological change, less conventional loyalty among workers, more lawsuits, and leaner staffing all contribute to tough times for human resources (HR) managers and executives. But there is great promise in the future for HR to play a role in organizational change and redefinition.

The new strategic opportunities in the 1990s and early 2000s are likely to be people-centered and therefore offer good opportunities and visibility for HR innovation. The key is the attitude of corporations and their senior managers toward innovation in human resources and their reactions to people-centered management generally. This attitude is changing. The arrival of Japanese-owned corporations in the United States and their approach to managing people, especially in the front line, is one application of human resources that has had a strong impact on U.S. management.

The task of reconstructing the American corporation in the 1990s to meet increasing worldwide competition will center largely on more effective use of material, financial, and human resources. This implies a strong role for HR planning and management. That new role will not necessarily be easy or congenial to many practitioners.

Human resources practitioners have often found themselves between two organizational poles as both advocates of the workforce who feed back to senior management the workers' reactions to management innovation and plead the workers' case and as agents of management whose job it is to see that individuals in the workforce accept company policy.

Their new role, as powerful actors in achieving organizational effectiveness through the best use of people, will call for earlier and more forthright anticipation and reporting of feedback. It will also call for spreading their ideas and plans for innovative directions around the company, acquiring support, and engaging in face-to-face exchanges. The alternative is to slide back into an auxiliary function, merely executing the initiatives of others.

Human resources finds itself in the unique bridging position of being able, on an ongoing basis, to gather, evaluate, and supply accurate information relevant to the effective use of people in the corporation. It can deliver this information at any level and to any group inside and outside the organization, but the most significant recipient is the executive team. How HR collects, manages, delivers, and takes initiatives based on this information is critical to its future organizational effectiveness.

People-Centered Developments for the Coming Decade

Four people-centered developments for the next decade are significant for the future organizational effectiveness of human resources:

- Total quality management (TQM), including continuous improvement
- Just-in-time (JIT) techniques
- Customer focus
- The high-involvement organization

Total Quality Management (TQM)

In the next decade or two, the current paradigms of management will be turned inside out. Although there are still consultants who complain that total quality management is not worth attempting—basing their warnings on a few well-publicized problem introductions—the powerful attractions of TQM are rebuilding American manufacturing, as they have already reshaped Japan's. In the next few years, TQM will be applied more extensively in the service sector.

How new management methods that are flooding through U.S. companies will develop and change corporations over the next ten to thirty years depends on many factors, including the economy. But the next ten years will see the evolution of continuous improvement processes as a few leading companies reach twenty years of experience with quality methods. Quality will take on a uniquely American character as the processes are shaped by the preferences of the U.S. organization, its culture, and the American worker.

TQM is only one of several terms used to describe methods of creating quality in products and services that does not depend on inspection and the enforcement of rules.

Besides being a method of management, quality is also being used as a metaphor for the struggle to reconstruct organizations into more effective, more competitive, and more personally satisfying places in which to work.

As many as three-quarters of U.S. companies claim to have begun a quality program, but some studies suggest that only a third believe that their programs have had good results so far ("The Cracks in Quality," 1992). Most U.S. companies have had only a few years' experience with quality management, and it probably takes more time than that to customize the precepts of TQM and make it their own. Some Japanese organizations have had more than thirty-five years' experience in doing this.

As might be expected, the attitudes of senior managers are extremely important. A change in CEO can lead to the end of a quality program, especially if it seems to reduce executive room to maneuver. Further, recession has cut some companies' enthusiasm for investment in quality.

It is worth noting that delivering an expanded flow of information to employees to enable them to improve the quality of their work often goes against the instincts of senior managers. Many senior people worked for years to reach positions where they would gain access to the company's business data. To them, information is a privilege, not a necessary condition for improving one's work.

Impatience with the sometimes slow gains of TQM may be a U.S. cultural failing. The American Quality Foundation's cross-cultural comparison of quality ideas shows that American workers are not inspired by many of the ideas borrowed from the Japanese, such as *kaizen* (continuous improvement), unless the concept is given a uniquely American spin. U.S. quality efforts must respond to the "What's in it for me?" challenge of the American worker. For example, a typical U.S. worker is less interested in making minor improvements to someone else's work than in creating something new and improved (Lamoglia, 1992).

Human resources must respond to this challenge. Sustaining the people skills involved in establishing and maintaining teamwork is one critical area. Another is in designing the collection of information, maintaining that collection, and expanding the flow of information to the workforce, internally, from outside the company, and from customers. This includes making information from human resources more available to individual workers, such as on compensation and benefits.

Just-in-Time (JIT) Techniques

The idea of having just enough materials available for production on any given day with delivery timed to the minute is proving to be a powerful and cost-saving concept that is being expanded well beyond its loading dock and inventory origins. Companies are using JIT to realign and radically change their relationships with suppliers of all kinds, including those who supply HR services. Training will be the first HR service affected by JIT concepts.

JIT has the potential for creating a revolution in the way organizations offer training. Traditionally, training departments carried out need assessments, designed courses, and produced a schedule of training sessions for the year. It was up to other departments to make time for their people to attend the courses when they were offered. And based on evaluations, the training department would revise the following year's schedule. Besides JIT, there are other forces influencing training in the corporation:

- Quality programs increase the demand for ongoing training.
- Existing workforces lack the skills to handle the quantitative tools of quality measurement and analysis. Extensive training may be needed so that workers can learn how to use quality tools (this has been Motorola's experience).
- Quality programs are pushing demand for new knowledge and skills down the organization, to workers who previously were rarely clients of the training department.
- New types of training and new approaches are needed to deliver the information.
- With leaner workforces, fewer managers want people to take time away from the job to attend a course.
- Yet more people want training, especially to improve their marketability and skills.

The training department will be expected to deliver the right amount of training at the right time and price and to meet customer requirements exactly. Some requests can be filled off the shelf, with training videos, books, and prepared courses. But trainers must become more creative in anticipating their customers' needs by having the right product available at the right time.

JIT will influence two other attributes of training: cost and value to the customer. In the past, courses were often well presented but not necessarily as immediately relevant as they should have been. In the future, customers will dictate content, presentation, and style and be prepared to pay, based on the material's perceived value to a particular objective.

HR may benefit from anticipating and applying the JIT philosophy to other functions such as employee communications that can be delivered as and when needed and personalized to the individual using computer access and software. Just-in-time staffing, orientation, and testing could also be explored.

Customer Focus

In services and manufacturing, corporations are gaining competitive advantage at two levels of customer service. One is delivering the product or service reliably, of a quality and at a price that the customer considers acceptable. This is sufficient to maintain an advantage if no one else is doing it better. Until recently, this was enough for the major telephone companies, for example. The second is to gain customer loyalty and recommendations to others by delivering the product or service as expected but then surprising the customer with something more. Southwest Airlines delivers service on time and at a competitive price, then goes out of its way to make the trip fun for passengers; as a result, the airline is profitable and highly regarded by its customers, despite its no-frills attitude toward service.

People want longer-term and closer, more personalized relationships in their customer interactions. This is true in businesses that deal with large industrial customers as well as the customers of the local Wal-Mart.

As U.S. businesses get better at delivering this kind of service, customer expectations will increase. JIT and TQM successes raise customer expectations of service, particularly among experienced customers.

Customer focus also educates; in providing a continuously improving service, it is essential to inform and work with customers so as to understand their requirements better. In the insurance business, for example, where customers are frequently resentful of what seem to be mysterious decisions to increase their premiums or cancel coverage, a major effort must be made by the insurers to educate their customers to be more sophisticated consumers of insurance products.

In the past, hiring people who would deal with customers directly was frequently casual and unrelated to their ability to manage the customer interface. Today, with everyone from the CEO on down clamoring for a stronger customer focus, HR will be challenged to come up with recruiting strategies to bring in people who can gain a competitive advantage through customer service.

One solution is to recruit according to the organization's strategic goals, style, and culture rather than for a specific job. Done successfully, any individual in the workforce can represent the company well to customers. Employees must be supported and upgraded through ongoing training. Efforts are being made in this direction at high-involvement companies.

The High-Involvement Corporation

High involvement intensifies the importance of finding the right people for the organization, not just warm bodies with exploitable skills. In a traditional company, the organization or its culture sets the rules, does the socialization, defines the behavior, and downplays individual differences in personality and behavior. A government bureaucracy would be a typical example of this process.

In a high-involvement company, individuals make the culture. The organization relies on the richness of the mix of people to produce profitable and satisfying outcomes. Some software companies are like this, as are many businesses that depend on the creativity of individuals. Even these, however, have traditionally had pockets of traditional culture, such as accounting and dispatching, where creativity has not been considered as necessary. The high-involvement company is an appealing model to firms that have worked through their first few years of TQM and are beginning to rely more on the creativity and commitment of their workforces than on the enforcement of their policies (Bowen, Ledford, and Nathan, 1991). It will be necessary to support and reinforce the wanted behaviors and characteristics to maintain them.

High-involvement organizations and the recruiting strategies necessary to staff them are only one example of the potential for radically different approaches that may emerge in the next decade as companies look for ways to train or build a world-class workforce.

Six Critical Stages for Senior Management in the 1990s

The changes that are occurring as the corporation struggles to redefine and reshape itself are altering the role and functions of senior management in ways that will have powerful implications for human resources. We will define six important decision stages for senior management. At each stage, the crucial factors in the executive's decision are the quality and the source of available information. Note that the innovations discussed earlier all involve information.

The six stages are as follows:

1. *Knowing what is going on now.* Managers must understand the present situation thoroughly. Frequently, what they think they know is filtered and revised by a variety of sources. These filters have the tendency to edit out bad news.

2. *Understanding the forces for change.* To understand what these forces for change are, senior management must listen to outsiders in addition to having an effective internal identification and scanning system.

3. *Understanding all the organization's options for managing change.* This requires generating, identifying, and analyzing information, some of which may not routinely reach top manage-

ment. Strategic thinking at this stage demands going outside the organization as well as using internal resources.

4. *Selecting the right option or options.* A carefully crafted vision of a future state of the business is often used as a guide to present actions. However, this requires that the vision be shared throughout the organization and anticipates an open system in which information flows up and down the organization. The right option must be more than a bottom-line choice to command wide support and effort in the organization.

5. *Implementing the choice.* Successful implementation strategies require a cohesive and coherent set of goals and must set in motion a process that enrolls everyone in the organization in implementing that choice. The executive must be able to influence others to make the same choice. Such consensus increases the chances that the chosen direction will survive changes in the executive team.

6. *Monitoring and measuring the results of that choice.* If the organization has established a quality culture, the systems and tools of measurement are at hand, and information will flow up through the organization.

At stage one, a senior manager knows that he or she is expected to master the current business situation and to provide direction for the people lower down in the organization. But the manager may not be aware that the emerging business environment requires everyone in the corporation to be an expert, and that can mean opening up access to information that previously only senior managers shared.

Stage two requires an open, questioning attitude to acquire the needed information. But the executive is caught between the traditional obligation to direct and control and the emerging expectation that executives merely lay down the strategic path that operations will follow. At stages three and four, in considering options, the senior manager must explore the organization from a new perspective. Success no longer depends so much on high-flying individuals as on perfectly functioning systems and processes. The complexity of these processes must be figured into the executive's thinking about options. Those options must engage the new culture of teams and cooperation.

At stage five, there is an even greater contradiction between traditional and new management. Trained as a fast and trenchant decision maker, the executive must accept that with tomorrow's more knowledgeable workforce, slowly building consensus will be a more effective route to implementing the chosen direction. In stage six, the executive must balance the demands of the shareholders and the stock market for fast results against the more complex and long-term outcomes of, for example, continuous improvement.

Implications for Human Resources. HR must anticipate and shape the executive's ongoing needs for information as the executive suite grapples with the shift to quality-based management. One direct avenue of influence is through the organization's management development program.

Two requirements are critical. First, senior managers must become more person-oriented. Tightly controlled organizations perform well in the short term but possibly less well in the long term. Continual innovation is likely to be essential to survival. An executive must choose a direction, gain support for it, and turn it into a successful new direction for the organization.

Second, managers must learn to operate in more open-ended, ambiguous situations. Traditional managers tend to favor careful and explicit job descriptions, hiring based on expectations of performance in the specified job, close supervision, and defined boundaries and expectations. The new person-centered managers prefer carefully defined cultural expectations, hiring based on personality and behavioral fit with the culture, individual responsibility for job performance, and loosely defined boundaries.

Critical Aspects of Information Flow

Various aspects of the flow of information between HR and senior management affect its value. We will examine a number of these factors.

Information Quality

In theory, at least, senior managers should get the best-quality information available. In fact, what they get frequently passes through many filters first. The impulse to protect the CEO from what everyone else in the corporation knows is sometimes so strong that even a CEO who wishes otherwise cannot get close to the sources of information. For example, a CEO who wants to visit a plant informally to get a firsthand view of the operation can do so only by arriving unannounced and in disguise. Otherwise, everyone will be prepared for the visit and on best behavior.

Further, the selection of information suitable for the executive suite is based on traditional management and cost-accounting systems that are rapidly growing less relevant to running a world-class business. Insistence on the bottom line frequently means that a complex picture has been reduced to a meaningless number. For example, it was recently calculated that if total quality management became part of every U.S. business, the United States could experience a 7 percent growth in GDP. What makes nonsense of this estimate is that a universal trend toward quality management would also involve a change in the way economic indicators are measured.

Implications for Human Resources. Human resources is likely to be caught up in the same information dance around the executive suite as everyone else. But because HR has key information not easily expressed in numbers, HR may have to be more forthright and more specific in presenting facts that executives need to know. For example, the effects on morale and performance of repeated downsizings should be made known to executives, just like the results of initiatives in health care cost savings.

Sources of Information

CEOs listen to other CEOs who are, like themselves, socially and functionally isolated. Even what they read is the same and reflects the opinions of a small group.

If the CEO relies heavily on one consultant or consulting organization as an information source, the company's strategic decision making is likely to be strongly influenced by that individual's world and business view.

Others may shade the truth to senior managers or be unwilling to propose an alternative if it seems to be negative. Everyone around the top team subscribes to certain cultural norms, or appears to, and thus new ideas have to navigate cultural and ideological barriers as well as logical and factual ones. In times of rapid change, there must be a pathway for negative or disagreeable information to be heard, examined, and used.

Implications for Human Resources. The HR executive must be highly visible, extremely well informed about the business, persuasive, and quick to introduce new information and to call attention to bias and premature closure in decision making. As a long-term strategy, the development of greater diversity in the executive suite can only benefit the information flow. The new members will have different sources of information and possibly a different set of business associates.

Information Flow and Access

Most large organizations are reorganizing their operations around a redesigned and expanded information flow. It is not yet fully recognized, however, that senior managers also need a great deal of high-quality information to plan strategy.

Executives need to know at least as much as front-line workers about how the business is meeting its goals—which, in a total quality environment, may be a great deal. This requires that information flow freely. The gatekeeping and channeling of information must be taken out of the hands of managers.

Implications for Human Resources. First, HR must make sure that it is in the mainstream of the information flow. Second, HR must feed information into the system. The information flow feeds back progress—the success of team performance, for example. Monitor the flow to make sure that the rewards and incentives carried in it are supporting the right goals and not inadvertently propping up undesirable ones.

The Need to Understand Systems

The only way to understand an organization's systems and processes thoroughly, several management researchers suggest, is to follow a process around personally until you know exactly what is going on and how resources, workers, managers, and customers are involved (Shapiro, Rangan, and Sviolka, 1992). As mentioned, this is a difficult task for a senior manager. But the guidance is clear. You should understand your organization's primary systems and their connections and interactions with other systems before you try to change them. Customers can give senior managers some insights into systems from their particular viewpoints, but much may still be hidden.

Implications for Human Resources. Encourage systemwide thinking and action through training and management development. Every senior manager from now on who enters the executive suite should be a structuralist, with a grasp of the company's major processes. It is all too easy for managers to rise through the organization without taking the time to follow all the systems that he or she is not particularly interested in or responsible for.

The Continuing Urge and Desire for Control

In today's uncertain business environment, tight, short-term control, such as is exercised in TQM, provides the necessary reliability and stability to produce consistent excellence in goods and services. If the same tight control is extended over longer-term options, however, the company's ability to meet change is compromised. Top and middle management's anxiety about losing control of operations will continue to manifest itself, even in highly effective TQM operations. The proliferation of PCs, E-mail, and distributed work may increase that anxiety because people will have means of communication out of their managers' sight.

The temptation to use the monitoring capabilities of information technology to reassert tighter control over the workforce will be great. Numerous ways of doing this are emerging. Here are some examples:

- All computing can be linked through networks (LANS, WANS, and so on), and access to software and files can be recorded.
- The use of electronic gateways, passwords, and encryption will guard and channel the flow of data and information.
- Monitoring technologies for counting and storing access records, monitoring individual computer use, tracking individuals in locations, and measuring departmental use of computer resources can be put in place.

Implications for Human Resources. Dealing with management concerns about control will be the most difficult during the transition to a more open style of management. When this is in place, a new understanding of the control of outcomes can be reached. In the meantime, managers may need new tools for problem solving, evaluation, the negotiation of satisfactory performance agreements, and other tasks.

The Persistence of Inertia in the Face of Change

Managers stonewall change for a number of reasons. One is that "it costs too much." For example, network managers complain that executives will not see the competitive advantages possible in networking, merely the cost. Innovation in human resources can trigger the same complaint because it involves spending more in an area where most executives are trying to cut costs. Another impediment is that the way things are currently being done is familiar and is comfortable. Organizations frequently adapt and add steps to their processes to meet internal needs, the convenience of individuals, and the demands of managers for information.

In short, managers may contend that everything is fine the way it is, that if they rock the boat, they won't know what's going on. Inadequate, false, or misleading information through the traditional methods of cost and management accounting may be contributing to this illusion. The choice of what is measured will tend to steer the company. Traditional measures tend to omit such important performance details as quality, on-time delivery, and customer satisfaction (Haskell, 1992).

Implications for Human Resources. One of HR's responsibilities is to make management aware of the need to anticipate and deal with consequences on the rest of the organization and to counter resistance. General Motors is an example of a large organization whose leadership appears only intermittently aware of or concerned about the side effects of its actions on the rest of the organization.

The principles and philosophy inherent in TQM provide

support for a systemwide approach to change if senior management is aware of them. Many of the critics of U.S. businesses' attempts to bring TQM into the corporation, however, say that the leadership often treats quality as a fad. HR has a huge opportunity to make TQM a lasting change in business style.

The Emerging Role of Human Resources in Corporate Strategy

In the large North American corporation, there is great potential for a new and stronger strategic partnership for human resources with senior management. Among the reasons why this is possible are these:

- TQM is an evolving new paradigm of management that requires a stronger people orientation to make it work.
- Continuous improvement implies long-term investment in the workforce. Greater emphasis will be on recruiting, training, and retention of employees.
- U.S. firms must develop sophisticated, knowledgeable, and empowered workforces to meet worldwide competition.
- Senior management must gain a deeper understanding of how to lead such an empowered workforce effectively.

HR executives, when surveyed, do not see the corporation becoming soft on people. CEOs of tomorrow's corporations will still be hard-driving, tough decision makers focused on shareholder return and the need to improve (SEI Center, 1990). CEOs advise HR managers to relate their people knowledge to the hard realities of the business:

"Know the business."

"Have a strategic focus."

"Be aggressive with information."

"Be my ear to the ground."

"Be a constant companion."

"Be sure I understand the value of HR to the business."

"Add value early to business decisions."

"Show that your mind extends beyond advising on HR
   issues."

"Know more about the business."

HR executives see their job today as redefining the employment contract in an emerging environment that offers less long-term shelter under the corporate umbrella for individual workers yet expects more autonomy and responsibility on the job.

Important factors in that task, as they see it, are these:

- Clarity in communication—being precise about the relationship between worker and corporation, for example, so that promises are not made that will not be honored

- Creating a new employee contract with different terms— employment for a limited time in exchange for an opportunity to develop skills and to be trained, for example

- Striking a balance between the flexibility gained by hiring, firing, and downsizing and the need to invest in training and educating workers to expand their responsibilities, which increases their value and cost of replacing them

- Reintroducing a sense of unity around shared values and a shared commitment to quality and customer value rather than a lifelong commitment to the corporation

Furthermore, the shape of the job is changing as large organizations shrink to a smaller generalist core surrounded by a variety of business alliances with specialists. It is suggested that in such an organization, the HR function will include marketing—anticipating needs and creating corporate program offerings to identify, attract, and retain employees.

Pay for senior HR people is up, and responsibilities are greater and expanding. HR executives must be prepared to contribute ideas on how to make the company more productive and more profitable. Their jobs, like those of everyone else, are no longer secure. To take advantage of the opportunities ahead, the future senior HR manager must have most or all of the following capabilities:

- Strong business knowledge
- Good knowledge of technology and familiarity with the ways in which information technology can be used to deliver and collect information
- A strategic and systemwide approach to human resources
- An aggressive and forthright stance
- Good connections with internal and external networks of information and relationships

No matter what else changes in the corporation, its senior managers must continue to deliver results that satisfy the various stakeholders in the organization. These include the board, the stockholders, the debtholders, customers, suppliers, alliance partners, the workforce, unions, and the public. People-centered strategies and innovations must produce outcomes that meet the need for results. Cost-cutting, downsizing, and trimming benefits may all produce quick results and seem to meet the need for immediate action. Building organizational effectiveness back up to where it was before the cuts and setting the foundations for improved effectiveness are long-term human resources strategies that may take five to ten years to pay off and will need a strong champion in the executive suite.

Finding a Place to Start

In the near term, HR must dig out opportunities for immediate improvement and act on them to gain credibility for a longer-term strategy. An important area of opportunity is the organization's information flow. It may be well designed and streamlined or haphazard and incremental. In either case, it is likely to include inadvertent, unclear, or negative information that could be hampering organizational effectiveness. These messages could be rewarding the wrong behavior, passing along misinformation about the company's products and services, or merely contributing to clutter and information overload. Review and evaluation of all HR communications should be part of this task.

The development of a more sophisticated workforce—empowered, responsible, and well informed—is likely to have long-term effects because such changes cannot be confined to the job and will inevitably have wider effects on the corporation, society, and the political system.

The future of HR in the large organization, therefore, is not as an advocate for a relatively powerless workforce or as an agent for the corporation's arbitrary policies but as an integrated partner in business planning at one level and as a timely supplier of services and people to operations at other levels.

References

Bowen, D. E., Ledford, G. E., Jr., and Nathan, B. R. (1991). Hiring for the organization, not the job. *Academy of Management Executive*, 5(4), 35–51.

The cracks in quality. (1992, Apr. 18). *Economist*, pp. 67–68.

Haskell, B. H. (1992, Jan.-Feb.). Performance measurement for world-class manufacturing. *Corporate Controller*.

Lamoglia, J. (1992, Oct.). Quality programs must focus on American style. *HR News*, p. 5.

SEI Center for Advanced Studies in Management. (1990). *Human Resources: Management for the 21st Century*. Philadelphia: Wharton School.

Shapiro, B. P., Rangan, V. K., and Sviolka, J. J. (1992). Staple yourself to an order. *Harvard Business Review*, 70(4), 113–122.

Part Two

Organizing for High Performance

The classic command-and-control organization with a hierarchical structure will soon be a relic of the past. In a traditional organization, the authority of control is articulated throughout many levels of management, each in control of a narrowly defined function and a limited number of workers. Control within the traditional context depends on close supervision, usually based on a classic span of control of six or seven direct reports. When companies reorganized, they shuffled the boxes on the organization chart but typically ended up with the same boxes aligned in a different reporting structure. Organization planning has been highly unscientific, although a series of principles has been widely followed.

Job design evolved out of the industrial engineering approach to job analysis, with its concern for efficiency and detailed documentation. Workers have been an extension of their machines, and the objective has been to systematize each step in the production process. This approach to job analysis concentrates on the movement of arms, legs, and hands but virtually ignores the mental state of the incumbent. So what if the workers are bored and frustrated by their routinized work activities? Their job duties have traditionally been stated in highly specific terms on the front page of lengthy job descriptions. Beyond this, the traditional organization has relied on a bureaucratic morass of rules and policies designed to control workers' behavior.

Since the 1980s, interest has been growing in transforming the traditional bureaucracy into a high-performance organization. More recently, the concept of the virtual corporation has gained acceptance as the model for the future. In Chapter Five, Fred Crandall and Marc Wallace compare the differences between these organizational models. The concepts have significantly different implications for managing employees.

In a high-performance work system, employees work in teams where they are collectively responsible for the activities and end results. They are expected to assume "ownership" of the process assigned to the team and to work to improve the process over time. A high-performance system requires fewer workers but multiple skills. One of the important new skills is the ability to work effectively as a team member. When a team learns to function as a productive unit, it leads to reduced cycle times, increased efficiency, and improved quality. Hundreds of successful companies have made the transition to the high-performance model.

The virtual workplace is defined by the process and the product. People do not necessarily work in teams; in some cases, they do not even work at the same location or at the same time. They are effectively tied together by their access to and use of an information system. The virtual workplace relies on specialists, rather than multiskilled workers, who are used on an ad hoc basis. Specialized skills command a premium but are not needed on a scheduled basis. The common skill is the ability to work as a member of a virtual team that exists only as long as needed. The workers have to be able to function cooperatively to solve problems without actually being present.

The infrastructure of a virtual work system is electronic. Because the system is not limited by time or place, workers have to be responsive to market and customer needs, and this ties workers together. Technology has made it possible for people to work from home or from any other location where they can link to the information system.

Another new concept in the management of work that has been covered extensively in the business press is reengineering. In contrast to the "do the old stuff better" marginal-improvement approach, the goal of reengineering is to design a business process from scratch to achieve significant improvement in customer service, efficiency, or process effectiveness. Chapter Six, by Al Walker, discusses the organizational implications of this new management tool. Although reengineering is not a model for organizing work, it will be used to revamp work systems and radically alter the way work is organized for some time to come.

Business processes exist at several levels, and each can be broken down into a series of subprocesses. A reengineering initiative studies the work involved, hoping to make it faster and cheaper. The individual worker can expect dramatic changes in the way the job is done. Reengineering has the potential to transform any work process, producing a turbulent change in the organization and in work relationships.

The redesign of work systems opens the door to consideration of the way work is supervised and of the strategies for staffing, developing, and rewarding employees. Some employees may not be able to make the transition to a reengineered work system.

Reengineering will normally result in the introduction of new work organizations and procedures and new technologies and the elimination or outsourcing of tasks. Many companies have experienced dramatic changes in the way work is performed. This is far more than a shuffling of boxes on an organization chart. The initiative can involve a significant investment of resources and take key people away from their normal roles, but the potential payoff is often substantial.

Chapter Seven, by Stu Winby, looks at the organizations that we can expect to see in the future. The sociotechnical organization model considers the integration of technology and organization structure. The high-performance workplace brings together technical, social, and business subsystems to optimize the congruence among them and support high levels of performance. The design of work systems requires simultaneous attention to all three subsystems.

Future organizations will view work organization and management as critical to success and competitive advantage. Technology cannot be separated from its human inputs and organizational context. New technology must be integrated into an organizational framework that makes full use of the knowledge, creativity, and initiative of human resources in the sociotechnical system. In the future, there will be less reliance on technology for competitive advantage and more on proprietary processes and knowledge-based core competencies.

As technology expands the role of technically trained employees, the human role will take on higher-order control functions necessary to deploy and use new technologies and to operate in a more complex environment. The new technologies will upgrade skill requirements and make the context in which the skills are used more complex and dynamic. Some existing tasks and responsibilities will be eliminated; skill development will remain a major focus.

The basis for designing organizations in the future will be "value chain processes." The value chain concept will shift the organization focus from vertical to horizontal. The unit of analysis shifts to the value chain, where work teams, networks, and organizations become the basis for organization planning. From the individual job to work teams to the network of work processes, organizations will be designed as integrated and self-regulating work systems.

Organizations are converging on a common structural format of interdependent networks of people, teams, and organizations. In turn, every organization is a member of a network made up of other organizations that are suppliers, customers, and strategic alliance partners. Interdependence will increase to the point where some companies no longer compete as freestanding institutions but rather as members of competitive networks. This will increasingly result in "virtual corporations," melding resources from several corporations. That will greatly increase the importance of sociotechnical systems in creating competitive advantage.

Chapter Five

Moving Toward the Virtual Workplace

N. Fredric Crandall, Marc J. Wallace, Jr.

The term *virtual reality* refers to a state that exists in effect but not in fact. Something "virtually impossible" is real to us but in fact shouldn't be real. For example, it is virtually impossible for people to exist physically in two places at once; however, in terms of virtual reality (VR), people may work in two places at once by using telephones (conventional or cellular), networked computers, fax machines, E-mail, and other visual and audio computer-aided devices. The use of picture phones, personal digital assistants (PDAs), laptop computer–based teleconferencing, cellular modem transmission, video E-mail, and a host of other soon-to-emerge technological tools will accelerate the process of breaking down the walls of time and space—reality as we have known it. This *virtual workplace* will provide the capability to be, meet, manufacture, contract, consult, educate, sell, and perform other tasks anywhere, at any time. Having the technology alone will not be enough to gain a competitive advantage. The components of workforce effectiveness (work design, skills, and rewards) must be deliberately configured to reflect the changes in the virtual workplace.

This chapter explores the revolution called the virtual workplace and the essential role that workforce effectiveness plays in making it function. We will describe the applications of today, the prospects for the future, and the reasons why the virtual workplace and the virtual workforce are driving forces for gaining competitive advantage in the twenty-first century.

Note: The authors wish to thank Daniel Cohen for his assistance in the preparation of this chapter.

Virtual Reality, the Virtual Corporation, and Virtual Products

Virtual reality is all about creating and transporting images and information through time and space to simulate the experience of "being there" (Reingold, 1991). VR technology includes such elements as audio and video transmission; head-mounted displays (HMDs); devices to guide computerized instructions such as keyboards, mice, and gloves; and electronic computerized systems to drive the devices. Behind the gimmicks, VR technology has two key components: *immersion*, the illusion of being inside of a virtual system, and *navigation*, the ability to move around, complete tasks, and access the virtual system. In effect, VR provides the opportunity to structure problems and their solutions in a digitally driven real-time analog to reality.

Virtual reality technology is being used in numerous applications to solve mathematical and scientific problems. Although still in its rudimentary stages of development and application, VR principles have begun to reshape social organizations and the work performed in them. The effect of VR on organizations has resulted in virtual corporations and virtual products. Organizations are being transformed by consciously applying the components of immersion and navigation to the workplace, discovering that VR is a means to get people together to share information, complete tasks, and greatly speed up the delivery of a product. For example, Dell Computer revolutionized the PC business using VR applications by putting the customer at the center of the production process. Prospective customers can call Dell on the telephone, discuss their needs with a sales engineer, and order a computer configured to their own specifications on the spot. Each computer is custom-designed and shipped within hours at a very competitive cost. It is a "virtual product"–the customer engages with the supplier to define the product together. The process is less of commodity sale to a customer than a joint problem-solving process, the creation of a product that never existed before. This combination of speed of execution and consultation with the customer, traversing time and space, are key components of VR at Dell.

The VR transformation will bring tremendous changes in the workplace, changes that will redefine work and what people do on the job (work design), the competencies they will bring (skills), and the best way to provide rewards.

Definitions

The virtual corporation as defined by Davidow and Malone (1992) has the following properties: "To the outside observer [the virtual corporation] will appear almost edgeless, with permeable and continuously changing interfaces between company, supplier, and customer. From inside the firm the view will be no less amorphous, with traditional offices, departments, and operating divisions constantly reforming according to need. Job responsibilities will regularly shift, as will lines of authority—even the very definition of employee will change, as some customers and suppliers begin to spend more time in the company than will some of the firm's own workers."

The virtual product or service is defined by its instantaneous availability "at any time, in any place, and in any variety." The *capability* to produce the product or service in such instant variety is its "virtualness." The product definition exists in virtual reality, and its real analog is produced instantaneously by people in the VR network. The advance of VR technology has created the ideation of the virtual product, and the development of the virtual organization has created the capacity to deliver the virtual product or service.

In many respects, the advent of virtual products and the virtual corporation is the hyperextension of the just-in-time revolution of the 1980s (Crandall and Wallace, 1994). Traditional bureaucratic organizations were transformed by customer-driven demands to deliver products and services of higher quality in reduced time frames. This led to restructuring around critical work processes—reengineering the organization—to rationalize the capability to deliver a defined product or service to a defined customer at a defined level of quality at a specific time.

The virtual product is produced by a cooperative *network* combining suppliers, manufacturers (providers), and customers. The virtual product can be delivered almost instantaneously because product specifications, production capability, and delivery are on-line and can be made simultaneously available to all network participants. Which individuals represent each organization may not be clear to outsiders. Roles in the process are defined at the moment the product is conceived. Relationships change and reshape for each successive product or service.

An example of how a virtual organization produces a virtual product is embodied by the role of an engineer named John Chabot, who works for a manufacturer of industrial valves, the Ross Operating Valve Company of Troy, Michigan (Neikirk, 1993). Chabot's work involves networking with suppliers and customers, engineering a product, and dealing with databases, as well as producing the valves themselves: "Not only does Chabot design valves . . . , [but] he also sells them to customers and works closely with the machinery and testing operations. He and his coworkers assist customers in designing their own valves for their particular needs. Then Ross produces and delivers them as fast as possible, sometimes in as little as 24 hours." Chabot describes his role in the following way: "I design it, machine it, test it, make sure it's ready to ship to the customer. And when the customer gets it, I interact with him to make improvements or change design. We're really more of a *process* than a product."

Components of the Virtual Workplace

The virtual workplace is where work is done to produce and deliver virtual products. It is defined by the same properties of immersion and navigation that define VR and is supported by VR technology:

• *Immersion:* the network of suppliers, producers, administrators, and users that engage in defining and ultimately delivering products and services. The network uses computer networks, as well as audio and video transmission linkages creating an illusion of a specific venue for work.

• *Navigation:* the process steps and protocols required to complete the product or service. The virtual workplace differs from traditional and high-performance workplaces. For example, for the engineer at Ross Valve to complete customer requirements, numerous high-technology applications are required to structure the workplace in VR. In addition, a new work role, skills, and rewards are required to define and stabilize the working environment.

Development of the immersion component has accelerated in the past ten years. First the cellular phone created the mobile office; then the laptop computer created mobile data transmission and analysis on a mass scale. In the near future, we will be using digital cellular audio, as well as data and video communications, in totally mobile networks, and work will be able to be done at any time and place. Companies such as AT&T have begun experiments with mobile offices and have found that a whole new social structure for work is required (Fitzgerald, 1991).

Working in the Virtual Workplace

How does an employee work out of a virtual office? What skills are required to produce the virtual product? How does a virtual team operate? There are no models to answer these questions in traditional organizations. Even high-performance organizations are based on common-site face-to-face relationships.

The virtual workplace is not bounded by visual and physical proximity. It exists as a platform to conceive, produce, and deliver the virtual product. It may involve individual contributors and teams from a number of firms. To understand the difference between the traditional and virtual workplace, consider how we express what we do in the traditional workplace. We characterize the traditional workplace in personal terms: "I go to work," "I finish my work." Work is centered around me; I go to a specific place to do it, and I leave that place when I am done. This is an ultimate simplification of the workday, in which work is defined in time and space and almost ceases to exist for us when we are not physically present. The personification of work and the attachment to time and space present tremendous productivity problems. For example, one of the greatest problems with shift work in manufacturing is the inability to capture and transfer experience and expertise gained on one shift to the next. Companies have attempted to deal with this problem by creating bridges: logs, notes on bulletin boards, periodic meetings, and electronic mail systems.

By contrast, in the virtual workplace, work may be independent of time and space, and what we do is expressed differently: "I join in an ongoing work process." Work centers around a process, the process is ongoing, and the work has no beginning or end. The emphasis shifts to joining a *group* activity, with the focus on a process-oriented continuous work flow.

In the virtual workplace, work is driven by the structure and dynamics of the virtual product. The process is repetitive, but the product differs to some degree with each iteration. Work is not centered on me, and I don't control it by my presence. The boundaries of the workplace are determined by the participants. These limits are most probably broader than "my" firm or "my" company.

Intel, a leading manufacturer of microprocessor chips, recognized this as a major productivity issue, especially in the initial manufacturing stage of a new generation of microprocessors when speed is crucial for recouping investment in technology—a significant competitive advantage. One solution involves "improvement teams" (members of cellular work teams from each shift) that meet weekly to coordinate their activities, discuss problems, and share solutions (Wallace and Crandall, 1992). The teams also meet *continuously* via E-mail to accelerate continuous improvement between meetings. In effect, the key to process improvement is the conscious application of disciplined E-mail communication in the coordination of intershift process improvements that is acted on between meetings.

Workforce Effectiveness in the Virtual Workplace

Our research and experience have demonstrated that workforce effectiveness has three major components:

- Work design—what people are asked to do and how activities are organized
- Skills—the competencies required to achieve desired work system outcomes
- Rewards—monetary and nonmonetary inducements for achieving work system goals and outcomes

These three components combine to drive performance and promote strategic objectives. We have found that an effective work system requires alignment of all three components (Wallace and Crandall, 1992).

The evolution from traditional to high-performance organizations has changed work roles from an individual focus to a team focus. In addition, people have acquired much broader skill bases, breaking down boundaries between nonexempt and exempt work or white-collar and blue-collar work. Finally, reward systems have been transformed, and broad-based incentives and competency pay programs are being developed to support the execution of high-performance work systems. In high-performance organizations, workforce effectiveness has enabled companies to achieve a competitive advantage through increased flexibility and speed, facilitating the transition to a process flow framework. Figure 5.1 depicts how the three components of workforce effectiveness affect the execution of strategy.

Our challenge is to develop models for work design, skills, and rewards to support virtual workforce effectiveness. Evolution to the virtual workplace will require some radical changes for these components of workforce effectiveness.

Evolution of the Virtual Workplace

The workplace has come through two major stages of development over the past forty years and is entering yet a third. Each is as different as night from day.

1. *Bureaucratic work system.* The bureaucratic work system was a product of the industrial revolution and the canons of scientific management. It was designed to be rational and economic. Work is divided into economic components called jobs. People are bounded by rules, policies, and a hierarchy of authority articulated throughout many layers of management, each in control of a specific function (accounting, operations, marketing, sales). In a bureaucracy, people work individually, in very narrowly defined spheres of activity. They don't ask questions and they do their work.

2. *High-performance work systems.* High-performance work systems evolved from research that began with the Tavistock studies in England during the 1940s and 1950s and came to fruition in the sociotechnical systems (STS) research and practice described by Lawler and others (Lawler, 1986; Kilmann, Covin, and Associates, 1987; Pasmore, 1988). The advent of high-performance work systems has been rapid and pervasive since around 1980. In such a system, people work on teams, in a highly coordinated fashion. They

Work Design	Skills	Rewards	Execution
What people are asked to do and how activities are organized	Competencies and skills needed to obtain results	Messages sent, behavior rewarded, career opportunities	Speed, flexibility, profitability, process improvement, customer responsiveness

$$\text{Work Design} + \text{Skills} + \text{Rewards} = \text{Execution}$$

Figure 5.1. How Workforce Effectiveness Drives Execution of Strategy.

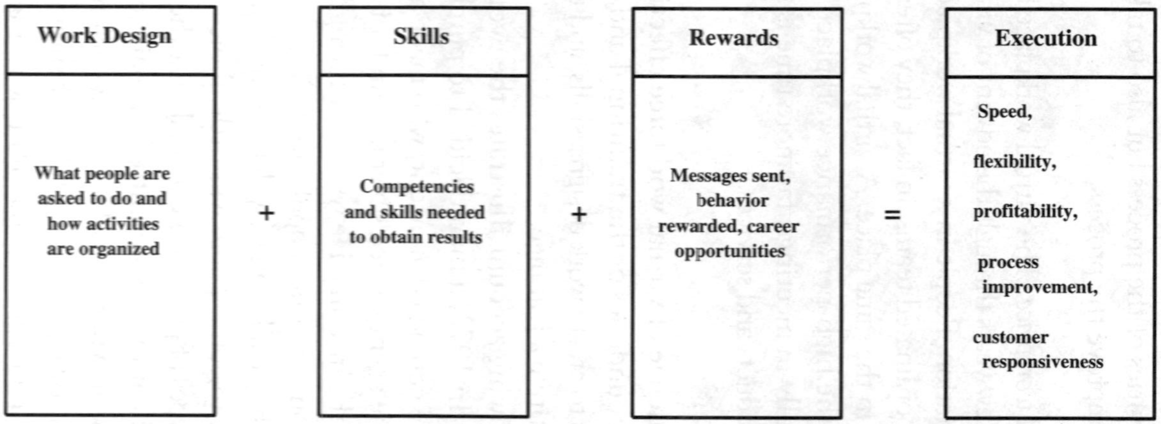

are collectively responsible for an entire set of activities that make up a particular business process. They are expected not only to conduct the activities of the process but also to take the initiative to change and improve the process.

3. *Virtual workplace.* The virtual workplace has been created in just the past few years through the advent of virtual reality and the virtual corporation. People in a virtual workplace do not necessarily work in coordinated teams; in fact, they often don't work at the same time or in the same place. A virtual workplace is not as labor-intensive as the high-performance workplace. Much less time is spent physically in meetings; far more time is spent creating and delivering products and services.

The challenge of virtual workforce effectiveness is to move beyond the boundaries of the traditional and high-performance organizations to create work designs, skills, and reward systems that boost competitive advantage.

The following account illustrates the evolution through the three stages. In 1972, a man decided to purchase homeowner's insurance. He contacted an agent, who made a date to visit three days later. The agent carried several pounds of binders, paper, and brochures to the meeting. He wrote down lengthy details concerning specifics on a four-page application. Many questions had to be answered with "I really can't say; let me check with the home office and get back to you." There was little choice in coverage—only three basic types of policy were available at the time.

The application was submitted by mail and put into a batch processing room, where it sat for two days before beginning a long, disjointed approval process. As Table 5.1 shows, no fewer than ten hands touched the application as it made its way from desk to desk.

Twenty years later, the traditional process had given way to a high-performance structure with fewer players and pass-offs. As the next column of the table shows, a team replaced individual

Table 5.1. Insurance Application Process: Yesterday, Today, and Tomorrow.

	Traditional	High-Performance	Virtual
Players	5: agent, application analyst, rate analyst, underwriter, application manager	5: application team (agent, processing team), team leader	3: agent, experts
Processes and procedures	1. Contact customer 2. Consider products available 3. Fill out initial application 4. Rate application 5. Review for approval 6. Issue policy	1. Contact customer 2. Input application 3. Review for approval 4. Issue policy	1. Assess customer needs and resources 2. Create product 3. Issue policy
Cycle time	2 weeks	1 week	30 minutes
Unit cost	$500	$300	$50
Work design	Sequential: individual participants make narrowly defined contribution needed	Coordinated team effort: team members perform broad range of activities, as needed	Collaborative virtual team effort: agent accesses expert system, calls experts

contributors, and productivity was improved by streamlining the process and introducing versatility of roles on the team. Cycle time and cost were reduced.

A virtual insurance application will radically change the way products are conceived, developed, and delivered. The agent will work with a laptop computer at the insured's premises to assess needs, draw up the policy, and issue it on the spot. The cost will be greatly reduced, and cycle time to policy issue will be almost nil. Instead of a work team at the home office, the agent will work with an "expert system" residing in the computer, as well as individual experts in the home office who will aid with on-line advice. As you can see from the table, the process has been streamlined again, and the high-performance work team has disappeared.

In this example, deliberate changes to work design, skills, and rewards were required to support the evolution of insurance sales. Work design moves almost completely outside the home office to the client's residence and the virtual reality represented by the laptop computer with its expert systems. Decisions are made on-site. And that is possible because all the information is also on-site. The skills required by the agent now not only include people skills but also computer skills, telecommunicating skills, and broader knowledge of insurance products. Reward programs will also change as whole departments of back-office functions disappear.

Work Design in the Virtual Workplace

Work design is the first element of workforce effectiveness. It involves the structure of work processes and the definition of work roles. Work design has three components (Wallace and Crandall, 1992):

- *People locus:* activities required to perform work and where they are located. It used to matter where people were located. In a virtual workplace, "where" is stretched beyond face-to-face relationships. The correct question is, to what extent can people be provided access to the process, regardless of where they are?

- *Decision locus:* the kinds of decisions that are required. In the virtual workplace, how can decisions be obtained on demand? What elimination of time and distance is required?

- *Information locus:* information required to complete work in the system. In the virtual workplace, massive databases are common. The major issue for workforce effectiveness is how to make all conceivably needed information accessible to all network participants, twenty-four hours a day.

Table 5.2 summarizes the difference in work design in traditional, high-performance, and virtual work systems.

Table 5.2. Work Systems and Work Design.

Element of Work Design	Traditional	High-Performance	Virtual
People locus	Low direct labor cost High division of labor with low task variety Individual contribution Work defined by function at a common site	High direct labor cost Little division of labor with much task variety Teams Work defined by process at a common site	Moderate direct labor cost Moderate division of labor with much task variety Individual contributors, team combination Work defined by process and product that transcend the boundary of the organization
Decision locus	Bounded by procedures and protocols Managed top-down High cycle time	Fewer procedures Self-managed teams Low cycle time	Fewer procedures Individual decisions aided by expert systems Instantaneous cycle time
Information locus	Information available on a need-to-know basis	Broad availability of information to support problem-solving efforts	Information on all aspects of the design, development, and distribution process available to entire network

In the traditional workplace, employees generally work at a common site with a high division of labor, conducting repetitive work. This approach—born in the industrial revolution and driven by the bureaucratic model—is aimed at achieving low labor cost. Decisions are made from the top down, with requisite layers of organization to drive the decision process. The decision process is supported (or bounded) by a highly structured set of protocols, tending to freeze the high cycle time. Finally, information is guarded, and data that do not support protocols are regarded with suspicion if they might upset the routine (Nadler, Gerstein, Shaw, and Associates, 1992). Traditional organizations supporting this approach to work design are structured around departments and functions.

As we have noted, the traditional model has been transformed into a high-performance or "lean" model. There are striking differences in people, decision making, and information. First, there is a reversal of division of labor. Teams are used to conduct work. Instead of a functional or departmental focus, work is organized around key processes, with individual members developing versatility and multiple skills. Direct labor cost increases on a per-head basis, due primarily to the requirement for multiple skills. However, work is still conducted at a common site. Indeed, project work teams and natural teams require significant interaction to achieve effective results (Osbum and Associates, 1990).

The overall objective of the high-performance or lean model is to reduce cycle time and increase quality. There have been hundreds of successful applications of this model, ranging from durable goods manufacturing to insurance operations and consumer customer service operations. To reduce cycle time, these organizations reduce the number of procedures and focus on decision making at the team level, cutting out numerous bureaucratic layers. It is a necessity for information to be broadly available to support problem solving and decision making.

The virtual workplace is defined by the process and the product and includes the chain of suppliers, purchasers, and manufacturers. It also relies on significant information databases and transmission capabilities. More specialists will be required in the virtual workplace than in the high-performance organization. This is not a return to traditional divisions of labor. Instead, the specialists will be available to the virtual network on an on-demand basis. These specialists will be linked in a number of ways, ranging from software support personnel accessed via toll-free telephone numbers to CompuServe-type network access arrangements. Thus there will be more individual contribution. Direct labor costs will be lower than in the high-performance organization because more flexible work arrangements will replace permanent employment. Being able to work anywhere at any time is already spawning a variety of flexible work arrangements, including working from home, permanent part-time work, job sharing, and contract employment (Patton, 1993; Mason, 1993). It was reported recently that the largest U.S. employer in 1993 was a temporary employment agency with a payroll of approximately six hundred thousand (Fierman, 1994).

Competencies for the Virtual Workplace

The virtual workplace will require a highly customized set of skills, ranging from deep technical specialties to the capacity to work independently yet in a network or on a string of virtual teams. As with work design, virtual competencies differ from those of high-performance organizations (see Table 5.3).

The skill sets used in the high-performance organization support the centralized role of teams. To operate effectively in common-site teams, specific roles for each member include technical skills, support skills (including activities that bridge departments and functions), and team skills (including those required to operate as effective team members and team leaders). Career paths are clearly

Table 5.3. Work Systems and Required Competencies.

Competencies	Traditional	High-Performance	Virtual
Required skill sets	Each person focuses on own function; functions segregated by occupational specialty	Bridge gaps of skill worlds; focus on multiskilling and versatility	Highly specialized, but person must be capable of operating in VR (new skills)
Career path	Rationed by the pyramid organization	Clearly structured; requirement for each team member to fulfill a role on team	Individual is much more independent; career path may traverse organizational boundary; independent contracting commonplace
Role of team	Secondary role to support individual contribution	Central to getting work done	Minimal maintenance of team and team management

defined, and all team members are required to function well in their role.

The virtual workplace differs in significant ways. The skill set required is not as stable or predictable as with high-performance work teams. Specialization is at a premium, but it is not needed all of the time. However, when a special skill is required, the individual must be able to operate as a member of a *virtual team*. Virtual team skills include a unique combination of cooperative problem-solving behaviors that can be applied even in the absence of experts. Substantial self-management and discipline are also required to accomplish tasks on a timely basis at remote locations.

Careers in the virtual workplace can take three paths. Some organizations will attempt to provide traditional careers, including hierarchical promotions for skill and authority. Taking this path would put strain on individuals who are working on a team with members from more than one company joining to produce a virtual product. A second path, in response to roles spanning companies, is to create new entities, such as joint ventures and partnerships, and place employees in them. This approach has been widely used in the cable and telecommunications business. Under the umbrella of a company such as TCI are numerous entities that focus on specific products and markets (Kneale, Roberts, and Landro, 1993). The role of individuals is shaped largely by the product subspecialty. A third path follows the approach of independent contractors who work for an organization for either a short period of time or on an ad hoc basis.

Rewards in the Virtual Workplace

Reward systems include the elements of base pay and pay progression (most often delivered in the form of merit pay), forms of variable and contingent compensation, recognition, and health and welfare benefits. All of these elements of the reward system will undergo change in the virtual workplace.

Base pay and pay progression will be a less prominent part of the reward system. People will be less focused on a long-term relationship with their employers and more concerned with the virtual organization—the tethering of suppliers, producers, and purchasers. Individuals will concentrate more on the value of each virtual interaction. Pay will therefore tend toward contract wages and salaries, commissions, and other types of contingent rewards. The temporary nature of the employment relationship will encourage more temporary compensation arrangements.

Employing companies will face a dilemma. On the one hand, employment relationships will be temporary or short-term. However, it will still be necessary for employers to maintain workforce skills and competencies. Thus we expect to see "skill-based" contingent pay arrangements wherein each contract will be priced according to the skill level or value of the work required.

Recognition will be a more natural part of the virtual workplace. Peers will share information, feedback, and performance appraisals as a means of maintaining and upgrading the quality of the virtual products and services. Finally, we expect benefits to be largely supplied by the contract workforce itself (see Table 5.4).

Making the Virtual Workplace Work

For managers hoping for some respite from change, the bad news of the virtual revolution is that work systems (including work design, skills, and rewards) must continue to change in order to achieve and sustain competitive advantage. The good news is that there are several things for you to do to prepare for and maximize the impact of virtual work systems in your organization. Based on the experience of organizations that have made the transition into virtual work systems, here is our advice:

1. *Stop force reductions and downsizing.* By reducing head count,

Table 5.4. Work Systems and Rewards.

Rewards	Traditional	High-Performance	Virtual
Base pay and pay progression	Grade structure, merit pay	Skill-based	Lower prominence of base pay in the total compensation mix
Bonuses	Reserved for management and top professionals	Broad-based, including goal sharing for production work groups	Greater focus on commissions and contingency pay; broader use of equity participation
Recognition	Minimal use	Broad-based	Peer recognition and acknowledgment within the VR network
Benefits	Noncontributory by employee	Contributory	Self-supplied

the organization reduces capability and makes it less able to develop and use the competencies it needs to compete. Downsizing is the corporate equivalent of anorexia nervosa. It may make sense as an emergency lifesaving tactic, but the longer term requires keeping and building on core skills. Organizations that are into successive waves of downsizing will eventually lose critical competencies and wither away. Energy should be spent on developing new markets, products, services, and growth.

2. *Prepare for a variety of workforce arrangements.* Traditionally, the choice has been full employment or unemployment. Anything else is considered abnormal, undesirable, or unnatural. For example, executives of some organizations have become concerned about the use of temporary or noncore employees. Not only are such arrangements responsible, but they are also both rational and compatible with promoting the virtual conditions necessary to create products and services "instantly."

Employment arrangements will be based on the types of skills each person contributes: core skills (full-time employees using core competencies continuously in the organization's operations), reserve skills (part-time permanent employees who represent a reserve of core competencies to be employed on an as-needed basis), ad hoc or specialized skills (subcontractors who supply highly specialized expertise whenever needed), and support skills (subcontractors supporting core processes but not integral parts of the process—for example, physical maintenance, cleaning, and food service). These alternative workforce arrangements will be the expectation, not the exception, in the virtual workplace.

3. *Rethink the use of teams.* Teams and teamwork are the hallmarks of the high-performance workplace. The advent of high-performance work systems has led to the creation of teams that work at a common site and are highly coordinated. This will not be the case in the virtual workplace. Technology will take us beyond the necessity to yoke individuals in time and place.

In the North American culture, the importance placed on individual accountability and contribution is as strong as ever. Group incentive systems such as gain sharing and goal sharing have provoked uncomfortable questions about losing track of individual merit. We will still have teams in the virtual workplace, but they will not have the identity and prominence characteristic of high-performance work teams.

4. *Expect virtual rewards.* Rewards will focus on incentives for individuals to develop and apply the competencies required to create immediate products and services. In addition, reward systems will become simpler, focusing on continuous reinforcement for achieving end-process results for customers. Accounting and information systems will be more powerful and user-friendly, allowing incentive systems to reflect entire business processes, not just parts of the process. The end result will be rewards occurring closer to the desired result in time and space.

5. *Expect continuous change and improvement.* The infrastructure of the virtual workplace is electronic. It is not based on paper; it is

not mechanical, nor is it bound to time or place. Work in the virtual workplace will continuously change as circumstances, threats, and opportunities evolve in often unpredictable ways. Workforce arrangements must adopt a capacity to change and evolve in the same unpredictable ways. The word *career* will no longer mean "the jobs you will have this year, five years from now, and so on until you retire"; *career* will mean "the platform of competencies you need to do your work now, destined to change in ways that cannot be defined much in advance." Prepare yourself to anticipate change and develop your skills accordingly. Your job will be to play a role in a virtual process. Both the process and the demands of your role will be in a continuous state of change.

References

Crandall, N. F., and Wallace, M. J., Jr. (1994). Alternative rewards in a time-competitive organization. In W. A. Caldwell (Ed.), *Compensation Guide* (chap. 31). Boston: Warren Gorham & Lamont.

Davidow, W. H., and Malone, M. S. (1992). *The Virtual Corporation.* New York: HarperCollins.

Fierman, J. (1994, Jan. 24). The contingency workforce. *Fortune*, pp. 30–36.

Fitzgerald, M. (1991, May 13). AT&T furnishing wall-to-wall laptops. *Computer World*, p. 41.

Kilmann, R. H., Covin, T. J., and Associates (Eds.). (1987). *Corporate Transformation: Revitalizing Organizations for a Competitive World.* San Francisco: Jossey-Bass.

Kneale, D., Roberts, J. L., and Landro, L. (1993, Oct. 14). Plugging in: Bell Atlantic and TCI are poised to shape new interactive world. *Wall Street Journal*, p. A1.

Lawler, E. E., III. (1986). *High-Involvement Management: Participative Strategies for Improving Organizational Performance.* San Francisco: Jossey-Bass.

Mason, J. C. (1993, Jan.). Workplace 2000: The death of 9 to 5? *Management Review*, pp. 14–18.

Nadler, D. A., Gerstein, M. S., Shaw, R., and Associates. (1992). *Organizational Architecture: Designs for Changing Organizations.* San Francisco: Jossey-Bass.

Neikirk, W. (1993, Feb. 22). Wanted: Skilled Jack-of-all-trades. *Chicago Tribune*, p. 1.

Osbum, J. D., and Associates. (1990). *Self-Directed Work Teams*. Homewood, Ill.: Irwin.

Pasmore, W. A. (1988). *Designing Effective Organizations: The Sociotechnical Systems Perspective*. New York: Wiley.

Patton, P. (1993, Oct. 28). The virtual office becomes a reality. *New York Times*, p. C1.

Reingold, H. (1991). *Virtual Reality*. New York: Touchstone/Simon & Schuster.

Wallace, M. J., Jr., and Crandall, N. F. (1992). Winning in the age of execution: The central role of workforce effectiveness. *ACA Journal*, *1*(2), 30–47.

Chapter Six

Reengineering: Improving Productivity Through Business Process Redesign

Alfred J. Walker

Reengineering entered the American scene with relatively little fanfare in the late 1980s and early 1990s, primarily as a computer systems initiative. It was billed as a new method by which systems departments could ensure that their efforts would not just install yet another mechanized system to perform the identical functions or work steps that had gone on before. Rather, it espoused that the technologist and the user engage in a rethinking—a "reengineering," as Michael Hammer called it (Hammer and Champy, 1993)—of the work process itself before automation is employed.

Although reengineering started slowly as a concept—systems analysts felt a little odd in their new role—it soon caught fire. Today, every company in America has at least heard of reengineering, if not actually gone through such a process. However, the experience of companies that have tried it appears to have been uneven. Some have had very positive results; others have had to abandon projects for a variety of reasons, some foreseeable and some not. What, then, is the future of this methodology? Is it just another fad, or are there deeper benefits to be gained from it than meet the eye? Is it the next wave of continuous improvement and total quality, and if so, where will it lead?

We will review the brief history of reengineering as it applies to the human resource area, explore the concepts and components of its underlying methodologies, and then highlight some areas where reengineering has been especially helpful. We will then go on to cite some lessons that have been learned along the way.

A Brief History of Reengineering

Reengineering can trace its roots to several disciplines, methods, and procedures: industrial engineering, operations research, computer technology, market research, management consulting, and, perhaps most important, the quality initiatives. It is a hybrid science to be sure—some wags refer to it as a "mutt science" because it is not a pure discipline in and of itself, and it had to be codified by such firms as mine (Towers Perrin) and the CSC Index to become usable. It was unique—or at least uniquely American—in that it took previous work and added some new spins and twists to solve the problems of the 1980s and 1990s. It updated work analysis techniques, customer sensing, cost-benefit analysis, and some work study tools to fit the problems of the day, and it packaged them with some new technologies and thinking that were previously unavailable, the result being a set of methods and tools that permit work to be studied and changed to benefit everyone involved.

Industrialized work—or "modern" work, as it sometimes is referred to—has been studied for quite some time, and the literature is fairly rich with the writings of Chris Argyris, William F. Whyte, Frederick W. Taylor, the Hawthorne Works studies, Peter Drucker, Frederick Herzberg, and others who have contributed much to the understanding of complex work environments. The methods that these individuals taught us to use showed us how to break work into tasks, how to group like work for greater throughput and job satisfaction, and the influences that pay and benefits may have on the workers.

These various writers guided us, with some ups and downs, through the growth years of American businesses—the 1950s and 1960s—as the economy expanded and prospered in the post–World War II era. There was little competition for North American businesses, as there was no Japanese or German manufacturing capability to speak of at the time. As a result, the primary interest for American companies was not being efficient or even being very good in terms of quality. Whatever they could make sold; the main concerns were quantity and distribution, not organizational effectiveness (other than on the factory floor). The development and implementation of manufacturing technology was tops on almost everyone's list because it was (and remains) one of the primary ways in which to manufacture and distribute vast quantities of goods at reasonable cost.

American companies were manufacturing and shipping automobiles, electronics, televisions, home appliances, telephone equipment, aircraft, pharmaceuticals, mainframe computers, and other durable goods worldwide. During the expansion years, little emphasis was placed on the overall structure of organizations or on the basic behind-the-scenes office and support work. Methods analysts usually operated as internal consultants (with an auditor's mentality); they drew up procedures and instructions on such matters as how suppliers were to be paid or the manner in which approvals for a purchasing requisition were to be obtained. They also used statistical analysis techniques from their industrial engineering backgrounds.

These discipline methods used work flow techniques to analyze work as it passed from person to person, and these serve as the basis for rearranging that work, whenever possible, to be more efficient. As the economy grew into the late 1960s, American companies discontinued or shuffled a large number of these methods and procedures specialists and industrial engineering analysts into other positions to make better use of their skills. A great many were moved to the hot new area of computers.

In the late 1960s, the first commercial business computers and computer-based systems were being introduced, and who better to help with this work than the procedures analysts? They became systems analysts and computer programmers. Unfortunately, strange as it may seem, many were never heard from again. The demands for this skill were so great that they were swallowed up by the business of building and installing computer systems. Suffice it to say that when we now need skills, methods, and procedures, twenty years later, few, if any, experts remain who have any knowledge of how to study work or write a procedures guide. We have systems analysts and some job redesign people but almost no one who really understands the basics of studying work, which is what reengineering is all about.

The good news is that more than enough gains were made in the computer field, operations research, and quality work during this twenty-year period to offset any lack of progress in methods work.

Another discipline that helped shape reengineering was operations research. Operations research work gave us a framework for analyzing flows and taking a horizontal view of a work process. Also, that discipline brought a strong focus in computer-based models for analyzing business problems, especially cost-benefit analysis.

But the quality work was unquestionably the force that enabled reengineering to mushroom as it did. The customer focus principles were new and powerful in their ability to get at the important aspects of concentrating on right work and satisfying customer demand: shortening cycle time and time-to-market principles, just-in-time techniques, continuous improvement ideas, quality circles to involve all areas and levels of employees in problem solving, measurements to guide us, and so on. If industrial engineering was the father of reengineering, quality work was the mother.

The newer technologies enabled reengineering to take place. It is one thing to envision the future and conceptually reengineer a process on paper; taking action is quite a different matter. Without the technologies we are using to bring about these changes—computer-based systems, local and global telecommunications networks, voice response systems, imaging, facsimile, scanning, and the like—few of the gains could have been accomplished.

These technologies were refined and perfected during the 1970s and 1980s, the same time during which the cold reality of competitive market forces caught up with giant, lumbering American companies. In their place, companies that were more focused on quality or lower cost suddenly became players and began to attract business. A new quality-conscious, sophisticated, and affluent buyer emerged. No longer did people just want an automobile; they wanted a solid luxury automobile with all the trappings–and they were willing and able to pay for it. However, the big monolithic American manufacturers found themselves lacking. Often their products were not as good or as specialized as the consumers wanted. Customers also wanted better service. They wanted the basic products and the whole "buying and maintaining" experience to be better. Our largest companies suddenly found that the German and Japanese industries, as well as smaller, more adept American companies, were serious competitors. The result was a series of recessions and layoffs in the 1980s as the big American corporations attempted to adjust their fixed, high-wage-scale modes of operation to more flexible, responsive styles. And the impact has extended into the 1990s. Out-of-date manufacturing and service methods were undergoing a profound change from the early command-and-control model of management typified by companies such as by AT&T, General Motors, and IBM to much more cohesive smaller units. These new companies were highly publicized by the authors of the day, including Peters and Waterman in *In Search of Excellence* (1982), as the new model of efficiency. Companies like Hewlett-Packard and Texas Instruments became the envy of all with flatter organizations and more entrepreneurship. The profit squeeze was on, and downsizing began in earnest in the 1980s.

Globalization also was thrust upon us during that time period as well. We could make a product in the United States, or we could make it in Korea—same product, same quality, much different cost basis. The message was clear: get smaller, get more efficient, and listen to the customer, or you will fail. People who did not believe that calamity could befall long-successful organizations got a rude awakening when revered companies like Sears, Roebuck and IBM lost money and almost went under. Both got caught overstaffed, complacent about their past success, and entrenched in their marketing, manufacturing, and style of management. But now they had to change.

It was onto this stage in the late 1980s that the reengineering players stepped. You can now appreciate why they were well received.

Concepts and Methodologies

A working definition of reengineering for this purpose is "the redesign of business processes to achieve significant improvement in one or all of the following areas: customer service, operational efficiency, and process effectiveness." *Significant improvement* is key in this definition because both the reengineering process and traditional quality programs have the same goal of improvement. What do we mean by "significant"? And when do we cross the line from continuous improvement to reengineering? The answers often lie in the objectives and goals of the project and the extent to which management is committed to change. *Significant* must be quantified early on by the sponsor of the project. How much gain in cycle time, reduction in cost, and the like are we looking for? This must be clarified up front.

Members of the press have latched onto the catchword *reengineering* and have used it as a substitute for downsizing, calling it "right-sizing." Although downsizing might be one of the outcomes of reengineering, it is not reengineering itself. To be a true reengineering project, a project must contain at least the following components:

1. A process orientation leading to the identification and selection of a set of processes to study

2. Alignment of processes with business strategy

3. Analysis of the current work, including process mapping and cost analysis

4. Customer involvement, including measures of satisfaction

5. Visioning and best practices

6. Options for proceeding, including outsourcing, technology usage, work elimination, and work restructuring

7. Benefits derived by improving the process and ongoing measures to ensure that the benefits are capturable

8. Recommendations for implementation and measures for future monitoring

Let us examine each in turn.

Process Selection

Business processes exist at several levels. For example, we might have a process called product distribution, which exists at a high level. It, in turn, might be broken into several components: ordering, shipping and delivery, receipt and accounting, and so on. And each such process can be further decomposed into microprocesses that are much more detailed. An example of this in human resources is a high-level process called staffing, which could be broken into subprocesses of internal sourcing, college recruiting, external employment, and temporary employment and contractor hiring, and each of these could be broken down further into more discrete processes. Internal sourcing could be subdivided for analysis into a set of microprocesses such as preparing a requisition, job posting, interviewing and selection, and transfer.

At the start of a project or shortly thereafter, the project team would select either all the processes for study or a sample. (A representative set of processes is easier to study than all the work processes in an organization.) Should a project team decide to study a sample, it might apply the following considerations:

- *Efficiency:* the process might be extremely inefficient by today's standards (too time-consuming or too complex, too many forms, too much paperwork, and so on).

- *Effectiveness:* customers may have been complaining about the work and the effectiveness of the process.
- *Cost:* the cost of the process may be too high for its value.
- *Importance:* the process may be critical to meeting business targets.
- *Dispensability:* for business reasons, the customers or the process owners may want to eliminate it altogether.

Although choosing a sample is easier than examining all the processes, care must be taken that the selections are truly representative of the whole and will enable the team to envision, determine costs and benefits, and design the new process to obtain significant improvement.

Processes are not to be confused with tasks, jobs, organizations, or functions. Let us explain by defining some terms.

A business *process* is a series of steps, actions, or tasks that lead to a desired result. In the course of business conduct, the steps, actions, or tasks in a process can be handled by customers, employees, agents, or contractors or by automated means (computers, telephones, ATMs, or other mechanisms). For example, making a cash withdrawal from a bank may require several actions, depending on the specific method chosen (see Table 6.1).

Although the methods of each *process* are different, they combine people and machines in a number of steps. The employee takes certain actions, which include verifying and updating accounts and disbursing cash. The *job* is that of teller. The *organization* involved is the National State Bank. The *function* here is the retail branch banking. This particular process might have been chosen if customers were complaining about the wait involved when trying to get cash, or the bank may have been trying to cut the cost of retail banking and the process was selected as one of the sample processes to be studied as representative of the whole. The purpose

Table 6.1. Cash Withdrawal.

Cash Withdrawal: Old Method	Cash Withdrawal: Reengineered
1. Customer writes check or withdrawal slip and submits to teller.	1. Customer inserts card into ATM and enters PIN.
2. Teller receives check and reviews for completeness.	2. ATM verifies card and PIN.
3. Teller verifies signature against signature on record.	3. Customer indicates amount to be withdrawn.
4. Teller verifies that balance in account is sufficient to cover disbursement.	4. ATM verifies that balance in account is sufficient to cover disbursement.
5. Teller disburses cash to customer.	5. ATM updates balance.
6. Teller updates balance.	6. ATM disburses cash to customer.

of reengineering here is to study not how the teller is performing but rather the entire process, including the computer systems behind the teller, forms, policies, and so on. The hope is that the ATM process delivers the same or better service at a lower cost when all aspects of the process are taken into account.

Be very clear on that: reengineering studies work, not individual performance. Confusion sometimes arises when the term is improperly applied to the assessment of how well John or Mary handles a particular job. Reengineering the process should make it better, faster, and cheaper, with greater customer satisfaction, and the effect on the incumbent will most likely be a change in work—perhaps for the better, perhaps not. But the assessment of John's or Mary's performance on the job is a management, employee, and customer matter and not a topic for study in the reengineering process per se. Setting out competencies is, but performance evaluation is not.

Strategic Alignment

All processes must be gauged for importance. This is especially true for the processes selected for analysis under a sampling approach.

They should be scrutinized to know how important they are to meeting business goals not only in the eyes of the process owners but also in the eyes of the customer. This is a critical stop, for we need to know which processes can be reduced in terms of resources and investment and which should be increased in light of the new business model. Therefore, this alignment step involves input from senior management and customers as well as the process owner. This input can be obtained through meetings or by careful assessment of the implications of the business strategies by the people doing the reengineering analysis.

Each step of the current process must be reviewed with the objective of the strategy in mind. Will this process, as it exists, help or hurt our strategy? Do we need it? If we need it, how can it be made better? Once the strategic alignment has been examined, there may be other reasons for retaining the process, such as legal and statutory considerations, but the business need will be reviewed and will result, ideally, in a clear indication of what work is important and where the process fits with respect to it.

Work Process Analysis

Analyzing the process as it exists today takes two primary forms: work analysis and cost analysis. Both are important because they address two complementary aspects of the process: the work and the cost.

Work analysis—studying the work itself—is further subdivided according to the two techniques that are used: process mapping, in which the current job steps and tasks are depicted in flowchart form, and task analysis, in which a given work task is described. Task analysis is used when a task has to be examined in greater detail than would be covered in process mapping.

The process flow maps highlight several key items for each process, subprocess, or microprocess:

- Process name

- Process objective (why it is performed and necessary)
- Primary customers and stakeholders and their issues and priorities
- "Hands-on" time of people in the process
- Current use of technology
- Cycle time (start to end, on average), as well as best case and worst case
- Issues and problems with the process from the worker's standpoint
- Measures or indicators currently used to gauge how well the process works
- Detail of the work (to permit assessment of its value) and level of work being performed, including control points
- Trigger points and end of process

These are all critical pieces of information for the people doing the reengineering; they now have some hard facts to work with. The maps may have to be verified or "fleshed out" at several sites to ensure that costs and timing are treated consistently and that the analyses are complete.

Task analysis concentrates more on the issues that are inherent in the conduct of each task for which more detail is required. These are normally conducted in one-on-one interviews with incumbents to gain a greater understanding of the issues and job steps.

Complementing the work analysis is the cost detail of the process. Values can be determined by summing the individual costs for all the subprocesses. Also, the team should uncover any additional costs to consider; quite often, additional costs are found in budgets that are usually not identified by process. They have to be prorated or allocated to the processes to which they apply.

The costs involved in the processes must be rationalized or normalized by volume estimates to cover a work period or site and then extrapolated for the division or company as a whole. That is why several site visits or verifications are needed to make the extrapolation reasonable if not all sites or work groups can be visited.

A valuable tool often employed here is activity analysis, in which all employees in a function, process, or organization complete a survey on how they spend their time. These data reveal where paid time is spent.

Customer Involvement

One of the most important steps that can be taken in the reengineering effort is to engage customers in a series of dialogues and discussions on their satisfaction level with the current processes and what they believe can be done to improve them. The input can be obtained through group feedback sessions, direct interviews, and telephone or written surveys.

Customers often view the process very differently from the employees involved. Customers may not see the rationale for the way the work is organized, why certain control points and audits are required, or why the tasks are done in a particular sequence. And they have little tolerance for inefficiencies now that they have been exposed to world-class operations for several years. They have learned to expect excellence in product quality and service, and if your process is not up to such standards, it is quite obvious to them. This feedback from customers will yield specifics on what to change and why—very often parts of the process quite different from those that the workers or process owner would choose. For example, process owners may concentrate more on internal controls than customer service. Feedback, then, is especially important because one area of improvement does not have to be sacrificed at the expense of the other; both views can be incorporated into the reengineered process.

Customers can also be engaged in a series of trade-off discussions to get at another critical piece of the reengineering effort, prioritization.

One of the problems with inefficient service functions and corporate back-office support functions, such as finance, human resources, information systems, legal, and purchasing, is that the workers in them are frequently working longer hours, often with frustrating results if customer complaints are rising, budgets are tight, and outdated technology is used to support the work. By reengineering standards, the total volume of work must be reviewed and simplified. However, when the entire process or set of processes cannot be improved due to budget or other limitations, choices have to be made: Which ones should be worked on? Which must stay the same for the time being? Can we make do with less than a total overhaul? The customer input to this set of trade-offs—what gets improved and when—can often be surprising to the reengineering team in that customers may place the most value on a part of the process that is easy to fix. This knowledge is obviously very helpful in guiding the implementation work.

Visioning and Best Practices

The part of the reengineering work that most people want to move to immediately—understandably, for it is at the heart of the charge process—is "visioning," whereby team members, process owners, stakeholders, and customers arrive at what they believe is the best way of handling the particular process in the future.

It is dangerous to begin visioning without fully understanding the current work—what is right with it as well as what is wrong with it. Without this information, we could easily lose parts of a process that are needed. That is why we must map the current work first to get at the detail, the cost, and the issues. These data then become the starting point for the visioning component. Following this, the objectives of the process must be reexamined in light of the business needs, strategic direction, and alignment. The issues, cost, and work details are brought to the forefront, and each proposed solution is tested against these pieces of information: Does the solution lower cost? Does it resolve all or most of the issues? Does it raise the value of the work, decrease cycle time, and increase customer satisfaction? Have we changed the process *significantly*? Visioning must also have a model to reengineer against. This is where the objectives of the project come into play. Is one objective lower cost? If so, how much lower? Is better service a goal? If so, how much better, and at what expense? This model must be known in advance if the reengineering team is to alter the work correctly.

During this exercise, it is valuable to understand what the best competitors or other industry leaders are doing with the similar process in their companies. This method of comparing one organization to another has been referred to as *best practices* or *benchmarking*. "Best practices" normally refers to the method by which you would find out through visits, discussions, face-to-face meetings, or telephone conversations with representatives of another company how they handle a particular process.

Benchmarking is actually quite a bit more complex than best practices in that it involves sharing information at a significant level of detail regarding costs, organization structure, manufacturing techniques, customer service, and work methods with the company you are benchmarking against.

Either method opens the eyes of the team doing the reengineering into a world where an alternative method of handling a process exists. Many companies feel that their way is the only way of approaching a problem, so it is helpful to learn that in dealing with the same issues, there is another, perhaps better way to reach the same objectives yet perform more effectively or efficiently.

Arriving at a new vision must begin with a rigorous examination of the process objective. What is the goal of the process? Why have it at all? Why not eliminate it or attach it to another process? Current methods must be rigorously challenged, and these questions must be asked by the team again and again. The processes become stuck over time, immersed in bureaucracy, plagued by delays, bogged down in paperwork and record keeping. The first priority of the reengineering team is not just to streamline or outsource existing processes but to eliminate them entirely or approach them in a much different way to gain a new level of effectiveness. The objective is not just to reduce steps in the handling of an invoice from ten to five but to eliminate paper entirely or eliminate the invoicing process itself if at all possible. To accomplish this, the policy, the practices behind the process, and even the culture of the company may have to be changed. Incumbents may feel threatened; after all, they may not have a job in the new process or may be shunted to positions of reduced power or influence. In any event, the process owners sometimes have a difficult time reaching a new vision without seeing themselves in it.

Visioning can be helped by including the people potentially affected in brainstorming exercises or by using best practices or customer suggestions as springboards. Customers generally view a process as a horizontal series of events, many of which they believe could be improved if handled by one individual or adapted to new technology. Today's work may be poorly designed, and process owners or incumbents who are part of the series may work in different organizations or at different locations. And when forms and paperwork are involved, delays and interruptions in the process will occur. Work proceeds in fits and starts—annoying to customers yet unnoticed by the employee performing the task. Here's where the input from the customer—"new thinking"—is helpful to get the team started on different ways to resolve issues and decrease expenses.

An excellent method to prompt visioning is to ask participants to clear their minds of the day-to-day constraints of time, money, and organization and begin listing different methods of handling the process. Once this session gets going, the team can begin to challenge some of the underlying policy issues and barriers.

Often the team will outline a number of improvements in the process that can be made in a relatively short period of time. These are referred to as "quick hitters" and usually require little capital investment. Management often has the authority to change certain practices or procedures that may be overly complex or involve double-checking—holdovers from an earlier time when the controls or automated systems were not as good as today's. The team should address how the new process should be measured—time, quality of service, cost, or some combination of the three—and if there is an initial target or standard for the measure, it should be indicated.

Finally, the requirements for the new vision must be listed. This might entail indicating policy changes, new technologies, new organizational alignments, and staffing or outsourcing arrangements that will be required to bring about this vision.

Options

The ultimate visions for the process will usually involve a combination of new work organization and procedures, technologies, task elimination, and outsourcing, often entailing some disruption to the work, change in procedures, or new investment. This is where the team must weigh the possible cost savings and increases in customer satisfaction against the initial investment and changes to the organization, policy, and procedures that will take place to arrive at an acceptable implementation approach.

Change for the better is always desirable, but if the gain is not worth the investment, the merits of the program are open to question. The particular packaging of the various options must be left to the team, but certain guidelines should be kept in mind as the team evaluates each of the potential options:

- Solutions should achieve the amount of change that management desires.
- Solutions should be practical, using technology that is appro-

priate and available, organizational alignments that will be accepted by management, and so on.

- At least one option should be bold in its concept and breadth—a real reach for all—while still being practical. An option can be practical no matter how far-reaching it is.
- There should be some "quick hitters" as part of each option to generate some savings as the project is implemented.
- Customer service should not decline beyond desired limits (at least not for long) under any option.
- Outsourcing should always be considered, even though it may not necessarily be recommended as the ultimate vision.
- The best practice or best company example from benchmarking and how that solution could work for your company should be discussed.
- Options should recognize and meet the most important business strategies.
- Technology should always be considered as a means to deliver better service and reduce cost. The price of computer technology and telecommunications continues to fall, while salaries and people-related costs continue to increase.
- There should be at least one low-cost option to give management a chance to save money.

Benefits

The team should also evaluate each of the potential implementation options in terms of time and resources. If the ultimate vision is very attractive but cannot be implemented for many years, management might be reluctant to back it as a serious plan. There are so many uncertainties with business plans—new approaches to handling work, outsourcing options, new technologies that are emerging—that a plan with a long time horizon will generally be unacceptable. The only exception might be if this option is integrally tied to the company's business plans. Similarly, the resources to be expended to get to the ultimate vision must be realistic in terms of people and cost. Tying up the most effective people in an organization or spending a lot of money on the project must be worth the gain. The impact of the new process, then, must be such in terms of return on investment or return on assets to persuade management that a given option is worth the investment and the risk.

Measures should be put into place to evaluate continually how the new processes are performing in terms that both customers and management understand and can live with. The benefits of change must be real, and the team's work is not complete without instituting measures for each new process proposal.

Recommendations

Following the evaluation of the various options, the team will generally decide that one option is more attractive than the others. This decision must be tested with several of the constituents—customers, process owners, and senior management—before it is finalized. This is especially true if the option contains anything that might be controversial. The team has to know the impact of the recommendations, just as management will invariably want to know the ramifications of its own decisions.

The time frame and discrete implementation steps should be noted in the plan, along with the schedule of expenditures and cash outlays that go along with the recommendations. Management will also want to know how much of the outlay, if any, is covered in the budget.

Displacement of staff and the potential costs of staff reductions must also be shown. Along with the implementation plan, a schedule of benefits should be provided. A month-by-month or step-by-step guide would reveal when the organization would gain from the implementation of a given feature in terms of cost savings, customer service, or new capacity.

The final recommendation must always be tested and evaluated in the light of other initiatives and requests that go to the senior management team for approval. How is this proposal going to be viewed? Is it strategic enough? Is it in line with current thinking? Is it bold enough? The team must determine how to package its proposal so that it has the best chance of success.

Impact of Reengineering

Reengineering and business process redesign have had an enormous impact on work. Application of the basic principles, including customer focus, reducing cycle time, and process owner feedback, has led to dramatic changes in the way that activities are handled. Steps in the process that were once thought essential have been removed. Processes with multiple approval levels saw many intermediate signatures eliminated. Costs have dropped. New technologies have been employed, with the result that elapsed times have often been dramatically shortened and customer satisfaction levels boosted. In essence, the processes were rethought and repackaged, with definite improvements made.

Some changes, though, have been painted in both good and bad light, and others are far less apparent. They should be mentioned because they will have as dramatic an impact as customer service increases and cost decreases.

New Working Relationships: Manager, Teams, and Compensation Links

Visioning and work redesign bring the opportunity to examine several other aspects of service delivery, including the role of the manager in light of these changes, the arrangement of work in self-contained positions or in teams, and the potential for new methods of compensation. Each of these topics is treated elsewhere in this text and therefore will not be gone into a great deal of depth here. However, it must be emphasized that process redesign will have a dramatic impact on the way work is performed and on the traditional boss-subordinate role, and the project team should be alert for them.

For example, reengineering, with its customer focus, may well result in new customer roles, backed by new technologies with direct customer contact. These new positions may be able to fulfill customer orders, answer customer inquiries, and clear customer complaints. Automatic call routing and tracking systems keep logs on call volume, waiting time, length of each call, and other details. Customer service satisfaction levels can also be computed automatically. In fact, most of the tasks once handled by several individuals can be performed automatically with better and less expensive results.

This type of working arrangement raises some thought-provoking questions; for example, what is the role of the supervisor? In the more traditional model, the supervisor would ensure a constant flow of work to the subordinate, ensure proper training, examine the quality of the work, handle interdepartmental problems, and respond to customer complaints. The newer work models used in reengineering change this relationship from a "boss as director" to a "boss-as-helper" role. Since the work is being heavily influenced by the customers, the boss can assist by ensuring that there is room for development by assigning the worker to some nondirect customer contact work from time to time to help build other skills or improve performance. In essence, the boss is interested in boosting overall worker performance, not "running interference" for the subordinate or engaging in territorial organizational battles.

Obviously, new skill sets are needed for this type of boss, more aligned with employees' skills as well as customers' needs and desires.

The teams that might be formed as a result of reengineering will also have to be aligned with customers' needs. Each team will require feedback on how the entire team performs. The newly designed process and systems should be positioned so that they support the team and provide sufficient data in such operational statistics as work volume, cycle times, errors and returns, customer satisfaction levels, costs, and waste. In essence, the teams should have enough information regarding their production or service to be able to monitor their progress and adjust to boost output or correct trouble areas.

Here, too, new roles emerge for the supervisor in terms of working with the teams to find the best workers for each task, making shifts or supplying training and guidance where needed. The boss as coach is the operating model that some companies use, altering the team mix and varying the level of investment needed to maintain supervisor results.

New methods of compensation might also be in order as a result of the reengineering work. Why use the same methods of appraisal as in the past, when the boss was entirely familiar with the work and, in a very real sense, the employee worked for the boss? In the newly designed processes, ideally, the employee works for the customer. Why, then, would our salary and incentive systems not reflect that? This is but one example of the need to rethink the plans and programs that are in place. What about a plan that rewards individuals who achieve better customer satisfaction scores? Companies are examining not only the compensation basics but also different forms of incentives, including time off, work at home, and pretax arrangements. Most compensation systems were developed for the individual, with little or no accommodation for the team concept or a process-driven, customer-focused environment. Obviously, this has to change.

Change Management

Reengineering is all about change—change for the better. The objectives of the reengineering effort may vary—cost savings and efficiency in one project, better customer service in another, building a higher value work team in yet another—but the result will be change: new work, new customer interaction, new teams, new methods of measurements, new pay options, new technologies, and so on. Not everyone involved in the change will welcome it.

Change represents uncertainty, and uncertainty will usually elicit resistance until the potential outcome is clear. Also, change brings a potential loss of influence and social structure. Most workers have developed a framework in which they operate: they have mastered their jobs and the process and actions they employ to get work accomplished, and they understand their co-workers. They may not like all aspects of their job, their boss, or their co-workers, but at least they are known commodities. Most people try to slow down change whenever they can in an attempt to control it. The same is true in the corporate world. When change is introduced, most people will try to control the pace; many will even resist. What will happen to my job, my co-workers, the influence I now have? All are natural concerns.

Managing these concerns, then, becomes a challenge for the people involved in reengineering. What types of changes are likely to occur? Will there be major upheavals in the way work is handled? Even if there are no layoffs or displacements, the workers will have questions. Will I have to move? What new job skills will I have to learn? What if I can't learn and perform them at an acceptable level? Will I have sufficient input and say in how the new work is to be handled? Will my new job be more stressful?

Open and honest communication with all concerned is best. Face-to-face meetings to discuss the reengineering process itself, why it is needed, and its goals are essential. Other forms of communication, such as memos, booklets, and internal company publications, are good too, but because objectives may change, caution is advised in putting into print anything that might be difficult to retract. Communicating the company's commitment to the basic principles of trust and caring for customers and employees, a deep-seated belief in top-quality products and services, and a need for competitive advantage should be good starting points; the reengineering efforts should be linked to those values. In any event, manifesting management's concern and strong support for the project helps greatly.

Right-Sizing or Downsizing

No treatment of the subject of reengineering would be complete without mentioning the loss of jobs attributed to it.

To be sure, jobs have been lost, but usually only when a sizable number of processes have been compressed, for it is rare that a change to one process would yield reductions of force large enough to generate cutbacks or layoffs that could not be handled through normal personnel processes such as job posting and other internal placement programs. When the reduction of workers is sufficiently large to warrant attention, it is usually symptomatic of other events, such as restructuring due to reduced product demand, planned technological improvements, or elimination of duplicate services as a result of mergers or acquisitions.

Competition *is* forcing businesses to operate with lower overheads and seek out methods of doing more with less, and this does lead to some worker redundancies. But generally, new processes are designed, tested, and tried out far enough in advance to permit arrangements to be made for handling workers ultimately displaced. Management can use the normal human resource programs to help them find alternative employment.

Dealing with workers affected only slightly has become more of a problem than first thought. In changing a process by reducing steps and eliminating tasks that are redundant, we can often obtain a marked increase in savings for the customer while reducing the hours of people involved in the process—but not by enough to eliminate one whole person. Even when a cluster of processes are changed, the savings may not equal one worker. How, then, to capture the savings from a reengineering effort when the impact is measured in partial people?

Companies have employed several strategies to deal with this issue. Some have reallocated the work to others if at all possible, thereby freeing up at least one whole person. This strategy works well where the work is similar and can be transferred to others without much difficulty.

Alternatively, work can be redesigned so that it is kept in one group or location and not passed along. This ensures a more complete set of tasks, reducing the fragmentation of a process. Such reassignment may increase the duties and responsibilities of one job while reducing or eliminating those of another, but with an overall saving of time and expense and improving the efficacy of the process.

Another strategy is to move affected workers to part-time status if the remaining tasks do not warrant full-time employment. As with job elimination, if handled properly and communicated early enough, employees may be able to make accommodations. And some employees would prefer this option to embarking on a job search in a difficult employment market and might even enjoy the benefits of part-time work.

In any event, although savings have been achieved through reductions in workers, making the process less costly to the organization, the disruptions to careers and the total level of employment due to reengineering initiatives are not as dramatic as the publicity would have us believe. The jobs would perhaps have been lost anyway due to more fundamental shifts in supply and demand. And if managed judiciously, disruptions can be kept to a minimum.

Conclusion

Reengineering is here to stay—at least for a while longer. It has a sufficient root structure from the earlier disciplines to remain valid; it has caught the imagination of many people in business who want to improve operating effectiveness and efficiency; and it has a heavy quantification orientation. It is also assisted by the fact that management now knows that there are no easy answers to complex business problems. The solutions require study, hard work, some new approaches, and, finally, choices. But improvements can be achieved if pursued properly—and the better we are at doing that, the more significant the improvements will be.

References

Hammer, M., and Champy, J. (1993). *Reengineering the Corporation*. New York: HarperCollins.

Peters, T. J., and Waterman, R. H. (1982). *In Search of Excellence*. New York: HarperCollins.

Chapter Seven

Integrating People and Technology: Sociotechnical Perspectives on the Structure of Work

Stuart S. Winby

New technologies and new organizational structures are converging to form the "high-performance workplace" of the manufacturing firm in the twenty-first century. By the turn of the century, manufacturing will have evolved from a mass-production system to a new highly integrated system designed for mass customization. This transition will bring about the integration of new production and communication technologies with innovative human infrastructures.

This chapter provides a broad vision of the high-performance workplace in manufacturing at the turn of the next century. Current trends are reviewed, and anticipated changes in work organization and management are discussed. A sociotechnical model of technology and organization design integration for the business enterprise of the future is presented.

The Global Context

The environment at the turn of the century will be significantly more dynamic than the one we face today. The scope of concerns and competitive requirements that must be addressed and the variability that must be accommodated will continue to increase. An environment beset by such rapid change will require the manufacturing organization to compete in many areas, beyond today's cost, quality, and time metrics. These additional competitive dimensions will include variety, customization, customer convenience, and customer relations. This new reality will marry the volume and productivity standards of mass production with the craft standards of quality, variety, customization, convenience, and timeliness. Competitive advantage will be gained by organizations that can compete on these multiple performance dimensions.

The successful twenty-first century manufacturing organization will have the ability to adapt simultaneously to many different business environments and also to anticipate and respond to customer needs and wants. It will constantly improve its capacity to innovate, to create new sources of value, and to incorporate new ideas and technologies quickly into products. Products will consistently satisfy customer expectations. The underlying competitive capability will be organization and individual learning in order to engage in systemic change and improvement on a continuing basis.

Eight emerging trends will likely characterize tomorrow's global environment:

1. *Internationalization and globalization.* Technology and markets will be worldwide; global networks that operate across multifunctional boundaries will replace corporate centers.

2. *Regionalization.* Countries will join up to form economic regions as a means to increase access to markets without tariffs.

3. *Fragmented, sophisticated, demanding customers.* The customer base will be more demanding and more sophisticated, and fragmented global markets will be served by fragmented media niches.

4. *Smart products and technical fusion.* All products will likely contain some electronic elements; smart products and the fusion of technologies will be the norm; a major component of many products will be software.

5. *Service growth.* Manufacturing will be viewed as a specialized form of service; customers will intervene in the production processes and in the design of the products.

6. *Value-added alliances*. Suppliers, manufacturers, distributors, financiers, and competitors will move away from operating as separate entities toward the formation of value-added alliances.

7. *Focus on relationships, interactions, and dependencies*. Given the high level of joint ventures, consortia, and alliances, it will be common for competition and cooperation to coexist; high levels of global interdependencies will require an emphasis on cooperation, trust, and relationship building.

8. *Green manufacturing*. Environmental responsibility will permeate all industries; manufacturing will be required to meet locally imposed constraints; environmental concerns will include safety and energy efficiency as well as social, political, and economic values.

The Expanded Concept of Manufacturing

The concept of manufacturing is expanding from a narrow focus on the production of goods to the comprehensive process of creating, developing, selling, and maintaining products over their entire life cycles (see Figure 7.1). This expanded concept will cover the entire value chain. Most noted differences from today will be the changes resulting from the product design segment on the one end of the value chain and the service segment on the other.

Manufacturers will operate more as a specialized form of service. Customers will more often intervene in product design and development processes in terms of both frequency and substantiveness. Information systems will connect the customer directly to the manufacturer, eliminating the need for intermediaries, which will reduce distribution costs. Manufacturers will bring new products out quickly, assimilate field experience, involve the customer as much as possible, and produce easy-to-modify new products that are designed to evolve. For many products, this will be extended by

Figure 7.1. The Expanded Concept of Manufacturing.

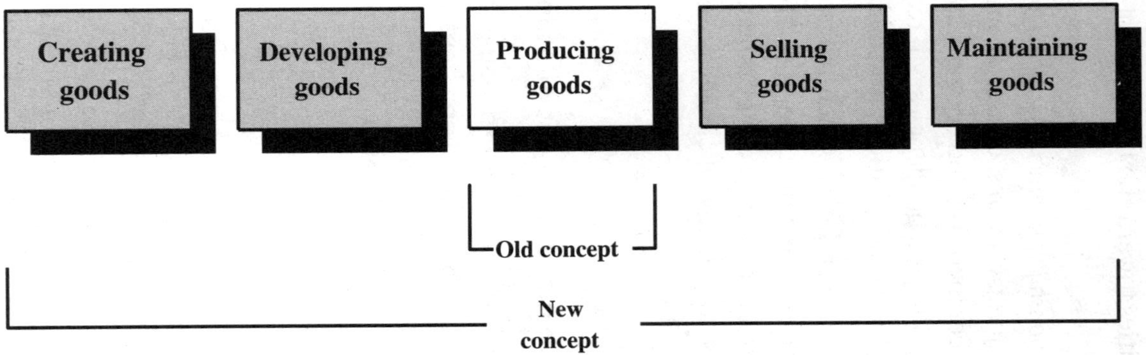

reconfiguration and upgrade capabilities. Also, software will be dominant in products and will be customized for and by users (Davidson and Davis, 1992).

Products will be made by flexible (reprogrammable and recon-figurable) production systems. Such a manufacturing system will produce to order and track quality from the customer's point of view throughout the life of the product. It may even communicate with these products while in the user's possession.

Sophisticated technical systems, however, will not be enough to ensure survival. Technology cannot be separated from its human inputs and organizational contexts. It must be integrated into orga-nizational frameworks that make full use of the knowledge, cre-ativity, and initiative of the human resources available.

Future manufacturers will view work organization and manage-ment as critical to competitiveness and sustainable advantage (Lawler, 1992). Effective organizations and management systems are difficult to imitate and serve as key differentiators. There will be less reliance on technology for competitive advantage and more emphasis placed on propriety processes and knowledge-based core competencies. Technology can be easily procured or, for that matter, brokered with a value chain partner, whereas critical work processes and core knowledge skills will reside in the organization and its peo-ple. Furthermore, effective work organizations will be viewed as more than just the sum of their parts; they will be regarded as a set of integrated policies, practices, and behaviors. When effectively designed and integrated, technologies and work organizations will jointly constitute the high-performance workplace.

The Bull's-Eye Model

World-class manufacturers constantly seek to describe and under-stand the interdependence of the many elements of the work orga-nization. The bull's-eye model (see Figure 7.2) is useful not only to describe the design of the workplace but also as a tool to design the

Figure 7.2. The Bull's-Eye Model of Work Organization.

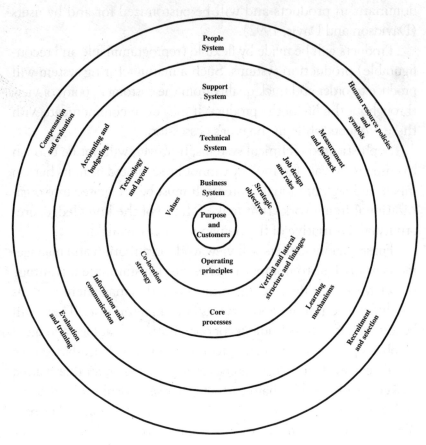

work organization. The bull's-eye is comprised of a set of infra-structure design elements that form a work system. Organizational effectiveness and performance are strongly influenced by how well these parts fit together. The design process starts from the center of the bull's-eye and moves progressively to the outer rings. The objective is to design the elements so that they complement or fit with each other and to optimize the whole rather than the separate parts.

Describing the future workplace by reviewing all the infra-structure elements of the bull's-eye would go beyond the scope of this chapter. However, a sociotechnical model in relationship to the bull's-eye tool is used to describe the high-performance workplace. The sociotechnical model presented in Figure 7.3 is the concept of two work system elements, social and technical, that are designed to fit one with the other and have congruence with business to achieve high performance. From a practical perspective, the sociotechnical systems model suggests that the design, planning, and implementation of social and organizational infrastructures is done simultaneously and in concert with technical (product and process) design. The high-performance workplace is then an organizational design that brings together technical, social, and business subsystems in a manner that optimizes the congruence or fit among them in order to produce high performance. High performance is defined as the effective response to customer requirements and other environmental demands and opportunities.

Earlier we cited such competitive requirements as adaptability, responsiveness, innovation, customer satisfaction, environmental anticipation, and learning. These qualities are critical to remaining competitive in the kind of dynamic environment the manufacturing firm will experience at the turn of the twenty-first century. The high-performance workplace is designed to meet these competitive requirements, respond effectively to customers, and adapt to a dynamic environment.

Sociotechnical systems theory allows us to examine the evolving tightly linked interactions between people (the social system), technical processes (the technical system), and business needs (the environment; see Figure 7.3). Designing work requires simultaneous attention to all three subsystems. It is my premise that the complexities of the new manufacturing systems at the turn of the century can be more fully understood through the adoption of a sociotechnical systems approach.

The business component of the sociotechnical model refers to the ongoing analysis of the organization's environment and customers, a mission and business strategy of distinct competency,

Figure 7.3. Work Design Subsystems.

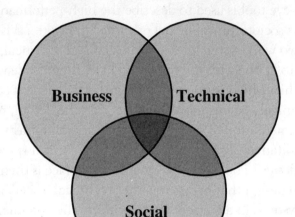

short-term plans and performance measures, and the design of business systems that support and reinforce the overall needs of the business, including technical and human dimensions.

The technical component refers to the capital equipment chosen (hardware) as well as the ways in which the equipment is organized and used (what tasks are done and by whom; the role of software, if used; job design and work flow; vertical and lateral structure and layout; employees' skills, knowledge, and methods). The technical system focuses on the organization's primary or core conversion process—acquiring inputs, transforming inputs to outputs, and providing outputs or services to customers (Pasmore, 1988).

The social (or human) component refers to the people aspects of the organization, such things as how employees are recruited, selected, oriented, and trained; the extent to which they are held responsible for decision making and problem solving; and how they are appraised and rewarded. It also includes personnel policies that affect behavior and work in the organization.

The bull's-eye model is used in the design process in sociotechnical design. The two innermost rings of the bull's-eye refer to the business subsystem, followed by the technical subsystem in the next ring, then the support subsystem, and finally the social subsystem.

I shall describe each of the subsystems of the sociotechnical model from the perspective of the high-performance workplace. This sociotechnical systems analysis presents a vision of what the business, technical, and social systems of the modern factory workplace will be like just a few years from now.

The Business System

In a knowledge economy, commerce in knowledge will fuel an unprecedented rate of start-ups and shifts in business strategies. For the most part, knowledge will be the core business of the knowledge economy, with information, its raw material, to harness into myriad products and services (Carnevale, 1991). How well a business scans its environment, exploits targets of opportunity, and makes adjustments to its business will determine its survival. Business strategy will be an ongoing process of deliberation and execution.

Organizations will define their mission as much by the markets they address as by the technologies in which they have technical competencies. Therefore, it may be common to see statements such as "to produce units at the lowest possible cost while producing far smaller quantities of high-quality (as defined by the customer) customized products and services."

Core Values. The organization's core values embody its beliefs about its work, people, and business. Here are some typical core values we might see in the future:

- *Customer focus:* the system and everyone in it must know their customers and must seek to satisfy the needs and wants of those customers and other stakeholders.

- *Continuous learning and improvement:* given that the rate of continuous learning and improvement is a key competitive differentiator, everyone will be on the learning curve and expected to improve processes continually.
- *Teamwork:* most work will be accomplished through groups, and teamwork to exploit task interdependence will be essential.
- *Flexibility:* rapidly changing environments and flexible technologies must be accommodated by operational and human flexibility.
- *Ethics (information):* the idea of sharing information and behaving properly with respect to proprietary information will be a major ethical issue and a value stressed by most firms.

Business Operating Principles. A number of strategic operating principles will dominate the future manufacturing organization.

1. *Manufacturing as a service.* Manufacturing will be the provider of quality customer services throughout the product's life, as well as the producer of quality customized goods. Consumer participation in production and service delivery will be common. Computer-based technologies will allow customers to participate in designing goods and services tailored to their own needs and preferences. Organizations will offer technology and service, not just physical products. Electronic self-design will allow customers to design products and processes themselves on remote terminals. This capacity allows customers to preview any potential product configuration and to submit orders directly to the vendor (Davidson and Davis, 1992).

2. *Mass customization.* Whereas today's operating formula calls for standardization of products and services, successful business at the turn of the century will offer individually customized products to mass markets. These customized products may be built out of

standard components, but they will be assembled as unique combinations of standard parts, designed by the customers themselves.

3. *Design for speed and flexibility*. Organization and business process design will be based on the criteria of speed and flexibility. Key capabilities in rapid and flexible reconfigurability, rapid prototyping, and rapid information handling and decision making will be critical to competitiveness.

4. *Direct communication*. Direct communication between customer and manufacturer will reduce the duration of the order entry and processing cycle. Response times will also be compressed on other fulfillment functions.

5. *On-demand production*. Key will be the ability to analyze and optimize the supply chain configuration of factories, suppliers, distributors, and retailers to meet fluctuations in demand variability, reduce inventory costs, reduce cycle time, and improve supplier performance. Manufacturers will not produce finished goods until after the customer has specified the precise configuration desired. On-demand production will dramatically shrink finished goods inventories while minimizing response time (Davidson and Davis, 1992).

6. *Electronic networks*. To facilitate on-demand production, suppliers and manufacturers will develop electronic linkages that permit coprocessing of information. Parties to these electronic relationships will transmit and receive information instantaneously and share access to operating systems and information resources. Customer orders to a vendor will trigger instantaneous requests to a supplier for the requisite parts and components. Suppliers will then deliver the required components with minimal delay using just-in-time or consignment delivery methods. Due to the sophistication of these electronic relationships, traditional functions will dramatically reduce cost and time in the transaction cycle (Davidson and Davis, 1992).

7. *Value-added alliances*. Companies will create technology alliances yet maintain a balance between competition and cooperation. The same company can be supplier, customer, and competitor.

8. *Global regionalization*. Manufacturers will optimize a business globally, to specialize in the production of components, to maximize economies of scale, and to move managers and technologies around the world to share expertise and solve problems. They will also have deep local roots everywhere they operate—building products in the countries where they sell, recruiting the best talent from local universities, and working with government to increase exports.

9. *Proprietary processes and key capabilities*. Emphasis will be on execution of strategy. Competitive advantage will be based on superior execution of core skills and waste-free business processes. Core skills are the fundamental institutional skills that make an organization capable of executing its strategy—organizational design and capabilities, skills of the people, and fit with technology.

10. *Green manufacturing*. Manufacturing processes will recycle everything and use renewable energy sources. This may not be easy, for new materials technologies will present unique disposal and handling challenges.

The Technical System

From a sociotechnical system perspective, the technical system of an organization is usually equated with the tools (hardware and software), techniques, methods, configurations, procedures, and knowledge used by organizational members to acquire inputs, transform inputs into outputs, and provide outputs or services to clients and customers. The technical system as defined here will include technology, job design and roles, work units and organizational structure (the second ring of the bull's-eye in Figure 7.2).

New Technology. In the literature as well as in practice, examples abound of the changes taking place in information and manufacturing technology. Machines for many processes are now very flexible and can be programmed to perform a wide variety of manufacturing tasks. What is new is that flexible manufacturing technologies are increasingly more capable in accommodating diverse product characteristics while providing both high quality and low cost.

Technology will be characterized by reprogrammable, reconfigurable, continuously changeable production systems, integrated into new information-intensive manufacturing systems that make lot size or customization irrelevant to cost. The new production technologies will be flexible, programmable machine tools grouped in reconfigurable, modular, and scalable manufacturing cells with "intelligent" manufacturing process controllers. These controllers are linked to closed-loop monitoring of the manufacturing processes, employing sensors, samplers, and analyzers coupled to intelligent diagnostic software (Iacocca Institute, 1991). As mentioned earlier, these new technologies must be linked to an organizational design that can exploit their power.

There will be an explosion of so many technologies that choosing among them and pacing their application to the ability of the workforce to manage and use them will be among the organization's most difficult tasks. Each firm will need a strategy to guide the discovery, development, and implementation of new technology. Technology will be more of a disadvantage than an advantage if not integrated with the people who must interact with it.

In the totally computer-integrated enterprise, technologies will of necessity change organizational arrangements within and between firms. The introduction of these new technologies will have pervasive implications for work methods and organizational structure. Instead of simply modifying a few work procedures, entire units may have to be reorganized and appraised in different ways, new cultural behaviors may have to be instilled, and everyone in the organization may need to be reskilled. The organizational changes entailed thus go far beyond today's conception of employee involvement to comprise new coordination structures, performance management systems, and skill and knowledge requirements.

Job Design and Roles. As technology expands the technical role, the human role will take on the higher-order control functions necessary to deploy new technologies effectively and to operate in a more complex environment. Therefore, advances in technology will not necessarily represent the growing dominance of machines in the future workplace. People and technology do not operate in a vacuum. When the complexity of work increases, a commensurate increase in the quality of both technical and human elements is usually required. It is true that the new automation will eliminate or subsume repetitive intellectual tasks in much the same way as previous mechanization eliminated or took over repetitive physical tasks. For every task surrendered, however, rare new responsibilities will be generated for exploiting the flexible capabilities of the technology. The more flexible and more powerful the machinery, the more that employees, work teams, and organizations must increase their skills to deploy it.

The new flexible technologies will change skill requirements and the context in which skills are used. Because of the new technology, some existing tasks and responsibilities will be eliminated, some will be subsumed, and some will be added. Ultimately, a whole new set of skills will be required, both deeper and broader than those currently sought. Low-skill entry-level jobs as laborers, material handlers, machine operators, and craft workers will be for the most part absent from the new factory. It is estimated that seven hundred thousand fewer laborers and operators will be required by the year 2000 (U.S. Office of Technology Assessment, 1988). However, technician responsibilities will replace these jobs and become the primary work on the factory floor. At least one hundred thousand new technician jobs are expected by the year 2000. The new manufacturing technician will assume an expanded scope of responsibility for productivity, quality, and speed, not only at an individual workstation but also with other people at various points in the work process. The manufacturing technician will work with powerful and flexible technologies that will substitute for a variety of current workers—laborers, material handlers, machine operators, repair workers, and supervisors.

The future factory will have few employees with jobs characterized as operative. Most factories will be organized into flexible manufacturing systems with robots and automated material-handling devices moving working product within and between systems. Most nonengineering or nonmanagerial positions will be in maintenance. Few such jobs will be required, however, because machine reliability will improve rapidly.

Jobs and skill requirements will converge and have a tendency to look alike. This will be mainly due to the increased mechanical and electrical task interdependence in the work flow. Throughout the factory, increased interdependence will make it difficult to maintain boundaries between jobs. Job design will have to take into account the risk of information falling between the cracks and causing variances in the work process. Therefore, the unit of analysis for job design will be the work team, and a network of interdependent individuals will be cross-trained to make certain that each has redundant skills necessary to act for the work team as required. Skills will be more hands-off, general, abstract, and personal or social in content and applied in the context of teams.

Sociotechnical theory has provided an alternative form of work organization based on the principle of redundant functions (Trist, 1981). Autonomous work groups, today referred to as work teams, have been the standard sociotechnical solution to building redundant functions in manufacturing organizations (Susman, 1979). The design of work teams focuses on broad, flexible jobs that allow people to learn multiple skills. The work team design allows functional knowledge and skills to be stored in excess capacity within the boundaries of the work unit. The redistribution of skills among team members improves the flexibility of the work unit and permits members to be self-organizing while satisfying their needs for learning and growth. Key is that redundant functions have reduced the need for elaborate controls and increased the team's capacity for self-control. The development of redundant functions also leads to flatter hierarchies as work group members are able to absorb more responsibility for coordination and decision making (Pasmore, 1988).

At the unit level, process-oriented high-performance work systems that embody elements of total quality will be the norm. This work design will be characterized by simplified business processes and work flows, advanced technological tools (expert systems, knowledge-based tools, and so on), and innovative work unit design (autonomous work teams, enriched job designs, flat hierarchies).

Within the enterprise, teams will be the norm at all levels. Rather than having a rigid formal structure, the organization will be more organic, adapting to changing conditions and the current workload. Most productive work will be accomplished by small teams assisted by technology support (augmented meetings). Ubiquitous electronic communications will allow the organization to be reshaped as the work requires. With large numbers of teams doing the work, norms and values rather than rules and direct supervision will furnish the cohesion necessary to provide direction and achieve coordination.

Both vertical and horizontal interdependence will increase significantly. Vertical interdependence refers to the links between hierarchical levels for planning and controlling the factory's production process. Horizontal interdependence refers to links between lateral levels within the factory. Interdependence will thus increase across functions as product design, manufacturing engineering, and other functions become more linked.

The new factory will have few levels of management. Middle

management will not be needed, thanks to sophisticated information systems. Delegating as much information as possible to employees at the lowest levels, where the product is made, will prove most efficient. To push decision making downward and the capability for variance control closest to the conversion process, the predominant work design will be what is referred to today as a "high-performance work system."

Structure. To compete in a global economy will require an organization that is designed for a global environment. A sociotechnical fit of a global organizational structure with information technology will form the basis of the competitive workplace. The global organizational structure will be able to integrate a network of assets and resources that can achieve global efficiencies and local responsiveness simultaneously. This new sociotechnical system will have the ability to develop and exploit knowledge on a worldwide basis. The predominant organizational work unit will be the work team, supported by network structures along the value chain enabled by the capabilities of information technology.

Organizations in the future must have structural flexibility to survive and will therefore be designed for flexibility. Formal structure will give way to more organic, fluid work structures. For example, individual job or work team assignments may change to meet changing customer needs; to meet multiple challenges an organization may assemble teams very quickly by combining people with different expertise from many locations around the globe; and product teams will form and re-form to capture new market opportunities and develop new products.

In his discussion of physics and its relationship to organizations, Fritjof Capra (1983) notes that it was once believed that you had fundamental building blocks of matter and that process happened through interactions. A more recent view, from the "new physics," and systems theory, holds that structures "are flexible yet stable manifestations of underlying processes" (p. 267). This accounts for the current trend in organizing by process rather than function. For example, instead of the research and development manager, there will be a product generation process manager; rather than a manufacturing manager, there will be an order fulfillment manager. Functional structure will not disappear; rather, it will become secondary to customer- and process-based structures.

Key value chain processes such as product generation and order fulfillment will be the basis for designing the organization. The demand for flexibility will require not vertical integration but value chain integration, where the emphasis is on process capabilities. This shift will move the emphasis in organizational design from vertical to lateral or horizontal. From a sociotechnical perspective, the unit of analysis now becomes the value chain, where work teams, networks, and organizations, whether suppliers or alliance partners, become the basis of design in relation to the value chain link of processes serving the customer.

Organizational models will be based on principles of sociotechnical systems and cybernetics; organization design will be based on work units conceived of as systems with self-regulating properties. In this respect, any part is like the whole, and vice versa—the smaller parts have similarities to the whole. From the individual job to the work team to the network of organizations, the principles of self-regulating work systems will be apparent up and down the business organization.

Organizations are converging on a common structural format of interdependent networks of people, work teams, and organizations. Organizations will be networks of work teams. In turn, every organization is a member of a network made up of other organizations that are suppliers, customers, and strategic alliance partners. Interdependencies will most likely increase to the point where organizations no longer compete as single institutions but as members of competitive networks. The ultimate expression of trust in new organizations will be the formation of "virtual companies." The virtual company is designed by selecting resources from different companies and then synthesizing them into a single electronic business entity. The objective is that the various distributed resources be "plug-compatible" so that they can perform their respective functions as if they were a single company. As long as the market opportunity lasts, the virtual company will remain in existence. When the market matures, the virtual company will dissolve, and the resources will be reallocated.

The Social System

Developing social system criteria is as important in organization design as developing accurate technical equipment specifications. The primary objectives in social system design are to foster high commitment and to sustain high performance.

Values. It will become apparent that to a large extent, an organization's culture can be designed rather than left to evolve on its own. Given the temporary nature of work units at all levels of the organization and the greater dependency on pulling together individuals from different backgrounds, cultures, and locations, the self-design of culture through shared values will be important. Values consistent with such a culture will be demonstrated as early as job hiring, team member selection, and orientation. A set of high-performance values will be sought to support the types of organizations described in this chapter. Values such as continuous learning and improvement, flexibility, teamwork, and recognition and rewards for achievement and loyalty will underlie the high-performance workplace.

Information and Decision Processes. The new information technology will provide tremendous knowledge processing capabilities. This new technology will enhance the capacity of organizations to develop and integrate needed knowledge. However, knowledge processing will remain a sociotechnical operation. Information technology will require people to operate it, and information and decision processes will therefore be subject to a wide range of individual and social system influences. At best, technology can help store, retrieve, and process more information more rapidly than humanly possible. But decisions regarding what information to store, retrieve, and consider in decision making will remain subject to human discretion (Pasmore, 1988; Zuboff, 1988).

Rewards. Reward systems will be designed to support behaviors and attitudes such as loyalty to the organization, commitment to the task, willingness to work with others, and on-task creativity. Reward systems will be crafted to elicit the required behaviors in line with the business strategy rather than a blanket corporatewide pay system. Most reward systems will focus on supporting teamwork, learning, and productivity improvement. People with the most education and access to learning on the job will do the best; those with the least will do the worst. Salary increases will be based on demonstrated learning rather than the passage of time. Pay for knowledge may be the preferred strategy to reinforce multiskilling. The use of team bonus pay and plans of the gain-sharing type will also increase.

New social contracts will be aimed to attract and retain employees. Employees will be tied to long-term benefits that anchor their loyalty in the face of routine participation in projects outside the boundaries of the company as traditionally conceived. The manufacturing organization will have invested a considerable amount of money training its employees and cannot afford to lose them through turnover.

Learning. The emphasis on individual skill acquisition and team responsibility for product and process will increase the value of learning. Sets of skills will have shorter and shorter life cycles, necessitating continued learning. All organizational members will be on the learning curve, on a track of lifelong learning.

The most profound social system design will be its organizational learning system. True competitiveness will be achieved by organizations that are learning-efficient. Organizations that are capable of anticipating shifts in their environments and increase their intelligence over time will be top performers. Consequently, organizations will experiment more and make more attempts at innovation. Emphasis will be on "failing faster than one's competitors" to speed learning, find solutions, and seize opportunities. Importance will be placed on reflecting and gaining insights from experiments, innovations, customer data, and projects to apply in improving the organization. Learning processes will be designed into the management of work.

The New Sociotechnical Imperative

Eric Trist first conceived of sociotechnical systems (STS) in 1951 as a new paradigm of work organization in the context of an industrial economy. Application of STS focused on shop-floor job design and self-managing work teams. Only recently has STS been widely acknowledged as the preferred paradigm of work organization and the basis for the popularity of high-performance work system design, self-managing work teams, high-involvement organizations, business reengineering, and empowerment. Although STS theory and practice have been applied to knowledge work settings using office technologies (Pava, 1983; Pasmore, 1988), computer and information technology was not fully realized, and the benefits of a "coordination technology" with global implications were not well understood. STS can have at least as much impact on organizational effectiveness in the emerging information economy as it has in the industrial economy. The high-performance workplace of the next century will embody the principles and practices of STS in its design and will cover a much broader systemic application to manufacturing at the enterprise level.

STS has been the central design principle for optimizing the fit between the social system and the technical system in a given environment. Where a high degree of sociotechnical fit was achieved, performance increased. The principle of joint optimization has traditionally been limited to the technology (technical subsystems) and human (social subsystems) fit in job design. In the future, the principle of joint optimization at the job design level will endure but will encompass a broader unit of analysis—the entire organization at the value chain level.

From a sociotechnical systems perspective, the high-performance workplace will view the value chain as the technical system. The technical system will include a linked chain of core product processes. The value chain will include a customer-to-customer set of processes such as customer solution, strategy planning, product generation, order generation and fulfillment, and customer support processes. From customer input to customer satisfaction will evolve one business learning cycle. A key design objective is to design the work organization for speed, flexibility, and learning, for organizations that can accelerate business learning cycles by providing increasing value to customers will have a distinct competitive advantage.

The value chain as the unit of organizational design analysis will be critical, given the deverticalization of the value chain. From an organizational perspective, emphasis will be placed on lateral or horizontal integration. The lateral emphasis of the value chain will bound all the owners of processes of the business system and also place a necessary focus on speed and learning by decentralizing decision making and learning to core processes. Sociotechnical fit will come into play in designing work team and network social systems through global electronic technical systems.

Enterprise-Level Design

To operate with high performance in an environment of uncertainty and intense competition, the global organization must rely on innovation and continuous learning by participating knowledge workers. And if innovation and continuous learning are to be possible, knowledge workers must be given sufficient flexibility to act and modify work processes to serve customers in the marketplace. Knowledge workers must have sufficient discretion to design their own work systems to satisfy customers.

At the enterprise level will be the need to design key infrastructures to support work team and network structures of knowledge workers. Management must provide minimal critical specifications regarding all areas of the bull's-eye infrastructure elements. This provides the boundaries of decision making and action for self-design at the unit level of work design. These shared infrastructures provide operational stability and permit groups of knowledge workers to effect coordinated outcomes. Providing minimal critical specs at the enterprise level places decision making regarding outcomes at the discretion of work teams and networks of knowledge workers.

Unit-Level Design

Unit-level design will be done through high-performance work systems and self-designing network structures. The design of high-performance work systems at the unit level will address the reengineering of work processes, the design of work teams as well as individual jobs, and the supporting bull's-eye infrastructure elements for support. Also, high-performance work system design usually involves the more formal, stable parts of the organization—the underlying hierarchy of the organization.

The design of network structures involves the people who constitute them, using many of the organizational design tools and technologies of high-performance work system design. The distinctive characteristic of networks is that network structures are less stable and more organic than the high-performance work system model; networks usually involve knowledge workers from dispersed form work units and employ a wide variety of information technologies to facilitate robust communication toward a common purpose.

The high-performance work systems model will work hand in hand with self-designed networks. Both share the minimal critical specifications of infrastructure elements at the enterprise level. A key distinction of the high-performance workplace will be its self-design attributes. The purpose of self-design is to enable its members to shape the organization to whatever is required to meet customer needs and environmental requirements (rings one and two of the bull's-eye model). The workers themselves design the work systems they need to implement business strategy. The self-design capability becomes a critical skill of the organization's workforce.

Unit-level design will frequently involve globally dispersed knowledge workers. For example, in the STS design process, once a technical core process analysis is completed, task interdependencies can be identified in order to design work structures. In a global environment, the probability that each of the interdependencies involves people from around the world would be expected. The design element of colocation would be reviewed to determine if employees should be physically colocated (if along the critical path) or virtually colocated. If virtually colocated, the employees themselves determine technology support systems (shared databases such as CAD systems, client servers, and groupware) and protocols. These virtual team units design their work system based on value chain metrics. All the design elements of the bull's-eye are used to ensure fit and high performance.

From a value chain perspective, designers will elaborate a work system that may involve multiple divisions or companies. The STS comparative will be to execute business strategy effectively through elaborate cross-functional business processes using sophisticated information technology (technical system) while satisfying the values, needs, and aspirations of the various stakeholders (social system).

Conclusions

This chapter has attempted to provide a vision of the high-performance workplace at the turn of the twenty-first century—a mere handful of years from today. It is almost certainly inaccurate, considering the rapid rate of change and uncertainty; however, current trends clearly point toward the situation described.

Sociotechnical systems theory and practice have provided the basis of a new work organization paradigm for the past forty years. The STS work organization paradigm (compared to the industrial economy paradigm of machine bureaucracy) has provided an alternative approach to effective organization and management in turbulent environments. However, only of late has ineffectiveness in the industrial model of machine bureaucracy, coupled with the high performance of STS applications, forced global industries to shift paradigms.

The information technology that links organizations and people globally will offer new challenges to organizational design and workplace operations. STS approaches to the challenges described in this chapter encourage hope for the realization of the high-performance workplace early in the twenty-first century.

References

Capra, F. (1983). *The Turning Point: Science, Society, and the Rising Culture*. New York: Bantam Books/Simon & Schuster.

Carnevale, A. P. (1991). *America and the New Economy*. Washington, D.C.: American Society for Training and Development/U.S. Department of Labor Employment and Training Administration.

Davidson, W., and Davis, S. (1992). *Management and Organization Principles for the Information Economy*. Los Angeles: Center for Effective Organizations, University of Southern California.

Iacocca Institute. (1991). *Twenty-First-Century Manufacturing Enterprise Strategy*. Bethlehem, Pa.: Iacocca Institute, Lehigh University.

Lawler, E. E., III. (1992). *The Ultimate Advantage: Creating the High-Involvement Organization*. San Francisco: Jossey-Bass.

Pasmore, W. A. (1988). *Designing Effective Organizations: The Sociotechnical Systems Perspective*. New York: Wiley.

Pava, C. (1983). *Managing New Office Technology: An Organizational Strategy*. New York: Free Press.

Susman, G. I. (1979). *Autonomy at Work: A Sociotechnical Analysis of Participative Management*. New York: Praeger.

Trist, E. (1981). *The Evolution of Sociotechnical Systems*. Toronto: Quality of Working Life Center.

U.S. Office of Technology Assessment. (1988). *Educating Scientists and Engineers: Grade School to Graduate School*. Washington, D.C.: U.S. Government Printing Office.

Zuboff, S. (1988). *In the Age of the Smart Machine: The Future of Work and Power*. New York: Basic Books.

Part Three

Providing Effective Leadership

Organizational change initiatives are unlikely to be successful without solid and ongoing leadership at senior management levels. Experienced managers and supervisors often have trouble accepting some of the newer work management ideas—they effectively relinquish control and thereby lose power—and their behavior can become an impediment to the planned changes. For example, the failure or limited success of many TQM initiatives has been attributed to a lack of support and acceptance by managers. Senior management leadership is the key; managers must make it an important company objective.

Chapter Eight, by Irvine Hockaday of Hallmark Cards, discusses the role of senior executives as leaders. His company has entered a transformational phase as a response to changes in its product markets. He argues that before a company can expect to be successful, it must have a shared vision grounded in a thoughtful long-term strategy capable of commanding employee commitment. Creating the vision and developing the strategy are important CEO responsibilities. Hockaday then traces the differences between the old Hallmark and the new. He uses a basketball team as an analogy. In contrast to a football team, which is hierarchical and autocratic, a basketball team is similar to Peter Senge's learning organization. Hockaday makes the point that basketball teams cannot have a highly detailed game plan; plays are selected and run on a real-time basis during the game. The coach cannot dictate each play, and the players have to adapt their behavior, as a unit, as the game progresses. Communication and teamwork among the players are essential for success.

In Chapter Nine, Richard Whiteley discusses the research conclusions from surveys conducted by his company, the Forum Corporation. The studies focused on the leaders of twenty-three companies that have successfully changed to become customer-driven. The findings revealed seven behaviors that characterize the key executives responsible for the changes in these organizations:

- They personally champion the customer.
- They create direction and alignment.
- They become "students for life."
- They believe in and invest in their people.
- They make teams work.
- They stay the course.
- They live the organization's purpose.

These behaviors differentiate the leaders in companies that have make the transition successfully.

Whiteley's focus is on a company's customer orientation, but his argument and research findings would be relevant to any organizational change initiative. If this type of leadership had been sustained in the companies that failed at quality management, they might have had different track records. To transform an organization, its leaders have to articulate and reinforce their vision of the future by their behavior at every opportunity. This role cannot be delegated to lower levels of management.

Chapter Ten is by one of the leaders in the quality management field, Philip Crosby. His is a practical view of quality management. From his perspective, there is no such thing as TQM; each initiative is different. Done properly, quality management is the most valuable action an executive can take; done improperly, it can damage morale and increase operating costs.

The culture of an organization is, in Crosby's words, "a portrait of the interests and concerns of management as seen by the people." The executives leading the organization play a major role in creating the culture and in establishing the priority commitments that drive performance. True quality can come only when top management makes it a fundamental objective of the organization and reinforces its importance by active participation in and support for actions to improve the quality of products or services. Quality is not a series of techniques and procedures; it is a way of managing that depends on top management leadership.

Chapter Eight

Creating a High-Performance Climate: A CEO's Perspective

Irvine O. Hockaday, Jr.

I have been asked to write about "achieving and sustaining a high-performance operation"—and I will do so. But I will conclude by returning to the broader point, a point that in a very genuine way converts you into "lamplighters" for society.

There is an underlying scaffolding that supports my remarks: institutions, including corporations, reflect a chosen—consciously or otherwise—and particular view of human nature. If that view of human nature is a prescient and sensitive one and if we bring our organizations into alignment with that view, progress results. Misalignment vitiates even the hope of progress.

Consider a few examples that illustrate the point. The Pilgrims' Mayflower Compact of 1620 created a communal economy: work according to ability, goods and services according to need, land owned in common. In the winter of 1622, one-third of the colonists starved to death. Colonial Governor Bradford abandoned the project, commenting that the concept did not jibe with the realities of human nature.

Contrast that idealistic view with *Federalist Papers* No. 10, a realistic—some would say cynical—view of man. Madison concluded that since you cannot change the contentious, competitive nature of man, you must control the impacts of that nature. The question was how to manage such a situation, and Madison's solution was to "establish a system which convinces people that their individual self-interests are best served by a combination of peaceful competition and cooperation."

Moving away from the political realm and closer to the corporate arena, reflect on a classic work published in 1776, Adam Smith's *Wealth of Nations*. Smith described what at the time was considered the best means of "achieving and sustaining a high-performance organization." He focused on the manufacturing of pins—the kind used in sewing—and described how the division of labor in factories could increase output at an astounding rate. Working alone with simple tools, an individual might produce one pin a day. Working in a factory, his share of the total output could be five thousand times that. No wonder this transformation in work methods was called a revolution. At the factory, processes were broken down into different and focused tasks. Each person performed the assigned task over and over, hour after hour, day after day. Employees were paid to follow directions. Creative thinking—if any was done—remained the prerogative of the people at the top.

The industrial revolution spawned this kind of functional-hierarchical model, and General Motors and other companies perfected it. Workers were extensions of machines; empowerment was anathema. It worked brilliantly for a long while. But as the reality of global competition came into being, our models began to produce inadequate results. The dramatic erosion of corporate America's global competitiveness is now apparent to all.

Consequently, today we seek a way to transform our corporate organizations. The phraseology has become a cliché. We talk about a radical retooling of business processes, about viewing employees as a company's most valuable resource.

Hallmark is in the midst of such a transformation, and our experience is, I suspect, rather typical. I see three stages of Hallmark's history, stages characterized by different views of the human factor in our organizational scheme of things.

Our company began in 1910 with the vision of a young entrepreneur named Joyce Hall. In its first phase, his company took one product, the greeting card, and built it into an entire industry. He served as chief executive officer, chief financial officer, chief operating officer, and all other things. The small company grew to meet exploding demand. The organizational approach was both paternalistic and autocratic: "We know what's best; do as you're told; you'll be well taken care of."

The second phase found Hallmark again strapped to a growth rocket, this time the card shop concept. Growth proceeded at such a pace that systems and focused functional disciplines became a necessity. Functional silos were firmly set in place.

We are now entering a third transformational phase, because our world has changed. The velocity of consumer taste change has sped up remarkably; where people shop and the time available for shopping are different, competition has improved, and technology offers new ways to communicate. The environment in which we operate became transformed, necessitating our own transformational response.

Although organizational transformation is admittedly difficult and success is by no means guaranteed, the conditions required are clear and precise:

• *A shared vision, not an individual one.* The vision must be grounded in a thoughtful, long-term strategy. Both vision and strategy must be worthy of employee commitment—and employees' standards are getting higher in that regard. Yet no company can succeed today without a strategy to which each employee willingly and enthusiastically commits. (By contrast, in the first two phases of Hallmark's life, strategy was irrelevant; only execution mattered.)

• *A link between vision and strategy.* The link between vision and strategy must be genuine and tight and can only be built on an open and honest dialogue among employees who understand the sacrifices being made and the opportunities being offered.

During Hallmark's current transformational phase, we are moving from looking at pieces and particular functions to looking at the entire whole organizational mosaic, from linear thinking to intuitive thinking, from assembly-line hand-offs to concurrent development, from specialization to an interdisciplinary approach, and from career elevators and functional silos to lateral movement of employees.

The difference is best described by football versus basketball. Football is hierarchical and autocratic. The coach is in charge; the team does what it is told. The game plan is preestablished and rarely varies. Execution carries the day. Basketball more nearly reflects Peter Senge's (1990) learning organization. An advanced game plan is impractical. Revisions are made on a real-time basis as play unfolds. The coach cannot dominate decisions. The players must adjust—as a unit. Consistent communication and flexibility are critical.

Being a learning organization is probably the only true source of a sustainable competitive advantage. In a learning organization, as with a successful basketball team, all participants must be involved as the company develops a culture of inclusiveness. And it is important to recognize that this transformation in the workplace is part of a larger societal phenomenon.

Social historian Riane Eisler (1987) suggests that societies around the globe are gradually transforming from a dominator model to a partnership model. The dominator social model has been the norm through most of recorded history; it places one half of humanity over the other half. Force and power are used to maintain superiority of position. It is a system marked by violence, authoritarianism, and ethnic conflict. Russia and China come to mind; so do Yugoslavia and Somalia.

The partnership model, in contrast, is based on the principle of linkage. In a partnership society, diversity is not equated with either inferiority or superiority; it is equated with opportunity. Nurturing is emphasized over aggression. Europe seeks this kind of union. Eisler suggests that all the post-Enlightenment movements for social justice, from the abolition of slavery to the women's movement to the ecology movement, reflect such a partnership thrust.

And so there is a convincing argument to be made that the way we design our societies and our institutions can have an important and beneficial effect on the realities of human nature.

One of the great pieces of all literature is a fable called "The Grand Inquisitor" from *The Brothers Karamazov*. In it, Russian novelist Dostoevsky paints a brilliant picture of the rationale for authoritarianism. The eponymous protagonist is an elderly cardinal in the church and a leader of the Spanish Inquisition. He is a man who holds absolute authority in matters of both church and state—a man who has personally directed the burning of hundreds of heretics. One day in Seville, Christ returns to earth in human form. Not surprisingly, this creates quite a stir, and he is ordered jailed because the Grand Inquisitor fears that he will unsettle the tranquillity established by the Roman church. Late that night, the Grand Inquisitor visits Christ in his cell.

The cardinal explains to his prisoner that God made a major miscalculation in giving humankind free will. Freedom is a "fearful burden," a burden that most humans would gladly give up for security and bread and a reassuring simplistic optimism in which to believe. The church provides all of those things, and the people gratefully accept its authority and compliantly give up their independence as a gesture of their appreciation. A powerful hierarchy is all that is needed to keep the sheep contented. The Grand Inquisitor would have admired Adam Smith's pin factory.

Contrast this view of human nature with the one found in Genesis, where human beings are created in the image of God and entrusted with the stewardship of the earth.

Our Declaration of Independence flows directly from that account of creation. "All men are created equal. . . . They are endowed by their Creator with certain unalienable rights, that among these are Life, Liberty and"—wondrous concept—"the pursuit of Happiness."

The Declaration's author, Thomas Jefferson, also wrote these words: "I know of no safe depository of the ultimate powers of society but the people themselves, and if we think them not enlightened enough to exercise their control with wholesome direction, the remedy is not to take it from them, but to inform their discretion." Whereas the Grand Inquisitor sees people as simple souls who long to be controlled, Jefferson sees them as beings endowed with the capacity for intelligent self-rule, individuality, creativity, and the potential to contribute in meaningful ways.

The Grand Inquisitor and the author of the Declaration of Independence would have run very different kinds of companies. Jefferson would have championed a learning organization. The trick is, of course, to get from one type to the other—to make the transformation.

Anyone who has spent time around young children knows that it is the nature of human beings to learn, to create, and to seek meaning. Yet somehow, by the time individuals come to work for our companies, their capacity for learning and creativity has been thoroughly suppressed. We are rarely able to reignite that flame, and their search for meaning must find its object outside the work environment.

What if the corporation could liberate those basic human impulses? What if it were a place where human beings could learn and create? What if they could find there a mission that meshed with their personal mission and aspirations?

As Bill O'Brien, CEO of Hanover Insurance, has said, "The ferment in management will continue until we build organizations that are more consistent with man's higher aspirations beyond food, shelter, and belonging" (Welter, 1991, p. 38). The transformative, partnership model could be the place for it to happen.

Transitions are never easy, and, ironically, transitions that move human beings into environments where they have more autonomy, power, and accountability can be particularly tough. Witness what is happening in the former Soviet republics and Eastern Europe. Witness IBM, DEC, and Salomon Brothers.

Initially, change breeds ambiguity, and ambiguity breeds anxiety. The corporate world is awash in transformational ideas, but the jargon is extremely risky if it is not anchored. It will only add to the anxiety if it is not based on the right assumptions, and organizational structure must logically and convincingly flow from those assumptions. And so we finally come to the roles of the CEO and the human resource professional.

A CEO has many responsibilities, but the three primary ones are to provide vision, to motivate all employees, and to develop leaders. Let me say a few words about each of these.

Vision

The vision is the galvanizing word picture of a desired future. It is where the company wants to be, yet it means little unless it is shared by employees.

People Express began in 1980 with a vision. The new airline would be the Ford of the air, bringing air travel within the reach of ordinary people: lowest fares, friendly, efficient, no-frills service. And it would do so with a host of innovative human resource policies that have since been adopted by many other firms—team management, universal stock ownership, and a flattened organization.

At first the airline was enormously successful. By 1982, People Express had more departures from New York airports than any other carrier. Morale was high. Employees shared the founder's exciting vision. Demand was so strong that the airline grew quickly, expanding its fleet and its schedule. But hiring and training employees didn't keep pace; soon one-fourth of the staff was temporary help. As a result, customer service went into a sharp decline. The original vision became blurred. The definition of victory was not clear. The company eventually collapsed.

There is another way to think about vision. If we've learned anything from the military, we've learned that unless we can agree on a definition of victory, we are unlikely to win the battle. Every company must thoughtfully craft a consensus on a definition of victory. Each company will have its own definition, but the process and conclusions are essential.

Motivation

A second CEO priority is to motivate employees. As John Kotter of Harvard describes it, leadership is the ageless process of deciding where a group of people should go, getting them lined up in that direction and committed to movement, and then energizing them to overcome the inevitable obstacles they will encounter along the way (Kotter, 1990).

To do that requires good communication—open, frequent, and flowing in both directions. It is the lifeblood of a high-performance company. Because at the end of the day, good communication has to do with human dignity, with valuing and understanding other people. It has to do with believing that all employees have the ability to contribute meaningfully. And it is the responsibility of the CEO not just to listen and communicate with employees but to foster an environment where everyone does the same.

Development

The CEO's third responsibility is to develop leaders—a responsibility shared with the human resource staff. At Hallmark, we have done this through the creation of what we call the Hallmark Leadership Development Institute, which is housed in our human resource division. It offers different programs for different stages in employees' careers. It is used not only to communicate about the visions and values of the corporation but also to elicit creative thinking about strategic business issues. The synergy of these leadership seminars has helped move our company forward in measurable ways while also helping develop the leadership qualities that we will need in the years ahead.

So a CEO in a transformed organization must communicate a shared vision, motivate a workforce, and develop leaders. What, then, is the role of human resources?

To my mind, human resources must be a major player in the transformation of our organizations. That is more true than ever as we move away from the dominator model, the industrial revolution model, and toward new models that view employees as a company's most significant competitive advantage. Human resources must be a full partner in the process of renewal, not just a resource to draw on.

That means that human resource professionals have to be knowledgeable about the strategic direction of the business and the plans designed to achieve victory. They must understand what it takes to reduce cycle time and to develop products concurrently rather than sequentially. They must understand the implications of using technology to bring company and customers closer together. And perhaps most important, they must understand the impact of change on the people who are investing their lives in the process of transforming an organization.

In the case of Hallmark, we have addressed these needs by decentralizing our human resource function and treating it as a partner in the business process redesign of our core business. At the same time, the head of human resources reports to me, sits on our strategic development and planning committee, and attends all meetings of the office of the chief executive.

Transformational issues are seldom easy. If your company is engaged in a process of transformation, you know the dilemmas all too well: How do you choose members and leaders of interdisciplinary teams? What are the implications for succession planning and seniority practices? How do you manage a matrix organization? How do you evaluate performance and compensate members of temporary teams? How do you encourage people to experiment if the experimentation may result in the disappearance of their job?

I don't pretend to have all the answers—nor do our HR professionals at Hallmark, though we're working on them. And work on them we must, answer them we must—we all must. Because the survival of our companies, in the competitive sense, depends on meeting these human resource challenges. Achieving and sustaining a high-performance operation isn't a choice, it's the centerpiece of survival. But there is something else at stake, something larger in scale. So I return, finally, to where I started.

With the collapse of communism, the West won an ideological victory, but we lost a common cause. As our populace becomes more diverse, different needs, agendas, and special interests proliferate. What is left to bind us together?

As individuals, we no longer know what we stand for. We are captives of our recurring dreams, but just what we are seeking in those dreams remains blurred and out of reach.

Corporations are not much different. What do they stand for? What is their mission, corporately but also socially? Surely, a purpose beyond year-to-year bottom-line improvement is part of the picture.

E pluribus unum once had profound meaning for Americans: "out of many, one." Our civic pendulum has swung toward the pluribus, with the resultant richness of potential that diversity brings. But what about that unum? How do we remain one?

Isn't that exactly the challenge that human resource managers face in their profession every day? Isn't it possible that companies are the laboratories where the aspirations, talents, and diversity of our individual employees are successfully blended with the vision of the whole?

Peter Drucker said it well: "The manager can no longer depend on the political process to be the integrating force; he himself has to become the integrator. Management may well be considered a bridge between a civilization that is rapidly becoming worldwide and a culture which expresses divergent traditions, values, beliefs and heritages."

Human resource professionals are the integrators. They build the bridges between diversity and common purpose. They insist on humanity as a credible part of any cost-benefit trade-off. In their companies, they reaffirm the wisdom of our *e pluribus unum* roots.

I am reminded of an elderly gentleman now deceased. As a child, he lived in a small village in rural England. In the evening, as dusk came on, the village lamplighter would appear with ladder and lamp. He would place the ladder against a lamppost, climb up, light the lamp, step down, and proceed to the next lamppost. My friend was fond of saying that after a while, the lamplighter would be out of sight down the street, but you could always tell which way he had gone from the lamps he had lighted. Human resource managers must be encouraged to be our lamplighters.

References

Eisler, R. (1987). *The Chalice and the Blade: Our History, Our Future*. New York: HarperCollins.

Kotter, J. P. (1990). *A Force for Change: How Leadership Differs from Management*. New York: Free Press.

Senge, P. M. (1990). *The Fifth Discipline: The Art and Practice of the Learning Organization*. New York: Doubleday.

Welter, T. R. (1991, May 6). A winning team begins with you. *Industry Week*, pp. 35–42.

Chapter Nine

Championing the Successful
Quality Effort

Richard Whiteley

Recently my company, the Forum Corporation, sent a questionnaire to hundreds of senior executives in the United States. One of the questions asked was, "What are your most important strategic imperatives at this time?"

Over six hundred people responded, and fully 86 percent used words or phrases that indicated a keen desire to improve customer-driven quality. This percentage was significantly higher than that of the second most mentioned imperative, "to increase profits."

At about the same time as we were conducting our survey, the *Wall Street Journal* was doing one of its own. The *Journal* asked typical customers like you and me if they believed that United States business is trying to understand and meet our needs. Only 5 percent responded yes!

What these two surveys tell us in dramatic fashion is that although customer-driven quality rates top-of-mind awareness with business leaders, precious few are actually concentrating on creating customer-pleasing products and services.

Today, sad to say, seven out of ten customer-driven quality initiatives undertaken by companies around the world are failing to achieve the desired results. The waste and disappointment engendered by such false starts have given quality a black eye. Indeed, today, many authorities dismiss serious quality work as just another ineffective fad, a sort of industrial hula hoop, that will soon fade away. In fact, a recent study by Ernst and Young, the consulting and accounting firm, suggested that many companies have wasted millions of dollars pursuing quality-boosting strategies that really haven't improved performance and may actually have hampered it.

One need only look at companies like Motorola, Saturn, USAA, and British Airways, however, and the positive results that they have achieved in customer-driven quality, to understand that it is not quality that is failing but rather its implementation.

There are many reasons why this is so: lack of proper customer connection, debilitating functional warfare, untrained employees, failure to integrate quality into business strategy. But far and away the most common reason is the failure of senior management to lead the effort.

This is repeatedly and graphically demonstrated by questions I receive after my speeches. No matter where I am, the number one question asked by far is, "How can we get our senior executives to lead our quality effort?"

In this chapter, I will answer that question. I will answer it first by examining what leaders who are successfully implementing quality specifically do that leads to their success. Second, I will present the three most common mistakes senior executives make as their organizations struggle to implement customer-driven quality. In addition, I will suggest preventive measures to eliminate these mistakes. Finally, I will present an approach designed to build the senior executives' commitment to customer-driven quality, commitment that is expressed in behavior, not just words.

Secrets of Success

What do leaders do that leads to success in implementing customer-driven quality? At Forum, we studied the leaders in twenty-three companies that have taken giant strides toward becoming customer-driven. The sample covered organizations with some of the most successful quality programs in North America, including three Malcolm Baldrige Award winners and a winner of Canada's Award for

Business Excellence in Quality. We conducted structured interviews with leaders in each organization to learn which practices set them apart and make them so effective. The results revealed that seven specific behaviors seem to characterize the pivotal people in a successful customer-driven organization:

1. *They personally champion the customer.* They profoundly believe in the core values of customer-driven quality. They spend time with customers, even to the point of becoming the voice of the customer in their own organizations.

2. *They create direction and alignment.* They make sure that their organizations have a clear and meaningful direction and that virtually every employee is aligned or motivated to move in that direction.

3. *They become "students for life,"* constantly acknowledging what they don't know and seeking new ways of learning.

4. *They believe in and invest in their people,* training them, educating them, preparing them to do more than they can do today. Then they give these people the permission to use what they've learned even to the point of remaking their own jobs.

5. *They make teams work,* first by bringing teams together from different parts of the organization to solve problems and then by giving their members the training they need—celebrating their success, using them as communication channels between different parts of the organization, and encouraging them to make decisions that will benefit the customer.

6. *They stay the course,* understanding that achieving customer-focused quality takes time. They continuously encourage others, even if results are slow in coming.

7. *They live the organization's purpose,* leading by example, being willing to get their hands dirty, and continually creating more leaders within the company.

People who behave in this way can lead anything from a two-person work group to the largest business in the world.

Championing the Customer

The title on the business card of Anthony Harnett, former chief executive officer of Bread and Circus, a Cambridge, Massachusetts–based health food chain, is "CEO and Customer Service Representative." No false humility here. Harnett liked to spend time at a vegetable stand, serving customers. That part of his job, he explained, showed both employees and customers what is really important in his company.

Harnett is a dedicated man. "Food is life," he says, "and life should be about passion" (Whiteley, 1991, p. 182). He believes deeply in doing right by his customers. By spending time with them, he gets to know their passions and see how they respond to his. This provides insight that no surveys could ever yield. Moreover, when he spends time helping customers, Harnett also demonstrates his passion to the people who work for him.

Forum research found, to no one's surprise, that the companies making real progress in serving their customers are led by people who themselves value customers as a high priority. More than that, these leaders believe passionately in giving customers what they want. They spend much of their time with their customers. They speak for the customer within their organizations—in a strong, compelling voice.

The successful leaders are people who have made the move that one top executive calls a "leap of faith." These people didn't calculate the amount by which quality would improve profits and then set out to improve quality on the basis of those calculations; not at all. These people came to the profound, intuitive realization that profitability is simply an indicator of how well you are treating your customers. If they could create happy customers, profit would take care of itself.

AMP, Inc., of Canada is the northern arm of a large electrical connector company based in Harrisburg, Pennsylvania. Barrie Whittaker, AMP's Canadian general manager, loves customers. And it shows. At his regular meeting of operating managers, he always leaves one seat empty. Symbolically, this seat is for the customer, a silent presence reminding these executives that the primary reason they are seated around that table is to make decisions that will serve the interests of their customers.

If there is a question about spending money, closing an office, or reorganizing the company, the premier business leaders always ask, "How can we deal with this issue in a way that will serve our customers best in the short and long run?"

Creating Direction and Alignment

In our most recent research on effective leadership, Forum found that outstanding leaders at all levels in an organization expend a great deal of effort interpreting the environment. It is a leader's responsibility to create stability by making sure that the organization has a clear picture of the future and that people know what that picture is and are prepared to work hard to attain it. Two important tools for making this happen are vision and values.

"Good businesses create a vision, articulate the vision, passionately own the vision, and relentlessly drive it to completion," says Jack Welch, CEO of General Electric (Whiteley, 1991, p. 184). Welch knows that an inspired view of the future has the potential to excite company personnel and give much more meaning to their work than simply seeking a paycheck.

The Ritz-Carlton hotel chain, a recent winner of the Malcolm Baldrige Award, has a succinct but powerful vision: "Ladies and gentlemen serving ladies and gentlemen." In just seven words, with great respect for the customer and great dignity for its employees, this grand establishment makes clear its fundamental purpose—to serve.

If vision is a picture of a desirable, exciting future state, values are the guidelines that govern behavior and aim people in an organization toward this future state.

Values may be explicit or implicit, but every organization lives by them. An organization's strategy—and values—are reflected in the behavior of its senior managers. One need only observe whom they listen to, what they approve or disapprove, how they spend their time, what they read, how they invest, whom they promote, and their values become clear.

At Saturn, the remarkable automobile company that is taking market share from Japanese competitors in the small-car market, there are five clear values: commitment to customer enthusiasm, commitment to excellence, teamwork, trust and respect for the individual, and continuous improvement. Each prospective Saturn employee is made aware of these values and is also told that if Saturn's values are not consistent with his or her personal values, Saturn will not likely be a place where that person would be happy.

Gemini Consulting is a company that appears to be taking the matter of values quite seriously. The Morristown, New Jersey, company recently named one of its vice presidents "values champion." Through training programs and one-on-one coaching, he'll devote all his time to helping Gemini workers get the word.

Remaining Students for Life

I frequently ask people to think of the best leaders they've personally known and then rate them, on a ten-point scale, for charisma. The average charisma rating for the best leaders is around six. In other words, the best leaders are no more than average on the charisma scale. How can that be? Isn't charisma—which I'll define as a sort of extraordinary personal magnetism—a major element in leadership?

Apparently not. Leadership, it turns out, actually depends on something quite different, something that charismatic people often lack: an openness to new ideas and, beyond that, an insatiable hunger for ideas that will help achieve goals.

There's a catch here, however. To become a student, one must admit ignorance. For the highly paid executive who's made the arduous climb up the corporate ladder, this is perhaps the most challenging vulnerability of all: After all, they're paid for brilliance, not ignorance, right? It is an ego trap, and too many executives get caught in it.

Customer-driven quality (and its implementation) need not be complex. But much of what is needed to accomplish this goal *is* different—so different, in fact, that today's executive will find that many of the tools available are ineffective. In the worst case, they may even be harmful to the creation of customer-driven quality. (Later I'll detail some of the most common mistakes in this often confusing area.)

Bob Galvin, the former CEO of Motorola, reflects on a time when his company needed to move in new directions. "I knew I wasn't smart enough to know how to get us to be competitive," he says—an amazing admission from someone who is paid to be smart, even omniscient (*Customer-Driven Quality*, 1993).

Did Motorola become competitive? The record says yes. Why? Because when he was able candidly to admit his own limitations, Galvin also was able to roll up his sleeves and become a student, and his entire company followed.

Craig Weatherup, president of Pepsi North America, offers his method of continuous learning: "Actually, most of my personal learning has been just going out and doing my own personal research. I did some benchmarking—I read every book I could think of, met with consultants here and there. But basically, you know, talking to people, benchmarking, consultants, a tremendous amount of reading. . . . So I'd say the bulk of it has been just my own personal kind of research" (*Customer-Driven Quality*, 1993).

Believing and Investing in People

"Commitment must go both ways," says Charles E. Horne, vice president of Amica Mutual Insurance Company, a firm that consistently achieves exceptional service ratings from its policyholders. "We want people to commit to us, but we are committed to them in the same way" (Whiteley, 1991, p. 190).

Just as the best leaders have made a leap of faith in believing that doing right by customers will in the long run cause profits to take care of themselves, so too they've typically decided to believe in and invest in their own people. After demonstrating that faith, these leaders have seen the results in higher morale, better work, and increased profitability. Dr. Thomas Malone, chief operating officer of Milliken & Co., the textile manufacturer that won the Baldrige award in 1989, said that the most difficult part of his company's transformation was actually to believe that his people understood how to improve the processes and to empower them to develop solutions and implement those solutions (Whiteley, 1991, p. 190). This, incidently, is exactly what you should do with customers—listen to them and jointly develop solutions to problems.

Forum found in its research that transformational leaders invest aggressively in training that supports their organization's vision and strategy. And along with that training comes empowerment, the permission—encouragement, really—for each employee to use his or her newly developed skills *and* personal judgment to reduce waste and serve customers better.

You get confidence in your employees by training them. That is the key responsibility of managers: to train the people who work for them. And once you've given your employees all the training that is necessary, you've got to have the confidence that they're going to do the job and empower them to do it. You can't be afraid that your subordinates are going to be better at the job than you are. Indeed, one of our division vice presidents advises that you should always have several people working for you who are better qualified than you.

Many successful leaders insist that managers themselves teach courses. While at Xerox, David Kearns not only vastly increased Xerox's investment in education and training but also presented the training to his organization in a "cascading" sequence. Xerox decided to teach people skills in leadership and quality. Kearns and the people who reported directly to him took the course first. Then they spent time using the skills and techniques. Then themselves—top executives of a $17 billion-a-year corporation—actually taught the techniques to the people who worked for them. They worked with trained facilitators, but the managers had to do the first part of the training themselves.

Then the next level of managers taught the techniques to the people who worked for them. That got people's attention. You couldn't very well treat training as something nonessential if the teacher of your training course was a senior manager and you knew you would have to teach it to your own people. Other companies, including AT&T, Milliken, and Motorola, have employed similar approaches.

The confidence that a leader *must* have in his or her people is perhaps best summed up by Sarah Nolan, former president of Amex Life Insurance Company. "You must give away some of your power," she says, "and you must expect the unexpected, and the unexpected will always be better than what you could have ordered" (personal communication, 1994).

Making Teams Work

Few techniques of management have caused more excitement in the past decade than the creation of teams to set direction, share information, and solve problems. Only a few years ago, it seems, books about management focused on how to run a hierarchy, delegate jobs, and manage subordinates. Although these subjects are still important, our research shows that today's managers succeed by developing and effectively using teams that possess considerable freedom in achieving excellence for customers.

Work groups in these organizations function as teams in which the ideas of low-ranking people frequently count as much as those of more senior members. Quality circles, customer action teams, quality councils, and cross-functional groups are constantly struggling to solve problems for customers and, in doing so, are helping people in each part of the organization understand the needs of the rest of the company.

At the same time, one of the most challenging tasks facing a leader is to make those teams work—to make them effective. Too often, employees who have suffered through management efforts to create teams tell tales of boredom and frustration. Is the camel a horse designed by a team? Probably so—if the team hadn't a clue what it was trying to create and was just going through the motions. Many meetings that are supposed to enlist people in a common purpose or convened to make important recommendations or decisions are too often viewed by their participants as a waste of time.

Why do some leaders create productive teams while others don't? A few years ago, Forum conducted research addressing this basic issue. We asked, "How does a person in an organization achieve influence—effectiveness in getting things done while working in teams with people over whom he or she may not have operating control?" We looked at people who were excellent with influence, and we also looked at those who were below average at influencing others. What were the superior influencers doing? We carried out our first research on this question more than ten years ago and since then have administered questionnaires to more than four thousand managers.

By studying people whom peers felt were influential, we made three important discoveries:

1. *Influence requires much more than powerful persuasion skills.*

Successful influencers use a sequential process to build, apply, and then sustain their influence. First, they establish an open and negotiated framework in which influence can take place. For example, they establish explicit ground rules for working together with others in their influence network. Only then do they actually use influence, working with a network to develop high-quality, creative decisions. After achieving this collaboration, they employ specific practices to sustain their influence, creating a basis for consistent execution by demonstrating openness and gaining confidences.

2. *Influential people have specific underlying attitudes about how people work together.* They appreciate the necessity for supporting and helping others, sharing power and building trust. In workshops, we find that these attitudes are likely to be missing in organizations where teams function poorly.

3. *Influential managers instill confidence in their employees.* When teams rate influence practices highly, the team members believe themselves significantly more innovative and better at continuous improvement. These are two of the most important and desirable outcomes for creating customer-driven quality.

It is crucial, of course, that a senior leader—one to whom other executives report—not tolerate wasteful and demoralizing functional or geographical rivalries that lead to debilitating "turf warfare."

If lower-level teams are to work effectively, the most senior team must be a model for all to see and emulate. It is not only "do what we say," it is also "do what we do."

Staying the Course

Efforts aiming at a corporate transformation often follow the pattern illustrated in Figure 9.1. When an initiative starts, it opens

Figure 9.1. Staying the Course.

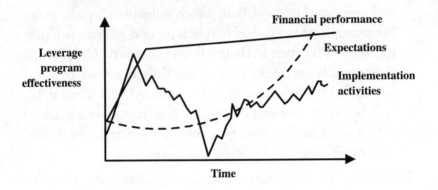

with a great deal of fanfare and excitement. People's expectations rise rapidly—and often continue rising. They're excited about doing a better job.

But that doesn't translate to increased financial performance right away. Your program costs money, and it takes a while before many of your most important initiatives begin to affect the customer. Even if customers quickly notice better service on the front lines, they won't automatically start spending more for your product.

After that initial push, moreover, the program will have problems—guaranteed. A lot of work is being done, people are "turned on," but typically the company hasn't yet developed an integrated cross-functional effort. Here's a typical result: an effort by a group of people in, say, a factory is defeated because some middle manager in the accounting or design department doesn't support it.

A common reaction is, "Why bother?" Work seems excessive, and people look for ways of reducing the effort they put into improvement activities. The whole program slows down. People feel frustrated, sometimes cynical.

When this happens, unfortunately, most companies and the managers in them back away from their quality programs. Leaders still talk about quality, but the references are perfunctory, a mantra. They start looking for an easier way to increase profits, and this usually means more cuts.

In such a climate, the leaders who succeed show their star quality. Their leap of faith is real. If they're facing financial losses, they may make cutbacks in areas that don't directly affect the creation of value for the customer. Their focus on becoming customer-driven continues. They keep on pushing, keep on selling their vision to people, keep on celebrating the successes that have been achieved, keep on working to learn how to use the tools to create delighted customers. The middle managers who succeed keep fighting for the vision, struggling with others in the organization who have become cynical. And then, preceded by some short-term results that can show up fairly quickly in isolated pockets, the entire organization begins to register a remarkable improvement.

Tom Malone of Milliken said, "It takes two or three years for it to really happen. You've got to get the scoreboards in place, and then the environment of applauding people for improving the characteristics you're measuring on those scoreboards. You can document all that up-front cost. The payback is later" (Whiteley, 1991, pp. 198–199).

You become a successful leader if, like Tom Malone, you persevere through the challenging times.

Living Their Purpose

Here's an axiom: all customer-driven companies are alike. Watch their leaders' behavior, and you'll understand what they value and see why they succeed.

In our research at Forum, we constantly hear people saying just that about the best leaders: they *are* what they want their companies to *become*. When Ray Kroc opened his first McDonald's restaurant, hundreds of other fast-food places already lined the roads outside most of America's major cities.

Kroc's franchisees could never tell when Kroc himself would show up in their parking lot, picking up hamburger wrappers that the franchisee hadn't bothered to sweep up. He always lived his business vision—providing "quality, service, cleanliness, value" to ordinary people.

Not long ago, our Building Customer Focus workshop was held at Corning, the first of many seminars scheduled for employees. Most impressive to us was that Jamie Houghton, Corning's chairman, attended the two-day program without interruption. He also attended the first presentation of each of the companywide quality programs created by Corning's quality staff. "That did us a lot of good when we wanted to present them at the plant level, and the plant manager said he was too busy to attend himself," says Joel Ramich, Corning's associate director of quality (Whiteley, 1991, p. 185). Houghton's message, delivered through behavior visible to all, was clear: quality at Corning is important, and it is worth your while to take time to learn about it.

David Weekley is CEO of David Weekley Homes, a Houston-based home builder that has experienced 40 percent growth per year for five years running. How has this company achieved such growth in the challenging Texas economy? One vital reason is that the employees love their customers and go out of their way to get customers to tell them how David Weekley Homes can improve.

The acid test for this builder comes several months after a new buyer has moved into one of his homes. This question is asked: "Would you recommend a David Weekley home to a buyer moving into this area?" Three answer options are offered: "no," "yes," and "maybe." In tabulating the results, Weekley considers "maybe" the equivalent of "no" because the buyer obviously wasn't delighted.

For every single "no" or "maybe" received, either Weekley himself or John Johnson, his COO, personally visits the homeowner and conducts an interview to learn what the problems are, how they can be resolved, and how they could have been avoided. Not so surprisingly, more than 95 percent of their customers respond with an enthusiastic "yes."

By making this effort, Weekley and Johnson learn about customer issues firsthand. Equally important, their behavior gives a strong, clear signal to their entire organization: quality and customer service are paramount.

The Three Most Common Mistakes That Senior Executives Make

As we work with organizations around the world that are struggling to become customer-driven, we see certain patterns emerging. The patterns seem to repeat themselves, regardless of an organization's size, industry, or country. Three of them are in fact mistakes.

Mistake No. 1: Focusing Only on Short-Term Results

Every executive should, of course, expect and even demand results from the company's quality work. Unfortunately, too often the emphasis is on the wrong results with the wrong timing.

The executive who is managing only by financial results is managing by a lagging indicator. In today's volatile, fast-moving business environment, this is a prescription for failure. By the time you've had a chance to react, the results are already posted. Donald Petersen, former chief executive of Ford, says, "I wouldn't play an important tennis match with one eye on the scoreboard" (personal communication, 1994).

Countermeasure: Focusing on Processes. All right, no scoreboard. But what should the alert executive keep an eye on? The answer is to watch the processes that produce the desired results, not the results themselves.

A process is a series of activities that takes input, adds value, and produces a result in the form of a product or service that is delivered to an internal (employee), intermediate (distributor), or external (consumer) customer. *All results are created by processes.* If you want to manage the results well, you'd better look upstream and manage the processes that produce them.

This concept of process management is very difficult for many executives to embrace. Why? Because we grew up with the now-obsolete concept of management by objectives. Pepsi's Craig Weatherup says his biggest challenge was convincing his board to think in terms of processes *and* results, not just results (*Customer-Driven Quality*, 1993).

Does this eye-on-the-process philosophy work? It does. I am told of a Sony plant that manufactures television sets. At the end of a production line, the desired result is a television that works perfectly. In the plant, workers are so confident of the upstream processes that when the TV comes off the line, they do not plug it in or turn it on—they just ship it!

Mistake No. 2: Being Unwilling to Break Down Functional Barriers

In a typical manufacturing company, a product is created as it moves horizontally through the organization. Raw materials enter the plant. They are worked on by a person or a team that adds value. When this step is complete, the product-to-be moves to the next person or team, which adds more value, and so it goes. In the process of being created, this product journeys throughout the organization, moving from one function or business unit to another. Ultimately, the finished product requires the effort of such diverse groups as purchasing, receiving, manufacturing, accounting, shipping, marketing, and sales. If these various groups collaborate well and operate as a smooth-functioning team, in all likelihood they will produce a superior product. But if they bicker, fight, protect turf, and cover their tails, what do you think the product will look like? A camel? Well, perhaps.

One of an executive's primary responsibilities is to ensure that functional barriers do not block the creation of customer-pleasing products and services. Yet all too often, ego-driven and politically motivated infighting creates impenetrable barriers at the top of the business. This internecine warfare serves only to signal people at lower levels in the organization—people who actually produce the products and services—that collaboration is, at best, optional.

This problem is particularly prominent in organizations that have decentralized into freewheeling, entrepreneurial, independent business units. To their leaders, collaboration often looks like the surrender of power. When this happens, customers always suffer.

Countermeasure: Smashing the Barriers. Management at British Airways (the world's most profitable airline) chips away at functional "chimneys" by assigning executives and managers from different functions to cross-functional teams. This serves to promote communication and understanding as they work on important projects aimed at improving processes and results for customers.

Establishing a subordinate goal, one that stands above individual or functional group achievement, also serves to unite people in pursuit of a common purpose. A clear, well-developed vision and statement of values will go a long way toward bringing people together, with this proviso: they must be real and be reinforced by the leader. At General Electric, for example, it is no longer enough just to produce numbers. Each executive is expected to live by GE's values as well, and doing so is considered every bit as important as making budget.

Of course, compensation is another lever. Many organizations are still caught in the old dilemma of providing products and services horizontally but rewarding people vertically. When this happens, it is possible for a function to be well rewarded even as external customers are being disappointed. That explains the move toward team bonuses. At Saturn, for example, world-class cars and service are being provided almost as a matter of course. There, every employee, from production line workers and administrators to the president, has the same compensation format. It consists of a base salary plus incentives for overall company quality, company productivity, and attainment of each individual's personal development plan. Other than for one's own personal development, there is not one single individual or departmental compensation incentive.

Mistake No. 3: Viewing Quality as a Program

I know of a company that proudly proclaimed 1993 "The Year of Quality." Although the intention behind this type of annual theme is obviously positive, its consequences may be negative. The theme could be interpreted as implying that quality is a program, is short-term, is separate from the regular business. Unfortunately, too many executives regard quality in that way—as an important or even vital add-on but separate from the business itself. Ted Levitt, professor of marketing at Harvard Business School, states that "the fundamental purpose of a business is to create and retain a customer" (Levitt, 1983, p. 5). If this is true, how can it be that creating customer-driven quality is *not* the business?

Too often, as soon as a quality department is set up, everyone in the organization who is not in that department stops worrying about quality ("That's *their* job, not mine"). The same phenomenon occurs upon the establishment of a customer service department. Suddenly, customer service is somebody else's job.

The problem with this add-on view of quality is that as soon as the "real business" heats up or runs into trouble, the quality work gets dropped. Or when the organization is anticipating a change of command at the top, quality work is slowed or put on hold "till we can see how our new leader feels about quality." What this really signals to the entire organization is that striving to improve quality is discretionary and dependent on other circumstances. It is not a fundamental need of the business.

Countermeasure: Adopting Customer-Driven Quality as Your Strategy. While creating a video seminar with *Fortune* magazine on customer-driven quality, I had the pleasure of visiting Saturn and interviewing Skip Le Fauve, the president. During the interview, I asked, "How does quality relate to your strategy?" He looked puzzled for a moment and then responded, "Quality *is* our strategy" (*Customer-Driven Quality*, 1993).

If you look at the winners of various quality awards—the Deming Prize in Japan, Canada's Gold Award for Quality, Hong Kong's HKMA award, England's quality management award BF5750—you will find they have many things in common. One is that they integrate: they do not separate business strategy and quality.

How can you do this? Review and, if necessary, revise your strategy to ensure that customer-driven quality is at its heart.

Understand that the CEO or senior executive on site is the senior quality officer for any organization. If the formal position of quality officer exists, it should report directly to the senior officer. And if quality departments exist, their purpose is not to produce quality but to help every person in the company produce it.

Start every board and executive committee meeting with a report on quality. Ideally, at such meetings, regular reports will include performance against key customer-driven-quality indicators. At British Airways, CEO Sir Colin Marshall receives such reports monthly. He is keenly interested in them because he realizes that the financial reports indicate what has been accomplished but the customer reports tell how tomorrow's financial reports will look.

Obtaining Executive Commitment:
A Formula for Success

At the beginning of a speech, I often say to members of the audience, "Raise your hand if you do not believe in quality." I've probably said this to over ten thousand business executives in locations as diverse as Singapore, England, Italy, the Czech Republic, Brazil, Canada, Japan, Venezuela, and the United States. In all this time, not one hand has been raised. What have I learned? That everyone professes to believe in quality. What do I conclude when seven out of ten quality initiatives fail? That most people who say they believe in quality are not truly committed to achieving it.

In our research at Forum, we have determined that two primary forces lead companies to embrace customer-driven quality. The first is a vision of the organization's founders so deeply rooted in customer and quality thinking that it both creates and sustains an organizational culture that puts the customer at its center.

When IBM CEO Louis Gerstner, the first outsider to run the company in its history, spoke at its annual meeting in April 1993, he mentioned several solutions to IBM's serious problems. One was to redouble the company's commitment to customers. "At one time," he said, "IBM understood the importance of putting the customer first. It will again," he added (Gerstner, 1993).

When the Walt Disney Company was producing the animated film *Aladdin*, the people involved decided that the story just wasn't working right. Even though the entire movie was on story reels, Disney tore the film apart, eliminating some characters and redesigning others, literally going back to the drawing board. The decision was extremely costly but "one we had to make." The emphasis in this case was on quality, not on the bottom line. As it turned out, *Aladdin* has been phenomenally successful—one more bit of evidence, if you will, that pleasing customers, more than any other factor, is what makes a business thrive.

The second force occurs when an organization faces a crises of such major proportions as to threaten its very existence. When companies like Xerox, Harley-Davidson, and Ford realized that business as usual meant no business at all, they had no option but to change—dramatically. In each case, survival and later success were gained by emphasizing the tenets of customer-driven quality.

Figure 9.2. The Manager's Dilemma.

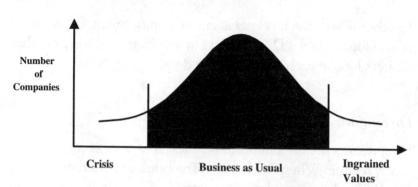

At one pole are visionary founders; at the other, major crises. The truth is that leaders of most companies today don't perceive their organizations to be at either pole; they place themselves somewhere in the middle. Performance is still good enough to be able to avoid the uncomfortable transition from the old ways to being customer-driven. Little wonder that executive commitment beyond approving slogans and budgets is hard to find. No vision, no crisis, no change. Figure 9.2 depicts the dilemma as a bell-shaped curve. The shaded area is where executive commitment is suspect and most implementation failures occur.

In the face of satisfactory results, executives will not be committed to lead the change required to become customer-driven. Their rationalization is, "If it ain't broke, don't fix it." Our question is, "How do we get these stand-pat executives committed?"

A succinct and imaginative answer to this question comes from Len Schlesinger, one of several professors and researchers at Harvard Business School doing outstanding work in the field of customer-driven quality. I have both borrowed and enhanced his approach (Schlesinger and Heskett, 1991a, 1991b; Fromm and Schlesinger, 1994). Basically, the question can be answered by a formula:

$$EC = (D \times V \times P \times L) > C$$

In other words, the level of executive commitment EC is a function of four variables D, V, P, and L when their total is greater than C. Let's look at each component in detail.

Discomfort

D represents the discomfort in business that the executive is currently feeling. When Ford was on the brink of bankruptcy in the late 1970s, there was a lot of discomfort—so much, in fact, that its executives were willing to bet their company on creating a total quality culture.

But if the crisis isn't already there, the job is to create discomfort. Larry Dille is the quality officer at UARCO, a company that specializes in document management. He explains, "My job at UARCO is to discourage comfort with the status quo. And that's hard to do because UARCO is a successful 100-year-old company" (personal communication, 1994). Dille understands that UARCO must change and adapt to a new business environment if it is to be successful for the next hundred years.

How does one get an apparently successful company to see that it is in trouble? There are several ways. First, get your executives to go on a customer-listening tour. The objective is for *every* senior executive, including the human resource manager and the chief counsel, to visit five to ten customers. They should listen and learn how these customers feel about doing business with their company. When the tour is complete, each listener should give a report at a meeting of all executives devoted exclusively to this topic. The energy generated is electric, and most participants will feel the discomfort resulting from hearing candid feedback from customers who are less than delighted.

By the way, during the tour, don't sell, don't solve problems, and don't let salespeople set up the customer meetings (they will send you to their happiest customers).

Another way to create discomfort is to calculate the amount of waste created by poor quality. Forum's research shows that for most organizations, this will average between 20 and 40 percent of revenues. A large manufacturing firm made such a calculation and realized that of its $4.5 billion in revenues, $950 million was waste. The discomfort was so great that it rendered management ready to act immediately.

Be careful of this calculation, however. It can lead to indiscriminate cost-cutting that does not focus on getting rid of waste (not all costs are waste) and provides no incentive to introduce customer-driven quality.

Vision

Back to our formula EC = $(D \times V \times P \times L) > C$. The V stands for vision. We now feel the discomfort, but if we do get rid of it, what is possible? In a way, it's not dissimilar to the sequence of events and emotions leading to a diet. First comes the discomfort—major discomfort: pants are too tight, the summer wardrobe doesn't fit, you feel like an overstuffed artichoke. When the discomfort gets strong enough, you decide to start a diet. Motivating you also is a vision of what's possible—you on a beach, tanned and trim, or you, fitting into your clothes again or perhaps buying a new wardrobe.

The most effective way to create a vision of what is possible is to send executives on site visits to other companies that are successfully implementing customer-driven quality. Ideally, these companies should not be in the same industry. That avoids ethical questions about visiting a competitor and prevents executives from talking shop and missing the opportunity to see and understand the principles that make customer-driven quality work.

In Japan, Mitsui Bank was moved to embrace total quality

management only after its president witnessed a quality circle presentation at one of Mitsui's affiliates. At Pepsi, Craig Weatherup visited five or six other companies both to build team motivation and to gauge Pepsi's initiative and learn where to place his leadership emphasis.

Site visits are important because they instill a vision of what is possible. Executives see extraordinary achievements accomplished by ordinary people. They witness the power, energy, and excitement of a customer-driven company and generally have two reactions: "I want this for my company" and "Their people are excellent, but no better than ours. This is within our reach."

Here are some hints for an effective site visit:

- Send executives in groups of three or four. Multiple sets of eyes will take in more.
- Send each team in with specific learning objectives. The purpose of the trip should be clear.
- Have the team write a report on its findings. The report should answer these questions: What do these companies do that makes them successful? What are the principles behind what they do? What can we take from this that will be useful for us?
- At a meeting convened solely for this purpose, have each team report its findings to the rest of the executives. Follow with a discussion.
- Communicate your findings to the rest of the organization.

Plan

The next element in our equation EC = $(D \times V \times P \times L) > C$ is P, which stands for plan—a plan that will guide your organization to become customer-driven. An effective plan is usually laid out in phases over a number of years. It should include significant events and milestones such as formation of a quality council, adoption of a quality policy, and initial team activities. In addition, the plan should focus on such processes as communication, measurement, and rewards and recognition. The importance of the plan should not be underestimated:

- It sets the clear expectation up front that this is not a program but rather a multiyear journey aimed at changing the culture of your organization. When he was with Xerox, David Kearns expressed this well when he said, "Quality is a race without a finish line. A focus on quality has made Xerox a stronger company, but we know we'll never be as good as we can be because we'll always try to be better. We are on a mission of continuous quality improvement" (personal communication, 1994).

- The plan lays out a sequence of steps that, when completed over time, sends a clear message to what is often a skeptical workforce tainted by too many "programs of the month." The message is that this work is real and is here to stay.

- It sets the expectation that a multiyear investment of dollars will be required to achieve success, and to cut the budget will jeopardize the chances for success.

- The plan makes it clear that a sustained commitment of executive time, interest, and involvement will be required for a company to become customer-driven. Don't take the first step if you don't intend to complete the journey.

Have your executive team create the plan. It won't be easy because initially, the team's members will have no idea what should go into the plan. So they will have to educate themselves. Executive seminars, reading, site visits, and interviews with customers and employees will be vital. Only after these explorations will they be in a position to create the plan.

Of course, things being as they are, most executives will want a plan presented to them by staff, a plan that they can then simply approve. That won't do. By insisting that they write their own plan, executive team members will have to become knowledgeable enough to create it in the first place; what is more, they will "own" what they create, psychologically and intellectually.

Leadership

The L in EC = $(D \times V \times P \times L) > C$ stands for leadership. When most organizations embark on the customer-driven journey, they must move from one place (existing culture) to another place (new culture). The purpose of becoming customer-driven is to improve market share, profits, responsiveness, and morale. These are the "hard" results that executives look for. But to achieve them, the "soft" aspects of culture must be considered. For most organizations, becoming customer-driven means changing the culture from what it is to what it needs to be. For most, it means moving in these directions:

- From motivation through fear and loyalty to motivation through shared vision
- From an attitude that says "It's *their* problem" to ownership of every problem that affects the customer; from "the way we've always done it" to continuous improvement
- From making decisions based on assumptions and judgment calls to doing it with data and fact-based decisions
- From the belief that everything begins and ends with management to the belief that everything begins and ends with customers
- From functional "stovepipes," where departments base decisions solely on their own criteria, to cross-functional cooperation; from being good at crisis management and recovery to

doing things right the first time; from depending on heroics to driving variability out of the process

- From a choice between participative and scientific management to a combination of participative and scientific management

This kind of movement simply cannot be achieved or sustained without strong leadership at all levels of the organization. The specifics of such leadership were described earlier in this chapter.

Costs

The last letter in the formula $EC = (D \times V \times P \times L) > C$ stands for costs. Executives will be willing to commit to change if the first four factors—discomfort, vision, plan, and leadership—are greater than the perceived costs of that change. There are three costs.

The first is direct cost. This might be the budget required to create quality, hire a consultant, review a seminar, serve customers, or institute quality awards.

The second is indirect cost. This is the opportunity cost of employees not doing their regular work while they're in training sessions or the time of executives who are on a site visit. Some executives—too many, in fact—tell me that they don't have the time for site visits. The underlying belief, obviously, is that this activity isn't as important as doing their regular job. If their regular job is to bring new ideas and innovation to their companies, aren't site visits a vital aspect of doing that?

The first two costs, let me stress, are minor when compared with potential gains. Study after study shows that investing in customer-driven quality is one of the best investments a leader can make.

It is the third cost that causes the most trouble, and that is personal cost or perceived risk. We cling to the familiar. For front-line employees, it means letting go of skepticism and embracing change.

It means making suggestions and taking the risk to innovate or improve the work they do. It also means believing (and this takes demonstrated assurance from management) that as waste is driven out, their jobs may disappear but they will not. Rather, they will be retrained and deployed elsewhere in the organization.

For middle managers, becoming a customer-driven company means empowering the people lower down the hierarchy. It means letting go of comfortable techniques like management by objectives and learning new ones. It means sharing the power they have fought so hard over the years to gain.

For executives, the goal of becoming a customer-driven company means investing in an all-out effort but not realizing many of the rewards for periods well beyond normal performance reviews. It means admitting ignorance and becoming a learner. It means staying the course, steadfastly investing in the process of becoming customer-driven long before the results begin to show.

Conclusion

So that is the formula for change: $EC = (D \times V \times P \times L) > C$. If it's a question of getting executives to lead or of developing the true commitment to lead, the answer may very well lie in using the formula.

In this chapter, we have taken a hard look at leadership, without question the most critical aspect of an organization on the road to becoming customer-driven. Without clear, purposeful leadership, the weight of "business as usual" supported by a resistant culture will suffocate any serious attempt to build a customer-driven company. And building a customer-driven company, there seems little doubt, is absolutely crucial for success in today's dynamic, turbulent global business environment.

References

Customer-Driven Quality. (1993). Boston: Nathan/Tyler Productions. Videotape.
Fromm, B., and Schlesinger, L. A. (1994). *The Real Heroes of Business . . . and Not a CEO Among Them.* New York: Currency/Doubleday.

Gerstner, L. V. (1993, Apr. 26). Remarks at the Annual Meeting of International Business Machines, Inc., Tampa, Fla.

Levitt, T. (1983). *The Marketing Imagination*. New York: Free Press.

Schlesinger, L. A., and Heskett, J. L. (1991a). Breaking the cycle of failure in services. *Sloan Management Review, 32*(3), 17–28.

Schlesinger, L. A., and Heskett, J. L. (1991b). The service-driven company. *Harvard Business Review, 69*(5), 71–81.

Whiteley, R. C. (1991). *The Customer-Driven Company: Moving from Talk to Action*. Reading, Mass.: Addison-Wesley.

Chapter Ten

Quality Management in the Real World

Philip B. Crosby

We live in this very real world economy where competitors, suppliers, and customers can be anyplace. As the Europeans are beginning to realize, 93 percent of the world's customers do *not* live in Europe. We see the Far East moving into many industries; we see Eastern Europe getting ready to participate in the world of business. The United States is beginning to create jobs again and is moving into a trade relationship with Latin America that will generate new businesses. Japan is in recession but is rapidly moving into Vietnam, Indonesia, Malaysia, China, and other areas.

The companies that will survive to grow into the twenty-first century are the ones that are willing to take a "greenfield approach," looking at the way they operate as though they were starting in business tomorrow. We have to take advantage of our assets and get rid of the management approaches that make us noncompetitive. This involves more than just improving productivity; it means changing managerial lifestyles. The most important of these changes is making quality a routine part of the business.

The usual way of handling quality has not changed much in spite of all the activities. In fact, it has deteriorated with the creation of ISO 9000 and other 1960s concepts of regulation and procedures. Like what is called total quality management, it does not represent a way of working that reduces costs and makes customers successful. Executives seem to think that TQM is some body of knowledge, like accounting, that can just be installed in a company. In fact, there is no such thing as TQM; look for a common definition, and you will not find one. Executives who install TQM feel that it is a matter of techniques and procedures applied to the lower part of the organization. This is like blaming the handles on a pot for making the soup too salty. Governments think that giving awards to people who nominate themselves and establishing mind-numbing criteria, as for the Baldrige Award, will lead to improvement. This has not been shown to be so. Also, these criteria are oriented toward quality assurance, which is old-fashioned containment. What we want is quality management, which is prevention.

Done properly, quality management is the most valuable action that an executive can take to move a company into the twenty-first century. Done improperly, it has an adverse effect on the morale and confidence of employees and increases the costs of doing business. The purpose of this chapter is to teach executives what they have to know to reap the benefits of quality management in their organization.

The only reason for installing quality management as part of the operating philosophy of a company is to make that company more successful and longer-lived. If the executive and shareholders are satisfied with the present condition of the company in this regard, no action should be taken. There is no need to follow a fad or do something that no one really understands. An executive should not "do quality" just because there is a stir about it or because some other function requires it. The decision should be based on clear-eyed reality, not fashion.

I like to say that there are three areas of primary concern to executives: finance, quality, and relationships. Most of their time is spent on finance; they like to turn quality and relationships over to someone else. If they had a firsthand comprehension of quality, they would be more likely to want to hang on to that and turn over the others. In truth, all three fit together. Quality is the structure of the organization, finance is the nourishment, and relationships are the soul. The eternally successful organization would have the characteristics described in Table 10.1. It is not difficult for people who know a company to find its current location in the table. Quality, growth, customers, change, and employees are all considered.

Table 10.1. The Eternally Successful Organizational Grid.

Condition	Comatose	In intensive care	In progressive care	On the mend	In perfect health
Quality (*Price of non-conformance*)	Nobody does anything right around here. (33%)	We finally have a list of customer complaints. (28%)	We are beginning a formal quality improvement process. (20%)	Customer complaints are practically gone. (13%)	People routinely do things right the first time. (3%)
Growth (*Return after tax*)	Nothing ever changes. (0%)	We bought a turkey. (0%)	The new product isn't too bad. (3%)	The new group is growing well. (7%)	Growth is profitable and steady. (12%)
Customers (*Customer complaints on orders*)	Nobody ever orders twice. (63%)	Customers don't know what they want. (54%)	We are working with customers. (26%)	We are making many defect-free deliveries. (9%)	Customer needs are anticipated. (0%)
Change (*Changes controlled by systems integrity*)	Nothing ever changes. (0%)	Nobody tells anyone anything. (2%)	We need to know what is happening. (55%)	There is no reason for anyone to be surprised. (85%)	Change is planned and managed. (100%)
Employees (*Employee turnover*)	Working here is a little better than not working. (65%)	Human resources has been told to help employees. (45%)	Error cause removal programs have been started. (40%)	Career path evaluations are implemented now. (7%)	People are proud to work here. (2%)

Companies that show up well on this evaluation can look forward to a long life. The table also provides a guide to what must be accomplished in order to stay healthy.

Executives must understand the practical concepts of quality management and recognize what can be accomplished by their proper application. These concepts were developed over a forty-year career of international "hands-on" work that saw them implemented in dozens of manufacturing and service businesses. I have learned that organizations can become quality-effective without having to set up a special department, embark on a complicated "certification" program, or even apply for an award. The same concepts apply to companies of all sizes. The application is in the hands of the executives; the operation looks like them. They need help in doing the task, particularly in the areas of education and communication.

In this chapter, we will discuss the *need* for quality management, the *content* of quality management, and the *leadership* of quality management. Need is viewed through the profile of a quality-troubled organization. Content is divided into four segments: management commitment, education, corrective action, and completeness. Leadership is briefly discussed in terms of what I call the absolutes of that subject: integrity, information, innovation, and incisiveness.

Need

It is possible to obtain a good idea of how a company is doing from a quality standpoint just through knowing what is going on every day. Here is a checklist to help you determined the status of quality in your organization. For each item, indicate (a) "That's us all the way," (b) "Some of this is true," or (c) "We're not like that."

1. Our services or products normally contain waivers, deviations, and other nonconformities.
2. We take a "fix-it" approach to our systems, procedures, products, and services.

3. Our employees do not know what management wants from them concerning quality.

4. Management does not know what the price of nonconformance really is.

5. Management feels that quality problems stem from sources other than management action.

Executives can review this checklist quickly using information from their own head. If you answered (c) to each item on the list, there is no need to read further. However, I recommend that each member of the management team make an evaluation before deciding that there are no troubles.

The key part for executives in this evaluation is item four, the price of nonconformance (PONC). If the executive does not know this figure, there is cause for concern. One reason why quality programs such as TQM do not become part of the organizational woodwork is that they do not relate to the real-world measurements that management uses to run the company. The primary one is, of course, financial. PONC has its origin in the definition of the word *quality*. It means conforming to the requirements that we have agreed on with our customers and co-workers. When requirements are not met, they must be done over in some manner. This interrupts the planned flow of work and adds cost—considerable cost. Manufacturing companies without an effective quality management involvement will spend 25 percent of revenues on the PONC; service companies waste 40 percent of their operation costs. If this figure is not calculated by the comptroller's department and used for corrective action, management will never take the causing of quality seriously. Executives know instinctively that there is no reason to get involved in quality improvement if it is not going to make a dramatic difference in the financial standing of the company. Why spend time and money doing something that we do not need?

Content of Quality Management

As mentioned earlier, content can be broken into four aspects: management commitment, education, corrective action, and completeness.

Management Commitment

The culture of an organization, as we all have experienced, is a portrait of the interests and concerns of management as seen by the people. The personality of the boss shines through into daily activities. Whatever he or she is interested in becomes the priority of the people who work in and with the company. A real commitment to quality will occur only when nonconformance is measured financially. Benchmarking won't do it. We can all find someone fatter and uglier than we are for comparison. True commitment must be displayed and reinforced in several ways:

- *Policy*. We will deliver defect-free products and services to our customers and co-workers on time, conforming to the requirements we have agreed on.
- *Improvement*. As we learn to do things better, or better things, we will formally change the requirements.
- *Participation*. Management must take part in actions for improvement and lead the way personally. It is not enough to be a cheerleader. Act the same way you do about profit.

Education

Each individual must understand the concepts of quality management and must recognize his or her personal role in making it all happen. People must be trained for their jobs in an atmosphere that respects education and skill. Things change so fast today that everyone needs help in keeping up. Most companies will need to get outside help from quality education companies, universities, and elsewhere. And executives cannot be taught by someone inside the company; they just will not listen.

The concepts of quality management are these:

- *Definition.* Quality means conformance to agreed requirements, not goodness.
- *System.* Quality is accomplished through prevention, not detection.
- *Performance standard.* Quality is being defect-free, not having acceptable quality levels.
- *Measurement.* The primary measurement is the price of nonconformance, not indexes.

Let's examine these in more detail.

Definition of Quality. When people talk to us about quality, we must ask them first to define their terms. The interesting thing about this subject is that people have some strange ideas of what quality is, most of them based on a sort of "goodness." However, as executives, we must be able to deal with subjects in a way that everyone can understand. We need a definition of quality that the shipping clerk can discuss with the CEO. "Conformance to requirements" eliminates the "good," "bad," "high," "low," and other modifiers of quality. Now we ask each other about the requirements and deal with real, measurable items: What time? How long? How many? Requirements are answers to questions. We do not need to create a whole bunch of new ones; we need only to take seriously the ones we already have.

System of Quality. For years, companies have used quality control, quality assurance, systems process control, and the like to find problems as early as possible. This requires inspection, testing, analysis, and continuous evaluation. Many manufacturing companies have one assessment person for every four or five productive persons. What we need is prevention. The thought of vaccinating a company, as we do our body, against the diseases of failure should be a primary one. Smallpox is gone because we learned how not to contract it. We can do the same thing to the list of problems that concern us in our business life. Exhibit 10.1 lists some of the situations that exist in a prevention-oriented company. Clear requirements, continuous training, and encouragement are the weapons of prevention.

Performance Standard of Quality. "Good enough" has been around so long that many executives do not realize that they are planning for failure in their processes. "Acceptable quality levels" (AQL) and "That's close enough" are the standards of organized waste. What we must do is insist that we try to do the right things right the first time. Then if there is a mistake—and there will be—it can be recognized and prevented the next time. Symbolically, this concept is called zero defects. Employees like and trust this approach because they do not have to live in a world where constant decisions about what is "good enough" are made. Executives get what they ask for. The thought of continuous improvement means that we will improve the requirements; it does not mean to drop six babies this week and only five next week.

Measurement of Quality. The traditional way of measuring quality is by indexes. Mushy information provides mushy comprehension, which results in people having no idea of reality. The true measurement is money, and that is not hard to achieve. Look at the accounting reports and identify the expenses that would not have to be incurred if we met all our requirements the first time. Don't overlook accounts receivable that are overdue because of disagreements or excess inventory held because suppliers can't be trusted. PONC must be included in the operations review data and used as the basis for corrective action. Quality should also be the first item on that agenda.

Exhibit 10.1. The Crosby Nonconformity Vaccine.

Integrity
- The chief executive officer is dedicated to having the customer receive what was promised, believes that the company will prosper only when all employees feel the same way, and is determined that neither customers nor employees will be hassled.
- The CEO believes that management performance is a complete function requiring that quality be "first among equals"—schedule and cost.
- The senior executives, who report to the CEO and the COO, take requirements so seriously that they can't stand deviations.
- The managers, who work for the senior executives, know that the future rests with their ability to get things done through people and done right the first time.
- The professional employees know that the accuracy and completeness of their work determine the effectiveness of the entire workforce.
- The employees as a whole recognize that their individual commitment to the integrity of requirements is what makes the company sound.

Systems
- The quality management function is dedicated to measuring conformance to requirements and reporting any differences accurately.
- The quality education system ensures that all employees of the company have a common language of quality and understand their personal roles in making quality routine.
- The financial method of measuring nonconformance and conformance costs is used to evaluate processes.
- The use of the company's products or services by customers is measured and reported in a manner that triggers corrective action.
- The companywide emphasis on defect prevention serves as a base for continual review and planning that uses current and past experience to keep the past from repeating itself.

Communications
- Information about the progress of quality improvement and achievement is continually supplied to all employees.
- Recognition programs applicable to all levels of responsibility are a part of normal operations.
- Each person in the company can, with very little effort, identify error, waste, opportunity, or any other concern to top management quickly and receive an immediate answer.
- Each management status meeting begins with a factual and financial review of quality.

Exhibit 10.1. (cont.)

Operations

- Suppliers are educated and supported to ensure that they will deliver services and products that are dependable and on time.
- Procedures, products, and systems are qualified and proven prior to implementation and then continually examined and officially modified when the opportunity for improvement is seen.
- Training is a routine activity for all tasks and is specifically integrated into new processes and procedures.

Policies

- The policies on quality are clear and unambiguous.
- The quality function reports on the same level as the functions that are being measured and has complete freedom of activity.
- Advertising and all other external communication must be in complete compliance with the requirements that the products and services must meet.

Corrective Action

The traditional method of corrective action is aimed at fixing the current situation enough to keep things moving along. The result is to learn how to repair the same condition over again effectively. This does not apply only to hardware. Relationships with employees vary with the situation. When things are going well, employees are ignored; when problems crop up, management is suddenly interested in their ideas and well-being. The pattern is stated clearly in Table 10.1. When programs of empowerment and quality circles are introduced, people see them as short-range "fix-it" actions. They recognize that management has not changed its spots. Relationships do not need programs with fancy names to be effective. They only need to be sincere.

Completeness

The dictionary meaning of *integrity* is "completeness." To manage quality in the twenty-first century, we must leap over executives' confused ideas about quality and set goals that can fit into the future daily operations of the company, based on these simple principles of completeness:

- Cause employees to be successful.
- Cause suppliers to be successful.
- Cause customers to be successful.

I chose the word *successful* specifically because it requires a lot more thought to accomplish than *satisfied*. In the global village, employees, suppliers, and customers all have many choices; they are under no obligation to deal with us.

For instance, employees are going to be harder to attract in coming years. The knowledge workers that modern business requires are already in short supply. We need to be able to select employees who can grow with their jobs, who can become veterans of the company, and who will feel a sense of accomplishment. Many companies, particularly in the service areas, have turnover rates of 30 percent a year. It takes a year to learn how to do even the most basic jobs properly. The key with employees is to create a climate of consideration. When they know that the company cares about their lives, they will give the company life.

Suppliers are the primary source of everything we use. We need to select them and help them furnish us with what we need. They have to enjoy prosperity with us; we make each other successful. The days of having a dozen suppliers for each item and then picking one on the basis of price are gone. To gain the best price and service today, we must give the supplier a sense of permanence. If you are concerned about having but a single source, I might point out that we usually have only one spouse at any given time.

Customers will stick with us as long as they are getting what they want. Knowing what makes them successful takes a concentrated effort that never ends. All the companies I know that began to wither and die were the ones that lost contact with the customer.

All of these principles require concern about relationships. At management seminars, I always ask group members to write their biggest problem on a card. At the end of the day, we take those problems and examine them to see if they involve finance, quality, or relationships. Without fail, all but a few involve relationships. Unfortunately, this is the area that most executives turn over to others. They assign the employees to human resources, the suppliers to purchasing, and the customers to marketing. These are natural enemies.

Leadership of Quality Management

Quality programs fail because they are programs. Companies that have mastered quality have done so through leadership. Of course, leadership is essential for a lot more than quality; that is why we need to think of completeness. Companies must be leaders as well as individuals. Those that can make it happen share some characteristics that I call the absolutes of leadership: integrity, information, innovation, and incisiveness.

Integrity

Integrity means much more than being honest most of the time. It means running a ship that doesn't leak anywhere, that is dependable at all times, that knows where it is going. People will not follow someone whose principles change regularly and who cannot be trusted. Even criminal organizations require that their leaders adhere to a code of conduct if they are to be taken seriously. When employees at all levels are asked to learn their job requirements, offer ideas for improvement, and do things right the first time, they want to know that their leaders really believe that this is the way to proceed. They want to see examples of integrity right there before their eyes. Many executives tell me that they have problems getting middle management interested. This can only be because middle management is not going to work for something that senior management is not willing to die for.

Information

At the request of a seminar group, I saved everything I read for a month and then weighed it. The total was one hundred pounds, made up of fifty-two magazines, five daily papers (*Wall Street Journal, Financial Times, New York Times, Orlando Sentinel, USA Today*), and a few books—all just to keep up. Unwary executives may focus too tightly on their particular niche of business. They fall behind on what is happening in the world; they miss any changes that are not displayed in their daily production report. Soon the business falls behind. We see one national industry producing automobiles, for instance, at half the cost of another. Benchmarking at work— the executives have been looking in the wrong places.

Innovation

Finding the right things to do and new ways to do them is the executive's absorption. Production lines hum with efficiency while white-collar offices plod along with duplicated efforts and poor communication. When I came up with the concept of zero defects back in 1961, the cry from quality control professionals was that it was impossible. Now they think it is routine, although they still like AQLs better. The true executive brings out innovation in people.

Incisiveness

Making decisions that last may be the toughest part of the executive's job. In terms of quality, this means sticking to the requirement or changing it forever. For years, executives wandered around the shops saying, "That's good enough," "This is OK to use," and the like. The result was that the customers never did get exactly what they ordered.

Quality management is not hard to do. It is not a series of techniques and procedural applications. It is a way of managing. The important thing is education and the executive must make certain that what will be taught is the proper information. Don't leave it up to some TQM package. Go to school yourself and find out. If you don't understand it, the employees certainly will not.

Quality is the quickest way to gain productivity and profit improvement.

Part Four

Developing High-Performance Management Systems

New organizations and the need for improved performance require new work management concepts. There is solid evidence that the potential for improvement in "doing the old stuff better" is often significantly less than when the goal is to find or develop new methods or practices. After decades of efforts to squeeze often negligible marginal improvements out of existing systems, the reengineering approach has become a new philosophy that frees managers and workers to throw out the old and to consider radically different answers. When everyone is a cog in an established process, it is very difficult to gain acceptance for different approaches. Now any established practice is suspect, innovation has become the norm, and we are trying to stimulate creativity at all levels.

The old hierarchical command-and-control model is doomed to failure in this environment. Both good ideas and mistakes can come from anyone. A great many stories tell of managers deciding to spend thousands and even millions of dollars on new plants and equipment that workers knew would turn out to be a mistake.

Similar tales have appeared in the business press about mistakes made by groups of empowered workers. The potential gains from new work practices cannot be realized without a few steps in the wrong direction.

The changes involve new behavior by managers and workers alike, and that is inevitably difficult to realize. Every organization has to learn how to make the transition from the old to the new. Despite the uniqueness of organizations, several common threads run through the plans and management practices of organizations that have successfully made the transition.

One of those threads is an objective to become a high-performing company. In Chapter Eleven, "Linking Business Strategy, Unit Goals, and Performance Management Systems," Craig Schneier describes how the practices in companies recognized for their performance differ from more conventional practices. The common objective in these companies is to get the most out of their people. Schneier's consulting and research experience confirms that high-performing companies do this differently.

The traditional approach has been to rely on a performance appraisal process that is typically limited to the completion of an appraisal form at some point each year. Over the past few years, these practices have been criticized severely, and this has prompted many organizations to look for alternatives. The problems with the conventional approach are widely recognized, the subject of numerous articles and books. It has become apparent, however, that there is no quick fix.

Despite the criticism, very few employers have eliminated appraisals. Companies do need to make decisions about their people. They have to decide whom to promote, whom to move to new positions, whom to train, and whom to pay more. They may also use this information in making downsizing or layoff decisions. Even W. Edwards Deming, one of the most outspoken critics of appraisal practices, did not have a viable alternative that could satisfy the need for appraisal information.

High-performing companies manage the process as a business improvement tool, not a rating mechanism. They move away from generic performance factors (such as teamwork) and work to translate their business strategy and operating plans into performance expectations. They then identify critical success factors that help everyone focus on what the company needs to do and the performance levels associated with success. As part of this process, they measure what counts, and they do this throughout the year.

This approach makes line managers responsible for the program's success. The orientation shifts from looking at performance management as a human resource practice to a tool that is used daily as part of the management process. It provides a basis for managers and their people to discuss and understand goals and performance expectations.

Another important innovation in the management of work is the shift to work teams. In Chapter Twelve, "Designing Work Teams to Fit the Organization," Susan Mohrman discusses the issues that have to be addressed in deciding how to take advantage of the team concept. The team concept emerged in manufacturing operations in the 1970s; it was rapidly adopted, spreading recently into the service sector and knowledge-based work groups.

Experience shows that a key element of work team effectiveness is the design of the team structure itself: what teams, for what purpose, and with what composition. Team design is critical to team effectiveness, but there are no generalized answers proven to work in all situations.

The prototypical work team is often referred to as "self-contained" or "self-managed." The self-contained team houses all the abilities and has access to the resources needed to accomplish assigned tasks. The self-managed team has the authority to handle tasks that would normally be managerial prerogatives, such as scheduling and purchasing. Not every team can be designed to be self-contained or self-managed, and deciding how to define the team's responsibilities is critical to its effectiveness.

Experience with teams has shown over and over that it is possible to achieve surprisingly high levels of performance. Most organizations, however, will have to stop short of the ideal model. Team design has to be tailored to the work system's requirements and the challenge of integrating the team in the work process. The constraints imposed by the work system may be limiting, but the advantages of moving to a team environment fully justify the investment in time and resources that may be needed. Few work systems would not be improved by reorganizing to take advantage of the potential benefits when workers look to one another to accomplish their goals.

One of the overriding issues in achieving high performance is the need to measure performance. Chapter Thirteen, "Using Measurement to Reinforce Strategy," by Carl Thor, discusses some of the issues involved in developing and using performance measurement data. The goal is to measure the right things for the right reasons in the right manner. High-performing companies measure what is important to their business strategy, and they do so continuously. Using the data to adjust and improve operations is the basis for day-to-day management.

Performance measurement starts with the customer and what the customer considers to be important. In some situations, that means quality; in others, it might mean service or delivery. The customers' needs are translated into strategic priorities, and measures are developed to track progress in satisfying those priorities.

"What gets measured gets done," the saying goes. If a company commits the resources needed to measure and communicate results, people understand that the matter is important, and that prompts them to pay more attention to the factors that drive performance. Unfortunately, not everything measured is important; tracking unimportant factors can defuse workers' efforts. Conversely, companies often fail to measure performance criteria that are central to the organization's success.

No organization can expect to get an adequate picture of its performance with a single measurement. The bottom line may be the overriding concern among investors, but every operation has a family of measures that would individually or in combination serve as early warning signals that precede a downturn in profitability. The family-of-measures concept can be useful in monitoring and assessing the performance of any work process or function. Ideally, there is a complementary family of measures at each level in the organization that are readily aggregated to track progress toward the achievement of operating goals.

The family of measures will normally include ones that track productivity, quality, and innovation. Each group must be represented to provide a balanced picture of important long-term performance issues.

The measures are in turn linked to the organization's reward system. Workers must understand the organization's priorities, and the criteria that trigger organizational rewards are always interpreted as an indicator of those priorities. Linking the measures to desired rewards provides a powerful engine that can drive work groups to progressively higher performance levels.

Chapter Eleven

Linking Business Strategy, Unit Goals, and Performance Management Systems

Craig Eric Schneier

Every company measures and evaluates the performance of its people. The owner of a small office supply store uses a very informal process. She certainly knows, based on observation, how well each of her four employees is doing on a daily basis. The owner's judgments determine who gets paid what amount, who does what job, who gets promoted, and who is laid off if business declines. The multinational pharmaceutical company, by contrast, has a formal system to measure, manage, and appraise performance of its hundred thousand employees working in sixty-four countries. The system is replete with "official" forms, procedures, policies, and computerized databases containing summary appraisals, developmental needs, and even statistics on ratings distributions. Results of the process provide a basis for merit increases, promotions, job assignments, terminations, stock options, and training. Performance is measured not only for each employee but also for every business unit, plant, department, cost center, and function. Hence whether the process is formal or informal, every organization assesses its performance and that of its people.

Performance measurement, management, and appraisal (PMMA) systems, as discussed here, are viewed broadly. They include determining what performance to measure, the rating or evaluation of performance, the ongoing management of performance, and reward allocation and development (see Figure 11.1). As noted, PMMA exists at the individual, team, unit, and organization levels. Motorola's corporationwide "six sigma"

Figure 11.1. Scope of Performance Measurement, Management, and Appraisal.

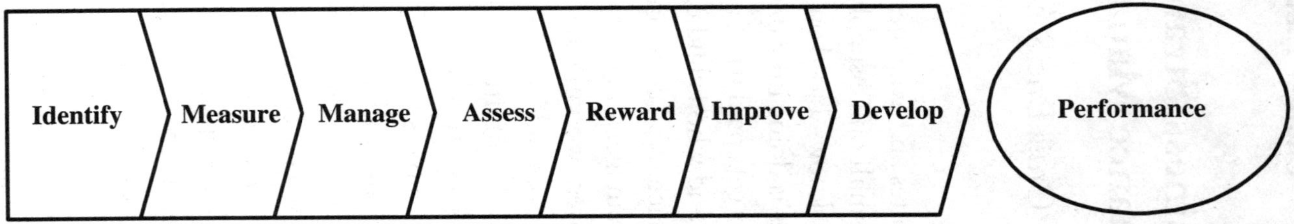

| Identify | Measure | Manage | Assess | Reward | Improve | Develop |

Performance

(99.9997 percent) defect-free goal is an example of an organizationwide measure, as are earnings per share, market share, revenue, stock price, and return on equity. Organization units are often measured on customer satisfaction or cost per unit; teams can be measured on cycle time; individuals, on such measures as collaboration.

The purpose of this discussion is first to describe the operation of typical PMMA systems—their objectives, impact, and problems. Second, examples are provided regarding how "high-performing" companies have addressed PMMA systems (for example, determining long-term financial success—earnings growth, returns, market value, industry leadership). The best companies make PMMA work by attacking its underlying problems (such as lack of managerial accountability) rather than treating its symptoms (such as complaints from managers about time-consuming forms). When PMMA works, it is used as a driver for strategy execution and culture change, not merely as a mechanism to generate a performance rating and a merit increase.

Why PMMA Is Important

PMMA is a critical organization process for at least three reasons. First, "what gets measured gets done." If something is important to a company—market share, profit, innovation, safety, customer service, community involvement, environmental protection, employee development, leadership—it will be measured. Everything that is truly important to a company is routinely measured; unfortunately, many unimportant things also get measured and hence get done! As Figure 11.2 shows, considerable insight into organizations can be gained from observing "what really counts," that is, what is measured. For example, companies that say that they value collaboration but do not measure it and reward it convince no one.

Second, studying the measurement cycle described in Figure 11.2 for a company provides an accurate window into its corporate values, beliefs, and behavior. Corporate culture can be described,

Figure 11.2. The Performance Measurement Cycle.

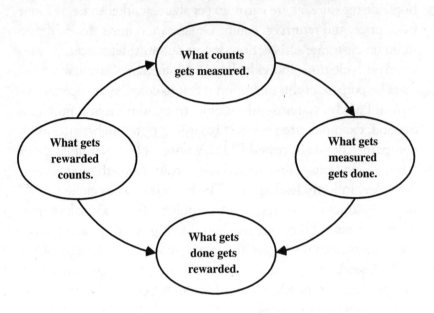

in essence, as "what really counts here." True customer-driven cultures obviously must measure customer expectations, as well as their success at meeting them. American Express and USAA, for example, consistently assess customer satisfaction. True values-driven companies should measure employee perceptions as to whether values are actually being followed. Levi Strauss and Johnson & Johnson are examples of companies that regularly poll their people to ensure that corporate values are operating. Innovation-driven companies like Sony and 3M both measure and reward innovative behavior. It is no surprise that this fosters entrepreneurism. Quality-driven companies like Xerox have numerous quality-based measures. Utilities are an excellent example of safety-driven cultures. How do we (and, more important, their employees and customers) know? In every utility, safety is tracked closely, and the safety record is well publicized. "Learning organizations" that do not measure (and reward) learning are hard-pressed to sustain the belief that learning counts.

The third reason why PMMA is important was noted earlier: both the small office supply store and the global pharmaceutical company must make numerous decisions about each of their employees that influence their ability to execute corporate strategies. They decide whom to pay more, whom to promote, whom to move to what position, whom to send to training, whom to hold accountable for what goals, and whom to coach. Many companies today are also making tough decisions about whom to lay off and whose job to eliminate, due to increased competition, merger, acquisition, divestiture, poor company performance, or declining markets. These critical decisions are made, to a large degree, on the basis of performance. They are not always made on the best measures of performance, and they are not always made accurately, but performance is still a key criterion for human resource management decision making about people. (Obviously, personality, potential, seniority, critical skills, and even gender are additional criteria used for making decisions about people in organizations. Some of these criteria are defensible and appropriate; others are not.)

PMMA decisions affect not only individual-level outcomes, such as pay and development, but company outcomes as well. Via PMMA goals—to broaden a product line, cut manufacturing costs, enter a new market—companies can focus their efforts. In this way, PMMA systems define success. They may also specify how well a company must perform against those goals—percentage of revenue from the new product line, percentage of costs reduced, share of the new market. PMMA processes hence communicate expectations about the level of success expected (Kaplan and Norton, 1992). Finally, as noted, PMMA systems are indicators of company values and beliefs and become mechanisms for attaining them. Values, such as customer service, typically show up as performance measures with goal defined. Performance against the goal is tracked and rewarded. Likewise, empowerment, participative decision making, integrity, and numerous other values, if truly important, would show up on the performance screens of individuals, teams, or units.

How Effective Are PMMA Systems?

PMMA systems are not very effective. Survey after survey indicates that PMMA is one of the most difficult management systems to operate. Further, it generates a great deal of dissatisfaction. More than 250 executives from large companies around the world recently rated their own PMMA systems on a five-point scale (one being the lowest). The average rating from the executives was a dismal 2.25, lower than ratings for their compensation, benefits, selection, training, or even diversity programs (Craig Eric Schneier Associates research, 1991–1993).

Why the dissatisfaction with PMMA? Among the reasons are these:

- Managers dislike completing PMMA forms; they are often seen as complex and time-consuming.
- Performance in many jobs (such as research chemist) or aspects of performance in many jobs (such as the coaching skills of a sales manager) are difficult to measure.
- Delivering negative feedback is never pleasant.
- It often makes little difference in pay whether a person receives a high or a moderate rating, so why bother giving a low rating and facing a disgruntled and less motivated worker?
- The rater may not be in the best position to judge performance, perhaps rarely observing the person on the job.
- Because appraisals are based on judgment, they are susceptible to human biases and errors, both intentional and unintentional.

PMMA Systems: Symptoms and Diseases

The typical reasons for ineffective PMMA systems are symptoms of underlying problems. For example, managers fail to complete PMMA forms not because the forms are complex but because managers see little real value in spending time on that activity; it does not improve performance, and it does not lead to significantly different consequences. Managers do not consider completing appraisal forms part of their "real" work of producing parts, delivering service, or earning profit. The PMMA system is consequently viewed as a personnel- and paper-driven exercise. Managers are not held accountable for its design, operation, or effectiveness. In short, PMMA is often little more than an administrative procedure required to process a merit increase. But as practiced in many high-performing companies like General Electric, Federal Express, and Motorola, PMMA is viewed as more than an individual-level rating and feedback process; it is seen as a way to shape culture and execute strategy (see Figure 11.3; Schneier and others, 1991). For example, GE's goal to become a "boundaryless" culture is well documented. It has a measurement process in place to track its large-scale culture change initiative called "Work-Out" (Tichy and Sherman, 1993). At GE, what counts typically gets measured, and what gets measured typically gets done and gets rewarded. Boundaryless behavior is spelled out, measured, and rewarded; consequently, it occurs.

The diseases underlying PMMA symptoms relate to a company's culture (how important is high performance?), its expectations for its managers (are they accountable for measuring, assessing, managing, rewarding, and developing performance?), and whether there are compelling business reasons (profit, revenue) for being effective at PMMA. If performance-based culture and values, managerial PMMA accountability, and individual-level performance linkages are the underlying causes of PMMA problems, they are also the keys to its lasting improvement.

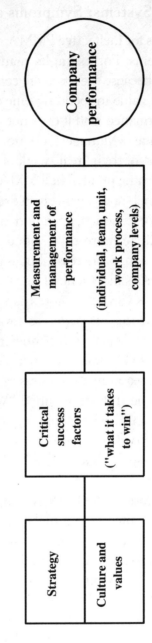

Figure 11.3. PMMA: A Management-Driven Business Process for Strategy Execution and Cultural Change.

High-performing companies have discovered this linkage and use it to make PMMA work.

What High-Performing Companies Do About PMMA

In a recent assessment of twenty-five high-performing companies, including Merck, PepsiCo, Asea Brown Boveri, Johnson & Johnson, 3M, Toyota, Federal Express, AT&T, Nordstrom, GE, Wal-Mart, Microsoft, Levi Strauss, Corning, Coca-Cola, USAA, and Emerson Electric, notable similarities in PMMA practices were found (Craig Eric Schneier Associates research, 1993).

1. *Measure what counts.* As Exhibit 11.1 indicates, high-performing companies take the measurement of performance very seriously. Overnight delivery at Federal Express, customer service at USAA, quality at Xerox, market share at Coca-Cola, drug development cycle time at Merck, and productivity at GE are examples. All of these high-performing companies have determined what is important, communicated it repeatedly, set a challenging target for it, and measure it incessantly. The measures are not just the aspects of performance that are easy to quantify but the softer cultural characteristics as well. At Levi Strauss, "aspirations" (values), not just profit, are measured. Top companies thus identify and communicate what really counts and then attach rewards and punishments to the results obtained. Further, high-performing companies expect their managers to operate the PMMA system via ongoing communication, coaching, assessing, feedback, reward, and development. PMMA is a process, not an annual event. They don't delegate PMMA to human resources; it is a managerial accountability.

2. *Benchmark PMMA practices.* High-performing companies are both learners and innovators. They continually search out best practices in all areas and compare themselves to the best. PMMA is no exception. Companies that make PMMA work search out the

Exhibit 11.1. Principles of High-Performing Companies' PMMA Systems.

1. *Determine what counts.* Identify the most critical determinants of success (to execute and live the values); communicate them effectively and continually so that everyone understands.
2. *Measure what counts.* Measure a broad but relevant spectrum of performance (quality, financial results, cycle time, customer satisfaction, innovation, capability development); measure both results and processes.
3. *Set the bar high.* Set very challenging (order-of-magnitude improvement) performance expectations.
4. *Tell it like it is, and tell it often.* Provide candid, constructive, ongoing performance feedback.
5. *Differentiate between poor, good, and great performers.* Allocate both positive and negative consequences, as appropriate.
6. *Expect managers to lead.* Hold managers accountable for effective leadership (setting direction, motivating), not just management (controlling).
7. *Set an example at the top.* Use the PMMA system throughout the organization, not just in the middle and at the bottom.
8. *Get "three-sixty" feedback.* Obtain performance feedback from all sources who have relevant data (peers, subordinate customers, suppliers, self, superiors).
9. *They who use it own it.* Hold line management, not human resource staff, accountable for PMMA process maintenance and improvement; allow flexibility in use by local managers.
10. *Give "grades."* Assess people, don't rate them. (No one wants to be a three on a five-point scale, no matter what the labels are.)
11. *Maintain credibility.* Monitor to ensure fairness and accuracy, as well as consistency in application.
12. *Make it better and better.* Assess how PMMA is working; identify best practices from inside and outside the company (benchmarking), and share the learning.

best PMMA ideas from their own experience and that of others. However, PMMA benchmarking is much more than a visit to another company. Deriving value from PMMA benchmarking, as AT&T, Motorola, and many others have recently demonstrated, requires considerable effort.

PMMA benchmarking consists of diagnosis, learning, and application (Schneier and Johnson, 1993). As many who have benchmarked will attest, most of the work occurs before the visit to a benchmark company. Careful identification of underlying PMMA problems, translating problems into areas of inquiry to focus data gathering, developing criteria for selection of relevant benchmark companies, and the logistics of scheduling, travel, and so on are all enormous tasks. Finally, extracting learning and actually applying what has been learned to improve the PMMA system is where the payback in benchmarking occurs.

3. *Set order-of-magnitude performance improvement targets.* High-performing companies set their sights high, and their performance expectations and targets reflect their confidence and optimism. The best companies know the value of order-of-magnitude improvement targets. They know that incremental improvement—even "stretch" goals—leads to a little more effort but rarely requires a rethinking of the status quo.

Improving cycle time, quality, customer satisfaction, or revenue by 3, 5, or even 10 percent is typically possible: work a little harder, work a little smarter, ask for a little more help, or measure results differently. But to improve 30, 40, or 80 percent, a fundamental shift in thinking is required; with an order-of-magnitude improvement target, after the initial shock, it becomes obvious to most people involved that "we can't get there from here; we have to figure out a new way." A zero-based approach to work process redesign leads to the real breakthroughs (Hammer and Champy, 1993).

Aiming high enabled Hewlett-Packard to cut the development time of computer printers from fifty-four weeks to twenty-two weeks. GE wants to put out new products in one-fifth the time previously taken. 3M has a goal to cut its development cycle time by 50 percent. Radical work redesign is no doubt mandatory to meet these performance expectations. The best companies, via their PMMA systems, keep measuring their processes and keep exceeding even their own outlandish goals. They know that doing so is not a luxury but a requirement for today's competitive companies.

4. *Measure performance of teams.* The competitive environment of most companies requires excellence not only in setting strategy but also in executing it. Execution speed necessitates collaboration across numerous boundaries: functional, hierarchical, customer supplier, country, division, region. Cross-functional teams can speed decision making, development, or process redesign (Katzenbach and Smith, 1992). However, participation on these teams cannot be seen merely as a committee assignment or an extra task; it must be regarded as a critical priority. To ensure giving proper weight to team work, team performance must be measured and rewarded. Measures can include team behavior (such as listening), team process (decision making), and team results (product design). Each measurement category can be defined and rewarded. Companies like Kodak have learned that rewards must come from teams, not functions, if teams are to prosper.

5. *Manage performance as a process, not an event.* Another vital PMMA lesson from the high-performing companies refers to the ongoing nature of PMMA. PMMA is a cyclical process: determine what and how to measure; link organization to unit to process to team to individual goals; set and communicate performance expectations; monitor, coach, and provide ongoing feedback; assess, develop, and reward performance. The high-performing companies expect their managers at all levels to manage performance all year rather than rate it once a year. They have found that if people do not know what counts and what is expected at the outset of a performance cycle, there is little chance they will attain (or agree on how well they attained) the goals at the end of the cycle.

The complexity of the PMMA forms, the length of time it takes to complete them, and disagreements over whether to use a four-point or five-point rating scale are not the key PMMA issues in high-performing companies. The key issues are managerial accountability for assessment, development, and differentially rewarding based on performance. If these are done well, the major problems of PMMA are alleviated. These issues also clearly demonstrate how PMMA can provide links from individual performance to business results. This gets people's attention.

A Business Improvement Tool, Not a Rating Mechanism

Based on what we have learned from high-performing companies, rather than expend effort on rating scales and their definitions, designers of PMMA systems would be wise to build linkages from company goals to business process (such as new product development) to unit to team and individual performance. PMMA, as noted, actually becomes a tool to facilitate strategy execution as companies use it to identify strategic goals to pursue, set accountabilities, and define success.

An illustration of PMMA as a strategy execution tool is outlined in Table 11.1. A global consumer products company we will call Consolidated Foods shifted its strategy in two divisions from commodity products to specialized ones. The strategy was now to gain market share via distinctive products that, if placed into the market before those of its competitors, could gain and protect market share and command premium prices. Like many strategies today, Consolidated's was in no way unique. But if executed effectively, a sustainable competitive advantage was obtainable.

Little about the strategy, however, ended up in the PMMA system for middle managers at Consolidated. They were still rated on "technical knowledge," "leadership," "teamwork," "work products," "report completion," and "work quality," none of which were defined differently since Consolidated adopted its new strategy. A survey of twenty Consolidated managers showed that *not one* indicated that he or she was personally expected to do anything different as a result of Consolidated's new strategy. They felt that the current performance measures were fine, even though the company was undertaking a major strategic shift. Consolidated's CEO

Table 11.1. Strategy Execution Through PMMA in a Global Consumer Products Manufacturing Company: Sample Performance Expectations.

Business Strategy	Potential Sources of Competitive Advantage	Critical Success Factors	Performance Measurement, Management, and Appraisal	
			Sample Performance Expectations (behaviors, activities)	Sample Performance Consequences
Gain market share via distinctive products launched first in the market	Technological innovation	Understanding of customer needs	Marketing research conducts "focus groups" with end-use customers, not distributors, to identify needs and issues instead of reactions to product ideas, then conducts focus groups with manufacturing and engineering "internal customers" to share learning, identify simpler manufacturing process, obtain patent.	Annual incentive
	Product quality	Reduced raw material costs	Manufacturing supervisor identifies one "preferred supplier" of vital parts in food "cookers"; long-term contract reduces costs, defects; quality improves.	Spot bonus
	Cycle time	Worldwide cross-functional teams	Marketing executive assumes leadership of global cross-functional new product development team; development cycle time is cut; new product is launched before competitors, market share increases.	Stock options

repeated in countless speeches that if the new strategy were to be executed, employees needed to understand their individual roles and how they added value.

The PMMA system at Consolidated was an untapped mechanism to help deliver the CEO's message. Consolidated hence decided to concentrate less on the generic performance factors in its PMMA system and more on translating its new strategic direction into specific performance expectations. First, sources of sustainable competitive advantage were extracted from the strategy. Then critical success factors—what it takes to meet the goals—were identified. These were illustrated in activities and in actual behaviors: what success looks like and what people must do differently now. Finally, consequences were attached to performance. Table 11.1, a portion of Consolidated's actual resultant PMMA system, links business results to the PMMA process. It was seen by managers as a tool to help them succeed, not merely as a form to complete. To make PMMA a strategy execution tool, key business processes such as procurement, selling, and capital expenditure decision making would be derived from the critical success factors, and new process measures would be developed. Then the processes would be redesigned to meet the new order-of-magnitude performance goals. Templates like the one in Table 11.1 (simplified here for illustrative purposes) were constructed for various parts of Consolidated and served as communication tools to focus effort on the right activities, clarify behavior expected, and specify consequences offered (Hammer and Champy, 1993; Schneier, Shaw, and Beatty, 1992). As Consolidated's managers constructed their own PMMA templates, they began to see how PMMA affected goal attainment and hence regard PMMA as managers' work, not human resource staff work.

Additional PMMA Best Practices

PMMA systems, like other managerial tools in high-performance companies, are in a constant state of assessment and improvement.

Exhibit 11.2. PMMA Practices That Work.

Company	Practices
Royal Bank of Canada	One list of performance criteria is developed for the top three hundred managers; results on the measures are used to determine pay and promotions.
USAA	A "family of measures" (customer satisfaction, quality, development of people) is used to guide performance reviews, updated monthly.
Levi Strauss	CEO is the model for "aspirations statement" (values)—evaluates and discusses performance with all direct reports after obtaining input from subordinates.
Campbell Soup	Fundamental assumptions about what counts (such as marketing budget increases each year) are challenged; new success criteria are articulated.
Corning	Managers are trained and evaluated on skills by "career coaches"; self-assessment is completed and used by managers.
General Electric	Managers—even officers—are measured and rewarded or punished on both hard (financial performance) and soft (candor in communications) performance measures; subordinates assess managers.
Conrail	One critical success factor—operating expenses as a percentage of revenue must equal 80 percent for earnings to exceed cost of capital—is used to assess top management performance.
Federal Express	Organization-level measures—Service Quality Index (SQI)—that drive customer satisfaction are identified and communicated to all seventy-five thousand employees daily via closed-circuit TV.
Citibank	Branch manager's bonus is linked to customer satisfaction ratings.
GTE	Satisfaction level of twenty-five thousand customers is measured and reported to the board of directors monthly.
Mobil Oil	Competencies are derived from the study of highly successful employees; lists and definitions are used to select, appraise, and reward employees.
Emerson Electric	Execution is emphasized: "Once we fix our goals, we do not consider it acceptable to miss them" (CEO); everyone has an order-of-magnitude cost reduction performance measure.

Note: This list is highly selective; each item is not necessarily representative of the entire process, system, or company.

These continual improvements have led to particularly effective practices for specific companies. A few of these practices are listed in Exhibit 11.2. What is most important about the exhibit is not how profound the practices are—most are frequently advanced as desirable PMMA improvements—but the fact that these companies have actually implemented the practices. There is considerable potential for PMMA learning here, as well as evidence that PMMA can affect a company well beyond linking ratings to pay increases.

Successful PMMA systems are powerful managerial tools. The best companies have shifted their approach from an annual performance appraisal to an ongoing process for executing company strategy and shaping corporate culture. To make the shift, it is critical to highlight the real business potential of PMMA—via its ability to identify what counts, communicate a new and higher set of expectations, focus effort on values and on what it takes to win, and link consequences to behavior. Staff units must turn over control of the tool to its users. When managers see PMMA's value to help implement business goals, they make it succeed.

References

Hammer, M., and Champy, J. (1993). *Reengineering the Corporation*. New York: HarperCollins.

Kaplan, R. S., and Norton, D. P. (1992). Balanced scorecard: Measures that drive performance. *Harvard Business Review*, 70(1), 71–79.

Katzenbach, J., and Smith, D. (1992). *The Wisdom of Teams*. Cambridge, Mass.: Harvard Business School.

Schneier, C. E., and Johnson, C. (1993). Benchmarking: A tool for improving performance management and reward systems. *ACA Journal*, X(1), 14–31.

Schneier, C. E., Shaw, D. G., and Beatty, R. W. (1992). Companies' attempts to improve performance while containing costs: Quick fix versus lasting change. *Human Resource Planning*, 15(3), 1–25.

Schneier, C. E., and others. (1991). Performance measurement and management: A tool for strategy execution. *Human Resource Management*, 30(3), 279–301.

Tichy, N. M., and Sherman, S. (1993). *Control Your Destiny or Someone Else Will*. New York: Currency/Doubleday.

Chapter Twelve

Designing Work Teams to Fit the Organization

Susan Albers Mohrman

Designing organizations in which the work team is the focal per-forming unit began in earnest in production settings, where "new design plants" (Lawler, 1978) or "high-commitment work systems" (Walton, 1985) emerged in the 1970s and are now widely used (Lawler, Mohrman, and Ledford, 1992). These plants created teams that are responsible for a "whole" product or service and perform many of their own management and support functions (Cummings and Griggs, 1977; Goodman, Devadas, and Hughson, 1988). The organizational context is designed (or redesigned) to support the team as the focal performing unit. The organization is flat; employ-ees receive extensive training; management jobs are redefined; and all systems, including information, reward, and decision-making sys-tems, are altered to support team effectiveness.

More recently, the work team concept has been expanding rapidly into the service and knowledge-processing components of organizations. Work teams are being employed in insurance pro-cessing units, sales and service offices, new product development projects, information systems, human resource departments, and many other areas. Organizations are striving to transport the con-cepts of teams, empowerment, self-management, and self-contain-ment from the factory floor to parts of the organization that employ quite different technologies.

The challenge of redesigning the service and information pro-cessing components of the organization is significant. The sound-ness of team effectiveness rests on an accurate analysis of the technology of the work system. Sociotechnical analysis is one approach. The analysis is geared toward the joint optimization of the technical and social systems by designing teams with control over their boundaries, feedback about performance, and the ability to adjust their work processes to correct and improve performance (Pearce and Ravlin, 1987). Teams are designed to encompass the key interdependencies and variances (places where the production process is likely to get out of range) of the production process (Cummings, 1978; Pasmore and Sherwood, 1978). Different technologies pose different design challenges. Because the technologies in the knowledge segments of organizations differ from production technologies to a certain extent, the notions embodied in the traditional team literature do not translate easily to these new contexts.

This chapter provides a framework for considering the design of work teams. It deals with teams that exist to perform the transformation processes of the organization. They turn inputs into the products or services that are the outputs of the organization, or they provide products and services for the internal customers who make or deliver the outputs. The chapter does not deal with the design of parallel teams (such as improvement, task, and other special-purpose teams) to improve the way the organization carries out its processes.

The underlying premise is that a key element of work team effectiveness is the design of the team structure itself: what teams, for what purpose, and with what composition. Appropriate team design is not a trivial issue—it is extremely important for successful work performance improvement but not always easy to accomplish. There is no one recipe for effective teams; one size does not fit all. The chapter spells out a way to think through the issues of team design.

Teams for Routine Work

The prototypical work team, described in the literature as the "self-contained" or "self-managed" team (Cohen, 1993), has been used primarily in production settings, largely with technologies that are relatively routine, where one of the major benefits of creating teams based on sociotechnical analysis has been increasing the degree of stability and reliability in the technical processes. These teams are established when employees perform interrelated tasks and are required to interact to produce a product or service (Goodman, Devadas, and Hughson, 1988). The ideal form of these work teams is characterized by self-containment and self-management. These characteristics are supported by a number of design features that will be described.

Self-Containment

Ideally, the team houses all the tasks required for the accomplishment of its mission to deliver a service or produce a product. This implies that team members possess the skills to perform all the tasks. Consequently, the team's effectiveness depends minimally on the task accomplishment of people outside its bounds. This has two implications.

First, tasks that have traditionally been performed by specialized support services such as maintenance or quality assurance are moved into the team, meaning that the team need not depend on services that emanate from a different organizational location or may not be attuned to team objectives or performance requirements. If such integration is not possible for economic reasons, specialty services that are shared across teams must be made accountable to the teams that are their customers.

Second, individuals in the teams are cross-trained for purposes of flexibility, to make sure that they can cover for one another, and to develop in each team member a broad understanding of the whole task. In fact, cross-training is sometimes economically bounded, with individuals being rewarded for learning multiple skills only to the extent that multiple team members are actually required to perform the task. The limitations on cross-training are particularly likely where certain tasks require a great deal of specialized expertise that would be very expensive to develop in all team members.

Some additional design features result from the effort to create a self-contained team. These teams tend to consist largely of dedicated members, who do not have split priorities between the work of the team and other assignments. Furthermore, the entire team generally reports as a unit to a common manager. Consequently, team members are not subject to direction by multiple bosses. Both these features reinforce the integrity of the team as a performing unit and enhance team members' abilities to focus on the team's mission.

Self-Management

Self-containment means that the team is capable, within itself, of performing all the tasks and roles necessary for it to accomplish its mission. Consequently, it can be the locus of most decisions relating to how it goes about its work. Management tasks that were traditionally performed by a hierarchical superior can now be performed within the team. If the team has clear goals that link it to the overall mission of the organization and if the organization has mechanisms for holding the team accountable for its goal accomplishment, the team can perform its own day-to-day management functions. The new role of management is to ensure that the goal system and accountability system are in place and to provide support to the team in the form of information, resources, training and development, and systems that are geared to support team functioning.

The prototypical self-managing team can manage three aspects of its functioning: its tasks, its boundaries, and its own performance.

Task management is the most fundamental form of self-management. A major benefit of the team structure is that teams can make decisions internally about how to apply their resources in carrying out their tasks. Within the constraints of the routinized and standardized aspects of the technology, the team can also set its own performance strategies (how it goes about its tasks). These decisions are made right in the group that is performing the work and can be responsive to the real-time requirements and issues that arise. Task self-management includes scheduling, integration of work between individuals, and responsibility for monitoring and improving the quality of the output.

Boundary management refers to the team's managing of interfaces with the rest of the organization and with its customers, both internal and external. If the team is truly self-contained, it relates to other teams in the organization that provide it with inputs or that it supplies with inputs. Boundary self-management tasks include making sure that agreed processes and standards govern the interfaces, monitoring the effectiveness of the transactions that occur, solving problems with the interfaces and improving their effectiveness, and dealing on-line with exceptions and required changes.

Performance management refers to the team's role in managing its own performance as a collective entity and the performance of its individual members. The team negotiates its objectives with the organization, manages the setting of objectives for its members, monitors and reviews its collective performance and that of its members, and finds ways to improve collective and individual performance. It may manage the way in which rewards are distributed internally within the team and may have primary responsibility for dealing with performance problems.

Each of these self-management areas requires skills that have to be developed within the team. Furthermore, they support the notion of self-containment in that tasks that used to be performed by external specialists (in this case, managers) are now performed within the team.

Self-containment and self-management reinforce each other. Self-management is made possible because the team contains the skills required to perform the whole task and is responsible for it. The team is not enmeshed in a complex web of interdependencies and conflicting priorities that must be resolved. Once self-management is in place, self-containment is more complete—the team not only has all the skills and resources necessary to do the entire job, but it also has the skills, authority, and responsibility to manage how it goes about doing it.

Work teams that approximate this ideal are most easily embodied in work settings that include routine technologies, where programs and procedures for completing the work are well specified, uncertainty and exceptions are not pervasive, interdependencies can be described and routinized, and the cross-training objectives are readily accomplished thanks to less reliance on a diverse array of specialties.

The important distinction here is not between production and other kinds of work. Rather, it is between routine work that can be well specified and nonroutine work that involves uncertainty, unique cases, and complex interdependencies among highly specialized contributors. As production processes become more automated and as flexible manufacturing capabilities are established, some observers contend that the remaining production workforce will increasingly be performing jobs that fall into the nonroutine category. In addition, much service and support work can be characterized as production work; it involves routine, highly specified work such as back-office paper processing. Next we will examine some of the design issues encountered in creating work teams in nonroutine settings.

Teams for Nonroutine Work

Let us look at the particular challenges of designing work teams in settings characterized by high uncertainty, complex and changing interdependencies, dynamic requirements, and extensive specialization. New product development, systems development, and technical sales are some of the areas that perform this kind of work. In such settings, it is hard to constitute stable teams and to predict the interdependencies within and between teams because the nature and duration of the projects they handle can be highly varied and tend to unfold over time. Some of the attributes that characterize the prototypical work team may be impossible to establish.

Self-containment, for example, may not be possible due to a complex array of interdependencies. Consider a project team that is designing an electronics system. The system consists of three integrated "boxes," two of which are composed of integrated software and hardware subsystems. Traditionally, the organization that handles this project has broken work down into discipline-specific packets that are then divided among the members of discipline-based work groups (see Figure 12.1.). The disciplines include software, electrical, mechanical, structural, and systems engineering. Here, the term *work group* is being used to denote that they are not work teams because the modus operandi has been for a manager in each work group to break the work down into individual assignments and to take responsibility for integrating the whole. Individual contributors are held individually responsible for their assigned work.

This program has forty-six members, including a program manager and a discipline-based manager in each work group. Each of the disciplines that are required to develop the system constitutes one or more work groups. A software work group develops the software for each of the two boxes that had integrated software. A quality and reliability work group provides specialized quality and testing support for the entire project, and a systems integration work group monitors and directs technical integration across the subsystems.

The double-headed arrows indicate the interdependencies between the groups, the places where work between the groups has to be coordinated on-line because what members of one group design has repercussions for the work of members of the other group. Thus these work groups are not self-contained because they do not contain all the tasks and skills required to produce a whole

Figure 12.1. Sample Electronics Program, Traditional Work Group Structure.

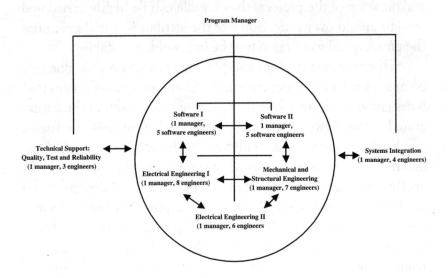

Note: Interdependencies are indicated by double-headed arrows.

product, nor can they be given complete authority over task-related decision making because decisions made within one work group have repercussions for all other work groups. For example, a design decision made in an electrical engineering group may have design implications for the work of the software groups, the other electrical engineering group, and the mechanical and structural engineers. In fact, a technical analysis indicated that the people in these work groups have at least as many technical transactions with people outside their work group as they have with people within. The technical support and systems integration groups, furthermore, provide services for every work group. Each of these services cuts across teams and has to be integrated for the entire set of teams.

In this traditional design, managers provide technical supervision and integrate work internally within the group, as well as manage the performance of the work group members. An advantage of this design is that each work group is composed of one specialty and can be supervised by one manager. Because of the large number of intergroup transactions, the managers are central to the boundary management process. Individual performers and even work groups lack the broader perspective required to make systemwide trade-offs. Many cross-boundary decisions ended up getting made by various assortments of managers thinking through the trade-offs involved in various courses of action or even by escalating the decision to the program manager. Each work group is continually affected by decisions made externally.

The notion that the design challenge in knowledge work settings is to create forums (such as teams) that include the stakeholders who are party to key deliberations (issues requiring ongoing resolution) underpins recent work applying sociotechnical system concepts to knowledge work settings (Pava, 1986; Pasmore, 1988). This company's decision to move to work teams required the program to embark on a technical analysis to determine the configuration of teams that most closely approximated self-containment in order to be able to move as many decisions and task interdependencies as possible into the teams and to decrease the number of decisions requiring intergroup and hierarchical decision making.

The task facing this program is to determine which transactions can be handled in a routine fashion (by specifications, change orders, and the like) and which require on-line deliberation. As many as possible of the latter should be located within teams; the former can be handled by procedures that can efficiently integrate across teams. In the case of this program, no solution provided complete self-containment. Figure 12.2 illustrates a design that combines hardware and software for the two component boxes where their integration is required. The assumption underpinning this design is that the key deliberations and task interdependencies have

Figure 12.2. Work Team Structure A.

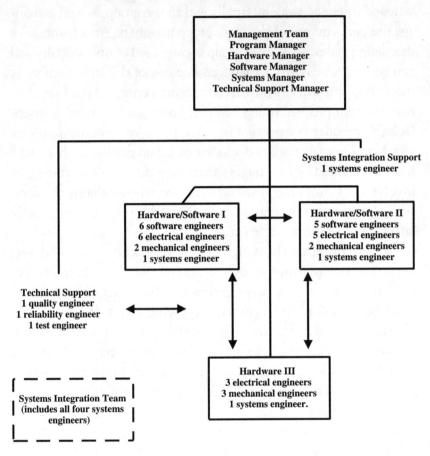

Note: Interdependencies are indicated by double-headed arrows.

to do with the fit and the functional trade-offs between hardware and software. This design raises an additional challenge for the organization because one manager can no longer perform the technical supervision for all team members in the teams that are composed of multiple specialties.

Figure 12.3 illustrates a design that combines all software into one team and creates three hardware teams, each of which designs

Figure 12.3. Work Team Structure B.

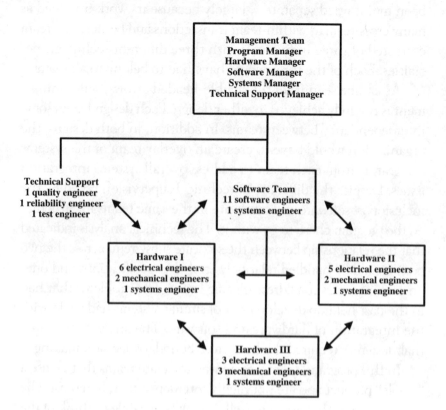

Management Team
Program Manager
Hardware Manager
Software Manager
Systems Manager
Technical Support Manager

Technical Support
1 quality engineer
1 reliability engineer
1 test engineer

Software Team
11 software engineers
1 systems engineer

Hardware I
6 electrical engineers
2 mechanical engineers
1 systems engineer

Hardware II
5 electrical engineers
2 mechanical engineers
1 systems engineer

Hardware III
3 electrical engineers
3 mechanical engineers
1 systems engineer

Note: Interdependencies are indicated by double-headed arrows.

one of the component boxes. Different disciplines are housed within the three hardware teams. This design provides for within-group creation of all software for the hardware in each box. The assumption underlying this design is that key technical deliberations and task interdependencies are within the development of the overall software subsystem and between the different disciplines designing the hardware for each box.

In both work team designs, the systems integration group has been dispersed into the teams. The quality group, by contrast, has been maintained separately, largely because its work involved as many cross-team as within-team transactions and because the team consisted of three individuals with three different technical specialties. Each of the three would have had to belong to all teams.

As can be seen from the double-headed arrows, self-containment is not fully achieved in either design. Each design leaves some interdependency between teams. In addition, in both designs, the organization would have to create an overlay team of the systems integrators from each team to address overall systems integration issues. Despite the difficulty of technical supervision posed by the inclusion of software and hardware in the same teams in Structure A, the program chose to go with it. The technical analysis indicated that the relationship between the software subsystems across the two boxes could be handled relatively easily by specifications and one-on-one meetings to address specific issues. The problems that had in the past held up development of similar systems had to do with the integration of hardware and software. The analysis indicated that design A required the least cross-boundary decision making.

In this program, there was no way to create teams that create a "whole" product and are not highly interdependent. In a sense, the natural team is the program itself. It may be possible to think of the program as the team and the others as subteams, but this does not resolve the coordination issue because the same integration problems exist across subteams. Thus the best that the designers can do is maximize the self-containment of deliberations and task interdependencies and find ways to address deliberations and interdependencies that cut across the resultant work teams.

Another factor that makes it difficult in this electronics firm to duplicate the prototypical self-contained team is the high degree of specialization. Key deliberations and task interdependencies crossed disciplines; consequently, multidiscipline teams were indicated. Although one advantage provided by a team structure is increased familiarity across disciplines, substantial cross-training may not be an option due to the extensive education that underpins each discipline. Thus these teams can provide increased ease of integration, but they offer less flexibility in resource utilization than is provided in the cross-trained team. Software engineers and hardware engineers may work better because they gain more familiarity with each other's perspectives, but they will most likely not receive the training that would be required for them to trade off tasks.

Another issue, illustrated in the example by the quality, reliability, and test engineers, concerns both the cost effectiveness and the technical desirability of placing each needed specialty within a team. Many technical specialties may exist in small numbers and be shared across a number of organizational units. Key contributors may not be able to be dedicated to a team; consequently, teams and these contributors will have to deal with their conflicting priorities. A test engineer servicing five teams will have to juggle the priorities of all five. Other specialties may handle work that is of necessity performed across units. For instance, quality may largely be an issue of fit across the whole system and thus may not be best achieved within a team that is designing a subsystem. These specialties perform work that has profound implications for the work of each team but is not dedicated to the team or perhaps not even located in it.

Finally, the team design options faced by the electronics program illustrate another area in which the self-containment model may be more difficult to achieve: the ideal of the team collectively reporting to the organization. The issue is the technical desirability of having specialists managed by managers who are not familiar with their discipline and the ability to define the role of the discipline managers so that technical excellence is assured at the same time that cross-functional integration and the integrity of cross-discipline teams is maintained. In some cases, dual reporting will be the solution. Some individuals, particularly those shared across teams, may maintain a discipline reporting relationship because they have multiple team affiliations. Others may be functionally managed because their discipline is so important to the organization's strategy that they are considered a core resource that has to be managed first and foremost for technical excellence. Clearly, certain issues can erode the concept of collective team reporting.

Thus a number of factors arising from the highly interdependent, nonroutine, specialized, and dynamic nature of the work may detract from the integrity of the work team as a self-contained performing unit. These factors increase the requirements for coordination across teams and different parts of the organization and result in the work of the team being affected by ongoing deliberations that occur outside the team. This reality has profound implications for the second key aspect that is sometimes presented as integral to the work team notion, self-management.

Task self-management within a team is constrained to the extent that it cannot routinize its interface with other parts of the organization, it is on-line interdependent with other groups, and it is both party to and subject to decisions that involve trade-offs between many different perspectives beyond the team. Regardless of the ideal of empowerment and self-management, the reality is that the team does not have control over decisions that go beyond its scope. The organization must find ways to resolve issues between teams and at the whole-system level. The decision-making forums that are set up for this purpose must contain the requisite variety of viewpoints to address the needs of the various performing units whose work must fit together. An example is the overlay systems integration team in the electronics program we have been considering. The task of the organization is to develop forums in which these broader decisions can be made with participation and representation of the viewpoints of the teams. Participative though they might be, these interteam and systemwide decisions constrain the teams and have implications for how they do their work. In some cases, the decisions made may mean that a particular team cannot optimize its performance vis-à-vis its own goals because a trade-off is made to enhance performance of the larger system.

Extensive specialization makes task self-management a greater challenge. Because different specialties have different languages and frameworks, the integration task will be more time-consuming and involve complex trade-offs between perspectives. It may be especially difficult when functional management maintains an active link to the specialists within teams, a condition that is highly likely because technical excellence and technical learning are fundamental to organizational success and because teams may not contain the skills necessary for technical leadership of their own specialists. The organizational design task is to define discipline management's role as providing services to the team—to foster discipline development and monitor discipline excellence in a manner that supports the ability of the team to manage accomplishment of its tasks. The same service mandate must be built into the accountability system of all shared specialized services. The technical services group in the electronics program is responsible for developing approaches and conducting analyses to evaluate the technical effectiveness of the products of the teams. The group's mandate is to provide these technical services in a manner that takes team needs into account and enhances team effectiveness—in short, to treat the teams as customers.

Boundary management by the team is obviously a very large challenge when the team is enmeshed in complex on-line interdependencies beyond its boundary. Interface relationships cannot be routinized, as in a less complex model where its major interfaces are with units that supply it with inputs or with units that receive its output. The software engineers in both teams in work team structure A, for example, must continually interact to ensure that their pieces fit together to create an integrated system. One is not the customer of the other. Here the team can establish a variety of linking mechanisms (Galbraith, 1994) that range from less formal approaches such as face-to-face communication between individuals or special liaison roles to more formal solutions such as cross-team linking positions, like the systems integration engineer positions in the electronics firm. Hierarchical mechanisms for the resolution of issues that cannot be resolved laterally because of conflicting priorities may have to be established. Manager roles or higher-level cross-functional teams may be required to perform this function, such as the management team in the electronics program.

The team's role in its own performance management is also affected in the nonroutine settings being discussed here. Extensive specialization, for example, means that part of the management of an individual's performance may have to come from outside the team. The team may not have the resources for technical supervision, including goal setting, feedback, and development planning, that pertain to technical competency. This supervision will have to occur in a manner that supports team performance goals rather than working at cross-purposes. In addition, if individuals are not fully dedicated to teams, mechanisms will be needed to permit team involvement in negotiating priorities across projects and assignments.

Because of the interdependencies between teams and the dynamic nature of the work that is done, management will have to manage the performance of teams in a manner that aligns their objectives with dynamic system requirements and with each other. Cross-team interaction will be required for the establishment of mutually supportive goals. The three teams in work team design A will have to interact to establish coordinated goals so that they are responsive to the others' priorities. Mechanisms for interteam feedback and input into performance evaluation will also be needed to supplement the team's internal performance management practices and the hierarchical evaluation of teams.

In summary, the nature of the technology may preclude the design of teams that fully fit the mold of the self-contained, self-managing team that has been described in the literature. Complex technical interdependencies and uncertainties may seriously erode the self-containment ideal; consequently, the team may not have control over many of the decisions that affect its work and how it goes about producing its product or delivering its service. This means that the team is constrained by decisions beyond its bounds and that the constraints cannot always be specified in advance. The additional design task posed by these conditions is to create mechanisms for making these more inclusive decisions. These mechanisms may be lateral (cross-team) or hierarchical (at the larger unit level). They may involve the creation of specialized roles, such as a management team or formal integrator positions. Or they may be representative cross-team teams. The design challenge for such organizations is to create a team structure that maximizes within-team deliberations and minimizes complex and expensive cross-team deliberations. The next section provides some guidelines for organizations moving to a team structure.

Design Choices: Trade-Offs and Guidelines

When designing work settings composed of work teams as performing units, it is wise to keep the ideal of the self-contained, self-managed work team in mind. There is evidence that these teams can achieve high levels of effectiveness if properly designed (Cohen, 1993). But the ideal cannot always be attained. In fact, most firms will find that their technology lies somewhere along a continuum from routine to highly complex, uncertain, and dynamic. Most organizations will have to stop short of the ideal model. But that does not mean that they will not benefit by creating a design that establishes teams that fit the ideal as much as possible.

Fully self-contained work teams will not always be practicable. Nevertheless, it may be desirable to work toward that goal. If the teams are properly designed and if interfaces are standardized as much as possible, most organizations can increase the extent to which teams make their own task decisions, set their own boundaries, and manage their own performance. Additional formal decision-making mechanisms may be required to provide cross-team integration, and hierarchical mechanisms will be required to resolve issues that cannot be resolved laterally.

There is no cookie-cutter solution. The design will have to be tailored to each organization's requirements and the integration challenges it faces. However, the closer to the ideal model, the greater the benefits of using work teams. If a decision has been made to move to work teams, it is important to keep that intent in mind. All design decisions involve a trade-off: ease of technical supervision is traded off against ease of cross-functional integration, hierarchical control is traded off for self-management, and so forth. Thus in designing team structures, it is important to keep the following guidelines in mind:

1. Let the team contain as much as is technically and economically possible.

2. Let the team manage itself as much as it realistically can, given the developmental stage of the team and the need to integrate the efforts of the team with the rest of the organization.

3. Substitute lateral integration mechanisms for hierarchical ones wherever possible.

4. Flatten the organization where possible.

5. Where total self-containment or self-management is not possible, develop integrative mechanisms that are as consistent as possible with the work team notion; in short, give teams a voice in decisions that affect them.

6. Assess the transaction costs of lateral coordination, and provide hierarchical mechanisms where the cost of lateral coordination outweighs its benefits.

7. Maintain a clear management responsibility for managing the overall performance of the organization and its teams and for creating a context in which teams can more fully

manage themselves and lateral integration can more readily occur.

Finally, it is important to note that work teams are not the solution for all organizations. Interdependencies may be so complex that lateral integration must occur higher in the organization, and the line workforce may be better off managed by function. Conversely, the work may not be interdependent; it may be performed by individual contributors who do not need to interact to perform a complete task. In the latter case, creating the extra transactions required to be a team may simply adds cost without a performance benefit. Thus the primary assessment to be made by any organization contemplating a work team model is whether it will benefit from such a model.

Conclusion

The work team model, initially developed and used in production settings and popularly referred to as self-contained, self-managing teams, may not be fully implementable or desirable in all organizations. Organizations performing nonroutine, dynamic, highly uncertain work involving complex interdependencies may be unable to contain the work entirely within teams. This in turn limits the amount of self-management that can be vested in the team.

This limitation does not necessarily mean that a work team design will not benefit the performance of the organization. However, it means that the organization will make a series of trade-offs in designing its team structure. It will have to design mechanisms that facilitate cross-team and systemwide decision making. One challenge will be to do so in a manner that supports team functioning. A second challenge is to do so in a manner that doesn't drown the organization in complex transactions that offset the advantage derived from the teams.

Arguments have been made that work team structures are not

always appropriate and that organizations should base their transition to teams on an analysis of their technology as well as the performance requirements they face, rather than initiate a transition because work teams are fashionable and other companies are using them with positive results. This is truly an area that requires local analysis and tailored design approaches.

References

Cohen, S. G. (1993). Designing effective self-managing work teams. In M. Beyerlein (Ed.), *Advances in Interdisciplinary Studies of Work Teams* (vol. 1). Greenwich, Conn.: JAI Press.

Cummings, T. G. (1978). Self-regulating work groups: A sociotechnical synthesis. *Academy of Management Review, 3*, 625–633.

Cummings, T. G., and Griggs, W. H. (1977). Workers' reactions to autonomous work group conditioning for functioning, differential effects, and individual differences. *Organization and Administrative Sciences, 7*, 87–100.

Galbraith, J. R. (1994). *Competing with Flexible Lateral Organizations*. Reading, Mass.: Addison-Wesley.

Goodman, P. S., Devadas, R., and Hughson, T. L. (1988). Groups and productivity: Analyzing the effectiveness of self-managing teams. In J. P. Campbell, R. J. Campbell, and Associates (Eds.), *Productivity in Organizations: New Perspectives from Industrial and Organizational Psychology.* San Francisco: Jossey-Bass.

Lawler, E. E., III. (1978). The new plant revolution. *Organizational Dynamics, 6*(3), 2–12.

Lawler, E. E., III, Mohrman, S. A., and Ledford, G. E. (1992). *Employee Involvement and Total Quality Management: Practices and Results in Fortune 1000 Companies.* San Francisco: Jossey-Bass.

Pasmore, W. A. (1988). *Designing Effective Organizations: The Sociotechnical Systems Perspective.* New York: Wiley.

Pasmore, W. A., and Sherwood, J. (1978). *Sociotechnical Systems: A Sourcebook.* San Diego: University Associates.

Pava, C. (1986). Redesigning sociotechnical systems design: Concepts and methods for the 1990s. *Journal of Applied Behavioral Science, 22*(3), 201–222.

Pearce, J. A., and Ravlin, E. C. (1987). The design and activation of self-regulating work groups. *Human Relations, 40*(11), 751–781.

Walton, R. E. (1985). From control to commitment in the workplace. *Harvard Business Review, 63*(2), 76–84.

Chapter Thirteen

Using Measurement to Reinforce Strategy

Carl G. Thor

Performance measurement is a critical part of performance improvement for an organization of any size and type. Just measuring gets an organization nowhere. Measuring the right things for the right reason in the right manner may make the difference between a completely successful improvement initiative that is easy to institutionalize and a random collection of good intentions and accidental insights that goes nowhere.

This discussion will consider a set of measurement principles that would apply to most situations; then it will move to specific types of measures that might be appropriate only in certain cases and at certain levels of the organization. Finally, the use of measures in goal setting, effective team activity, and motivation and reward will be considered.

Principles of Measurement

The proper role of measurement has to be considered in the context of the whole organization. Everything in a modern organization starts with the external customer. A supplier stays in business only if it satisfies its customers at least as well as its competitors do. Satisfying the customer is more than the simple will to do it by customer-contact employees. Smooth-working "upstream" systems are required, and they must be carefully planned and improved.

An organization's strategic plan (or the equivalent) sets the priorities for making improvements. It is both a filter and a funnel. It receives the customers' requirements as expressed in many ways, directly and indirectly, and filters out the nonessential many to bring concentration on an essential few. It then funnels the expressed needs into an organized project structure that allows concentrated effort, involving all levels of the organization. All the tools at the organization's command are then appropriated to make the improvement happen and communicate the improved state to the customer.

Out of this simple model of organizational improvement come three principles pertaining to performance measurement:

- What to measure is ultimately determined by what the customer considers important.
- The customers' needs are translated into strategic priorities so that the strategic plan indicates what specifically to measure.
- Supplying improvement teams with measured results of key strategic priorities contributes to further improvement by providing both team motivation and information on what works and what does not work.

No department or division, no business process, no group or team is doing work so simple that it can be described and evaluated in a single measure. As work operations change, some aspects of the operation get better and some may get worse. Trade-offs abound among cost, product quality, timeliness, safety, and the like. What is desired in any organization, at least in the long run, is balanced improvement among many interrelated parameters. The most diagnostic value comes from a family of measures, each of which helps describe what is happening with the organization in question.

Similarly, it is necessary to have measures at many levels and in many parts of the organization. There should be multiple families and multiple measures in each family, providing measures appropriate to each level and each cross-cutting business process. Measure types will differ from level to level. One convenient classification differentiates planning, screening, and control measures. At the top of the organization, the measures should be oriented toward the big picture, the macro idea often expressed in financial terms. Key issues here are new products, market share, major investments, and, of course, profitability. At the other extreme are control measures. These are found at the elemental bottom of the organization. They are physical, frequent, and transparent, and they deal with very small parts of the organization—one machine or one workstation. Between these opposites are screening or diagnosis measures. A screening measure may be a control-type measure that is aggregated throughout a whole organization —for example, covering all machines in the organization instead of just one. Or it might be a multiple-cost look at a small part of the organization rather than just a profile of labor costs. Screening measures are the most challenging because they can lead directly to important action but are often obscured by being cross-departmental or having components found in several sources.

Closely related to the foregoing is the idea that measures must be "in the language" of their user. Planners need planning measures, operators need operational control measures, and screening or diagnostic teams need screening measures. Measures must be simple enough to be understood but not so trivial as to have no meaningful information content. Sometimes measures can be no more than approximate. Whereas precision is possible in the control environment, elsewhere it is better to be approximately right than to be precisely wrong. It is easy to underestimate the ability of workers at all levels to understand a measure that they perceive to be important and useful to their work. A little stretch in understanding goes a long way in diagnostic value.

Out of these points on the structure and nature of measures come another three performance measurement principles:

- A family of measures is needed to describe and analyze any organization or group.

- There should be a family of measures at each level and for each group and key business process in an organization.
- Each measure should be understandable to its users but still provide as much diagnostic value as possible.

Measures should be developed participatively. Much more improvement interest and initiative will come out of a situation where the improvers developed their own measures than where the measures were handed to them from above or from outside experts. Senior executives frequently apply this principle to themselves but not to the employees below them.

- Measures should be developed participatively.

So far, this discussion has concerned groups and departments. Measurement is done at the individual level also, but not always successfully. Measures of individual education and experience are relatively easy, but measures of actual performance are usually limited to rather subjective supervisor ratings. If an organization is transforming itself into a team-driven organization, it is clearly inappropriate to continue to concentrate on individual measures except as related to the individual's role as a team member. But one of the dilemmas of team-based organizations is how to notice and recognize unusually effective individuals.

- An appropriate balance must be struck between individual and group measures, depending on the target corporate culture.

Finally, most performance measurement is of improvement trend. This is reinforced by the common emphasis on "continuous improvement." The basic finding from a family-of-measures reading is that there has been an *x* percent overall improvement, and this is proper. But the *level* of performance is important too. An organization can improve very rapidly from "poor" to "fair," win continuous improvement awards, and still not be at a competitive level of performance. So it is necessary to supplement the basic trend measurement with appropriate attention to the performance level in key areas as compared to other organizations or to predetermined standards or goals. Most organizations can continuously improve most of their processes and be forced into "breakthrough" improvement in a few key areas only where their benchmarking studies show them to be lagging too far behind.

- A comprehensive performance measurement system includes an understanding of both performance trend and level.

Meeting all nine principles may seem a lot to expect, but typically they fit together naturally once the first few are in place. All that is really being described is a transparent and communicating organization. The needs of all stakeholders—customers, owners, and employees—are respected. Finally, firm principles are allowed to be addressed in a flexible manner.

Types of Measures

Anything that is important to at least one group of stakeholders should be measured somewhere. However, the key measures of most organizations can be grouped into a small number of basic categories. Three key groupings are productivity, quality, and innovation.

Measures of Productivity

"Pure" productivity ratios present a relationship between the output of an organizational unit or business process divided by one or more of the inputs required to produce that output. If just one input is involved, the ratio is called "partial." If all the perceived inputs are included, it is a "total" productivity ratio. More than one and less than all gives a "multiple" ratio.

Historically, most productivity ratios were partial labor productivity ratios because the only input considered was labor hours or number of employees. More recently, partial ratios have been developed for materials, capital, energy, and other catchalls such as "business services" or "information cost." Clearly, there are trade-offs between partial ratios. Labor productivity will increase, everything else being equal, as automation capital investment replaces manual workers. Capital productivity will go down unless there is a large increase in usable output tied to the automation project. Was the investment good on a net basis? This can be determined only with a multiple or total productivity calculation that includes both labor and capital.

Some thinking is also necessary regarding the output. The output is clearly understood in most manufacturing processes, but in service or support areas, identifying exactly what is the measurable output can be a challenge. What is an "idea" or a "unit of support"? There is also an issue on the frequent need for weighting of outputs; a unit produces both big and little products (or services); a simple count of number of products could be badly affected by a shift in output mix, so it may be desirable to give extra weight to large or difficult outputs so as to control this possible distortion.

It is important to differentiate between output and outcome. Many processes, especially in service areas, cannot be fully judged at the time of output delivery. Much of the measurement in education, health care, and basic research is of the delivery, whereas the producers of the service would much rather have measures of the final outcome. Did the students actually learn something they can use? Did the new cure actually work, meaning that the patient can walk again? Will the reduction of this form of emission actually improve air quality? Will the new ad sell any toothpaste? For current feedback, we are usually limited to outputs and milestones toward outcomes. But it is still a good idea, off-line, to keep track of newly reported outcomes, even if they pertain to work completed years ago, because this information can still reinforce good practices or help undermine faulty traditional practices.

Most productivity ratios are made of physical data: pounds, hours, square feet, people, linear feet, cartons, gallons, kilowatt-hours, and so on. It is not unusual, especially in service or support environments, to compare a physical output with a multiple input cost. The cost of service thus created may be the most important single measure for that organization or support process. A total productivity ratio must also deal with financial inputs (and possibly outputs, too), since you cannot add together work hours, tons of materials, kilowatt-hours of energy, and the like except by converting them to dollars. This in turn requires attention to inflationary effects. A trend measure involving financial data often has to have the specific inflation effects removed by conversion to constant dollars by means of indexes developed in-house or obtained from associations or government agencies.

It is widely recognized that the productivity or efficiency of many production and service units can be largely dictated by the basic design of the system of work rather than the diligence with which the workers apply that system. Attempts at continuous system improvement should be promoted, but fundamental redesign of the process in question to eliminate unnecessary steps and delays may be more fruitful. It can be useful to count the moves, steps, transfers, planned interruptions, tests, and reviews that are specified for the system in this form of measurement.

Utilization of fixed resources belongs in the productivity grouping. It compares the time used against the total time available. It says nothing about how well the time was used, but it can give clues about investment options. This sort of measure is used with floor space, vehicles, process equipment, and computers.

Measures of Quality

Quality is fundamentally the prevention and elimination of waste, where waste is broadly defined as anything that does not add stakeholder value. Variation reduction in production and support processes is one form of quality improvement, but not the only one.

Measuring the extent of the use of variation reduction procedures and the degree of variation in the ultimate product or service are both useful performance measures.

One comprehensive approach to measuring quality is called the cost of (poor) quality. It is made up of cost of internal nonconformance, cost of external nonconformance, and the cost of conformance. These calculate what would have been the (much lower) cost of performing the organization's activity in a perfect-quality manner throughout. The difference between the zero-defects cost and the actual cost is presented as a percentage of sales or of total costs, and it is often surprisingly high (20 to 40 percent). This type of measure is a good indicator for general awareness and strategy setting but must be decomposed into screening measures to obtain diagnostic data for improvement projects.

The main stakeholder concerned with quality is the external customer, so measures of customer satisfaction are critical quality indicators. They are usually derived from customer surveys or other means such as focus groups. They measure what interested customers (those who have bothered to respond) think about the product or service. Clearly, it is necessary to sell to disinterested customers also! So customer "joy sheets" must be supplemented with data on how product or service delivery went with all customers as measured by the supplying organization itself. These measures of service quality are easily misinterpreted. Delivering the (apparently) right service on time and within specifications ought to be enough. But there is often an intangible extra something that the customer perceives and does not articulate very well. The customer is "always right" but might also be careless or too busy to say much. So customer satisfaction survey data must be combined with factual data collected by the supplying organization dealing with what actually happened in order to make a full analysis of this aspect of quality.

Most quality organizations go beyond the customer survey to find other ways to dialogue and cooperate with their customers.

Carefully designed focus groups can not only identify discontent but also help determine source and cause. A critical distinction often missed by surveys is that between design and delivery. A survey response may show that a supplier frequently ships the wrong part. In a discussion between supplier and customer, it comes out that there are two similar parts that could be standardized into one with very little effort, saving production cost and eliminating the risk of misshipment. One of the major features of the new "agile" manufacturing is that suppliers and customers work together on product design from the beginning, often through networked computer information systems.

Timeliness is usually classified as a quality measure. Certainly, timely performance is often an important customer perception. But on-time statistics are difficult to diagnose and lend themselves to excuse making: if only the upstream supplier in the chain had delivered on time, we would have been on time also! A more useful diagnostic measure is process cycle time: how long did the activity take to be completed once all the prerequisite components were present? The ultimate customer may have difficulty seeing or even understanding all the components of cycle time, but it is the basic tool for the supplying organization to understand a complex process and to design improvements.

Two other behind-the-scenes measures that are sometimes used are housekeeping and documentation. It is easy to assume these away by saying that they are somehow included in the more direct measures of quality, but if either is a problem for an organization, it ought to be highlighted by appearing in some families of measures. Housekeeping appears most in production or research situations where a controlled environment is needed or in services where the end user is physically able to see the "production floor," as in a hotel or restaurant. Documentation, both its completeness and accuracy and its promptness, can also be important in research and technical service areas, not to mention accounting organizations.

Measures of Innovation

Innovation is a subtle concept. It is usually associated with counting "special" results, above and beyond what could normally be expected. Measurement is always more difficult when one slips outside normal activities, but in fact most organizations have this sort of measure somewhere.

Many of the innovation measures are associated with employee activity or behavior. As more and more organizations are moving to a team structure, the profile of the work being done in teams gives interesting data. How is the work shared, and how many jobs can each person do? At what level are certain typical decisions made? What are absentee and turnover rates? Is quality training being applied?

It is also possible to focus on the innovative outcomes often associated with teams. New products or services, voluntary product revisions, suggestions for process changes, voluntary customer and supplier contacts, patents, publications, and presentations might all be signs of innovation.

There are other profile measures. Does the organization have the targeted number of approved suppliers for each major purchase? Does it have the right configuration of academic background and business experience to meet its personnel needs of five years hence?

A safety program becomes a generator of innovation when safety problems are solved by foolproofing innovations. Similarly, with environmental initiatives, it is possible to start by solving a regulatory problem and end up with a process or cost improvement. A defensive-looking measure such as pollution fines per time period may stimulate proactive improvement efforts.

Finally, it does not matter whether a measure fits neatly into a category. An organization should measure what is important to it at each level of the organization. What is important will usually turn out to be several things, and the goal will be balanced improvement in several different but related areas. The family of measures for each department and each business process should both reflect the strategic interests of the whole organization and also be expressed as variables understood at each respective level of the organization. The typical family of four to six measures would have some that are clearly related to higher-level issues but also some that are of primary concern only to one specific group or process.

Benchmarking: Joining Level to Trend

Benchmarking is the systematic comparison of one organization to another with the aim of mutual improvement. Through benchmarking, an organization can set improvement goals and thereby judge the adequacy of improvement rates in the context of what needs to be done (Thor, 1993; Camp, 1989). Continuous improvement is the basis for most of the organization, but breakthrough improvement becomes the basis in the aspects of the organization discovered to be seriously behind current (and future) best practice.

For many years, in many nations, interfirm comparisons have been conducted by productivity centers or specialized consultants to allow participants to see where they fit in the performance of their industry group and to give the sponsoring organization some insight into the condition of the industry as a whole. Most of the data compared are in financial terms and give insight into alternative strategic approaches such as degree of vertical integration, maintenance policy, or product line proliferation.

These studies in turn provide information on where in the organization more detailed operational improvement studies might be conducted. The new quality benchmarking movement assumes that the organization already has a good idea where its problems lie, either through executive intuition, strategic planning, or wise consultants. It proposes interorganizational studies of process elements. If interfirm comparisons can be called "strategic benchmarking," this new form of sharing process information might be called "operational benchmarking." As the former can aid an organization in goal setting at the top of the organization, the latter specializes in putting new life into the middle of the organization and its major cross-cutting processes.

What is difficult about operational benchmarking is that proper metrics do not spring out of joint deliberations without a great deal of adjustment work to make different approaches comparable. Two organizations' approaches to the same activity may well differ in the relative completeness of purchased components, the extra features offered to the final customer, the amount of review and testing thought to be required, documentation practices, the relative training of the workers involved, and even outside-imposed restrictions on the operations. However, with patience, teams from different organizations can arrive at a consensus best practice. This can then rather directly provide the much-needed level indicator or goal that in turn helps pace the improvement effort in the organization.

Though goal setting is an important output of benchmarking, the outcome must be improved organizational processes. It is important that "floor workers" from the process being benchmarked be a part of the study team so that when it comes time to implement the redesigned process, the practical eye (and persuasive ability) of the local worker can be used for a smoother transition.

Benchmarking fills an important gap in trend-oriented performance measurement practice. But benchmarking could not be conducted without using measures of productivity, quality, timeliness, and so on to select best practices. In fact, determining what is best practice is essentially the same issue as deciding how to weight the components of a family of measures. Which of these variables is the most important after all? Just as performance measures are often classified as strategic or operational, depending on where in the organization they are found and acted on, two forms of benchmarking can be similarly characterized. Strategic benchmarking (interfirm comparison) and operational benchmarking are both needed in the organization, as are their measurement counterparts, with the strategic usually giving valuable direction to the operational.

Using the Measures

Each member of a family of measures can be analyzed and interpreted on its own, but usually there is also an interest in a "bottom line." Has there been a net improvement or not? The individual measures can be aggregated simply by weighting each measure according to its relative importance to the group in question and then combining the individual trend rates. But a serious difficulty is created by the fact that some measures can be improved substantially without much effort (say, from 50 percent on-time delivery to 70 percent on-time delivery), whereas other measures are much more difficult (from 99.0 percent accurate paychecks to 99.5 percent accurate paychecks). What is needed is the ability to scale effort toward balanced goals regardless of the magnitude of improvement called for.

This feature is provided by the objectives matrix, an aggregation technique that combines weighted individual measures based on relative progress toward preset goals for each measure (Thor, 1991; Riggs and Felix, 1983).

The objectives matrix format provides an excellent way of giving feedback of results to the relevant employee group. Each new set of results should provide the occasion for a careful review of progress against schedule and a rethinking, if necessary, of the improvement approach. The main feedback should be basically horizontal, to the people directly involved in the work of that department or process, whether as participant, manager, or customer. Summary feedback can be given to higher organizational levels along with proposed changes decided on after reviewing results, but if it is perceived that the main reason for measuring is to give higher-level executives ammunition to attack prevailing activities, measurement will not be accepted or used constructively.

Measured results are not secrets. They should be fed back primarily to the workers directly involved in the relevant process, with some summarized results sent upward in the organization. And there is great additional value in displaying on bulletin boards the main local charts for everyone to see. Workers in adjacent processes may have their own suggestions for your process or might be able to borrow something from you. Modern production and service processes tend to be complex. It is up to all of us to fight this by making the internal operations of an organization as transparent as possible to allow improvement efforts to succeed.

Measurement systems, or at least criteria, must change as the organization changes. New leaders have new pressure points to work on. The organization changes its product line or its overall strategy. Improvement has been so great in one area that it is time to proclaim satisfaction and move on to something else. As major issues are better understood, pressure can be focused on a critical subissue. Measurement systems, like all other basic systems, need regular review, and change must be provided for.

A measured trend starts from a baseline. The base measure has to be a reflection of normal. Agreement on what is normal is rare, but the first rule of trend analysis is that consistency is more important than accuracy. If the measure is always made in the same way using the same assumptions, at least it can be readily analyzed. So a "close enough" baseline often is close enough!

A frequently overlooked application of performance measurement is to use measured results directly in the compensation system. Variable group incentive plans, such as gain sharing, can be fed directly from the bottom line of the objectives matrix, for example. (For more on gain sharing, see Chapter Sixteen.) Senior executives are accustomed to having performance incentives; evidence is abundant that incentives are equally effective in the lower reaches of the organization, if the organization is reasonably open and communicative by nature.

Conclusion

Five essential points were made in this chapter:

- Measures have their origin in customer needs as filtered through the supplier's strategic plan.
- The purpose of measures is to provide clear feedback to the organization's "improvers" at all levels.
- A family of measures is essential, for nothing is so simple that it can be understood with one measure.
- Separate but related families of measures are needed in each department, cross-cutting process, and key group.
- Measures of performance trends that identify continuous improvement must be supplemented with benchmarked level measures so that breakthrough strategies can be employed where needed.

References

Camp, R. (1989). *Benchmarking: The Search for Industry Best Practices That Lead to Superior Performance*. White Plains, N.Y.: Quality Press.

Riggs, J., and Felix, G. (1983). *Productivity by Objectives*. Englewood Cliffs, N.J.: Prentice Hall.

Thor, C. G. (1991). Performance measurement in a research organization. *National Productivity Review, 10*(4), 499–507.

Thor, C. G. (1993). Cost-effective benchmarking. In D. J. Sumanth, (Ed.), *Productivity and Quality Management Frontiers* (vol. 4, pp. 350–356). Norcross, Ga.: Industrial Engineering and Management Press.

Part Five

Linking the Reward System to High Performance

The way in which organizational reward systems are designed and managed is being transformed. One of the most important aspects of this transformation is the recognition that organizational rewards are broader and more numerous than base salary or wages. Recognition is also growing that, designed and managed effectively, rewards can serve as a powerful management tool to help accomplish operating objectives.

Traditionally, the majority of employees have been paid only a base salary or wage, based on the time they spend at work. Effectively, our pay systems have purchased the employee's services by the hour, week, or month. Only a small number of senior executives—typically less than 1 percent of the workforce—have been eligible for cash incentives or stock ownership opportunities. The obvious assumption has been that organizational success rides on the efforts of this small group. That assumption is now being questioned, and this has opened the door to a search for new ways to reward employees below the executive level.

Another aspect of the transformation is the recognition that organizations have changed dramatically since the almost universal model for salary programs was developed in 1930s and 1940s. That model was developed at a time when organizations and jobs were essentially static. Once the organization structure was defined, human resource specialists set to work to analyze the content of each job and to determine its relative internal value. The administrative systems, particularly the basic job evaluation methods, were developed to fit this model and the needs of organizations in the post–World War II period. The pay program was designed, maintained, and controlled by the personnel department, as human resources was known at the time.

These traditional pay programs were realistically intended to control wage and salary costs; providing a financial incentive for employees was a secondary priority. Despite announced commitments to merit pay, virtually all employees—good and poor performers alike—were granted essentially the same increase. This problem was aggravated by the prevalence of cost-of-living salary adjustments during periods of high inflation and by the "keep them whole" philosophy that led to general pay increases. The failure to introduce meaningful pay-for-performance systems led to entitlement cultures in which employees absolutely expect an annual salary increase. It has become obvious that we cannot afford the costs of entitlement.

The need to develop more effective programs was triggered by the recession of the early 1990s. Corporate leaders focused on the need to hold down labor costs to be more competitive and to find ways to stimulate productivity increases. It is now widely acknowledged that traditional pay practices have never lived up to expectations, but the downturn in business made finding better answers a survival issue for many companies.

One of the overriding characteristics of the new wave of compensation programs is the emphasis on flexibility. This is a reflection of the increasingly dynamic nature of our organization structures and of the roles that workers are expected to play. The rate of change has made organization charts, with their boxes to delineate workers' jobs, increasingly irrelevant. Jobs that cannot be forced into tiny boxes cannot be "measured," to use the jargon of job evaluation specialists. The new program concepts introduce considerably more flexibility than is typical in a traditional salary program.

Another pervasive trend is the shift in accountability for pay program management from HR specialists to supervisors and line managers. This shift was prompted by the emerging understanding that management accountability includes people management. If we are going to hold managers accountable for results, we have to give them the tools to tap the full capabilities of their staff. They are in a much better position that the human resource staff to evaluate the needs of their work group and to determine how to allocate organizational rewards.

Chapter Fourteen, "Base Pay: Rethinking the Basic Framework," by Howard Risher, provides an overview of the strategy considerations relevant to developing a wage or salary program to fit the new work environment. The chapter reviews the traditional practices and the strategic considerations involved in rethinking base-pay programs. The field of salary management has seen little change in over four decades, but there is now broad-based recognition that the traditional practices are not working. This chapter provides an overview of some of the emerging ideas.

The new model for wage and salary management downplays the nuances that make jobs different and that have been important in job evaluation. Many companies have concluded that the time and resources committed to documenting jobs in detail and to job evaluation did not add sufficient value to justify the time and expense of the program. Organizations have also come to appreciate that traditional salary programs placed too much emphasis on the job hierarchy. As a response, interest is high in salary or grade banding. This concept solves several of the basis concerns with traditional programs and introduces a new management philosophy.

In Chapter Fifteen, "Developmental Pay: Aligning Employee Capabilities with Business Needs," Richard Beatty, Boris Dimitroff, and Dennis O'Neill discuss a new rationale for handling salary increases. By focusing on the skills and competencies needed to be successful, employers can reinforce the value of each worker and provide an incentive to the worker to develop and use his or her full capabilities.

Under the developmental pay concept, workers are effectively paid for what they can do, based on their skills or competencies, not on their supposed performance last year. This concept emerged in part as a response to W. Edwards Deming's criticism of traditional merit pay and performance appraisal practices. Workers start at competitive entry-level salaries and are granted pay increases as they develop and demonstrate enhanced skills or competencies.

Chapter Sixteen, "Group Incentives: Improving Performance Through Shared Goals and Rewards," by John Belcher, develops a framework for designing and managing nonexecutive group incentive plans. Gain-sharing plans are the best-understood plan concept, but increasingly, group incentive plans are moving away from the classic gain-sharing formula to provide greater flexibility and to fit a wider range of circumstances. One of the goals for introducing incentive compensation is to change compensation expenses from fixed to variable costs. Another goal is to provide meaningful financial incentives for improved performance.

Group incentive plans create a common focus for group efforts—employees all know what they have to accomplish—and reinforce the feeling that "we're all in this together." Research has confirmed that group incentive plans can have a profound impact on an organization's performance. If the recent past is prologue to the future, group incentive plans will soon be a standard component of every employee's pay package.

Chapter Seventeen, "Rewarding Special Performance: Low-Cost, High-Impact Awards," by Jerry McAdams, makes the case for relying on a broad definition of rewards to encompass the almost endless ways in which performance can be recognized and rewarded. People like to celebrate their success and to have their contribution acknowledged when they or their organization reach important goals or go beyond expected levels of performance. Noncash awards can include valued merchandise, paid time off, travel opportunities, symbolic awards (such as parking spaces and pins), and social reinforcement (such as pats on the back, award ceremonies, and public recognition). The variety of noncash awards and their modest costs provide considerable flexibility. When properly managed, noncash awards have been found to provide more "bang for the buck" than equivalent cash awards.

Chapter Fourteen

Base Pay: Rethinking the Basic Framework

Howard Risher

One of the "hot button" concerns of senior management is the need for organizational change. In many situations, the concern was triggered by the recession and the need to reduce or control expenses for survival. This has resulted in force reductions, often with an emphasis on delayering. In other situations, the concern reflects an attempt to respond to changing market conditions. These changes have involved innovative work management practices such as self-managed work teams and flexible job design as well as new strategies such as total quality management (TQM). American industry has never experienced a period of more dramatic or widespread efforts to reconfigure the way work is organized.

One of the functions that has experienced the least change until recently is wage and salary management. The policies, program concepts, and methods that are widely used were introduced over fifty years ago in a very different era of management. The overriding objective has been program control, with at least superficial concern for consistency across the organization.

A basic premise of the conventional approach to managing salaries is that once a job is understood by a human resource specialist, the program methods and procedures can systematically determine the job's ranking in the hierarchy, which is in turn used to establish the appropriate rate of pay for the job. The emphasis has been on analysis and documentation and on centralized management.

Wage and salary program concepts evolved out of the early

industrial engineering efforts to analyze and plan production systems. The past few years have seen a proliferation of software packages to automate and facilitate decision making and record maintenance, but the basic program logic is unchanged. It has become increasingly obvious that the traditional program concepts are incompatible with emerging organizational paradigms and work management practices. The purpose of this chapter is to explore the recently conceived alternatives.

Conventional Salary Management Concepts

The heart of a conventional salary program is the salary structure, composed of a series of overlapping salary ranges. Although there are minor variations in structure design from employer to employer, virtually every salary program relies on a basically similar structure.

The two key design issues are the percentage difference between range midpoints—typically 8 to 10 percent—and the percentage difference or "spread" from the range minimum to the maximum. Surveys show that most organizations rely on a spread of 50 percent for nonmanagerial, exempt positions, increasing to as much as 65 or 70 percent for managerial and executive positions, and a spread of 40 to 45 percent for most nonexempt positions. The latter numbers have been increasing in recent years as firms have eliminated or reduced the differences between exempt and nonexempt programs.

Jobs are assigned to salary ranges based on their relative value—or, more accurately, their position in the organizational hierarchy. Starting with the time-and-motion studies in the early 1900s, compensation specialists have emphasized the analysis and documentation of job content, in the form of a job description, as the basis for these decisions. This information serves to define and all too often to lock the incumbent into a set of job duties. If it's not on the position description, it's not part of the job! Ostensibly, it is the value of these duties that determines a job's ranking and the appropriate salary range.

The problems involved in measuring or determining a job's value have been an ongoing concern for over half a century. A number of job evaluation methods have been developed and tested, with emphasis in recent years on the use of computers to speed up the process and on statistical techniques to enhance a system's reliability and precision. In the past decade, the interest in pay equity has been an important stimulus to the development of better systems.

Despite these efforts, job evaluation has never been fully accepted as a necessary management system. In recent years, a number of leading corporations have dropped their job evaluation system and are now relying on market pricing. The number of critics is also increasing; the most prominent voice is that of "management guru" Ed Lawler (author of Chapter Three).

Lawler accuses job evaluation systems of the following sins (Lawler, 1986):

- Promoting bureaucratic management and inflating administrative costs
- Reinforcing and overemphasizing the job hierarchy
- Discouraging organizational change and individual initiative
- Emphasizing stated job duties rather than individual capabilities or performance
- Emphasizing job changing rather than skill development

The role and importance of the job evaluation system are appropriately treated as strategic issues to be addressed by senior management. The bottom-line question is, do the time and resources committed to job evaluation represent value added to the organization? If the response is no, it may make sense to reconsider the basis for assigning workers to salary ranges. That issue is discussed in more depth later in this chapter.

The conventional program concept provides for new hires or promoted employees to be paid a salary at or close to the range minimum. Pay is then adjusted upward, typically on an annual cycle, based on "merit." In theory, the employee's relative salary within the range reflects his or her individual value. Typically, the range midpoint is aligned with market pay levels so that as an employee's salary progresses through the range, it is possible to track his or her pay relative to the market.

The basis for the annual adjustment has traditionally been the supervisor's assessment of the employee's performance over the prior year. Even though researchers have spent years studying these decisions and developing procedures to improve the process, it remains inherently subjective and difficult to defend.

Virtually all corporations rely on merit pay policies to manage salaries for at least the white-collar segment of their workforce. Again the framework for these policies is generally consistent from employer to employer. The supervisor looks back over the employee's accomplishments or comparative performance for the year and, using a rating scale, specifies a performance level. This is in turn linked to an increase policy that provides for specified merit pay increases at each rating level. Some employers also consider the employee's position in the range, expressed as a ratio (employee's salary divided by the range midpoint), and provide for larger increases if the employee is low in the range and smaller increases if high in the range.

The intent is to provide a framework within which supervisors can manage subordinates' salaries and to establish controls that will ensure consistency throughout the corporation. At the same time, merit policies limit the supervisor's discretion and make it difficult to respond adequately to unforeseen individual circumstances. In many organizations, supervisors or managers have less discretion in managing their payroll expenses than they do in any other aspect of their budget.

The traditional program concept also builds the merit adjustment into the employee's salary, making it a fixed cost that continues until the employee retires or leaves the company. This effectively means that the employee is paid for the prior year's performance year after year into the future. This is a decidedly different philosophy and certainly has different financial implications from the variable-pay concept reflected in an incentive pay program, where money has to be earned each year. The fixed-cost nature of wage and salary programs is one of the reasons why employers are seeking alternatives.

Strategic Considerations

Salary management practices are at a point of transition. Many employers are looking for innovative concepts and practices. They have concluded that the traditional practices are not meeting their needs, and this has triggered a search for alternatives.

In considering program changes, several traditional questions must be addressed:

• What caliber of workers do we need to recruit? Does our business strategy suggest that we need better people in some job families than in others? Have we experienced any problems attracting adequately qualified candidates? Is our current staff sufficiently competent to accomplish our objectives?

• Do we understand our labor markets in terms of competing employers? Do we understand competitive pay levels and practices? Have we articulated an adequate strategy to link our pay programs to market levels?

• Do current salaries reflect an internal hierarchy that is consistent with management's understanding of the relative importance of jobs and job families? Do we want to give formal recognition to the hierarchy? What do we mean by "internal equity"? Is the program appropriately balanced between internal and external considerations?

• Is pay for performance an important policy issue? Are we rewarding the right behaviors? Is the performance assessment process perceived to be credible and fair? Is our merit pay policy compatible with our TQM initiative?

• Would it be advantageous to reorient the program to reward team or group performance? Should this involve a shift of funds into incentive plans? If so, how should we balance the risk and reward elements?

• Are our administrative costs to maintain the salary program at acceptable levels? Do we know how much time is spent on program administration? Would it be possible to eliminate or reduce the time needed for any of the administrative steps?

• Have the program and the administrators been sufficiently responsive to recent organizational and job changes? Is the program designed appropriately to accommodate and support anticipated changes in the way we organize and manage work? Would it be advantageous to decentralize program responsibility?

• Is the message to employees consistent with our strategic and program objectives? Does the message provide an accurate understanding of how the pay program is linked to the business strategy? Do employees understand what determines their "value" and their compensation?

The answers to these questions provide a strategic framework for evaluating the strengths and deficiencies of the existing program as well as for designing program changes. In keeping with the view that pay programs are management systems, it is useful to ask the users or "customers" if the program is meeting their needs as supervisors. While it is essential to get feedback from top management, it is also useful to consider the viewpoints of lower-level managers and supervisors. The program's effectiveness can be assessed best at the work group level, where it affects employee behavior.

Salary or Grade Banding:
An Alternative Structure Concept

Grade banding or broad banding is an alternative to the traditional salary structure. The concept was first introduced in a federal government research facility in the early 1980s. Aetna and Citicorp adopted the concept a few years later. In the 1990s, it has been adopted by a rapidly increasing number of corporations.

Grade banding involves a simplified salary structure. In contrast to a traditional structure that can involve twenty or more salary ranges for exempt employees, a banding structure can reduce the number of ranges to five or six. Although there has not been enough experience to develop rules of thumb, the number of salary bands or ranges is designed to accommodate the number of organization levels or tiers or, for nonmanagement positions, the number of levels in a career ladder. From this perspective, the concept provides a solid foundation for career management.

In contrast to a traditional salary range, the width of a band might be 75 percent to 100 percent or more. This means that a traditional range of, say, $40,000 to $60,000—a conventional 50 percent spread—would be increased to $80,000 or more. In this example, the band covers the same dollar range as three to five traditional grades.

The banding concept emerged as a response to a number of organization problems.

1. The traditional job evaluation process has focused on and served to formalize the job hierarchy. Employees certainly know that at least an informal hierarchy exists, but the knowledge that their job has been evaluated and points have been assigned makes

them decidedly more sensitive to their place in the hierarchy. They also, of course, appreciate that the evaluation points are important and that it is to their benefit to develop a personal strategy to justify an increase in points. More important, they develop greater sensitivity to the relative ranking of other positions. In some organizations, job evaluation points become a basis for assessing individual status. This attention to the hierarchy can affect working relationships. The banding philosophy is based on the recognition that organization level is important but that within each level, the distinctions between jobs are secondary to the value of the individual.

2. The recent emphasis on reorganization, downsizing, and delayering triggers an ongoing and intensive effort by compensation specialists to reevaluate newly created or redefined jobs. This opens the door to confrontations and "games" involving affected employees who want to avoid having their jobs downgraded. This resistance to organizational change often impedes and reduces the expected benefits of the reorganization. Banding diminishes the prospects for downgrading (as well as upgrading) as a result of a reorganization. It also reduces dramatically the level of administrative paperwork to support the reorganization.

3. Downsizing, with its diminished prospects for organizational expansion, translates into fewer promotional job openings. To provide new job challenges and personal growth opportunities, organizations are relying more often on lateral transfers to new assignments. The traditional structure and job evaluation logic would require an analysis of each job change to determine if it warrants a higher or lower salary grade. Needless to say, employees are always going to be reluctant to accept a transfer to a lower-rated position even if it will enhance their career prospects. The banding concept facilitates lateral job changes.

4. In the same way, the increasing emphasis on flexibility and

responsiveness means that job incumbents need to be able to react to changing circumstances. This spawned an emphasis on flexible jobs where employees are expected to do "whatever needs to be done." The traditional job description and the job evaluation logic are premised on the idea that job duties can be specified and remain static over at least some period of time. Flexible job duties are incompatible with the traditional administrative mechanisms. Banding places considerably less emphasis on job documentation and evaluation.

5. The current interest in quality management has triggered a high level of interest in team performance and cross-discipline cooperation. Realistically, the ability and willingness of workers to function as a team is affected by differences in status and perceived power, which are in turn affected by job evaluation distinctions. The banding concept should facilitate team cooperation and improved effectiveness.

6. The traditional process is the responsibility of designated compensation specialists. They normally have considerable authority to evaluate and assign jobs to salary grades. They are in many organizations the detective, the judge, and the jury. Their role involves enough win-lose confrontations with line managers that they can easily fall into disfavor. Supervisors and job incumbents need to devote more than a few hours to completing the paperwork required to provide requested job information to ensure that jobs are properly evaluated. Banding basically eliminates most of these confrontations and the inevitable ill feelings. This can represent a dramatic reduction in the time and resources needed to maintain a wage and salary program.

Grade banding represents a very different program concept. Although it may still make sense to use a job evaluation system to assign positions to bands, the rationale is not premised on measuring differences in job value. The banding rationale is simple:

jobs at each level in the organization are roughly equivalent in importance and should be in the same salary band.

Too often, the problems associated with job evaluation offset any possible benefit. Too much emphasis on distinctions in job value diminishes the prospects for teamwork and cooperation. At the extreme, job evaluation results, usually expressed as points, can become a more important measure of status and importance than an individual's contribution to the organization's success.

The message flowing from the banding program is this: "Everybody at your level in the organization is expected to work together and contribute to our success. Our salary program is designed to pay you appropriately relative to your level and the labor market for your experience and credentials. Our rewards are driven by performance and individual value, not artificial distinctions between jobs."

Experience with banding is still preliminary. An increasing number of prominent corporations, including General Electric and Xerox, have begun the transition to a banding program, but experience is insufficient to indicate preferred strategies or approaches. It will be several years before we understand what works and what doesn't.

The experience so far confirms that grade banding provides a sound foundation for simplifying salary administration practices and supporting organizational initiatives. Adopting banding makes sense in combination with an organization strategy to decrease the layers of management and to diminish the administrative burden. Banding makes fewer distinctions than traditional work classification systems and gives managers more discretion on how their subordinates are paid.

Market Pricing Strategy Issues

The concern with operating costs makes it important to align salaries with market levels. This is an important strategic decision because payroll is typically the single largest operating cost (except in financial service companies), often accounting for 50 percent or more of variable costs. Market pricing, which is the phrase commonly applied to analyses of market pay levels, can involve hours and hours of staff time in large, multiple-location companies.

One of the problems in understanding competitive pay levels is the wealth of available survey data. Thousands of surveys are conducted annually, covering different occupations, geographical areas, and industries. Many can be purchased for less than $100. Each is based on data from a different sample of employers. This means that published surveys covering the same occupations in the same urban area often show different results. None of the results may be a completely valid measure of competitive pay levels if the labor market is not properly defined.

The alternative is to conduct or sponsor private surveys that make it possible to study pay practices in specified labor markets. Although private surveys are more valid, they can cost $10,000 or more. For large employers with multiple locations, the cost to generate adequate survey data can be significant. Of course, a 5 or 10 percent error in estimating competitive pay levels—which flows directly into payroll—can easily offset the cost of accurate survey data.

Another consideration in using survey data is the distribution of pay levels above and below the mean. Some companies pay employees more than others, and this presumably enhances their ability to recruit higher-caliber employees. Salary surveys tend to focus on averages and in some cases fail to report any other statistics. If the caliber of employees is an important business issue, relative pay levels should be considered in planning the pay program.

With a strategically driven compensation program, it makes sense to start with the business strategy and consider which, if any, job families are critical to the organization's future. For those that are, the organization may want to pay employees in these job families above-average salaries. For example, if research personnel are crucial, it may make business sense to recruit world-class prospects and to pay these people at the 90th percentile. Looking first at the business strategy and analyzing the relative importance of job families provides a basis for a differential pay strategy. Few employers can afford or need to pay every worker above-average wages—that is simply not justified—but it may be essential to have high-caliber workers in selected positions.

With a conventional salary structure, salary range midpoints serve as the link to market pay rates. Jobs are assigned to the range that has a midpoint that best approximates the planned pay level for the job. This is a simple rationale that assures both management and employees that their pay is aligned with market levels. It assumes, of course, that the midpoint is the right pay level for job incumbents.

With a grade banding structure, however, application of the traditional market pricing strategy is no longer possible. Salary bands now have one or more control points that are used to monitor the progression of salaries through the band. Market data can still be used to track benchmark pay levels relative to prevailing levels, but the middle of each band—which is analogous to the midpoint concept—cannot be used as the basis for linking the program to market rates.

An alternative strategy has been adopted by Merrill Lynch. The company assigns jobs to bands based on their internal value to the organization, but each band is divided into three sectors, and jobs are grouped according to market data. Jobs such as systems analyst that command high market rates are assigned to the highest sector. Other jobs are assigned to sectors on the basis of market data. The jobs in each band are considered equal and are accorded similar internal status, but the use of bands makes it possible to differentiate salaries to reflect market differentials.

Banding provides considerably more flexibility to respond to market trends and to pay employees appropriately relative to their individual competencies. Too often with traditional salary structures, when the labor market pushes salaries for a specialized occupation up rapidly, organizations have trouble staying competitive. The only recourse over time is to move the jobs to higher grades or, as many hospitals have done for nurses and other allied health occupations, to establish separate salary scales. With banding, managers and supervisors can work with compensation specialists to determine appropriate starting salaries and manage wages and salaries to remain competitive. The decisions to allocate pay increase funds are driven by strategic correlates, and managers come to appreciate their responsibility to maintain an appropriately qualified workforce.

In the future, the trends to increase the number of employees with part-time schedules, contract workers, and employees with flexible job duties will force companies to adopt new market pricing strategies. The traditional logic is based on the assumption that there are generic or commonly defined jobs with a large number of employers. The market pricing process assumes that these jobs can be identified and matched for survey purposes. Traditional market pricing is not feasible if the jobs are not comparable.

Individual Salary Management Issues

The bottom line for any compensation program is the need to recruit and retain adequately qualified employees. Periodically, employees read or hear about alternative employment opportunities. Pay is a focal consideration in comparing job alternatives. Each time, the employee has to determine the adequacy of his or her current compensation. These are individual decisions, and realistically, this amounts to an ongoing assessment of the program.

As programs are modified to introduce variable-pay plans and lump-sum payments, the comparison with other job opportunities shifts to cash compensation and take-home pay. The employee wants to know, "How much can I expect to earn? Am I better off staying here or taking another job?" Variable pay introduces a level of uncertainty and makes it difficult to compare job opportunities.

A key issue is that the employee's circumstances change over time as he or she gains experience and develops new or improved skills. This makes employees more valuable and warrants progressively higher salaries. The traditional merit pay philosophy implicitly accounts for the enhanced value, although the rationale for the increase is treated as a reward for the prior year's performance.

Traditional salary management practices make the value of the job—as opposed to the value of the incumbent—the most important pay determinant. Unusual qualifications are sometimes reflected informally in starting salaries, but thereafter, virtually everyone is granted salary increases that fall within a narrow range. Moreover, the increases are granted almost automatically, year after year, pushing salaries progressively higher in lockstep.

Our salary management thinking has unfortunately been dominated by experience born in union settings (or under fear of unionization). The emphasis on equal treatment was further exacerbated, as mentioned earlier, by high inflation in the 1970s and early 1980s when managers opted to "keep employees whole" by granting increases equivalent to the rate of inflation. This experience created feelings of entitlement, and companies have found it difficult to back away from employee expectations that they deserve an annual pay increase. Pay for performance is espoused in virtually every North American corporation, but in reality, outstanding performers make out only marginally better than poorer performers.

In adding the pay increase to the current base, the employee is effectively paid for last year's performance until he or she leaves or retires. Not only is next year's payroll higher, but the higher salaries translate into higher pay-related benefit costs (retirement income, life insurance, disability income, time off with pay).

Over the past few years, merit pay policies have been attacked by advocates of W. Edwards Deming and his total quality management principles. Deming refers to traditional merit pay and performance appraisal practices as among the "deadly diseases" of management. The basic problem, according to Deming, is that the typical policy places too much emphasis on individual performance and too little on team performance.

His criticism is difficult to refute. Most employers acknowledge that their appraisal and merit pay policies "need improvement" and recognize that Deming's criticisms are to some degree valid. For many organizations with TQM initiatives, this realization has prompted a reconsideration of policies and a search for better ways to recognize and reward performance.

The easiest response to this criticism is to fall back on the general or step increase approach, eliminating the linkage between pay and performance. The increase in pay for performance has prompted most employers to move away from general increases, but the Deming advocates apparently want to ignore individual performance. This is a fundamental compensation strategy issue.

One alternative is to modify the appraisal system to recognize team performance issues and other TQM-related criteria, such as customer service. It is possible to split the merit increase pool to allocate a portion to reward individual performance and the balance to reward team performance. Realistically, some employees work as a member of a team throughout the workday, while others rarely work in a team. Human resource specialists, for example, commonly work as individual specialists in one-on-one situations. The balance of individual and team performance can be documented, if necessary, in job descriptions.

A basic Deming concern is the reliance on performance rating scales (five points for "outstanding," one point for "unsatisfactory") in the appraisal process, particularly when the rating is the basis for merit increases. In response to this, several prominent companies have eliminated the use of a rating scale and now give supervisors the discretion to determine increases. Rating scales were originally introduced to enhance consistency and to systematize the allocation of merit increase funds. Eliminating the scale gives supervisors considerably more latitude and makes their job more difficult. This also runs contrary to the consistency goal.

A related change is the shift to a three-point rating scale: outstanding, meets standards, needs improvement. Research has shown that people generally agree on the extreme cases, the best and the worst. By using a three-point scale, companies can more easily identify individuals who warrant special attention; because 75 to 85 percent of the workers tend to meet expectations, they are rated in the middle category, thereby minimizing the problems associated with subjective ratings that make finer distinctions. For the great many organizations with an interest in identifying poor performers and to giving recognition to outstanding workers, the three-point scale seems to work.

A final alternative that is consistent with the TQM philosophy is asking individuals other than an employee's immediate supervisor to assess and comment on performance. Each employee's situation is different, so it is important to focus on the individuals who have opportunities to observe performance: co-workers in the same work group, peers in other units, subordinates, external customers, internal customers for whom the employee provides a service. This recognizes that the supervisor may not have the best vantage point for assessing a subordinate's performance. It also serves to diminish the adverse consequences that can be triggered when the supervisor is the sole source of performance feedback. However handled, the assessment of an employee's performance results in a decision to increase his or her salary.

Some companies have decided to pay all or a portion of the increase as a lump sum to avoid or reduce future salary escalation. Employees will benefit by receiving the salary increase sooner than having it paid incrementally in future paychecks, but they lose the value of compounding with future increases and the increase in the value of their benefits. When employees realize the consequences of this policy change, it could create morale problems. The cost savings over time can be significant.

A very different approach to wage and salary management is

skill-based pay. In contrast to the past-oriented philosophy of the traditional merit increase policy (the merit increase is a reward for last year's performance), skill-based pay has a future orientation. The message of skill-based pay is that the employee's value depends on what he or she can do. The more employees can do, the higher their value, and this will be reflected in their salary. The concept is also compatible with the TQM philosophy in that it deemphasizes past performance and conceptually reinforces the importance of continuous skill improvement.

Skill-based programs are normally designed to cover a specific job family. The first step is to identify the skills required to work at each level in the relevant career ladder. In most job families, entry-level workers are expected to demonstrate a limited number of skills and then to enhance those skills and develop new ones with experience. In designing the skill-based program, management has to decide how important each skill is and how many performance levels need to be recognized. Management must also decide how skill attainment is going to be confirmed and documented. Many organizations rely on skill testing for this purpose, but that can grow into an administrative bureaucracy. More than one authority in the compensation field has characterized skill-based programs as "a compensation techie run amok," referring to the time needed to administer such a program. For each demonstrated skill, the worker earns an incremental wage or salary increase.

A similar program concept is competency-based pay. Skills are normally thought of in the context of hourly or nonexempt workers who focus on manual tasks. The concept of a skill is less relevant to jobs involving cognitive use of professional or technical knowledge. For some job families, mental capabilities and expertise—competencies—are the relevant basis for assessing individual value. Competency-based pay is conceptually the same as skill-based pay. For each family, management has to identify the relevant competencies and define performance expectations. These may be specific to the job family, such as knowledge of Securities and Exchange Commission reporting requirements, or more generic, such as verbal communication.

The goal is to provide an incentive for workers to increase the depth and breadth of their skills. In the same way, the most competent workers can be expected to make the most significant contribution. As they improve, workers can both expand the scope of their jobs and perform at a higher level. In some organizations, hourly workers have added skills normally expected of supervisors and managers, such as scheduling. This provides staff utilization flexibility and may reduce staffing requirements. However, it also increases the average pay level, so it is important for management to make full use of the new skills.

With each of these alternatives, management should consider the possible benefits that could be derived by adding group incentive plans such as gain sharing. As with management compensation programs, the balance between the base-pay program and incentive pay is a basic strategy issue. Cash compensation levels—base pay plus cash incentives—must be managed relative to competitive market levels. Adding a new incentive plan on top of already competitive base salaries inflates operating costs, so it may be important to phase in the incentive payouts over a year or two. The important issue is the need to manage total cash compensation and to ensure that employees' pay is consistent with the compensation strategy.

Whose Program Is It?

Traditionally, the human resource function has owned the wage and salary program. The increasing emphasis on merit pay over the past twenty years and the concomitant decreasing reliance on general or cost-of-living increases are gradually shifting program management from human resource specialists to line managers and supervisors. Managerial discretion is still constrained by policies and procedures controlled by the HR function. Managers who may have the authority to spend thousands or even millions of dollars cannot grant a subordinate an extra 10 percent without securing human resource approval.

With the trend toward delegating day-to-day operating decisions to the lowest management level, it is probably inevitable that line managers will want, and possibly demand, the expansion of their responsibility for salary management and for the introduction of new work unit incentive systems. If they are accountable for their unit's performance, they need to control the tools that influence employee behavior.

Managers and supervisors also have a better understanding of the situation in their units, their subordinates' individual circumstances and career aspirations, and their relative contribution to the unit's success. The employee relations philosophy that emerged from the period when unionization was an ongoing threat made consistent treatment an overriding concern. This orientation has begun to change over the past few years as the recession prompted many employers to look for ways to control or reduce fixed payroll costs and to introduce financial incentives. A rapidly growing number of employers have recently introduced individual, team, or work unit incentives that will generate unequal payouts even within small operating units.

In this evolving context, managers and supervisors need increased control over the reward system. It makes little sense to maintain centralized control of the rewards if the plans and programs are soundly designed and budgeted at appropriate levels. In this era of "nanosecond management," day-to-day program administration is best delegated to managers and supervisors who fully understand local organizational needs. When managers understand the program objectives and the potential consequences of their decisions, they should be fully capable of managing the pay of their subordinates within budget constraints. Compensation specialists can continue to play what is essentially a consulting role to help managers deal with pay problems, but final authority must remain with line managers.

Suggestions for Designing and Maintaining an Effective Base-Pay Program

Base-pay programs should be considered in terms of their impact on the organization. The cost is of course an important consideration. However, since the labor market dictates pay levels, it is the deviation from market levels that is a key policy issue and warrants in-depth consideration. The program also has the potential to influence the working behavior of every covered employee. This warrants continuing top management attention and ongoing efforts to assess and enhance its effectiveness. If there is any truth to the axiom "You get what you pay for," the link to the business strategy should be an important management concern.

Important new concepts may strengthen a wage and salary program. A number of these concepts are not yet fully tested. The high level of interest in them is surprising in light of their limited track record but points to dissatisfaction with traditional programs. It is probably appropriate to proceed cautiously, with careful consideration of the possible ramifications. All employees can be expected to react to a new pay program, and it is difficult for management to back off a newly implemented program that proves disastrous.

Compensation programs are best viewed as management systems that must be designed to fit the organization, its value system, and its compensation strategy. Not only does the pay program represent a significant cost item, but it can also be used to provide an incentive to meet organizational goals. Management must decide what it wants to accomplish and then link the pay program to the achievement of the objectives.

The compensation program is of course only one component of the reward system, which can be broadly defined to include anything awarded or presented by management that is perceived by a recipient to have value. Cash compensation is the most obvious, but almost anything can be a reward, from a pat on the back to the golden bananas awarded by a company mentioned in the now-classic book *In Search of Excellence* (Peters and Waterman, 1982). Management should consciously assess the existing reward system and decide if the events that trigger rewards are consistent with the business strategy.

The reward system exists, whether understood and manipulated by management or not. Somehow the organization manages to bestow the benefits of the organization on employees, even if it is done unsystematically. People are promoted, moved to new offices, given new titles or new responsibilities, recognized with favorable comments from managers—organizational life goes on. The key is to ensure that the rewards are granted to employees contributing to the organization's success.

Reward systems continually send messages to employees: "This is what we in management value. This is what we want you to do." Undesirable behaviors that are rewarded are more likely to be repeated. Company communication efforts can influence the employees' view of the pay program, but employees will ordinarily pay more attention to management's statements and behavior. When employees learn what they need to do to be in line for rewards, they will likely act in their own best interests.

No one understands the existing reward system better than employees and supervisors. They have a useful, practical understanding of how the formal and informal systems function as well as an important perspective on company policies and practices. They know how well the formal system is functioning. And if they do not understand an aspect of the policy or an existing practice, it is evidence that the program has not been adequately communicated.

Although it has not been part of the tradition in designing wage and salary programs, in today's climate, with the emphasis on empowerment, it makes sense to involve employees and supervisors in assessing and designing pay programs. The assessment can be done through focus groups or surveys. In both situations, the questions should relate to an evaluation of what is and what should be. In light of the purpose—to change or influence employee performance—it is only reasonable to explore their perceptions of how to make the program more effective.

If supervisors or workers are to be involved in designing a new program or developing changes for the current program, they must first be made to understand the organization's needs, management's goals, any program constraints such as funding, and the alternative program concepts. Salary management is not rocket science, so no more than a meeting or two should be required before they are ready to consider and evaluate possible program changes.

The prospect of employee involvement would be alien in some environments and expected in others. If the organization subscribed to the empowerment philosophy, employees could demand to be involved. Employees can be trusted as long as they know the rules.

There are decided advantages in carving out a role for employees. First, the members of the task force can be expected to accept and embrace the new program. They will support and defend it in discussions with co-workers. Second, they will understand and communicate both the efforts involved in designing the program and the management's goals for the new program as it emerges. They represent a credible and dependable source of information and are certainly more likely to be trusted than management. Finally, the resulting program will reflect the employees' view of the problem and the optimal solution, and they will work to ensure that the solution works. Despite the traditional reluctance to involve employees, there is little downside risk.

Pay programs are only as effective as they are perceived to be. Even the most technically sound programs will prove to be ineffective if they are misunderstood or seen as unfair by employees. The purpose again is to influence their view of the job and organization and to contribute to improved performance. That depends on how they view the program and their prospects.

The TQM emphasis on customers and their satisfaction is a useful philosophy for designing and maintaining any human resource program. Pay programs should be responsive to the needs of managers and employees. Employees and managers have somewhat contradictory needs in that the former speak from the perspective of an employee and the latter seek help in accomplishing organizational goals. The realization that traditional salary programs were not meeting organizational needs led to the search for new program concepts.

Conclusion

Managing an employee's base pay involves several basic policy decisions. How are the overall program and the pay for this position going to be aligned with prevailing market pay levels? Do planned pay levels properly reflect the internal job hierarchy? Do we want to develop the program around the hierarchy? How are entry or starting salaries going to be determined? What is the rationale for determining annual or periodic salary increases? Is the program supportive of our career management plans? Is the program consistent with our employee relations philosophy?

Management has to be confident that the program represents an appropriate response to these questions. The problem is that the administration of the program involves decisions by supervisors and managers across the organization. That requires effective policies and procedures to ensure consistent administration. This must be balanced by sufficient flexibility to meet evolving organization needs. The need for balance is the heart of the program management problem.

References

Lawler, E. E., III. (1986). What's wrong with point-factor job evaluation. *Compensation and Benefits Review*, 18(2), 20–28.

Peters, T. J., and Waterman, R. H. (1982). *In Search of Excellence*. New York: HarperCollins.

Chapter Fifteen

Developmental Pay: Aligning Employee Capabilities with Business Needs

Richard W. Beatty, B. Nicholas Dimitroff, Dennis J. O'Neill

Workers have been paid primarily by time (hourly, daily, weekly, monthly, or annually) or by piece (from traditional piece-rate systems dating to biblical times to contemporary piece-rate systems for sewing machine operators, shoemakers, rock groups, concert pianists, and tennis pros). In the context of large, modern organizations, compensation is often determined by an incumbent's job or the title, which carries with it a "rate of pay." The efficacy of traditional pay practices is being questioned as large organizations confront rapidly changing environments and new ways of competing. Among the new forms of compensation created in response to these changes is the concept of developmental pay.

The philosophy and implementation of developmental pay are elaborations and expansions of certain elements of what has traditionally been called skill-based pay, a method of compensation to encourage skill acquisition or enhancement to accelerate employee efforts to meet current job requirements. In skill-based pay systems, work is often aggregated into "skill blocks," which may be thought of as expansions of a traditional job (see Figure 15.1). Each block represents a set of skills required to perform at a certain level. As the employee masters additional skill sets, pay is increased. The expansion of work may be horizontal or vertical, but the focus is on the skill required to perform the tasks in a current assignment or job. The philosophy of developmental pay is to develop employees beyond the here and now of narrow job descriptions to develop a more flexible, broadly focused, customer- and future-oriented

Figure 15.1. Skill-Based Pay.

Skill Variety

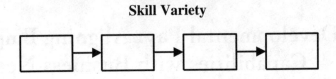

Job Skill Blocks

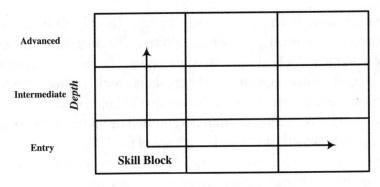

Breadth

workforce. Employees are encouraged to become active learners who continuously improve themselves and the organization, whose horizons are broader than merely getting "up to speed" to meet current performance requirements.

The shortcomings of skill-based pay in many organizations became more apparent as various team-oriented approaches were introduced, often reflecting the traditional top-down focus. Each team member had a specific job title and performed only the tasks required in a position's job description. In some organizations, employees resisted performing work outside their job description ("It's not my job"); in others, employees acquired a virtual monopoly on specific tasks under the illusion that possessing a narrow competency would provide job security. At a minimum, team members were trained to back one another up, an obvious advantage in the event of absenteeism, tardiness, or turnover. But as competition grew more intense, employers and employees in a growing number of organizations discovered that this notion of a team was insufficient. Narrowness was expensive and inflexible and put organizations at a competitive disadvantage against organizations possessing more supple workforces, as often found in high-performance work teams. Employers wanted to encourage a broader set of competencies in the workforce, to foster an overarching competency of "learning how to learn." Organizations began to realize that, ultimately, the only source of security is the customer and that to survive and thrive, the workforce had to become better positioned to meet changing customer needs. The advantage for employees would be increased mastery of skills and competencies and expanded career opportunities.

Developmental pay is focused on something deeper than specific work results and task-related skills in the current job. Developmental pay is rooted in the answers to two fundamental questions: What do we *really* want from our workforce, and what are we willing to pay for? The responses generally fall under the rubric of the "five C's": contribution, competency growth, creativity, collaboration, and commitment. The five C's are broader than the skills required to permit current job performance. Figure 15.2 illustrates that work actually produced is not only a function of an individual's successfully performing a set of tasks that requires special abilities, such as hand-eye coordination, spatial relations, or intelligence or learned skills (knowledge through experience and the like), but also a function of overarching competencies that facilitate task performance—the five C's. Developmental pay focuses especially on employee growth, creativity, and collaboration to enable the development of a fungible and flexible workforce.

Developmental pay systems often share components of skill-based pay, but they tend to home in on identifying *future* competencies required by an organization irrespective of job title. Such

Figure 15.2. The Iceberg of Competencies.

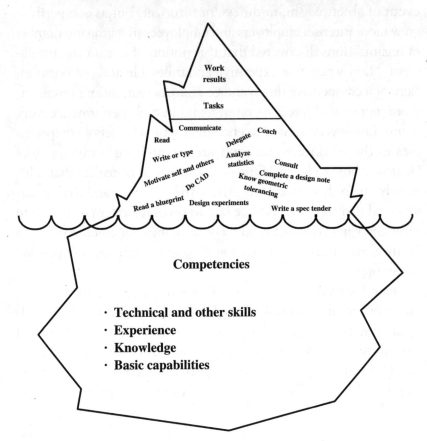

systems center on preparing an organization to respond to environmental contingencies and strategic initiatives through its existing workforce in ways that are faster, of higher quality, more cost-effective, and more customized than those of its competition. Developmental pay, then, is the embodiment of the popular concept of human resources as a competitive advantage (Pfeffer, 1994), not an expense to bring employees up to speed to meet current requirements but an investment in building a world-class workforce to create a world-class organization that can win in its markets and sustain its competitive position through world-class human resources over time.

Let us examine the competitive notions that undergird developmental pay plans—the five C's—and their implications.

The concept of *contribution* is broadened beyond traditional work results to consider whether the value added by each employee augments the organization's competitive advantage in the marketplace. In intensely competitive environments, employee contribution is seen as *only* what the customer is willing to pay for. If an organization is not smart enough to provide *only* such work and to remove work that adds no value, it will ultimately fail. Thus an important aspect of developmental pay is devoted to identifying and removing non-value-added work, expanding and enhancing work that customers presently value, and collecting intelligence on what customers may value in the near term. This is a very different way of thinking about work and has profound implications for such traditional human resource practices as job descriptions, performance measurement, and rewards. Most job descriptions are historical, based on how people use their time, energies, and efforts at work. Developmental pay attempts to take the focus off history—what work *was* valued or how things *were* done—and put it on designing work (not jobs) around the customer's requirements and identifying the core work of greatest value to the customer. All noncore work should be eliminated unless it is required by a regulatory body or is in some way supportive of a firm's core competencies. The philosophy also brings employees into the process of determining the "right" work. Involving employees requires of them a very different level of competency and mind-set to facilitate breaking vertical barriers in organizations (flatter organizational structures) as well as horizontal barriers to understanding a customer's (internal or external) requirements and how the customer measures suppliers' performance. Such employees are oriented to include their customers' viewpoint in the measurement of their own contribution.

Competency growth relates to winning and keeping customers—

what it takes to be world-class at present and to sustain the highest levels of performance into the future. Not only must every process and system continuously improve, but also, more important, every individual must grow. Competency growth is the building of broad-based knowledge and skill sets to respond optimally in meeting the customer's changing needs. It involves providing what customers value in unique and different ways so that an organization can distinguish itself from the competition, not merely survive but thrive in its chosen markets, and force its competition continually to react to its initiatives. Thus employees must become flexible, active learners and must continuously improve and expand their skills and competencies to meet, if not exceed, customer requirements.

The *creativity* envisioned goes beyond enhancing individual competencies to enhancing the processes and systems required to produce at higher levels and provide more unique outputs for customers. Thus processes and systems must be fashioned to foster a workforce that has the opportunity to think "out of the box" in new and different ways, continually question the value of work, and use customer intelligence to discover unique methods to delight customers before such ideas have crystallized in the customer's mind (Handy, 1990; 1994). Creativity requires a climate and a culture in which innovation is not merely tolerated but actually venerated, where critical questions are explored nondefensively and enthusiastically.

Collaboration takes on added importance in building future world-class organizations. In an environment more and more dependent on teams—especially transitory teams—the ability to engage immediately and collaborate with others is absolutely essential. Collaboration requires basic skills, such as good oral and written communication, providing support and help to one another, sharing information and resources candidly and openly, and articulating customer requirements in terms that can be understood and operationalized by others. Collaboration also requires interfacing and working with the customer and building relationships more aptly characterized as partnerships—sharing information, risks, and rewards. By helping their customers win, firms come to recognize that true competitive advantage lies not in merely satisfying customers but in making them successful in *every* interaction with the company. This requires a strategic unity (Ulrich, 1990) with the customer and the utmost collaboration within and throughout an organization and thus necessitates the breaking of vertical and horizontal barriers. Organizations must identify members of a work group who are essential to enhance change efforts or to deliver new processes. Only individuals who effectively model the collaborative spirit and its associated behaviors can survive in the most competitive organizations of the future.

If organizations work at developing contribution, competency growth, creativity, and collaboration in their workforce, the result should enhance the *commitment* of the workforce, developing employees who will remain with the organization and serve it well for many years. Whether or not this occurs depends not only on employee satisfaction but also on employee success within the organization, a concept that parallels the objective of developing customer success (Schlesinger and Heskett, 1991). Employee success requires meeting employee needs through the sense of self-worth that comes from making a contribution, the ego fulfillment that comes from competency growth, the excitement generated through creativity and innovation, and the gratification of collaboration in a collective effort. If these can be realized, obtaining committed employees may follow.

Developmental Pay Plans

Organizations need systems and processes to ensure contribution, competency growth, creativity, collaboration, and commitment in the workforce. Rewards and recognition systems should reinforce such accomplishments. The consequences for employees for achieving organizational objectives, if not substantial, will create perceptions of inequity and can stunt the developmental growth of the workforce. We will examine some of the systems used by organizations to motivate developmental growth in their employees. The discussion starts with traditional skill-based concepts and moves to examples of newer, sometimes more elaborate developmental pay systems. This will be followed by an exploration of the reward and recognition consequences associated with developmental growth.

Traditional skill-based pay systems resemble the examples in Exhibit 15.1 from a recently opened General Electric plant. GE's skill-based pay approach emphasizes learning basic skill requirements to "get up to speed," perhaps with off-line educational experiences, such as GEDs, technical courses, or directly related college courses or special seminars, and even extends to learning to speak a job-related foreign language. Such systems are described as primarily vertical, with the employee essentially climbing a ladder to meet the requirements of an existing job title. For each step in the ladder, compensation is provided.

Such jobs may be compensated horizontally as well, as was done by the integrated horizontal and vertical compensation system of a financial services institution in the Midwest in its "learning a living" approach. In this system, once individuals reach a particular level, say, Secretary I, they can begin to expand horizontally to meet Secretary II requirements; once the Secretary II requirements are met, they can move on to meet Secretary III requirements, and so on. Thus employees move up and over in a pattern in some respects more accurately described as diagonal than horizontal. In other words, there may be limited supervisory responsibilities such as training and coaching others (vertical movement), but most of the growth is greater depth of skill in a specialty or function.

In both examples of skill-based pay systems, the primary focus is on enabling near-term employee contribution rather than competency growth, collaboration, creativity, or commitment. Of course, a focus on skill growth does not imply that broader

Exhibit 15.1. Pay Progression, Segment II.

Materials Management (New Employee)	Minimum Qualifications: Attainment of skill level 9 in Production Control
Voluntary Progress Pay Rate	
Skill Level 10	Entry level
Skill Level 11	Complete 6 months OJT, receive no unsatisfactory performance appraisal, and complete Information Systems course
Skill Level 12	Complete 6 months OJT, receive no unsatisfactory performance appraisal, and complete Material Requirements Planning course
Skill Level 13	Complete 6 months OJT, receive no unsatisfactory performance appraisal, and complete Problem Solving and Decision Making course
Skill Level 14	Complete 6 months OJT, receive no unsatisfactory performance appraisal, and complete Production Management course
Skill Level 15	To be determined

Technician (New Employee)	Minimum Qualifications: Attainment of skill level 9 in Electronic Technology
Voluntary Progress Pay Rate	
Skill Level 10	Entry level
Skill Level 11	Complete 6 months OJT, receive no unsatisfactory performance appraisal, and complete Hydraulics and Pneumatics course
Skill Level 12	Complete 6 months OJT, receive no unsatisfactory performance appraisal, and complete Electronics II course
Skill Level 13	Complete 6 months OJT, receive no unsatisfactory performance appraisal, and complete Problem Solving and Decision Making course
Skill Level 14	Complete 6 months OJT, receive no unsatisfactory performance appraisal, and complete Communications Systems course
Skill Level 15	To be determined

employee growth is not taking place, but competency growth is not the intent or the target of system design. For example, collaborative skills are often a component of a skill-based pay system, especially when employees are part of a process performed collectively. But creativity may be somewhat limited by such semirigid approaches because the employee's focus may be on the relatively short-term financial gain for task mastery rather than creativity in meeting customer service demands.

Some developmental pay systems may be primarily horizontal, as shown in a proposed system from Honda (Exhibit 15.2). The system is designed to ensure basic competencies to meet the requirements of several jobs so as to maximize the interchangeability of the workforce. This approach is similar to one used by Nissan in Europe, shown in Figure 15.3. An *I* represents a beginner in a particular job, an *L* represents someone who is becoming competent, a *U* represents someone who is fully competent, and a square represents someone who is not only fully competent but also able to teach others the job. In this system, individuals may move horizontally or vertically to acquire competencies that fit their growth needs and learning objectives *and* the organization's competency growth requirements, as determined in consultation with the team leader. Employees may even pursue several competencies simultaneously. Such a system is particularly advantageous when there is considerable day-to-day variability in the work that must be performed. With a multiskilled workforce, work activities for a unit or team will vary according to different customer requirements. A unit or team would be assessed for its flexibility and resources allocated to different skill blocks that enable the organization to meet a given day's production demand. This is truly a fungible workforce, in which the effort is not simply to get people up to speed to meet job requirements but to meet the requirements of ever-changing customer demands.

The benefits of these two systems are manifold. Not only do they increase the potential of employee contribution, but, more

Exhibit 15.2. General Capability Factors: Supervisory/Management-Level Chart.

Level / Factor	Level 1 Team Leader	Level 2 Supervising Coordinator	Level 3 Assistant Manager	Level 4 Manager	Level 5 Senior Manager
Planning and Organizing Projecting needs and requirements and developing appropriate courses of action for self and others to accomplish objectives.	Plans and prioritizes own work within context of team or group objectives.	Plans and prioritizes own and others' work within context of departmental objectives.	Plans and prioritizes own and others' work by seeking out needs and requirements of other departments; applies judgment in balancing conflicting needs.	Plans and prioritizes own and others' work by weighing and balancing conflicting needs for all operations.	Has capability to develop strategic plans and priorities.
Adaptability/ Flexibility Modifying behaviors in response to change; effectiveness in performing work under varying conditions; open-minded approach to situations; coping with unforeseen emergencies.	Minimal flexibility required because most circumstances within scope of own control.	Must adapt to changing priorities and requirements from customers or clients.	Must be proactive in anticipating conflicting needs and priorities and developing contingency plans for changing conditions and circumstances.	Capable of seeing big picture and evaluating the total effects of change.	Change agent for company in response to fluctuating worldwide market and economic circumstances.

Exhibit 15.2. (cont.)

Level / Factor	Level 1 Team Leader	Level 2 Supervising Coordinator	Level 3 Assistant Manager	Level 4 Manager	Level 5 Senior Manager
Leadership/ Mentoring/ Influence Others Influencing others to strive toward accomplishment by sharing know-how, encouragement, and guidance with other associates.	Minimal leadership required due to task focus of job; teaches others how to do his or her tasks and processes and how to organize priorities.	Effects behavior change in others by example; teaches planning/problem solving; explains application of policy and procedures to area of expertise.	Shares knowledge of organizational dynamics at all levels to help associates get things done; shares deeper expertise gained through experience.	Develops broader awareness and understanding of how areas of business interrelate; shares this broader perspective with all associates.	Offers vision for future of the organization and direction for how to accomplish and attain strategic goals.
Problem Analysis/ Solving Diagnosing and evaluating alternative courses of action and developing appropriate counter-measures to control or eliminate undesirable causal factors.	Diagnoses problems and develops effective countermeasures to problems related to own job processes.	Diagnoses problems and develops effective countermeasures for department systems.	Utilizes potential problem analysis to anticipate and prevent problems that may result along interface between departments.	Anticipates potential problems and risk and develops systematic countermeasures to control or reduce disruptive effect.	Anticipates potential problems and risks throughout operations and initiates strategic action to minimize the effect.

Exhibit 15.2. (cont.)

Level / Factor	Level 1 Team Leader	Level 2 Supervising Coordinator	Level 3 Assistant Manager	Level 4 Manager	Level 5 Senior Manager
Judgment/ Decision Making Crystallizing main issues, concerns, and alternative choices; weighing the benefits and costs associated with them and following through to reach final decision.	Makes decisions from application of established policy and procedural guidelines; capable of some narrow policy interpretation.	Develops new policy and procedural considerations from company principles and values; interprets existing policy and procedure to apply to new or unusual circumstances.	Evaluates policies/ procedures for completeness, currency, and consistency with organizational principles and values; drafts new policy guidelines to direct or control company activity.	Makes decisions and establishes policy that significantly impact organization's competitive or strategic position.	Anticipates potential strategic decisions that may greatly impact competitiveness and profitability.
Interpersonal Communication Expressing ideas both orally and in writing by preparing reports, making formal presentations, and keeping others informed.	Generates reports and makes formal presentations related to own job or team activities.	Develops and presents information related to analysis of interdepartmental concerns or activities.	Develops and presents information related to analysis of interdepartmental concerns and activities to associates at all levels and from all areas.	Develops and presents company-wide announcements and position statements related to policy and procedural matters.	Develops and presents announcements and position statements related to strategic matters.

Exhibit 15.2. (cont.)

Level / Factor	Level 1 Team Leader	Level 2 Supervising Coordinator	Level 3 Assistant Manager	Level 4 Manager	Level 5 Senior Manager
Interdepartmental Cooperation/ Teamwork Participating in group activities to achieve mutual objectives; responding to, cooperating with, and covering for other associates toward mutual job accomplishment.	Cooperates with and covers for other associates in team or group.	Is proactive in anticipating needs of other associates in department and accepts mutual responsibility.	Routinely anticipates needs and concerns of other areas; looks for ways to facilitate process changes/ improvements to help organization be more responsive to customer expectations.	Habitually anticipates changing needs of customers/client organizations and acts as example and advocate for organizational consensus building and cooperation at all levels.	Decision-making process exemplifies consensus building with all levels of associates and customer and client organizations.
Technical/ Professional Competence Demonstrating specialized job knowledge and requisite skills and applying them appropriately.	Demonstrates knowledge and capability typical for entry level.	Demonstrates greater depth of understanding and breadth of application in field of specialty; has demonstrated capability in many department area functions.	Demonstrates broad theoretical understanding and application of expertise to business situations; thoroughly understands most of departmental functions.	Demonstrates "state of the art" command of specialized field of expertise.	Possesses companywide recognition as expert in business or professional discipline.

Figure 15.3. Job Design Model Based on Employee Development
and Job Allocation Requirements.

Job Name	A	B	C	D	E
Jerry	I	I	☐	L	U
Jan	U	L	I	I	L
Sam	U	U	U	I	☐
Glen	I	I	L	☐	L
Terry	I	U	I	L	U
Nicky	I	U	☐	U	L

I = beginner; L = employee with minimum proficiency; U = employee with complete
efficiency; ~ = employee qualified to develop and train others.

important, they also explicitly stress the collaborative aspects of
work and incorporate the necessity for supervisors to know the skill
and competency level of each employee as well as to understand
their explicit responsibility to develop employees. Creativity may
also be enhanced, especially when flexibility is provided, as in the
Nissan system (Figure 15.3), because employees have an opportunity to experience unique combinations of skill and competency
requirements. This provides the organization with flexibility but
also allows employees to experiment with task combinations that
break rigid paradigms of how work should be done. Thus the
employee may be able to improve work, perhaps even redesign the
job itself. When such designs are combined with a horizontal
approach to work design that includes customers, the work may

actually be reallocated across customer-supplier boundaries in unique ways that enhance the competitive advantage of both firms.

The example from Intel Corporation (Figure 15.4) resembles the Honda system in that it begins to expand jobs horizontally and vertically by stressing the components of a high-performance organization, namely, the movement toward self-directed or, in Intel's terminology, self-sustaining work teams and ultimately to self-managing work teams. Self-sustaining work teams are concerned with maintenance of quality and process improvement; the scope of the self-management stage includes scheduling and staffing decisions— in other words, empowered work teams. Self-directed work teams have managers who provide resources, team members who collaborate in carrying out a variety of activities, and technical experts who operate as advisers, teachers, and coaches for the team. Decisions are made primarily by empowered teams, and all information required to plan, schedule, and staff work is provided to the team (Wallace and Crandall, 1992). Intel's approach is a contemporary design that we expect to see adopted in many other organizations.

An even more sophisticated and challenging design is seen in the example from Du Pont shown in Exhibit 15.3. Du Pont's objective was to push far beyond existing requirements by building and sustaining a world-class technical workforce. Du Pont had found itself with a number of senior scientists who had not grown as customer demands had shifted. This presented Du Pont with a very difficult business decision: what to do with senior scientists, employees originally envisioned as mentors to junior scientists but whose skill levels were exceeded by those of their mentees? Should the company reinvest in these senior scientists and bring them up to world-class levels by sending them back to universities to re-earn a Ph.D., or should it start from scratch by raiding college campuses for the very best scientific brain power? More important, how could the organization keep this situation from recurring? The resulting system was designed to pay for the development of scientists through a progression system as opposed to a promotion system. In other

Figure 15.4. Skill and Competency Evolution.

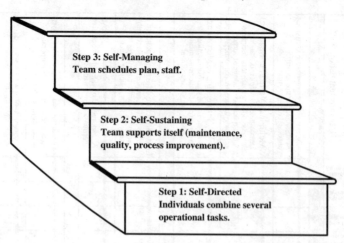

words, a job vacancy did not have to occur for scientists to enhance their competencies and be compensated for doing so.

Du Pont's matrix gives no explicit attention to performance (contribution); the emphasis is on competency growth, as one would expect given the rationale for its design. Du Pont's system is designed to stretch scientists to the limits of their scientific capability, culminating in the level of Departmental Fellow. The approach also makes explicit recognition of collaborative and creative growth essential for progression and subsequent pay treatment.

Nissan Motor's research and development system shares common aspects with Du Pont's but also adds unique elements that grow out of differing circumstances. Nissan R&D is charged with designing vehicles for the North American market, and although technical and research skills are a critical component, the organization operates in a different environment than Du Pont does. In the United States, Nissan, a Japanese firm, is attempting to develop world-class engineering and design skills in a foreign country and has had to grapple with cultural issues as well. The goal was to design a pay system to operate in a country where it might not always have the opportunity of selecting the best brain power and

Exhibit 15.3. Guideline Attribute Matrix.

	Engineer (3)	Process Engineer (3A)	Area/Development Scientist/Engr/Chemist (4)	R&D Scientist/Engineer/Chemist (4A)	Senior Scientist/Engineer/Chemist (5)	Research/Engineering Associate (5A)	Senior Research/Engineering Associate (6)	Research Engineering/Fellow (6A)	Senior Research/Engineering Fellow (7)	Departmental Fellow (7A)
KNOW-HOW										
DEPTH *How well you know it*	(Basic — Knowledge consistent with a current technical BE/MS degree									Extensive) — Recognized for this expertise outside the corporation
BREADTH *How many areas are you proficient in*	(Single Focus — Knowledge of a single science/ technology focus; basic understanding of general science/ technology business and economic principles									Multiple & Varied/Far Reaching) — Demonstrated excellent understanding & application of a multiple of disciplines & the application of advanced science/ technology business & economic principles
INTERPERSONAL RELATIONS *How effectively you communicate the above*	(Basic — Basic courtesy; basic interpersonal skills/good team player									Influencing & Motivating) — Motivates others across functions & across corporation; communicates effectively with management
PROBLEM SOLVING										
THINKING ENVIRONMENT *Degree of independence & breadth of environment*	(Most Structure Least Independence — Successfully completes projects with some guidance									Least Structure Most Independence) — Successfully completes projects with minimal guidance; contributes to setting division policy & direction
THINKING CHALLENGE *Degree of complexity and creativity called for*	(Least — Effectively solves routine problems									Most) — A track record of valuable, innovative contributions to business
ACCOUNTABILITY										
FREEDOM TO ACT *Latitude of actions within corporate ethical boundaries*	(Least — Operates well with supervisory guidance									Most) — Acts effectively across corporate & department boundaries
MAGNITUDE *Size of individual's sphere of influence*	(Low — Responsible for a narrow, well-defined area of focus									High) — Responsible for division level programs
IMPACT *Degree of direct influence*	(Most Direct — Direct impact in a narrow, well-defined area of focus									Indirect) — A documented record of highly valuable business impact

comprehending differing traditions, history, and so on. In addition, the Japanese believe in the continuous improvement not only of all systems and processes but also of all employees. Thus for philosophic reasons, Nissan R&D wanted a system to improve *everyone*, giving rise to the development of a system that includes *all* technical, secretarial, managerial, and other positions. This is a very different human resource strategy from one focused on core competencies alone. It is an attempt to build world-class competencies in *all* aspects where competition may be possible. The expectation is not only that everyone must contribute but also that everyone must grow continuously. The compensation system is designed to support that philosophy.

Nissan's system emphasizes competency growth and creativity. Each employee is rewarded separately for competency growth annually and receives special compensation when moving from one level to another. Contribution is rewarded through the traditional performance appraisal process: competency growth review and compensation treatment are part of a separate process at a different point during the year.

Conclusion

Developmental pay compensation systems offer several benefits. First, they force an organization to focus on its primary source of competitive advantage—human resources—and forecast *future* competencies required to win increasingly competitive markets, a process very similar to strategic planning efforts for other organizational resources. Second, an organization that wishes to compete on speed, flexibility, and quality soon finds that it cannot simply "buy" a workforce already imbued with the "five C's" but rather must grow it, leading to a new regard for human resources (at least in staffing core competencies) not as a commodity but as a resource that must be challenged and nourished. Third, to make prudent decisions concerning human resources requires some means of assessing broader competency growth; a method to ensure feedback is given to employees, and appropriate teaching and coaching efforts are deployed. Fourth, growth for its own sake may motivate employees in the short term, but it soon loses its motivational impact. Thus the recognition and reward system must be revisited to ensure that what is valued and enhanced is accurately and adequately rewarded. Finally, such systems must foster more prudent management of the organization's human resources. Managers must be educated to regard their responsibility to human resources with the same sense of fiduciary duty they demonstrate toward the company's financial assets. The investment in high-value-added human resources must be assessed from a financial standpoint to ensure that the risk-adjusted return is optimized. Managers must thus be much better assessors of human talent both over the short term and over the long term. Only by becoming proficient at some system to measure, value, and reward competency growth can managers gain and sustain competitive advantage in the marketplace.

References

Handy, C. B. (1990). *The Age of Unreason*. Cambridge, Mass.: Harvard Business School Press.

Handy, C. B. (1994). *The Age of Paradox*. Cambridge, Mass.: Harvard Business School Press.

Pfeffer, J. (1994). *Competitive Advantage Through People: Unleashing the Power of the Workforce*. Cambridge, Mass.: Harvard Business School Press.

Schlesinger, L. A., and Heskett, J. L. (1991). The service-driven company. *Harvard Business Review*, 69(5), 71–81.

Ulrich, D. (1990). *Organizational Capability: Competing from the Inside Out*. New York: Wiley.

Wallace, M. J., Jr., and Crandall, N. F. (1992). Winning in the age of execution: The central role of work-force effectiveness. *ACA Journal*, 1(2), 30–47.

Chapter Sixteen

Group Incentives: Improving Performance Through Shared Goals and Rewards

John G. Belcher, Jr.

The practice of management has changed dramatically over the past decade. As the momentum for change continues to gather, the roles of management and the employee are being fundamentally redefined.

- It would be hard to find a company that has not incorporated into its lexicon such phrases as "cultural change," "employee involvement," "empowerment," "self-direction," or a hundred other variations.
- Entire layers of management have been removed, leaving front-line workers to pick up many of their former supervisors' responsibilities.
- Teams are slowly but surely replacing individuals as the fundamental work unit in organizations.
- Management and unions pursue "partnerships" in which the two parties agree to develop nontraditional relationships with a focus on increasing performance and competitiveness.

The common theme is maximum teamwork, minimum bureaucracy, and continuous improvement to ensure survival in a world economy. These outcomes in turn require a common-fate mentality and a joint effort by all parties to maximize the performance of the organization.

These efforts represent strategic change initiatives, as their objectives involve nothing less than a fundamental restructuring of organizational philosophy, policies, and practices. The desired outcome is a reengineered organization that is lean and mean, focused from top to bottom on key business objectives, and adaptive to change. This transformation is viewed by those pursuing it as critical to their future success. In many cases, the organization's very survival is at stake.

The Role of Alternative Rewards in Supporting Change

Managers understanding these initiatives to transform the organization's culture eventually learn a fact that is well known to change experts: new behaviors will not become ingrained unless all organizational systems are aligned with the management philosophy and reinforce the desired behaviors.

Of all the systems that need to be brought into alignment, the reward system is among the most important. Reward systems send a strong signal about management priorities and reinforce desired behaviors. After all, people do what they are rewarded for doing. It would be unrealistic to expect people to adopt certain behaviors if the organization's reward system reinforced a different set of behaviors.

Unfortunately, our traditional reward systems fail the test of alignment with the principles underlying high-commitment, high-involvement organizations. Base pay is fixed and tied to rigid job classifications. Merit increases are doled out to salaried employees in a way that does little to differentiate performance. For workers paid by the hour, increased pay basically comes with inflation, longevity, and seniority. For the vast majority of employees, there is virtually no link between pay and organizational performance. There is no incentive for employees to take the initiative to improve the performance of the business.

It is therefore not surprising that the growth in nontraditional or alternative reward systems in recent years has paralleled the growth in organizational change initiatives. New management philosophies require new reward systems. Whatever behaviors our traditional reward systems reinforce, they are not the behaviors required to be a world-class competitor.

Of the variety of alternative reward system options, *gain sharing* probably has the broadest application and is one of the most effective when designed and implemented properly. Gain sharing will be broadly defined here as any variable-pay system that supports an employee involvement process by rewarding the members of a group or an organization for improvements on predetermined measures of organizational performance. This definition encompasses other commonly used terms such as *variable compensation* and *group incentives*.

Our definition contains some key distinctions. Gain sharing is a *group* reward system and therefore focuses on teamwork in the pursuit of business objectives rather than on individual performance. Because it rewards performance improvement (or, alternatively, the achievement of goals), it is a *self-funding* pay system that reinforces continuous improvement. It requires a predetermined *formula* to provide a clear focus on the appropriate performance variables and to increase employee trust by taking management discretion out of the system.

Perhaps most important, gain sharing supports a participative management process. The research findings are clear: the risk of failure is great when gain sharing is implemented in a traditional, autocratic organization that is not pursuing an improvement process designed to increase employee commitment, participation, and teamwork. By this definition, gain sharing isn't gain sharing unless it is used as an organizational change vehicle.

All of this, of course, raises questions about an organization's readiness for gain sharing. We will address that issue after some discussion of practical matters relating to the design of gain-sharing systems.

Who Participates?

The first challenge faced by designers of gain-sharing plans is to define the boundaries of the participating group. This decision is normally addressed first because we cannot proceed with the design process until we have identified the participants in the plan. For example, how can we intelligently establish measures if we do not know whose behavior we are trying to change?

There are really two decisions here. The first relates to the breadth of coverage. It is not uncommon to find gain-sharing programs that apply only to the hourly or nonexempt workforce (or the bargaining unit in a unionized organization), particularly in plans that were developed a few years ago. This decision usually stems from a felt need to focus involvement and improvement activities on the lower tiers of the organization or from a perception that salaried compensation systems must somehow be separate and different from those of the hourly workforce.

This logic, however, fails to stand up to scrutiny. If the purpose of gain sharing is (as it should be) to foster greater involvement and teamwork, how can we leave out a substantial portion of the workforce? Does employee involvement apply only to the hourly or union worker? How can we convince employees that we want a team-oriented organization when we maintain different reward systems for different groups?

The more likely decision today with respect to gain-sharing participation is to include all employees in a given organizational unit, with the possible exception of senior management. The exclusion of senior managers is often justified on the basis that their pay should be tied to broader financial measures and that their compensation should have a much higher variable component than is appropriate for front-line workers. This exclusion should involve only a small number of people, and it should be ensured that the gain-sharing program and the executive pay systems are mutually reinforcing.

An all-inclusive gain-sharing program sends the message that we are all working toward the same objectives, regardless of level or pay classification, and that our collective fate is tied to the success of the business.

The second decision with regard to group boundaries is perhaps a more difficult one: should all employees be covered under a single gain-sharing formula, or should there be a separate formula for each department or team? The latter option is often referred to as *small group incentives* and at first glance appears to offer significant advantages over the one-formula-covers-all option.

The obvious benefit of small group incentives is that the reward is tied more closely to the individual's efforts. Clearly, an employee will feel that he or she has more impact on a gain-sharing formula as one of twenty-five people being measured by the formula than as one of five hundred people being measured.

This advantage is gained, however, only at the expense of some significant trade-offs:

- The participants' focus will be on the performance of their teams rather than on the performance of the overall organization. This can lead to poor interfaces between teams and lack of concern for the impact of one team's behaviors on another team's performance. Thus the organization's performance may be *suboptimized*.

- The *complications* associated with both the design and the ongoing administration of the system are considerably increased.

- There will inevitably be *perceptions of inequity* due to differentials in payoffs among teams. Teams that consistently receive poor payouts can be expected to find fault with the system and withdraw their support from the gain-sharing program.

In view of these potentially serious problems, the small group incentive approach should probably not be undertaken unless the organization is very large or there is little interdependency between teams or bonus groups. For an organization containing a few hundred people or less, the all-inclusive formula probably makes more sense.

The Gain-Sharing Formula

The heart of any gain-sharing system is the formula, the measure or measures whereby the relevant improvements in performance are quantified. Formula decisions should not be taken lightly, for they will set the agenda for employee improvement activities.

Consequently, it is critically important that the formula be customized to meet the needs of the business. There is an unfortunate tendency among designers of gain-sharing plans to adopt standardized approaches, such as the historic Scanlon Plan, or to implement, with minor modifications, formulas that have been developed elsewhere in the company or in the industry. Though it is understandably tempting to shortcut the design process and avoid the hard work associated with developing a formula from scratch, this behavior eliminates the opportunity to develop a system that creatively meets the unique needs of the business. There are no rules in gain-sharing system design (other than those dictated by common sense and legal requirements), and there is no need to stick with preestablished models.

Until recently, most gain-sharing formulas tended to be structured around measures of labor productivity or cost. Those oriented toward labor productivity typically used or modified existing productivity measures that are in widespread use in industry. These included measures such as units per hour or comparisons of earned hours (based on labor standards) to actual hours. Improvements in these measures could easily be translated into the number of labor hours saved, which in turn could be translated into dollar savings, which could then be shared.

Formulas that focus on costs—the second traditional option—

are popular because of the recognition that employee contributions are not limited to improvements in labor productivity. People can reduce waste of raw materials and supplies, conserve energy, and save on various categories of overhead costs. There are a wide variety of possible cost formulas; a common approach is called the *multicost ratio*. A simple form of the multicost ratio is presented in Table 16.1.

The starting point for the formula is sales (or, in manufacturing, sales value of production). An "allowed cost ratio" is determined for costs that are to be included in the formula (usually those that employees have at least some degree of influence over). Although this ratio is often derived from an analysis of previous years' cost performance, it could also represent the current year's budget assumptions or some other target. The allowed cost ratio is then multiplied by the actual sales in each payout period to obtain "allowed costs." All that remains to quantify the gain is to subtract the actual costs incurred. A predetermined company share is subtracted from this gain, leaving the employee share, which is then distributed to participants in some fashion.

In practice, multicost ratios are generally somewhat more complicated than the example shown in Table 16.1. For example, they often have a *deficit reserve*, which is a mechanism that serves to protect the company against paying gains that are later offset by losses.

Table 16.1. Multicost Ratio.

Sales	$1,000,000
Allowed costs (70%)	700,000
Less: Actual costs	− 640,000
	60,000
Less: Company share (60%)	− 36,000
Employee share	24,000

They may also have separate allowed cost ratios for different categories of costs, or there may be an attempt to deflate sales and costs.

Other variations on the cost theme are cost-per-unit formulas and costs versus budget. Whatever the precise formula construction, all such gain-sharing programs have the common theme of cost reduction or control.

Productivity and cost formulas are still very common today, and no one would deny their importance. But these formulas suffer from a serious shortcoming: they do not allow for the inclusion of non-cost variables that may be very important to the success of the business. These variables fall into several categories:

- *Quality.* The quality of products and services as delivered to the customer has important implications to the viability of most businesses.

- *Customer satisfaction.* This is one of the most critical non-cost issues for many companies; cost reduction cannot compensate for a failure to meet the needs of the customer. Quantitative indicators of customer satisfaction include percentage of delivery schedules met, number of customer complaints, response time to complaints, turnaround time in processing orders, customer retention, and customer survey results.

- *Safety.* Because industrial accidents carry costs, a safe workplace is a value that goes beyond the effect on the bottom line for most organizations.

- *Environmental compliance.* Reducing or eliminating environmental incidents carries a high priority in industries such as chemicals and petroleum.

- *Organizational change initiatives.* Total quality management (TQM), employee involvement, and work redesign are examples of change initiatives that could have strategic importance to the organization. It may well be appropriate to reward employees for their support and active involvement in these processes.

For the company that wishes to broaden the scope of its gain-sharing program beyond productivity and cost control, a formula approach called the *family of measures* may make sense. A family-of-measures formula is simply one that contains multiple measures. For example, a manufacturing plant might choose to measure productivity, scrap, customer returns, delivery performance, and safety in its gain-sharing program. A service business might measure cost per unit of service, service delivery time, and customer complaints. A gain or loss would be calculated for each of the measures independently, and these figures would then be aggregated to determine the bonus pool.

An instructive example is provided by a plant that manufactures components for the automobile and appliance industries; the elements of its formula are presented in Table 16.2. Three of the measures—productivity, supplies usage, and raw materials usage—are legitimate cost issues that could have been covered in

Table 16.2. Family of Measures.

Productivity:	$\dfrac{\text{Weighted units produced}}{\text{Total hours worked}}$
Quality:	% defective parts
Supplies usage:	$\dfrac{\text{Manufacturing supplies}}{\text{Sales}}$
Materials usage:	$\dfrac{\text{Raw materials}}{\text{Sales}}$
Schedule performance:	% delivery schedules met
Customer complaints:	Number of complaints received

a multicost ratio. However, they are much more explicit as performance issues in this system because they are not lumped together and lost in a single cost measure.

The quality measure is a different animal. Yes, an outcome of reduced product defects would be lower costs, which presumably would show up in a cost formula. However, the connection is not nearly as direct as it would be if it were measured separately, and not all employees would appreciate that a cost-oriented gain-sharing formula would be improved by lower defects. And it would be a mistake for any quality-oriented company to implement a gain-sharing program that did not clearly and explicitly reinforce quality performance.

As we continue down the list in Table 16.2, the link to costs becomes more and more tenuous. Failing to meet delivery schedules probably has few short-term cost implications, yet it represents a major customer satisfaction issue for many companies. Likewise for quality complaints: the effect on costs is minimal, but the implications for the long-term success of the business are great.

Of course, using noncost measures in a gain-sharing formula raises a new challenge: how do you place a dollar value on the improvements so as to be able to share the gains? There are several possible answers (including using purely arbitrary values); in the case under discussion, the plan designers chose to treat both schedule performance and quality complaints as *modifiers*. Rather than contribute dollars directly to the gain-sharing pool, they modify the pool that represents the aggregate gain from the other measures. Positive performance on the modifiers expands pool size; negative performance reduces or even eliminates the pool.

An interesting example of a family of measures in a service business is presented in Table 16.3. The company in question provides computerized payroll services to outside customers. With offices around the country providing these services, management chose to pilot gain sharing in one location to gain experience with this alternative reward system before implementing it elsewhere.

Table 16.3. Family of Measures: Service.

Cost per processing
Controllable expenses as % of revenues
Number of credits issued
Customer retention
Number of suggestions submitted

The first two measures shown in Table 16.3, cost per processing and controllable costs as a percentage of revenues, are straightforward cost measures and require no further elaboration. The other measures, however, are unusual and reflect the trend toward the use of creative indicators that are not necessarily tied to hard dollar savings.

It was a management requirement that the gain-sharing formula incorporate some measure of quality, and after much deliberation, the task force charged with designing the system selected *number of credits issued* to meet this need. The rationale for this unusual measure was as follows: when a credit is issued to a customer, it is almost always an indication that something has gone wrong. Perhaps the service as delivered did not meet the customer's requirements, or perhaps it was not quoted properly by the salesperson. The invoice itself may have been incorrect. Whatever the cause, the result is a service failure and an unhappy customer.

Any business can lose a customer to competition, but there are some additional challenges in this business. Any customer could choose to bring payroll processing in-house at any time, for example, if not satisfied with the cost or the service. Since it is obviously very costly to lose customers, the plan designers chose to include a measure of *customer retention* in the family of measures retained. If a lower percentage of customers is lost from year to year, the associated gains are added to the bonus pool.

The final measure does not reflect performance at all, in the traditional sense, but rather rewards employees for increasing their involvement in the improvement process itself. Using an existing companywide suggestion system as a vehicle, additional money was contributed to the bonus pool based on the *number of suggestions submitted*. Presumably, an increase in suggestions submitted would result in improved performance. To reinforce the importance of teamwork, only suggestions submitted by a team qualified for gain sharing.

This unique plan also used modifiers in a manner similar to that described in the earlier example. Of most interest is a *customer satisfaction* modifier. Based on a regular customer survey, the gain-sharing pool is increased or decreased, in 3 percent increments, on the basis of overall survey responses. In this way, a critical but highly intangible performance variable is clearly linked to employee pay.

A variation on the family-of-measures theme is a *goal-based system*. Also known as *goal sharing*, this approach differs in that in this case gains are not quantified and no pool is shared. Rather, a series of goals is established, and a fixed, predetermined amount is paid to employees for each goal achieved. For example, an organization might establish goals for productivity, quality, schedule performance, safety, and customer satisfaction, with each goal paying a 1 percent bonus for its achievement.

More elaborate forms of goal-sharing might have multiple levels of goals for each variable, with a predetermined number of points associated with each level. The bonus would be determined by multiplying the points by some fixed factor, such as 1/4 percent. These features greatly increase the flexibility of goal-based systems by providing a weighting system for the variables and allowing for proportional rewards based on good, better, and outstanding performance.

The principal advantage of the goal-based approach to the family of measures is its relative simplicity. The system designers are relieved of addressing such potentially complicated issues as how to value gains in financial terms and how to share the gain-sharing pool between the company and employees.

Another variation on the family-of-measures idea is what we call a *financially funded* family of measures. Here the multiple variables do not directly determine the payout level; rather, the size of the pool, and hence the potential payout, is a function of the performance of some cost or profitability measure. The role of the family of measures is to determine how much of the pool is actually paid out to employees.

Let's take a simple example. A company sets aside a certain percentage of profits for potential bonus payments. If this money were paid out without any other conditions, it would be a simple profit-sharing program. To increase employees' focus on controllable performance issues, however, the firm could set four organizational performance goals and tie 25 percent of the pool to the achievement of each goal.

Motorola adopted this approach as part of its Participative Management Program, a twenty-year effort to transform the company to a team-oriented, high-involvement organization. Each of its five business sectors establishes, on a semiannual basis, a bonus pool based on that sector's return on net assets (RONA). These pools are not distributed automatically, however; each sector is free to make the payout contingent on achieving other performance goals of its own choosing.

Another example of a financially funded system is that of a Michigan-based supplier to the auto industry. The potential bonus size, as a percentage of gross pay, is determined by a comparison of operating profits to the annual plan (see Table 16.4). Fifty percent of the potential bonus is paid automatically, with the remaining amount tied to the achievement of six goals, as follows: productivity (20 percent), scrap (20 percent), rework (20 percent), customer rejects (10 percent), safety (20 percent), and attendance (10 percent).

The financially funded approach has an advantage that is important to some companies: whereas a performance focus can be established on softer issues such as quality, service, or customer

Table 16.4. Financially Funded System.

Division Operating Profit Versus Plan	Potential Bonus (%)
115% or more	8.00
112.5% but less than 115%	7.75
110% but less than 112.5%	7.50
107.5% but less than 110%	7.25
105% but less than 107.5%	7.00
102.5% but less than 105%	6.75
100% but less than 102.5%	6.50
97.5% but less than 100%	6.00
95% but less than 97.5%	5.50
92.5% but less than 95%	5.00
90% but less than 92.5%	4.00
87.5% but less than 90%	3.00
85% but less than 87.5%	2.00
Less than 85%	0.00

satisfaction, bonus payments are always justified on the basis of profitability or hard dollar savings in costs. The risk of paying bonuses when it is financially disadvantageous to do so is essentially eliminated.

The foregoing discussion of gain-sharing formulas reinforces the notion that there is great opportunity to be creative and to design a system that meets the unique needs of the business. In fact, given the importance of aligning the reward system with the business philosophy and strategy, it is imperative that the formula be congruent with the key business objectives.

Are You Ready?

Any organization contemplating the use of an alternative reward system would be well advised to consider its readiness for such a system. As an organizational change vehicle, gain sharing should not be expected to be effective in a very traditional organization that is not oriented toward change. There are simply too many impediments to employee commitment, empowerment, and teamwork in a traditionally managed, autocratic organization; gain sharing or any other alternative reward system cannot by itself overcome them.

In contemplating the readiness of its organization, management should evaluate the following issues:

- *Commitment to change*. Above all else, the people who control the organization's systems, policies, and practices must be committed to support change. If senior management is only lukewarm to the fundamental changes that are required to create a high-involvement, team-oriented organization, change will not occur.

- *Improvement process*. Performance improvements don't just happen; some formalized process is necessary to provide the tools, the techniques, and the focus. Any of a variety of improvement processes, such as employee involvement, total quality management, or the team concept, can be a good basis for gain sharing.

- *Middle management and supervisory support*. The people between senior management and front-line employees are crucial to the success of gain sharing (and the entire change process, for that matter). They can effectively undermine the best-intentioned involvement effort by not communicating with and empowering their subordinates.

- *Trust*. If trust of management is low, employees will be skeptical of management's intentions and will distrust the gain-sharing program. They will fear that it is a ploy to avoid paying a fair wage or that management will manipulate the system in some way to avoid paying fair bonuses.

- *Business conditions*. If the business is operating in crisis mode or if some major upheaval, such as layoffs or restructuring, is in the offing, the timing may not be right for gain sharing. People will be distracted, and unpleasant management actions may appear to be incongruent with the expressed desire to increase employee commitment and involvement in the business.

• *Union receptivity.* It is unrealistic to expect gain sharing or employee involvement to succeed if the union leadership is not supportive of, or at least receptive to, the process.

There are a variety of ways to assess the organization's readiness, including surveys and focus groups. Any assessment technique that does not obtain data from lower-level employees is of questionable validity, as the upward lines of communication are usually inadequate to allow management to reach a sound conclusion on its own.

Ultimately, of course, readiness is not a black-or-white issue but rather a judgment call. Readiness is not susceptible to precise quantification, nor is there any accepted cutoff point that clearly delineates the ready from the unready. But if the commitment and the improvement process in place and there are no glaring negatives relative to the other issues, the organization may be reasonably ready for gain sharing.

Keys to Success

Alternative reward systems like gain sharing are powerful tools for supporting the kinds of cultural change efforts that are critical to survival in a turbulent and demanding business environment. And these systems have stood the test of time: a few companies, such as Atwood Industries in Rockford, Illinois, have had gain-sharing plans in place for forty years or more; many more have used them for ten to fifteen years.

But they must be done right, and that is a bigger challenge than many companies realize. First of all, these plans are pay systems, and poorly designed and supported pay systems can do more harm than good. Second, they are *nontraditional* pay systems, which means that they represent change. And change is difficult and fraught with pitfalls under the best of circumstances.

It is apparent after years of experience with gain sharing that there are a handful of key success factors:

• *Commitment to change.* The number one readiness issue, a true commitment to create a high-involvement, team-oriented work environment, can overcome a lot of impediments, including relatively low readiness on other counts. Gain sharing just doesn't fit the traditional, autocratic management model, and it is unrealistic to expect it to overcome all of the barriers to involvement by itself.

• *Well-designed system.* There are innumerable examples of gain-sharing programs that failed because of poor system design. There are many subtle traps into which the unwary system designer can fall, and a failure to model the system under a variety of scenarios and contingencies will likely result in unpleasant surprises down the road. Designing a gain-sharing program under time pressure or a tight deadline is extremely risky; taking the time to think carefully through the design decisions is time well spent.

• *Procedures for maintaining and modifying the system.* In today's era of rapid change in markets, technology, and customer demands, any gain-sharing system will need to be modified to maintain its effectiveness and its relevance to the business needs—perhaps as often as once a year. In addition, circumstances may arise that demand an immediate modification to the system. Companies that have failed to create an expectation among the workforce that the system will be adapted to changing business needs and have not provided a mechanism to make these changes in a manner that maintains the equity of the system will almost surely have problems maintaining the viability of the system over time.

• *Commitment to education and communication.* The success of gain sharing is dependent, in no small part, on the level of employee involvement in the system and the ability of employees to relate the program to their actions on the job. These outcomes are in turn a function of the efforts made to educate employees on the basics of the program. A reward system cannot change behaviors if people fail to appreciate what behaviors will be rewarded. Attempting to save time and resources by shortcutting the education process is a false economy if it militates against the success of the gain-sharing program.

• *Continual attention to the improvement process.* Gain sharing does not produce gains by itself. It will remain effective only so long as management continues to enhance the improvement process and increase the empowerment of its employees.

A company that attends to these issues and is reasonably ready in the first place will likely enjoy the benefits of better organizational performance, a more committed workforce, and an enhanced cultural change process through gain sharing.

Chapter Seventeen

Rewarding Special Performance: Low-Cost, High-Impact Awards

Jerry L. McAdams

Mike Phillips is the division general manager of the claim servicing operation of a major insurance company in the Midwest. The compensation plan for his 750 employees is a common one—base salary, yearly merit increases (based on the individual performance review), a profit-sharing plan deferred into a 401(k) account, and a recognition program for the employee of the month and year. None of these plans seemed to focus his people on what the division had to accomplish to be successful—improvements in productivity, quality, and cost reduction. Although he was beginning a reengineering effort and creating some quality teams, as part of a total quality management plan, the organization wasn't working as a team. Purchasing was its own little world, as was each type of claim processing (dental, surgical, and so on), and data processing didn't seem to talk to anyone. Each department had its own goals but didn't relate to any other department. It was like having fifteen companies in one operation.

Phillips decided to use a performance reward plan for all employees to lead a change to a more integrated, "we're all in this together" environment. He also had to improve on the objectives so critical to remaining competitive in a very difficult market.

Because he didn't want to change the compensation plan, Phillips decided to use noncash awards rather than cash for improved performance against the objectives. He established a cross-functional design team, which established productivity (departmentwide) and quality (divisionwide) measures and baselines. Each month, employees would receive points (in the form of a check) based on performance against the baselines. They were also given a catalogue of merchandise awards and could use their points for awards each month or save them for a bigger award. In addition, a team suggestion plan was developed to address the cost reduction objective (and the reengineering effort), also using noncash awards.

After the first year, Phillips was delighted with the results and the attention the plan had gotten. With a solid plan design, a lot of communication and feedback, and the team suggestion plan as an employee involvement effort, he was able to get everyone to work toward a common goal, one in which everyone would win. The key to the plan, Phillips said during a plan reassessment meeting, was the use of noncash awards. "It gave us the extra sparks we needed—focus and excitement. We've begun our journey to a more integrated, team-based organization. The biggest surprise to me is the additional leverage I got from the awards. I think I got a lot more bang for my award buck than I would have had from cash. There's a recognition value, both for the employees and the objectives, that the equal amount of cash can't buy."

American industry is learning about the additional leverage to be gained by using noncash awards instead of, or in addition to, cash to improve an organization's performance and competitiveness. These nontraditional awards are being used in every sector of North American industry—manufacturing, health care, service, distribution—to reward employees for performance improvement of productivity, quality, education, cash flow, cost reduction, return on net assets, and lost-time accident reduction. Cash awards, in the amounts that organizations can afford to pay, often do not have the leverage of noncash awards of equal cost.

For years, noncash awards were used only for sales contests or recognition programs to celebrate length of service or honor as "employee of the month." Many of these programs did not demand financial justification and were considered pleasant but not essential to the success of the business. Noncash awards are now being used as powerful motivators for productivity (gain sharing, success sharing, goal sharing, and so on), safety, team and individual suggestion systems for quality and cost reduction, attendance, sales improvement, market penetration—objectives usually incorporated into an organization's strategic business plan.

Performance Reward Plans to Improve Organizational Performance

These plans are not designed to duplicate traditional compensation strategies, and noncash performance awards are more powerful when earned in addition to the existing compensation plan. The majority of alternative reward plans (referred to as performance reward plans in this chapter) are in addition to the existing compensation plans. Those few with a trade-off for existing compensation (so-called at-risk plans) generally reduce future merit increases rather than take away any existing base salary.

North American business has a long history of using compensation and human resource practices to attract, retain, and develop individual employees. Competitive base compensation, the promise of fair merit or cost-of-living adjustments, and benefit packages continue to be refined to "attract, retain, and develop." Human resource and compensation professionals have worked with line and executive management to make organizations fairer, more secure, and better places to work.

It is unfortunate, however, that the majority of these compensation and HR practices are now taken for granted or perceived as entitlements by much of the workforce. After fifty years of constant refining, we are realizing that improving an organization's competitiveness will not be accomplished by focusing on the individual or the small work team! Though we must continue to improve our efforts on this level, it is an *organizational-unit focus* that will make the difference in today's competitive market. That is why the business community is introducing performance reward plans (in addition to base pay, traditional merit increases, and COLAs) to improve performance. These newer plans actually connect strategic organizational performance with rewards for most of the employee population. They lead organizational cultural change rather than lag behind it, as most compensation plans do. They encourage organizations to treat their employees as assets rather than as an unavoidable cost of doing business. They demand continual reassessment, a new degree of openness and receptivity to employee feedback, and they involve employees in making meaningful contributions to the organization's success.

Despite their reward element, these plans are most effective when approached as business strategies for organizational performance improvement rather than as extensions of the compensation plan. Treated as business strategies, performance reward plans are proving to be an effective way of motivating employees to address the strategic objectives of organizations. Though the majority of these plans use cash awards, an increasing number are taking advantage of the extra leverage of noncash awards.

Performance improvement in the traditional compensation mind-set focuses most of its attention on individuals or small work groups in the head or tail of a performance distribution curve (see Figure 17.1). We spend most of our energy being concerned about poor performers who should really be in another line of work. We also spend an inordinate amount of time focusing on the outstanding performers, believing that if we create role models, the majority of the population will be inspired to follow in their footsteps.

The problem seems to be that most organizations have all the time and money they need but nowhere near enough energy. If they focus their energy on employees at the head or tail of the distribution curve, they will have little left to improve the performance of the majority of the people that can truly affect an organization's performance. The real value to the organization is to get the majority of the employee's efforts and creativity focused on

Figure 17.1. Performance Distribution Curve.

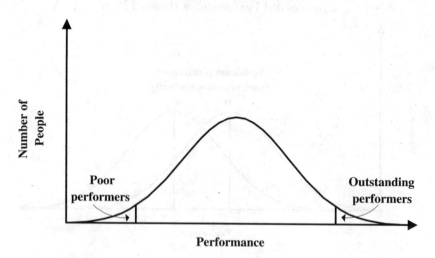

what is important to the organization, moving overall performance a few points to the right (see Figure 17.2).

In their quest for greater competitiveness, organizations are increasing their use of performance reward plans as a business strategy to focus on improving their performance and leading change. The majority of these plans are cash-based, but there are compelling reasons to consider the use of noncash awards to increase the leverage from the cost of the awards.

Proven Success with Any Kind of Award

Performance reward plans were the subject of great deal of experimentation in the 1980s, as reported by O'Dell and McAdams (1987). Their report predicted that the 1990s would be a time of broad implementation of performance reward plans, and this is proving to be true.

Organizations are taking lessons from the old piece-rate plans, executive compensation, behavioral science (B. F. Skinner's research), experimentation with sharing plans (gain sharing, goal

Figure 17.2. Performance Distribution Curve Under
a Successful Performance Reward Plan.

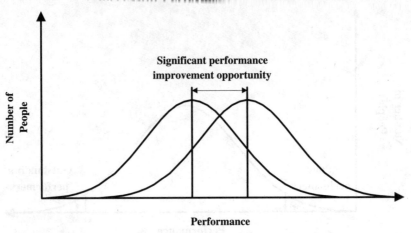

sharing, success sharing, and so on), a good deal of "common people sense," and a driving desire to make their people work as assets on what is good for the organization as a whole.

Before 1990, we had no substantive data on the effectiveness of performance reward plans to improve performance. As U.S. and Canadian businesses moved from experimentation to broad-based implementation, the need for such data, along with design, implementation, and support information, became important.

In response to this demand for "hard data," Elizabeth Hawk of Monsanto (now of Sibson & Company) and I formed the Consortium for Alternative Reward Strategies Research (CARS) in 1991. This nonprofit research project was established with the financial support and expertise of the American Compensation Association, GTE, Maritz Inc., Monsanto, Motorola SPS, and the Travelers Insurance Companies. In addition, we have as advisers Dick Beatty and Charles Fay of Rutgers University and Ed Lawler of the Center for Effective Organizations at the University of Southern California, plus a number of leading consultants in this field.

After months of discussion, we created a framework for the evaluation of performance reward plans designed to improve organizational performance. It has given us measures of effectiveness to determine what works, what doesn't, and why.

We started with eighty thousand contacts. After some basic cleaning, we made sixty-six thousand screening calls that identified ten thousand possible plans. (This research is based on plans, not organizations. One organization could have several plans, although it worked out to about one to one.) An additional screening effort applying our research scope requirements reduced that number to twenty-two hundred plans.

Some of the scope requirements can also be considered the critical success factors in plan design. These criteria will help ensure that an organization's performance will be positively affected by the plan. They are the plan design basics that make sure that a plan can do what it is designed to do—improve performance.

1. The plan must involve the rank-and-file employee population, although managers and executives can be included. Obviously, these plans address the majority of an organizational unit's employees and do not simply focus on the top and bottom performers. (Plans for sales employees have been excluded.)

2. The plan must have a preannounced performance reward formula or linkage. Management cannot determine award size after performance, only in the design stage. Once the plan is announced, everyone included knows what he or she will earn at each level of performance. (This eliminated merit pay, spot bonus, key contributor, and outstanding employee recognition plans, all of which are dependent on management discretion.)

3. The measurement of performance can be at any level of the organization: corporation, division, facility, work group, special team, or individual (at least twenty individuals have to be measured under the same rules to be included in the research).

4. The plans must have been in operation for at least a year,

368 The Performance Imperative

and the awards have to be paid out in real time, not deferred into a savings plan, 401(k), or the like.

5. Skill-based pay plans were not included because they generally do not have a performance element. Suggestion plans and executive compensation were also dropped because we have a lot of information already—in some cases, too much.

6. Any type of award can be used, as long as it has significant financial value. This includes cash, merchandise, travel, time off, and stock. Symbolic awards (plaques and similar items) were not considered. Regardless of the type of award, the design of the plan must be such that it can influence performance.

We can further differentiate plans according to what they are designed to accomplish—what business objective they measure and the performance on which they reward. There are three kinds of plans:

- *Financial* plans use profit-and-loss measures (profits, return on assets, and so on). These are typically cash (or current) profit-sharing plans.
- *Operational* plans use one or more operational measures (productivity, quality, safety, attendance, cost reduction, customer satisfaction, projects, output). They are often called sharing plans (gain sharing, success sharing, win sharing, goal sharing).
- *Combination* plans use both financial and operational measures. An example is the family-of-measures approach, in which rewards are based on a combination of financial and operational measurements.

The results of this research are found in *Capitalizing on Human Assets* (McAdams and Hawk, 1992). We found that performance reward plans can have a profound positive effect on the organization's performance objectives. Some plan types, however, are able to prove their effect better than others. The measures of effectiveness are as follows.

1. Gain—the dollar value of the performance improvement to the organization.

Findings: Operational plans usually had three measures on which rewards are made. (An example would be quality, cost reduction, and safety.) Generally, a dollar value could be put on one or perhaps two of the measured improvements. The median gain was $2,000 per employee per year. The $2,000 is clearly an understatement of the real gain due to the inability of the organizations to assign a dollar value to important performance improvements, such as customer satisfaction, projects, attendance, and, sometimes, quality.

So few financial and combination plans were able to report a dollar value gain that it would be misleading to report them. Combination plans with most of the reward opportunity based on operational measures reported gains far more frequently than those with a focus on financial measures.

Interpretation: Operational plans improve the measures on which they reward (productivity, quality, safety, cost reduction, and so on). There is less evidence that combination plans have an effect. It appears that financial plans are primarily for awareness of the importance of profit to the organizations but do not have an effect on profits (except occasionally in small organizations).

2. Payout—the dollar cost of the awards paid to employees for the improved performance.

Findings: Operational plans paid out $660 per employee per year (2.5 percent of base pay); financial plans, $930 (3.5 percent); and combination plans, $1,310 (5 percent).

Interpretation: These payout amounts are considerably less than expected. Traditionally, 8 to 15 percent of base pay was considered the minimum necessary to motivate employees. It appears that when combined with improved communication and employee involvement efforts, the financial value of the award may not be as important as the fact that it exists at all.

3. Return on payout—the closest we can get to a return-on-investment calculation, relating the cost of the payout to the dollar value of the gain.

Findings: Organizations with operational plans earned $3 and paid out $1, for a net of $2, or a 200 percent return on payout. (Financial and combination plans, which cannot calculate gains, are unable to report return on payout.)

Interpretation: Involving employees in an organization's strategic objectives and rewarding them for attaining those goals has always made good intuitive sense. Now there is evidence that properly designed performance reward plans make good business sense as well.

4. Satisfaction—the opinion of plan designers or administrators and management, rating the plan's effectiveness on a scale of one (very dissatisfied) to five (very satisfied), with three being neutral.

Findings: Operational plans scored 3.7; financial plans, 3.4; and combination plans, 3.8. Only the score for financial plans was statistically significant.

Interpretation: Ratings in the 3.0 to 3.5 (neutral to marginally satisfied) range suggest an entitlement mentality. Ratings in the 3.5 to 4.0 (marginally satisfied to satisfied) range suggest that the plans are having a desired effect, but not enough to warrant dancing in the streets.

5. Nonfinancial aspects—the opinion of plan designers or administrators and management, rating the effect of the plan on a series of outcomes. These results were subjected to cluster analysis and then correlation analysis to reveal statistically significant relationships.

Findings: Operational and combination plans had a positive correlation with the nonfinancial result of improved business performance. Financial plans did not.

Interpretation: Combined with the satisfaction ratings, operational and combination plans, containing as they do an element of operational performance (productivity, quality, safety), have a greater effect on the organization's objectives than financial ones.

We concluded that performance reward plans should be considered business strategies, designed to meet specific business objectives through people. They should not be treated or administered as compensation plans, even though they do include a reward element.

Communications, employee team involvement, management involvement (particularly that of first-line supervisors), and regular reassessment significantly affect satisfaction and the nonfinancial results of business performance, teamwork, and performance reward–linked outcomes.

In short, for a performance reward plan to affect organization performance directly, it must involve rank-and-file employees, have a preannounced performance reward linkage or formula, pay out in real time, and reward on measures that reflect strategic objectives. Performance reward plans are defined by what they are intended to improve: financial, operational, or combination measures.

The research also shows that performance reward plans tend to lead organizational change and should not be considered or treated as an extension of a traditional compensation plan, which tends to lag.

Communication, employee team involvement, management involvement, and regular reassessments are important to a plan's success.

Emergence of Noncash Awards

Some research suggests a change in the types of awards being used. Traditionally, awards in all types of performance reward plans have been in cash. O'Dell and McAdams (1987) found that in 1985, only 2 percent of the plans had noncash awards of significant value. In the latest research (McAdams and Hawk, 1992), 16 percent were using noncash awards in combination with cash awards. (The following is more of a general observation than a research finding, for we are comparing three different study populations. It does reflect a trend, however, that we have observed in combination and operational plans as we continue our research. Financial plans tend to stick to cash or, in rare cases, stock.) A recent study (Troy, 1991) reported that a majority of operational plans use noncash awards rather than cash.

Why the apparent trend? One explanation is the need to focus on less familiar measures such as productivity and quality. Focus requires an award that generates as much attention as possible. Merchandise awards of significant value, travel awards, and the like seem to fill that bill. Although cash is a valued award, it can get lost in the normal compensation process. The use of an award medium that provides additional recognition of the objective makes a lot of sense, particularly when you are trying to teach people how to affect and understand productivity, quality, cost reduction, safety, attendance, project milestones, and other strategic objectives.

It is easier and more effective to promote the excitement of a noncash award than its cash equivalent. Noncash awards have built-in excitement and recognition factors that cash simply doesn't have. In this way, noncash awards boost recognition of the importance of the objective.

Another reason may be reflected in the relatively low payout in operational plans—$660 per employee per year, or 2.5 percent of base pay. Operational plans tend to pay out more frequently (monthly or quarterly) than financial or combination plans, which pay out annually. If you break down $660 into monthly payments and take out taxes, the net award is about $40 a month. That may not be terribly motivating: funds would have to be accumulated for a long time to put them toward the purchase of something memorable. Forty dollars' worth of points, however, *will* tend to be accumulated for the TV set, camcorder, or VCR that will be remembered and appreciated by the individual and the family for a long time to come.

The research also revealed that the primary reason noncash awards of significant value ($600 is the average award value in merchandise) are used is their *trophy value*. Every time an employee sits in that lounge chair or plays with that set of golf clubs, the employee is reminded that it was *earned* for a *personal* achievement in improving performance. That memory can last for years, reinforcing the employee's belief that he or she can continue to improve performance. This continual reinforcement pays far greater dividends than a cash bonus that is barely remembered two or three years later.

Because these awards are not cash, they cannot be confused with the compensation plan. There can be little or no entitlement. The use of noncash awards allows the organization to adjust measurements and objectives, within reason, without argument from people who would be upset if they thought that their cash income standard of living might be reduced.

There is some evidence that plans using noncash awards can produce the same results as those using cash awards, at a lower cost (McAdams and Hawk, 1992). The research on the cost effectiveness of different types of awards covered 330,000 sales employees from 607 organizations. We have reservations about applying research findings on sales employees to nonsales employees, but in this case, it seems reasonable. The biggest differences between sales and nonsales employees are style, the degree of risk that sales employees are willing to take, and the availability of individual measures. Style would have little effect on the acceptance of a particular type of award. Risk acceptance is already covered by the fact that 70 percent of the sales employees are paid on a salary-plus-commission basis. Measurement is individually based for sales, whereas the performance reward plans we are discussing are generally group-based. And there is one more compelling reason to look at the sales performance reward experience and apply the appropriate portions to the nonsales employee population: sales staffs have a fifty-year track record.

The research revealed that cash incentives, over and above the base-salary-plus-commission plan, improved sales performance 13 percent. Noncash awards (for the perceived equivalent value) improved performance about the same amount, 13.3 percent. The cost of the cash awards is approximately 12 cents on every additional dollar in sales. The noncash awards cost approximately 4.1 cents per incremental dollar, a significantly better return on payout. This is not to suggest that noncash is three times better for all performance improvement efforts, but it is clearly a powerful type of award.

To sum up, the use of noncash awards in performance reward plans is increasing because noncash awards provide more focus on less familiar measures, trophy value, little risk of entitlement or confusion with the compensation plans, and the possibility of greater cost effectiveness.

Effectiveness of Noncash Incentives

Do plans using noncash awards work for nonsales employees? The oldest sharing plan in North America is the suggestion system. If an idea to save money or improve performance is accepted by management, the originating individual or team receives a share of the savings or dollar value of the gain. *Capitalizing on Human Assets* did not study these plans directly, but suggestion plans were considered as a form of employee involvement. We found that performance reward plans are more effective if they involve employees. "More employee team involvement plans" and "high participation rates"

**Figure 17.3. Participation in Suggestion Plans
and the Value of Suggestions Made.**

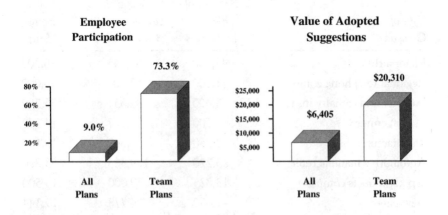

correlate with higher plan satisfaction and improved teamwork. Thirty percent of the organizations in our research have team suggestion plans with the highest participation of all employee involvement efforts, including quality teams, individual suggestion plans, and ad hoc problem-solving teams. Effectiveness data were supplied by the Employee Involvement Association (formerly the National Association of Suggestion Systems). In addition, a privately developed database of 166 team suggestion plans, exclusively using noncash awards, provided some strong evidence that nontraditional awards are effective (see Figure 17.3).

Comparing employee participation in individual and team suggestion plans predominantly using cash awards with team plans using only noncash awards shows a significant difference in participation rate. Most of the team plans were for a span of less than a year. When these plans run for longer periods, the participation drops to 40 to 60 percent—still considerably higher than the 9 percent for all plans.

The most important measure of effectiveness is the dollar value

Table 17.1. Team Suggestion Plans, 1983–1992.

Type of Company	Number of Eligible Employees	Total Value of Savings or Gain ($ thousands)	Average Value
Major airline	42,800	53,345	46,200
Regional telephone company	21,500	72,500	48,000
Property and casualty insurer	3,600	31,351	35,789
Manufacturer	1,500	7,137	14,500
Manufacturer	2,280	14,869	19,136
Automotive manufacturer	3,220	109,383	53,800
Wood products company	13,823	39,000	13,500
Newspaper	1,650	4,778	19,344
Branch bank (1988)	3,600	8,213	16,626
Branch bank (1990)	4,265	8,034	19,266
Foreign bank	9,000	£11,300	£12,500
Savings and loan association	1,600	5,700	14,748
Total for 166 plans	654,000	1,659,751	23,100

placed on the suggestions adopted. All plans using primarily cash awards are outperformed by noncash team plans by 3.2 to 1. These noncash suggestion systems operate in most business environments. Table 17.1 is a representative sample of the plans in the database.

If noncash awards are effective in suggestion systems, how are they used in operational plans? Table 17.2 is an example of a plan operating in a service center for equipment repair. After rounding the monthly payout value, it is converted to points (award credits) at the rate of two hundred per dollar (see Table 17.3). All taxes are paid by the company and have been included in the value of the payout. Noncash awards should be essentially tax-free to employees. They are grossed up in the employee's W-2 statement. Table 17.4 tracks performance for one year.

Table 17.2. Operational Noncash Award Plan for an Equipment Repair Service Center.

Service Center	Measurement	Participation
Quality	Cost of rework per unit serviced (see below)	All service center employees
Customer satisfaction	Determined by customer survey	All service center employees

Salaries:	$7,500,000 (600,000 labor hours: ⅔ service; ⅓ support)
Expenses:	$12,500,000 (including $8,000,000 in parts)
On-time delivery:	75%
Rework:	80,000 labor hours: $1,000,000 parts
Units serviced:	100,000
Employees:	300

Cost of Rework per Unit Serviced

Service center:	80,000 labor hours @ $12.50 per hr =	$1,000,000
+ Parts		+ $1,000,000
Total:		$2,000,000
Units serviced:	100,000	
Period:	1993	
Baseline:	$2,000,000 per 100,000 units = $20 per unit serviced	
Goal:	30% reduction; $600,000 savings, or $14 per unit service cost	
Participation:	All service center employees	

Required for motivation at target of 30% improvement: 3% of base pay value, or $7,500,000 × 3% = $225,000 in noncash awards

Return on payout:

$$\frac{(Gain - payout)}{Pay\ out} = \frac{(\$600,000 - \$225,000)}{\$225,000} = 166\% \ (37\%\ employees,\ 67\%\ company)$$

Table 17.2. (cont.)

Financial Overview

Improvement (%)	Cost per Unit ($)	Total Yearly Savings ($)	Total Payout ($) (% of base pay)	Yearly Payout per Employee ($)	Quarterly Payout per Employee ($)	Monthly Payout per Employee ($)
Baseline	20	0	0	0	0	0
10	18	200,000	75,000 (1%)	250	62.50	20.83
20	16	400,000	150,000 (2%)	500	125.00	41.67
30	14	600,000	225,000 (3%)	750	187.50	62.49
40	12	800,000	300,000 (4%)	1000	250.00	83.33
50	10	1,000,000	375,000 (5%)	1250	312.50	104.16

Table 17.3. Monthly Award Credit Payout for Rework Reduction.

Improvement %	Cost per Unit	Payout per Employee (award credits)
Baseline	20	0
10	18	4,000
20	16	8,000
30 (goal)	14	1,200
40	12	16,000
50 (cap)	10	200

Our research shows that when used in a sharing plan, such as a suggestion plan, team suggestion plans outperform plans that focus on individuals and teams and make awards in cash. The design of an operational or combination performance reward plan is the same regardless of the type of award used. Basic sound design principles and solid financial rationales are essential.

Types of Noncash Awards and How to Use Them

The most popular noncash awards for improved performance are social reinforcers, earned time off with pay, merchandise, and travel.

Table 17.4. Annual Summary of Noncash Award Plan Performance.

Period	Performance on Rework Reduction (%)	Savings or Gain ($)	Award Credit Payout per Employee
January	14	23,000	4,000
February	20	33,000	8,000
March	-20	-33,000	0
April	-6	-10,000	0
May	35	58,000	12,000
June	45	75,000	16,000
July	50	83,000	20,000
August	25	42,000	8,000
September	-10	-17,000	0
October	16	27,000	4,000
November	28	47,000	8,000
December	0	0	0
Total		328,000	80,000

Total payout = 80,000 credits × $\dfrac{\$1}{200 \text{ credits}}$ = $400

+ 20% for taxes   +   + 100
                                                                  500

+ 15% for transportation and sales tax ($400 × .15)   +   60
                                                                  560

× 300 employees   × 300
                                                               $168,000

Return on payout:

$$\frac{\text{Gain} - \text{payout}}{\text{Payout}} = \frac{\$328,000 - \$168,000}{\$168,000} = 90\% \ (51\% \text{ employees, } 49\% \text{ company})$$

Symbolic awards are more usual for awareness (focus on a specific objective or message) and role modeling.

Social Reinforcers

Social reinforcers include involvement, listening, pats on the back, respect, feedback, training, activities (picnics, tailgate sales, charity days, and the like). They should be an integral part of all management practices. Most such awards reflect management's style and can be used to boost morale and to acknowledge the value that the organization places on its employees.

Earned Time Off

Americans value their leisure time more than ever. With the increasing demands of work, time off can become an award in itself. Having an unplanned day off is becoming a very attractive award. Vacation, by contrast, is an entitlement and is planned in advance.

Most companies continue paying wages during time off because it would be hard to consider it an award otherwise. Time off without pay, however, can be a positive way of capturing productivity improvements. Many employees might appreciate having a day off even without pay if it would not jeopardize their job status.

Selectively used, earned time off can be a very powerful group incentive. It has been used in two ways. One way is for all employees to take one or more days off when a specific goal or objective has been reached. Some companies allow employees to accumulate days to add to vacation. However, a philosophical conflict could arise over earned time off. What message does such a plan send? Do we really want to reinforce the idea of not coming to work? Some experts believe that such a plan should be applied only in organizational units in which attendance is not a problem or customer contact is not part of the job.

A second way to use earned time off is through company celebrations that take people, as a group, off the company premises. Most of these activities are considered entitlements, such as company picnics, but they can also be effective awards. When goals are met, everyone gets to celebrate. If your company already has traditional events that are not considered awards, it would be unwise to try to convert them into awards. Some creative thinking, however, can bring a company real benefits through group activities. One firm uses special team-building training as an award. The event takes place in the Rocky Mountains, lasts a week, and is highly prized both as a benefit to the company and as an award to the employees. To be the latter, however, participation must be purely voluntary. Even implied pressure to participate eliminates the award aspect of such an activity.

Administration for this type of plan must be handled by the company and tends to be more complex with nonexempt and shift workers than with the exempt and professional ranks. Unlike the other types of awards described, the cost of this award is something to consider.

Because of the limitations of accounting systems, the real cost of this award gets lost in the system. Many firms consider professional, exempt, and management earned time off to be of no cost to the company, depending on how much time off is given. Nonexempt and shift workers' earned time off is generally considered to carry a real cost. Earned time off is probably most effective when used on a limited basis, driven by the nature of the operation, timing, workload, and indispensability. Also, earned time off generally has no tax repercussions for the employee.

Merchandise Awards

Merchandise awards are given for improved performance, and they can consist of preselected items or a broad offering of merchandise. The merchandise award is of significant financial value, usually totaling over 2 percent of the employee's annual salary. Merchandise certificates that can be redeemed at a local branch of a national retail chain often are used as awards, although merchandise awards are generally most effective when delivered via an award catalogue.

There are two types of merchandise catalogues: the award catalogue and the general-purpose catalogue. Some catalogues offer as many as eighteen hundred items of the highest quality, selected as appealing awards for a wide range of tastes. Though they offer a broad selection of functional items, their intent is to focus on items with special value to the individual or family. Recently, these catalogues have evolved to reflect the new lifestyles of employees. Health and other forms of insurance, education and training, memberships, and access to specialty catalogues are now included. The next smaller catalogue generally has about eight hundred items and is limited to quality merchandise. The smallest catalogues are really "booklets" that feature ten to fifteen items, in value groupings of $25 to $500.

Accompanying the catalogue is a price list in points or award credits. When a plan is introduced, levels of performance are directly related to the award value in points. Checks are issued by the agency for the appropriate number of points. The employees can redeem them immediately or accumulate them for a larger award. About 90 to 95 percent of employees accumulate the checks to get the award they have selected. The award catalogue itself enhances the merchandise as an award by providing an attractive and exciting promotional vehicle. Of the two ways to offer and promote merchandise as awards, the award catalogue is the more popular and has the higher motivation appeal.

Award catalogues are supplied by full-service performance improvement agencies. They issue and mail the point checks, based on performance information supplied by the company or the participants. They handle lost checks and refunds (when participants send in more points than necessary for an order). All record keeping, tax and management reports, order entry, shipping, customer service, auditing, and billing is also handled by the agency.

Some agencies also offer a bank account system. The agency deposits points in an account in the participant's name, issues balance statements, and allows ordering by telephone or mail.

To award earners, service is critical. People have higher expectations of product quality, delivery, and customer service when redeeming award credits than when buying something for cash. They have earned the award, and they want it as soon as possible and without hassle. If there are any problems, they demand quick, fair, and empathetic service. A good agency will stock items that make up from 60 to 75 percent of their orders. Some items, such as clothing, furniture, and large appliances, have to be shipped from the factory. The size and buying power of the agency has a strong influence on the service that an award earner will receive on these drop shipments. Some agencies offer a special ordering service for items not appearing in the award catalogue.

Employees earning merchandise awards feel that they have been cheated if they have to pay taxes on the awards. For this reason, firms "gross up" the award value when reporting it on each W-2 form and pay the federal tax, usually based on 20 percent withholding. Assuming that this does not move an employee into a higher tax bracket, there is little or no tax cost to the employee. Many firms extend this practice to cover state and local taxes as well.

Agencies usually bill the firms for the award points *redeemed* plus transportation and sales tax. This gives firms a cash flow benefit unique to merchandise incentives. The vast majority of merchandise award earners save their checks until they have enough to get their selected (and often larger) award. This time lag between actual performance improvement and billing for awards can be as much as a year. During that time, performance is better and the company has the benefit of that improved performance without even paying for the award. Depending on the interest rate, the positive cash flow can be significant. By contrast, there is no cash flow advantage when the award is made in cash: bank accounts are generally billed at the time points are issued, yielding no cash flow advantage.

The second type of merchandise award catalogue, a general-purpose catalogue from a traditional department store, is designed to meet everyday, functional needs. These catalogues provide a range of items in each category, from basic TVs to expensive big-screen models. The majority of the catalogue items, however, are low-end merchandise and would not be considered awards. Employees may find desirable items in the catalogue, but the catalogue is not designed to be an award vehicle.

Firms using this type of catalogue issue merchandise certificates redeemable at the store. As opposed to the award points approach, merchandise certificates are essentially "directed cash" and have far less appeal than award catalogue programs.

Most retail stores with catalogues do not offer administrative services for certificate issuance, record keeping of participants' performance, stop payments, tax reporting, or other administrative demands. If a company arranges its fulfillment directly with a retail store, the company handles all administrative duties. Also, the tax considerations are not the same as those associated with the book-of-awards program. Merchandise certificates are billed on issuance, eliminating any cash flow advantage. The service that employees get from the store is purely a function of the store itself. As with the agency approach, the service, good or bad, will be perceived as reflecting on the sponsoring firm.

Companies can also buy merchandise awards directly from a manufacturer. Many major manufacturers of popular consumer goods (GE, Motorola, Sony, Thomasville) have an incentive division that focuses on selling a limited selection of their products directly to companies for incentive plans. The buyer, in this case the company, has to decide what will be most appealing to the targeted population. A common approach is to create a booklet of a few items (TV, VCR, camera, golf clubs, and so forth), at least one of which will be of interest to everyone in the audience.

The risk with preselected items is that they might not be appealing to the people who are targeted. If you already own three TVs, it is hard to get excited about earning another. Trying to guess what is valuable to people is frustrating. Offering a broad range of awards is the safest approach.

Agencies are generally not involved in the incentive plan when companies purchase merchandise awards, although brokers often represent a number of manufacturers for the incentive market. Generally, brokers do not offer any additional services.

If a company decides to purchase merchandise from a manufacturer, the company handles all the administrative work. This may not be very burdensome if the number of items is limited and all merchandise is drop-shipped. If the company buys a number of items and stocks them for redistribution, it must take all of those costs into account when designing the alternative reward strategy. Because of the complexities involved, few firms take this approach—at least not the second time around.

The tax considerations are the same as described for the award catalogue approach, and unless the purchasing arrangement is drop-shipping only, there is little cash flow advantage with this approach because awards are paid for at the time of shipment to the company. Demand for good customer service is high with a preselected merchandise approach and when the company's staff is responsible for providing the service.

Travel Awards

Trips can be awarded to an individual or a family. An alternative is travel certificates of $50 to $100 that can be accumulated over a period of time and applied to a trip, just like saving up for a vacation.

Travel awards are becoming popular because they offer many of the advantages of an award catalogue plan. Travel certificates can be issued in various denominations of "travel value" according to a preannounced schedule that relates levels of performance to a number of certificates. A book of travel destinations is given to the employees at the beginning of the program. Certificates are accumulated by the award earners and redeemed for the travel awards. The certificates may be used to pay for part or all of the cost of the award.

One of the appeals of this approach is its ability to offer a wide range of destinations (a hundred or more) in a promotional kit given to the participants. All administration services, including redemption and travel arrangements, are generally made by the individual award earner directly with the airlines, hotels, and tour operators. The certificates are used in payment directly to the travel supplier.

Full-service agencies offer a catalogue of travel destinations designed to promote those destinations. They specialize in serving award travel participants around the nation or even the world. Customer service is a function of the travel supplier, with the support of the agency. In either case, in the participant's mind, the sponsoring company will be held responsible for the quality of service.

Taxes can be handled by grossing up. Billing for the cost of the travel certificates is done on issuance, so there is no cash flow advantage. If the certificates are issued in exchange for points, however, the cash flow advantage is the same as with the award catalogue plan.

Symbolic Awards

Symbolic awards, also known as recognition awards, have an emotional value far in excess of their intrinsic value. Examples include plaques, coffee mugs, desk sets, photographs, T-shirts, jackets, hats, rings, pins, mementos—the list is endless. The fact that these awards have little financial value does not mean that they have to be inexpensive. Company rings or pins can cost hundreds of dollars, but the average symbolic-award budget per person is $8 per year.

Symbolic awards are used for two purposes: awareness and recognition. Awareness is acknowledging the importance of an objective or a goal. A company could have program themes printed on selected items to distribute to all members of the organization, regardless of performance. These items are excellent communication tools and tangible, ever-present reminders of the company's focus.

The more common use of symbolic items, however, is for recognition. Offering a T-shirt or coffee mug to each employee who reaches a preestablished goal is an inexpensive way of getting focus. Few would argue that this award is significant enough in financial terms to get people to improve performance, but often dynamics and pride take over. The symbolic award is a way for employees to tout their accomplishments in public. Most companies have some forms of individual recognition for display in the workplace—plaques, photos posted in the cafeteria, and so forth.

Membership on advisory councils, upgrades in company cars, reserved parking places, free lunches, special business cards, and similar "perks" are also used extensively as symbolic awards for recognizing outstanding individual performance. (A word of caution about such programs as "employee of the month": the concept is great, but the execution is generally poor. Employee nominations from management often degenerate into a lottery or a rotation. Credibility and the reinforcing power of these programs tend to erode. Unless you truly can identify and defend the nominations to the rest of the employees, the worth of such programs is questionable.)

Hundreds of advertising specialty and promotion brokers can supply symbolic awards. Full-service agencies offer symbolic awards as an accommodation to their clients. They also offer artistic symbolic awards rarely available elsewhere, such as limited-edition sculptures designed and produced for the company or event. As with the award catalogue approach, these full-service agencies offer design, communication, promotion, and distribution services not available with fulfillment sources.

Administration of symbolic awards is much the same as for the award catalogue plan. Because the value of each item tends to be low, many firms stock the awards and handle most of the administration themselves, particularly if the awards are issued throughout the year. If the plan is to send out the awards all at one time, it is considerably easier to have the full-service agency or fulfillment sources handle the distribution from a mailing list supplied by the company.

Symbolic awards rarely cost more than $25 each and are tax-free to the employee. Under certain conditions, the tax-free allowance goes up to $600. The tax law tends to be interpreted differently over time, so be sure to consult your firm's tax attorney.

Conclusion

Noncash awards include social reinforcers, earned time off, merchandise, travel, and symbolic awards. Each type has its own intrinsic power of motivation and recognition.

Whether you call it leverage or getting more bang for the award buck, the use of noncash awards, either alone or in combination with cash, can make performance reward plans more effective. Whatever is used, it is critical that a plan be designed with the organization's strategic objectives in mind and be operated as a business strategy to attain or exceed those objectives in a cost-effective manner.

References

McAdams, J. L., and Hawk, E. J. (1992). *Capitalizing on Human Assets*. Scottsdale, Ariz.: American Compensation Association/Consortium for Alternative Reward Strategies Research.

O'Dell, C., and McAdams, J. L. (1987). *People, Performance, and Pay*. Scottsdale, Ariz.: American Compensation Association/American Productivity and Quality Center.

Troy, K. (1991). *Employee Buy-In to Total Quality*. New York: Conference Board.

Part Six

Moving Beyond Confrontational Labor/Management Relations

Unfortunately, the clashes between labor and management in the 1930s and 1940s continue to influence the way companies are required to deal with their employees. The primary federal labor and employment laws were enacted during this era and have guided labor/management relations ever since. The initial legislation was drafted during the Great Depression, when pitched battles frequently broke out between workers and their employers. The legislation passed during this period established unemployment compensation and the minimum wage and gave workers the right to bargain collectively and the protection of required overtime pay. As necessary as this legislation may have been at the height of the Depression, circumstances have since changed dramatically, making some of the provisions of these laws unnecessary and in some circumstances an impediment to effective workforce management.

One of the more important trends is the mushrooming interest in employee participation or empowerment. Workers have opportunities for input to a wide variety of operational decisions, and this is generally viewed as a win-win change for the company as well as the employees.

Despite the positive impact of this trend on participating employees and on the performance of their work groups, the National Labor Relations Board (NLRB) ruled in its 1992 decision involving Electromation, Inc., that employee committees in certain situations violate the National Labor Relations Act (NLRA).

The decision was based on the board's interpretation of congressional intent in 1935 in enacting the NLRA. The case has been viewed as a landmark in labor law because of its impact on the trend toward increased employee participation and empowerment. It makes it difficult for companies to involve employee groups in decisions related to grievances, labor disputes, wages, rates of pay, hours of employment, or conditions of work, even in nonunionized settings.

In Chapter Eighteen, "Legal Aspects of Employee Participation," Jim Redeker and Dan O'Meara discuss the implications of this case and related decisions. They review the NLRB's conclusions and provide guidelines for employers who continue to rely on employee participation. The authors argue that employers should plan carefully to avoid problems but that strategies can be developed to provide for continued employee participation.

The Electromation decision is important because it effectively limits opportunities for employee participation and because it highlights the need for new labor laws. At a time when employee interest in unions is at its lowest point in more than half a century, the framework of federal statutes supports unionization and precludes discussions between workers and management on certain topics that are directly relevant to their relationship. For example, it is a violation of the law for groups of workers to discuss working conditions in a management-sponsored forum unless they are formally represented by a recognized union.

Significantly, unions are beginning to appreciate and accept the importance of employee participation. In Chapter Nineteen,

"Making Everyone a Stakeholder: Strategies for Addressing Conflicting Needs," Lynn Williams, who recently stepped down as international president of the United Steelworkers, provides a labor view of employee participation. The Steelworkers have promulgated policy statements supporting employee empowerment and have negotiated significant changes in local labor agreements providing for increased worker participation. Williams reviews the history of his union's experience with worker participation along with that of the steel industry.

The problems experienced by the steel industry were in part responsible for negotiated agreements starting in the 1980s that provided for union participation in what had previously been treated as management prerogatives. These local agreements have provided for participation in—and in some cases control of—training programs, progression, and pay schedules. Workers may also determine work and vacation schedules and have assumed a role in deciding work methods and operational changes.

Williams cites the adage "No one knows the job as well as the person doing it." In making the case for participation, he points out that worker participation has enabled steel companies to realize savings that can be measured in the millions of dollars. He argues that in his industry, worker participation has been an important factor in helping American companies reestablish their competitive position in world markets.

The experience in the steel industry is not unique. Other industries have come to realize that their relationships with employees are adversely affecting their ability to compete both locally and globally. The choice is between adopting autocratic policies to reduce payroll costs and taking advantage of the wealth of job knowledge possessed by the workforce. The former policy will almost certainly produce quicker results, but the potential improvement in the bottom line (looking at payroll costs relative to total operating costs) is rarely as great as the potential improvement in productivity if the company is able to take advantage of the untapped expertise of its workers. Unfortunately, quick-fix actions can be expected to antagonize workers and almost certainly make it impossible to take advantage of this expertise for years to come.

To be sure, relatively few U.S. companies have to worry about unions or even the immediate threat of unionization. That era seems to have come to an end. However, federal labor and employment laws limit an employer's right to manage workers in every workplace. As global competitiveness continues to be a critical factor, U.S. employers need laws and regulations that facilitate and encourage worker participation. "We're all in this together" must be the governing philosophy for employers and their employees.

Chapter Eighteen

Legal Aspects of Employee Participation

James R. Redeker, Daniel P. O'Meara

Many employee participation plans (EPPs) are vulnerable to legal attack. For the purposes of this chapter, EPPs are considered any organized effort to obtain nonmanagement input into the running of a business. Such EPPs include quality assurance programs (under their various names), safety committees, workplace policy committees, and discharge review committees.

The primary basis for legal attack is the National Labor Relations Act (NLRA). The specific problem is that the unilateral establishment by a company and continued implementation of an EPP constructed along the lines of the most popular models may be considered the unlawful establishment and domination of a "labor organization" under the NLRA. This vulnerability to legal attack exists regardless of whether the employees involved in the EPP are union or nonunion, whether the employer intended to violate the NLRA, and even whether the employer knew that the NLRA might be implicated.

Electromation and Du Pont

Although the relevant legal standards have changed very little over the past several decades, the National Labor Relations Board (NLRB) focused considerable attention on the legal aspects of EPPs with its 1992 *Electromation, Inc.*, and 1993 *Du Pont* decisions. In *Electromation*, the NLRB held that various nonunion employee committees that had been established by an employer were unlawfully dominated labor organizations. In *Du Pont*, it came to the same conclusion about various union employee committees established at one of Du Pont's plants. In both cases, the NLRB ordered the committees disbanded.

In finding the committees at issue to be labor organizations, the board relied on the broad definitions in NLRA, Section 2(5), reprinted in Exhibit 18.1. The board stated that an organization is

Exhibit 18.1. Relevant Statutory Language.

Section 2(5) of the National Labor Relations Act

The term "labor organization" means any organization of any kind, or any agency or employee representation committee or plan, in which employees participate and which exist for the purpose, in whole or in part, of dealing with employers concerning grievances, labor disputes, wages, rates of pay, hours of employment, or conditions of work.

Section 8(a) of the National Labor Relations Act

It shall be an unfair labor practice for an employer
(1) to interfere with, restrain, or coerce employees in the exercise of the rights guaranteed in section [7 of the National Labor Relations Act];
(2) to dominate or interfere with the formation or administration of any labor organization or contribute financial or other support to it: *Provided,* That subject to rules and regulations made and published by the Board pursuant to section [6 of the National Labor Relations], an employer shall not be prohibited from permitting employees to confer with him during working hours without loss of time or pay; . . .
(5) to refuse to bargain collectively with the representatives of his employees, subject to the provisions of section [9(a) of the National Labor Relations Act].

a labor organization if (1) employees participate; (2) the organization exists, at least in part, for the purpose of "dealing with" employers; and (3) these dealings concern conditions of work or concern grievances, labor disputes, wages, rates of pay, or hours of employment. Such organizations cannot, under the NLRA, be dominated or interfered with by the employer; see Sections 8(a)(1) and (2) of the act in Exhibit 18.1.

After determining that employee committees were labor organizations, the NLRB in *Electromation* and *Du Pont* turned to the question of whether the committees were in violation of the NLRA—whether they had been interfered with or dominated in their formation or administration. In addition, in *Du Pont*, since the employees were represented by a union, they had to determine whether the company had violated the additional requirement of Section 8(a)(5) that the company negotiate in good faith with the union concerning the terms and conditions of employment in establishing and implementing the EPP. The board stated that if a committee is a creation of management, its structure and function are essentially determined by management, and its continued existence depends on the fiat of management, it has been dominated within the meaning of NLRA Section 8(a)(2). Consequently, both Electromation and Du Pont violated Section 8(a)(2) through their dealings with their employee committees and, in addition, Du Pont violated Section 8(a)(5) by refusing to negotiate with and involve the union representing its employees concerning the establishment and operation of the committees and the subjects with which they were concerned.

Defenses Certain to Fail

The NLRB in *Electromation* and *Du Pont* specified a number of legal defenses commonly raised by employers when their systems are challenged that, as a matter of law, the board will reject. These defenses include management's lack of intent to form a labor organization, management's lack of intent to break the law, the committees' lack of intent to be labor organizations, and the lack of perception by uninvolved employees that the committee is a labor organization. Although some courts of appeals can be expected to rely on good-faith intentions in refusing to enforce NLRB orders, the board will not honor these defenses. (Note that the rules of law in the text come for the most part from the principal decision of the NLRB in *Electromation* and its unanimous decision in *Du Pont*. There were three concurring opinions in *Electromation*, however, and numerous appeals have taken different positions on these issues.)

Although not discussed specifically by the NLRB in *Electromation* or *Du Pont*, some employers have argued in similar cases that their EPP is not a labor organization because the EPP does not bargain or attempt to bargain with the employer, and its only role is to make recommendations or proposals to the employer. Because the NLRA definition of labor organization uses the broad phrase "dealing with employers" and not the more narrow "bargaining with employers," this argument has been consistently rejected. Further, the U.S. Supreme Court clearly rejected this defense in a 1959 case, *NLRB* v. *Cabot Carbon*.

Nor is the lack of formal trappings typical of a union a defense. A committee or group may be a labor organization even if it lacks a formal structure, has no elected officers, has no constitution or bylaws, and does not meet regularly. A committee or group can be a labor organization even if it does not require the payment of initiation fees or dues and even if there is no formal framework for conducting meetings among the represented employees or otherwise eliciting employee views.

Legislative History of the NLRA

The NLRB in *Electromation* looked to the 1935 legislative history of the NLRA for guidance in its decision. After extensive discussion, the board concluded that Congress specifically intended to prohibit employee representation committees at nonunion employers because these committees were in 1935 used to defeat outside union organizing. In short, the board concluded that Congress intended to outlaw anything that might resemble a company-run union.

Debate over NLRB Policy

The heightened attention given by the NLRB to the legal issues surrounding employee participation plans has in turn heightened public attention concerning NLRB policy.

Dialogue among human resource professionals concerning the *Electromation* and *Du Pont* decisions has included criticism of the NLRB for jeopardizing win-win vehicles of employee empowerment. The dialogue has also included concerns that the board has impaired the ability of American businesses to compete with foreign operations. Finally, critics have accused the NLRB of perpetuating Depression-era assumptions that adversarial employer-employee relations should prevail at all American businesses.

Defenders of the NLRB assert that *Electromation* and *Du Pont* were correctly decided because the function of the board is to interpret the NLRA and not to rewrite it. They further add that the language of the statute is plain on its face, and the legislative history supports this conclusion. These defenders of board policy assert that whether the current policy is the best policy is for Congress, not the NLRB, to decide.

Employer Options

Political debates about past decisions do little for employers looking to the future. Employers wishing to structure and use EPPs lawfully should consider the steps outlined here.

Consent

If employees who will be participating on or directly affected by the decision of the committee are represented by a union, the union's consent should be sought and obtained. Failing to obtain the implied or actual consent of the union before establishing an EPP that deals with mandatory subjects of bargaining is arguably a violation of an employer's duty to bargain with the union in good faith. To be effective, the union's implied consent (waiver of its right to be involved) must be clear and unmistakable. Obtaining a written agreement is preferred.

In practice, the EPP should not circumvent the role of the union as the representative of employees. The employer might even consult the union as to which individuals should be involved in the EPP.

Decision-Making Committees

The NLRB in *Electromation* and *Du Pont* embraced a line of cases in which employee committees that made final management decisions were found *not* to be labor organizations. If these committees are "limited to performing essentially managerial or adjudicative" functions, the board concluded that they are not dealing with management but rather acting as management.

An example of this type of EPP would be a peer review or discharge review committee composed of a group of employees to which an employee can appeal a disciplinary or discharge decision. If the committee's decision is final and binding on the employer, the committee is not dealing with the employer but acting on behalf of or as the employer. If, conversely, the committee's decisions are subject to veto or approval by management, it is in fact making a proposal to management and would be a labor organization.

A difficult issue concerns whether *intracommittee* communications constitute "dealing with" the employer for the purposes of the

NLRA. If management representatives, as a practical matter, can reject employee proposals on the committee, intracommittee communications may be considered dealing with the employer, thereby transforming the employee component of the committee into a labor organization. If, however, the committee is governed by majority decision making, management representatives are in the minority on the committee, and the committee has the power to decide matters for itself rather than simply making proposals to management, intracommittee communications will not be dealing with the employer, and neither the committee nor any portion of it would be deemed a labor organization. Similarly, if management representatives participate on the committee as observers or facilitators without the right to vote, there is no dealing and hence no labor organization.

Brainstorming, Informal Meetings, Informational Committees, and Other Unilateral Communication Devices

The NLRB in *Electromation* and *Du Pont* discussed employee activity that it described as a unilateral mechanism and therefore not within the meaning of "dealing with" the employer. The board gave as examples the use of a suggestion box, brainstorming groups or meetings, and analogous information exchanges. Apparently, however, if any suggestions or proposals are given "real or apparent consideration" by the employer, the process will be deemed bilateral, and the group will be a labor organization.

Indeed, Electromation, Inc., prior to establishing its employee committees, had conducted group meetings with randomly selected employees (half of high seniority, half of low seniority) to discuss wages, bonuses, incentive pay, attendance programs, and leave policy. The employer met with the employees in these groups on an occasional, irregular basis. There was no contention that such meetings violated the NLRA. The board stated that these group meetings were not committees created specifically for the purpose of reaching mutually acceptable solutions to identified problems but were characterized simply as "employee communication meetings." They did not meet the threshold of "dealing with" the employer.

The NLRB in *Du Pont* gave further guidance as to the difference between bilateral and unilateral dealings. A bilateral mechanism ordinarily entails a pattern of practice in which a group of employees, over time, makes proposals to management, and management responds to these proposals by acceptance or rejection by word or deed, even if compromise is not required. A unilateral mechanism exists if there are only isolated instances in which the group makes ad hoc proposals to management, followed by a management response of acceptance or rejection by word or deed. In such a case, there is no dealing, and there is no labor organization.

Informational committees are also lawful. If a committee exists for the purpose of sharing information with the employer, the committee would not ordinarily be a labor organization. That is, if the committee makes *no proposal or suggestion* to the employer and the employer simply gathers the information and does what it wishes with such information, there is no dealing and hence no labor organization.

Finally, a suggestion box is not a labor organization, even though employees make proposals to the employer. That is because the proposals—the dealings with the employer—are made *individually* and not as a group.

Safety Conferences

The NLRB in *Du Pont* made clear that a safety conference can be lawful, even if the conference involves unionized employees giving input on safety, which is a mandatory subject of bargaining. Du Pont's daylong safety conferences, held quarterly, were seen by the board as, in essence, extended brainstorming sessions. The board emphasized that the task of the employee groups was not to decide on proposals to improve safety but rather to increase personal commitment, responsibility, and acceptance of safety as Du Pont's primary concern. The board went further and said that similar conferences could be held on other mandatory subjects of bargaining. Ongoing safety committees, as envisioned by the proposed Occupational Safety and Health Administration (OSHA) rules, however, would appear to be labor organizations.

Nonrepresentative Employee Committees

The NLRB in *Electromation* and *Du Pont* raised the possibility—but did not conclude—that if an EPP is not *representative*, it might not be an NLRA labor organization. If this view ultimately prevails, employers may wish to structure their EPPs to avoid a finding of representative status. One technique of showing that there is no representative status is to include *all* employees who might be affected. Members of such a "committee of the whole" speak for themselves and represent no one else.

Another method is to establish a committee that may not include all employees but whose members speak only for themselves. If committee members are not elected, serve for only clearly defined terms, cannot succeed themselves, and, preferably, are told that they are not to act in a representative capacity and are not to solicit the views of other employees on any subject, the employer will have the factual basis to assert this defense.

Avoiding Mandatory Subjects of Bargaining

Section 2(5) of the NLRA states that the organization, agency, or committee can be a labor organization only if it exists for the purpose, in whole or part, of dealing with the employer concerning "grievances, labor disputes, wages, rates of pay, hours of employment, or conditions of work." The NLRB emphasized that nothing in its decisions would limit employer-initiated programs concerning efficiency, quality, productivity, and other essentially managerial issues. Hence a committee focused exclusively on improving the quality of the employer's products or services or on the efficiency or productivity of the employer's operations would be lawful.

To come within this safe harbor, an employer seeking to limit a committee's domain should do so in writing to the committee, informing it that no suggestions on subjects related to conditions of employment will be considered. Employers will have to exercise vigilance in enforcing such restrictions because changes in production or quality improvement processes can directly affect conditions of work.

Keeping the Employee Committee at Arm's Length

The existence of an employee committee with the characteristics of a labor organization does not, in and of itself, violate the NLRA. Only if an employer has dominated, interfered with, or given impermissible support to the formation or administration of a labor organization is Section 8(a)(2) violated.

In determining whether an employer has dominated, interfered with, or given impermissible support to the formation and administration of an employee committee, the NLRB will examine whether the committee is a creation of management, whether its structure and function are essentially determined by management, whether its continued existence depends on the fiat of management, whether members of management attended meetings or sat on the committee, whether management determined the size of the committee or how members were selected, whether members were paid for committee time, and whether office space for meetings and materials were supplied by management.

In *Electromation*, the NLRB inferred that if the formation and structure of the organization are determined by employees, employer domination is not established merely because the employer has the *potential* ability to influence the structure or effectiveness of the organization. In addition, paying members for time in meetings and giving office space and supplies would not per se be an unlawful contribution of support, especially in the context of an amicable arm's length relationship with a legitimate representative organization.

However, as a practical matter, this safe harbor would seem to require what is in effect a traditional labor union—something with which most employers would not wish to deal voluntarily. Even if an employer is successful in showing that it did not dominate, interfere with, or give impermissible support to the EPP, it may be vulnerable to a charge that it illegally recognized the labor organization without a sufficient show of majority support by employees.

Moreover, most employers would have difficulty avoiding a finding that they dominated or interfered with an EPP as currently set up and functioning. This difficulty, combined with the possibility that a legitimate in-house union may affiliate with an unfriendly outside union, urges many employers to concede the finding of domination and become closely involved with the creation and day-to-day affairs of the committee. Such employers may then attempt to minimize their legal exposure by disestablishing the committee if any outside organizing begins.

Risk Assessment

Absent corrective legislation, employers that use employee participation programs or are considering adopting such programs should undertake a risk assessment analysis. The benefits of such programs should be balanced against the likelihood of the possible penalties and their severity (see Exhibit 18.2). If changes are considered necessary in light of a possible legal challenge, the employer should balance the legal benefit of such changes with the detriment that they might cause to the program's goals.

One factor to be considered is the likelihood of union organizing. If organizing efforts are possible, unfair labor practice charges are far more likely, and the legal implications are far more serious.

Exhibit 18.2. Consequences of
an Unlawful Employee Participation Plan.

Establishing an EPP that is deemed to be an unlawfully established, assisted, or dominated labor organization can have a variety of negative consequences for the employer.

The most serious negative consequence occurs if the EPP votes to affiliate with an outside union. Because the employer has already recognized the EPP as a representative of employees, it arguably cannot withdraw that recognition simply because the EPP has affiliated with another labor organization if the leaders of the in-house organization continue in a similar leadership role with the affiliated entity. As a result, the employer might have to recognize and negotiate with an outside union without an election among employees. The employer could refuse to recognize the outside union on the basis that the EPP was never recognized pursuant to a show of majority support among employees, and therefore the EPP was never properly recognized as a union.

Potentially, a "Gissel bargaining order" by the NLRB, directing the employer to bargain with a union that has never won an election, may result. For example, the unlawful formation and domination of an "employee works committee," along with other serious unfair labor practices, resulted in Camvac International's being required to bargain in 1988 with the Teamsters, even though the Teamsters never won an election among Camvac employees.

A more likely negative consequence is the direction of a new election following a management victory in an NLRB-supervised election. If the board concludes that fair election conditions were destroyed by the unlawfully established, assisted, or dominated EPP, the employer may have to post notices of its violation and endure a second election.

The remedy in many EPP cases is the issuance of a cease-and-desist order. This occurs if the employer has unlawfully interfered with or assisted the labor organization but not dominated it. The cease-and-desist order may ban all management representatives from the EPP. If the employer has gone beyond simple interference or assistance and has dominated the EPP, the board will issue an order disestablishing the EPP altogether. Ironically, the employer may be better off with an order disestablishing the EPP than with an order banning the involvement of management representatives. Thus the employer would be better off committing the more serious domination than the less serious interference or assistance.

Indeed, some nonunion employers have for many years used employee participation programs that could be deemed labor organizations. But because no outside union has ever attempted to organize the workforce, NLRB charges have never been filed.

Another decision is whether to hold the committee close or to keep it at arm's length. Placing management members on the committee, monitoring its activities closely, providing support services, and paying for time spent on committee matters will ensure that its focus will be on the best interest of the entire enterprise and that it has the resources to accomplish its objectives. Such actions, however, effectively concede that the employer dominates the alleged labor organization.

Unionized employees are well advised to gain the union's consent to the EPPs and, indeed, to make the union a shareholder of the EPP.

A Garden-Variety Violation of NLRA Section 8(a)(2) Through Use of an Employee Participation Plan

Company X is a small manufacturer with two hundred employees at one production plant. The employees are not unionized, no union has attempted to organize them in recent years, and no union is planning to organize them.

One day, several of the rank-and-file employees approached the plant manager to ask why they did not have an employee handbook. They pointed out that they have friends who work for other employers that have employee handbooks outlining company policies, practices, and expectations. The plant manager said that there is no particular reason that Company X had no employee handbook and that he believed that it was a good idea. He asked the three employees who had approached him if they would be interested in writing the employee handbook. The three employees were not just interested but enthusiastic.

The plant manager then established an employee handbook committee comprised of the three employees who approached the plant manager plus three other employees, one elected from each of the plant's three departments. Also on the committee was a department foreperson.

The committee met immediately after work every Wednesday for ninety minutes. Committee members were paid at the overtime rate. Company X provided pizza and refreshments for each meeting. In addition, the company provided office supplies, the conference room in which the committee met, and clerical support.

The task of the committee was to write an employee handbook. Members began by codifying existing practices in the plant. On any existing practices they deemed undesirable, they discussed them as a group and then consulted with the plant manager. Where practices were undefined, the committee members adopted ones that they felt were fair to both employees and employer. The plant manager reserved the right to reject or change the handbook but said that he would exercise this right only if there was something "really off the wall" in the handbook. In the end, he approved the handbook exactly as the committee proposed it.

Company X had absolutely no intent to violate the National Labor Relations Act and, moreover, absolutely no idea that establishment of the employee handbook committee might violate the NLRA. Neither the employer nor the employees on the committee nor any other employees had any idea that anyone would consider this committee to be an illicit labor organization within the meaning of the NLRA or in any other context. None of the employees had the intent to act as a union or belong to a union. There was no intent to break the law by any party or any awareness that anyone might be violating the NLRA.

The establishment of the employee handbook committee by Company X nevertheless constituted a garden-variety violation of Section 8(a)(2) of the National Labor Relations Act.

The employee handbook committee is a labor organization

because (1) it is an organization or an employee representation committee; (2) employees participate on the employee handbook committee; (3) the committee exists for the purpose, at least in part, of dealing with Company X; and (4) those dealings concerned conditions of work.

This would likely be the result even if no members of the employee handbook committee were elected by other employees. The committee is a labor organization even though the plant manager reserved the right to veto its work product, which in effect rendered its powers advisory and nonbinding. Indeed, if the employee handbook committee were not subject to override by the plant manager, it might not be a labor organization.

Company X dominated or interfered with the formation or administration of the employee handbook committee and therefore violated Section 8(a)(2), in that it established the committee, paid overtime to the members, provided the pizza and refreshments, provided the office space and office supplies, provided clerical support, and had a member of management on the committee.

This NLRA violation occurred despite the lack of any bad intent by anyone involved with the committee and despite the lack of intent by anyone that the committee should be considered a labor organization or union.

Chapter Nineteen

Making Everyone a Stakeholder: Strategies for Addressing Conflicting Needs

Lynn R. Williams

As the president of the United Steelworkers of America, a large industrial union, I, like many of my counterparts in other unions, have looked at the concept of employee empowerment and participation with mixed emotions—not because the idea in itself is not progressive and vastly superior to the traditional adversarial approach but because of managerial intent. When management proposes implementing such programs without input from the union and without including the union as an equal partner, the necessary negotiated guidelines needed to change from a traditional to a participative effort are not addressed, which causes the union to doubt the sincerity of management's intentions. History shows that this unilateral approach simply does not work. However, when management includes the union from the outset and treats it as an equal partner, respecting the collective bargaining process, the likelihood of success is greatly enhanced.

There is no question that an effective worker-empowering, fully participative process should become the modus operandi of the future in regard to labor-management relations. How successful we will be depends on how we interact. If we are to survive in a global economy, both parties must be able to change. Unions must accept responsibility, and companies must accept and respect the rights of workers, including their right to organize. Together, and with a responsive government that puts a priority on fair trade and other appropriate policies, the future can indeed be bright.

The Environment Demands Change

As we approach the twenty-first century, it would be wise to reflect briefly on the past before we address the future.

The decade of the 1980s was the most painful and wrenching of times for organized labor in America. Industry after industry either went out of business or contracted in size. The numerous plant closures threw thousands of Americans out of work, the subsequent loss of income and health coverage destroying for the displaced the American dream. Countless communities suffered drastic reductions to their tax base as a result of these closings at a time when they were most needed.

I would be remiss if I did not make a few observations on this extraordinary period in our history. If we look back in time, all traumatic events—social upheavals, wars, and the rest—occurred not for any one single reason but due to a number of interacting causes. Likewise, the massive loss of industries and jobs during the 1980s did not occur for any one reason.

For example, much was written about the closing of steel facilities. Many observers unfairly blamed the allegedly overcompensated, unproductive, recalcitrant steelworker. Precious little was written about the disastrous effect of our government's stimulative fiscal policy (tax cuts) or the Federal Reserve's restrictive monetary policy (manipulating interest rates and money supply) and the large account deficits that followed. To pay for these large deficits, government had to borrow massive amounts of money from home and abroad, at high interest rates, causing the U.S. dollar to appreciate relative to foreign currencies by 40 percent or more. In effect, the steel industry, as well as numerous other American industries that compete in a global economy, had a 40 percent or greater tax placed on their products almost overnight. At the same time, the domestic steel industry was not modernizing its facilities, while the steel producers in Europe and Japan were installing the latest steelmaking technology and equipment. In this atmosphere, the lack of investment in new, more productive steelmaking technology simply made the situation worse. Domestic producers had to compete against foreign concerns at a double disadvantage: weak currency and antiquated equipment.

Needless to say, these two situations alone would have sufficed to bring the steel industry to its knees. However, at the same time, newer steel facilities were being brought on-line around the world. Most of these facilities were financed by the World Bank and the International Monetary Fund at very low interest rates back in the 1970s. These new facilities had the latest steelmaking technologies, and of course, the people who ran these new operations were paid very low wages. When the new facilities were brought on-line, they simply added to existing world steelmaking capacity. Initially, it was believed that worldwide demand would grow and that most of this new capacity would be consumed internally by the new producers. Unfortunately, the projections were wrong. Steel prices plummeted further, adding to the woes of the domestic steel industry.

A number of foreign governments subsidized their domestic operations by allowing them to continue to produce beyond internal consumption needs, dumping the remainder in other countries—the first country of choice being the United States.

Concurrent with these episodes, newspaper articles and books were published chastising the United Steelworkers and the steel companies for being unable to work together to reduce costs, enhance quality, improve productivity, and generally improve relations among themselves. Unfortunately, at the time no labor-management cooperative system existed in the industry. However—and this is the point I am trying to make—even if it had, it would have at best delayed the inevitable, given the externalities at play. Although labor-management cooperation is certainly a desirable goal that we should all be striving for, unless other mechanisms are in place to complement and facilitate the participative process, this desirable goal cannot, in and of itself, save industries and jobs, given the realities of global commerce. Consequently, lost industries and jobs, like revolutions and wars, are caused by reasons born of more than one mother.

Joint Problems Require Joint Solutions

The idea of management and union working together toward a common goal is not a contemporary idea. Phil Murray, founder and first president of the United Steelworkers of America, envisioned a three-step approach to contemporary unionism, embodying the concept of "industrial democracy." The first step was to have the companies recognize the union as the lawful agent of its employees for reasons of collective bargaining. The second was to seek a binding agreement (labor contract) that would spell out the terms with respect to wages, benefits, working conditions, and grievance and arbitration procedures. The third was to enter into a joint labor-management partnership dedicated to making the enterprises viable and profitable. Murray rightly theorized that if the companies could not remain competitive, all of the titanic struggles to obtain the first two goals would eventually go for naught. Unfortunately, this goal languished in obscurity for many years, and for a number of reasons, including World War II and the predominance of American industry for many years following the war, abetted by the fact that the economies and productive capacities of Europe and Japan lay in ruin.

The rigid authoritarian management structure, which always existed, simply became more entrenched, causing union militancy to increase proportionately. The parties continued their arm's length relationship through the 1950s and 1960s. In 1971, the steel companies and the union agreed to a new collective bargaining concept known as the experimental negotiating agreement (ENA). This agreement ensured that the union would not strike the industry and that the companies would not lock out the union. The contract continued to be negotiated every three years by the parties, providing minimum assurances absent agreement, but there would be no stoppage of work. In a way, this was the first step toward participation.

In the 1980s, the pressures alluded to earlier came into full force. These circumstances caused both parties to examine their relationship yet again. It was becoming increasingly clear that our relationship was sorely in need of change. Both parties realized that a movement toward cooperation served the needs of all. As a result, the Labor-Management Participation Team (LMPT) process was introduced into our basic labor agreements with the steel industry.

The language gave the local parties the option to adopt this new process. Where agreement existed, the process was implemented. Elsewhere, rejection could be attributed to the mistrust and antagonism that had built up over the years. At some locations where the parties adopted the LMPT process, there was a genuine effort to change the adversarial relationships that had developed between them. Initially, changes came slowly at some locations. However, at other sites, productivity improvements were made from the very inception of the process. Some of the improvements were small, but at some locations, the savings from this joint endeavor could be measured in the millions of dollars. It was becoming increasingly clear that where management listened to and confided in workers, positive results could be shown. These situations gave impetus to expanding the participative process.

In 1985, the United Steelworkers of America and LSE (a joint partnership between LTV Corporation and Sumitomo Metals) agreed to a novel four-year agreement based on labor-management cooperation and employee empowerment. When it came time to negotiate the next agreement, the local union insisted that the joint partnership concept be strengthened. The parties subsequently agreed to have bargaining-unit people make more of the day-to-day decisions in daily operations. The unionized workers at this facility now develop training, progression, and pay schedules. They also determine work and vacation schedules. Through the use of integrated process controls (IPCs), they have implemented a number of method and operational changes, making the facility more efficient. *In effect, they have changed the way work has traditionally been done.* This facility has made a profit every year since its inception.

Cooperative Partnership Is a Joint Solution

In 1986, National Steel Corporation and the United Steelworkers entered into an equally innovative labor agreement based on "cooperative partnership," providing the foundation for conduct during the term of the contract. The guiding philosophy agreed to by the parties is embodied in the agreement's simple preamble: "National Steel Corporation and the United Steelworkers of America recognize that in order for the Corporation to meet the challenge of survival and the need for long-range prosperity, growth, and secure employment *each must be committed to* a partnership that extends from the shop floor to the executive office to solve problems quickly and in a cooperative manner."

It was further recognized that if this approach were to develop and mature, a primary condition had to exist: since people would be encouraged to become directly involved in all aspects of the production process through employee empowerment, the assurance of not being laid off was central to both security and motivation. As a result, the following language was negotiated into the labor agreement: "Employees covered by this Employment Security Plan ('Plan') will not be laid off except in the case of a disaster. If a disaster occurs resulting in the layoff of employees, the Plan will be terminated for all plants and the provisions of all SUB Plans will apply." Additional language spelled out the definition of *disaster*. Other considerations for employment security, dealing with seniority requirements, were also included. It was further understood that any decrease in staffing would be accomplished only through attrition for the duration of the agreement. A contract subsequently negotiated has extended these terms.

Although changes did not occur overnight, gradual progress has been made on a continuous basis, to the extent that National Steel Corporation was the only domestic integrated steel producer to post a profitable quarter for the year 1992.

The aforementioned examples constitute only two success stories; there are many more. At the same time, I should note that we also have many contracts that have language alluding to some form of labor-management participation, which regrettably amount to little more than words in a labor agreement.

The Union Must Be a Full Partner in Managing the Enterprise

As can be seen from the LSE and National Steel agreements, two extremely important prerequisites come into play. In the first, management recognizes the union as a full partner in promoting the participative process by agreeing to certain parameters established through the collective bargaining process. In my opinion, the greatest mistake that management can make is to exclude the union from being an equal partner in this process. Bypassing the local union officers and the international union and attempting unilaterally to impose quality control circles and the like that lack the principles embodied in a true participative system simply run contrary to the objectives of such endeavors. Experience has shown that a one-sided approach is doomed to fail. The implicit strengths of a union and the protections provided in a labor agreement counterbalance single-purpose management initiatives in changing work practices. However, when the union is included in changing how work is to be performed, these same contractual protections serve as a "power equilibrium" that drives the parties toward common goals and objectives, minus the baggage associated with traditional systems.

The other important factor that I alluded to earlier is the guarantee of not being laid off as a result of agreeing to a new way of doing things. If people are to be truly empowered to make decisions, learn new skills, and assume new responsibilities, it must be done in an environment where people are not fearful of losing their job or of causing others to lose theirs. Consequently, an employment guarantee is a must.

Other Factors

Five other factors of great importance should also be integrated into any viable attempt to promote and produce a truly workable participative and empowerment process:

- The people at the top of both organizations (company and union) must make a total commitment to making the participative process the cornerstone of the labor agreement.
- Management must be willing to share its authority in regard to strategic and workplace decision making.
- Management must be willing to share information with the union.
- Workers must be properly trained and compensated for learning new skills.
- Workers should share in the increased profits generated by the efficiencies of this new system.

Commitment from the Top

The decision-making structure of all management organizations tends to be top-down. Because ultimate power rests at the top, any decisions involving major change must come from the top. Consequently, it is imperative that management's desire to change from a traditional model to a participative model be initiated at the highest echelon of the company.

Any plant manager who would attempt to initiate a participative philosophy without the blessing of top management would be hindered from taking the innovative steps needed for a successful program. Because successful implementation normally involves modifying portions of the labor agreement, the plant manager could end up in conflict with corporate human relations policy. Second, the cost associated with training union and management people in this new process, as well as the added cost of upgrading and expanding job skills, could bring the manager into direct conflict with the chief financial officer of the company. For these and other reasons, support at the top is an absolute must.

On the union side, we are more of a bottom-up organization. The wishes of our members are directed through their local union officers and eventually to the union's executive board. Bargaining goals in all industries, large and small, are formulated by elected representatives who make up a policy committee for that industry. The union's executive board, technical staff, and servicing representatives serve as support groups in formulating bargaining goals.

With the advent of greater labor-management participation, it was becoming increasingly evident that the international union had to train and use headquarters technicians to assist members in the nuances of this new concept of performing work. Traditionally, this same resource group had provided training to our membership in pensions and insurance, safety and health, wages, and other areas. As more and more locations began to experiment with this new process, it became apparent that there was a need to provide technical assistance to the local unions. As a result, we created an LMPT task force from our international headquarters office. This group assists local unions from many different industries and works with management to develop participative programs.

At a union convention held in August 1992, our membership approved Resolution 15, "Workplace Democracy." This resolution is a distillation of our experiences and desires in developing a truly democratic work environment for our membership. We feel that in such an atmosphere, both the company and the union will benefit—the company through better product quality, increased productivity, and higher profit, the union through workplace empowerment, added job skills, and a share of increased profits.

Our 1993 Basic Steel Policy Statement incorporated the guidelines of Resolution 15. As a result, the cooperative and participative process is now a legitimate bargaining goal of our union.

Sharing in Decisions

Once a truly democratic and participative environment has been created, one that draws on the experience and knowledge that workers bring to the process of producing a product or service, the meaningful sharing of day-to-day workplace decisions can begin.

The old adage "No one knows the job as well as the person doing it" can take on a more positive meaning in a participative process. In realizing this new freedom, the people closest to the production process tend to apply all of their inherent skills and knowledge. As this new force is unleashed, product quality and productivity increase. Studies have also documented an increase in worker morale, a reduction in absenteeism, and a decrease in the number of grievances filed.

Workers must also have a say in the long-term planning and decision-making process. Because of their close proximity to the critical points of production and their knowledge of what is needed to improve the quality of product and methods of operations, workers can contribute immeasurably to future financial planning and new product design. At locations that truly democratize the workplace, worker councils can aid management in making present and future decisions, as both parties now have a greater shared stake in the future of the enterprise.

Sharing of Information

Just as it is important that workers share in workplace decisions, it is equally important that management share all information with the people who ultimately produce the product. To deny workers such information is simply silly. Under traditional management systems, information is compartmentalized and stored in separate bureaucratic layers, creating inefficiency and false fiefdoms. Managers protect their own turf—probably out of insecurity—to the detriment of everyone involved in the enterprise. This behavior might even be taken as proof of the bankruptcy of autocratic management.

It stands to reason that better-informed workers, using their inherent skills, can be a positive force. Simply stated, when the workers who have the "how" are given the "why," a new dynamic is created.

New Skills and New Compensation Systems

Unions have often been criticized for adhering to rigid job description and work rules with limited scope. However, what the critics fail to mention is that such limited and rigid job descriptions and practices were a creation of management.

The philosophy of relegating work assignments to limited activities was developed by Frederick W. Taylor, the father of time and motion studies. His system was based on the theory of management controlling all aspects of the production process. Managers would do all the planning and thinking; workers would follow orders, leave their brains at the plant gate, and obey all directives with little or no input into the enterprise.

Some authorities would argue that this theory worked well for most of the twentieth century, given America's strength at the time in the world's economic arena. Others would contend that this approach simply perpetuated the European caste system, which developed during the medieval age and was imposed on the fledgling American industrial complex at the turn of the twentieth century. I tend to think that the latter was the case.

A master-serf relationship developed between managers and

workers. Workers were relegated to performing repetitive or limited tasks. Seldom were they asked for their opinion on anything. Taylorism separated workers from the total process, institutionalizing managerial control of the enterprise.

Today, Taylorism is dead, industrial class society is in retreat, and a new reality is upon us. This new world cries out for fundamental change. For domestic industry to survive and compete in today's world, workers must be trained in new and old skills. Cross-training of people assigned to a specific area must encompass the duties of more than one classification, and new skills must be learned because of changing technology.

In the past, when management would attempt to negotiate job changes with the union or unilaterally impose "job combinations" on the workforce, the union would inevitably resist, for obvious reasons: the combining of jobs normally coincided with the loss of employment. However, with both an employment guarantee and an effective employee empowerment program in place, worker fears are alleviated, and a more responsive atmosphere results.

Finally, the parties must develop a compensation system to reward people for learning new skills. This can be accomplished by using the job evaluation manuals that are incorporated into the labor agreements or by other creative means.

When workers are trained in new skills, empowered in the workplace, made part of the decision-making process, and compensated for the same, the results can only be positive.

Sharing in the Profits

The direct result of all the aforementioned changes should be greater profits. Obviously, the workers who have contributed to that result should receive their fair share of the increased earnings. To deny them would constitute a great injustice and could imperil the continuity so important to the long-term process of profit maintenance.

Gain sharing and profit sharing are the two most popular methods of sharing in the improvements and the subsequent increase in profits that normally follow.

Note that neither of these methods, nor any others that might be created, should be considered as the only means for workers to receive future additional compensation. As has always been the case, future general wage increases and benefit improvements should be left to the collective bargaining process.

The United Steelworkers and the New Workplace

As previously stated, working with management has always been a goal of the United Steelworkers of America. In 1992, our union saw fit to institutionalize the cooperative and empowerment process through our bargaining and policy statements. These positions were not developed to be taken lightly. We are sincere in working with all the companies where we represent employees who wish to adopt this new democratic process. We simply ask to be full partners in bargaining, implementing, and executing this new process. How we deal with one another in the future and how democratic we make the workplace will in many cases determine the future viability of different industries and whether or not good-paying jobs will continue to exist. Historically, democracy has shown itself to be the political and social system of choice to all who have had a choice, and for those who have not, it is the ultimate dream.

If we can transfer these same democratic rights and freedoms that we enjoy as citizens into the workplace, why should we not expect the same human responses? The answer truly is obvious.

We face an uncertain world. Survey after survey shows that more and more people see less of a future for themselves and their children. As a nation, we have lost many jobs, good-paying and otherwise, and every day we continue to see them erode. Some observers attribute these job losses to changing markets, flagging competitiveness, technological changes, and other circumstances. To a certain degree, they are right, for historically, displacement has always been associated with economic change. During the 1980s, the downsizing of many industries was attributed to "rationalization."

Conclusion

At the beginning of this chapter, I touched on the ill-fated economic policies of government that contributed to industry and job losses. A lack of government and industry economic planning caused further decline, and the rest was, for the most part, unavoidable. The task before us now is to learn from our past mistakes.

Considering that capital and technology are portable, that many people in the world are willing to work for less than Americans expect, and that certain governments are willing to look the other way when it comes to polluting their lands, all in the name of economic development, it is clear that the tasks of modern developed industrial societies are immense.

We in advanced societies are revolted by the conditions that have led to our decline. But like it or not, we must face the realities in a coordinated and concerted manner if people are ever to believe that there is a better future.

Much can be done by democratizing the workplace. Numerous examples have shown substantial productivity increases, lower labor unit costs, and quality improvements. All of this has been done while maintaining good-paying jobs in viable, profitable industries. However, there are other elements that must be part of any overall equation with respect to competing in a world economy.

We must have international laws that prohibit multinational companies from exploiting workers by paying them low wages with no benefits, world standards with regard to pollution, trade laws that level the playing field for all, and laws that protect workers and their right to organize. A more humane and democratic worldwide policy dealing with worker rights should be adopted along the lines of the conventions adopted by the International Labor Congress.

These conventions should be incorporated into all future trading agreements such as GATT and NAFTA.

On the national scene, government, industry, and labor must work together in developing apprenticeship programs for new entrants into the workplace and training centers that teach the latest technologies.

Unions will continue to be a voice for social justice; from that we will never waver. We will continue to petition the various branches of government and to persuade any forces, in and out of government, that are unsympathetic to the equality of all of our citizens.

Some fifty-odd years ago, unions led the fight for livable wages, decent working conditions, and human dignity. We stand ready to work with management in developing a democratic process that will unleash the imagination and ingenuity of the men and women of our union, whom we so proudly represent.

Our task is great, but there is still time to change. There is no doubt in my mind that together we can do it.

Part Seven

Next Steps

Chapter Twenty

Managing Employees as a Source of Competitive Advantage

Howard Risher, Charles Fay

Organizations have taken big strides in the past few years to move away from the work management practices that emerged in the 1930s and 1940s. Markets have become too complicated and demanding to rely on the command-and-control model, in which a few senior executives make the key decisions. This model assumed that workers were extensions of the machines that dominated the industrial scene and our management philosophies until recently.

This thinking has still not completely disappeared. Over the past couple of years, workforce reductions have become an almost weekly occurrence. The actions are normally announced as a cost control decision. Many employers have used some version of the "People are our greatest asset" statement in their advertising, but there is never any reference to the value of the assets that are lost in the layoffs. It is all too apparent that employees are a cost to be controlled and, whenever possible, reduced.

If workers were actually managed as an asset, the concern would shift to measuring return on investment and strategies for increasing the return. That would open the door to a different view of training expenses and to policies and practices to make workers more productive. When we invest in an asset, we want to make sure that we will be able to take maximum advantage of its inherent capabilities. Integral to business planning is the effective utilization of assets. Yet we are too often content to limit employees to roles that barely tap their capabilities. We would never manage other assets that way.

The view that employees are a potential source of competitive advantage is not widely held at the senior management level. The idea that they will be the "only sustainable source" of competitive advantage, to use Lester Thurow's (1992) argument, is a new concept. That view has important ramifications for our management policies and practices.

Among those ramifications are the logic and benefits derived from layoffs. Payroll costs rarely exceed 50 percent of operating costs and in some industries are as low as 10 percent. A layoff of 10 percent of the workforce translates into at most a 5 percent reduction in operating costs and in reality far less because the layoffs typically hit workers at the lower pay levels.

Studies have shown that layoffs have a demoralizing effect on the workers who keep their jobs. The feelings of fear and anxiety and loss of trust persist long after the layoffs occur. It may well be that the negative consequences of a layoff measured in individual employee productivity and reluctance among employees to recommit to the organization and its goals offset the immediate saving in dollars.

The view of employees as a cost rather than an asset also helps explain our reluctance to invest in employees. American companies spend less on training than companies in Japan and Germany (Thurow, 1992, p. 54). When American companies do invest in training, it is generally focused on the specific skills needed to perform a current job or the next job in a career path. Very little is spent on broader training that would prepare the workforce to absorb new technologies. Training that has an immediate payoff helps improve current productivity or quality, but it is not an investment in the future.

Employee training as an investment for the future is an important public policy issue. There is solid evidence that investing in basic background knowledge and skills makes an economy more competitive. Recognition that employees can be a source of competitive advantage would help justify increased public and private expenditures for training.

Employees can be a sustainable source of competitive advantage if work and workers are organized and managed to tap their full capabilities. Individuals who have worked as supervisors know that workers hold back knowledge that could improve their unit's performance. This is attributable in part to the "us versus them" culture that prevails in all too many organizations and has been aggravated by the recent wave of layoffs. It is also attributable to the recognition that managers have low expectations and to work management practices that have ignored possible worker input. Scientific management principles focus on workers' physical capabilities, essentially ignoring their mental capabilities, and that continues to permeate our supervisory practices.

Empowerment

A few organizations have tried and benefited from "participative management" over the years, but empowerment is a new phenomenon. It goes beyond simple participation and carries the connotation that workers are expected to use their brain. It also suggests that workers should be held responsible for solving operating problems and for making their work unit successful. Empowerment has become the avowed management philosophy in numerous organizations, even though many managers and supervisors are still resisting the perceived loss of power.

The impetus for empowerment was the rush to quality management starting in the late 1980s. The foundation of Deming's philosophy is the worker's commitment to quality and customer satisfaction. An empowered workforce is essential to a successful quality program. The decisions needed to satisfy a customer's needs or to correct operating problems without costly delay have to be made as the need arises, and that can only be done by front-line workers.

Empowerment also gives workers at least an implied obligation and responsibility to correct other organizational problems.

Realistically, they are in the best position to see and assess the immediate implications of management's decisions. The rationale for empowerment is the worker's value in improving operations and in contributing to the organization's success. When supervisors or managers or co-workers make mistakes, it would be advantageous to encourage workers to offer suggestions and to play a role in correcting problems that arise outside their formal job responsibilities.

Empowerment is not a contractual right, but once this door is opened, it is difficult, if not impossible, to close it and revert to the control-oriented supervision that was common until recently. We have to appreciate, however, that employees may not be immediately comfortable with an empowered environment or have the skills to work effectively in one. An analogy would be the first experience with freedom and a market economy at the end of Communist rule in the former Soviet states. The initial faltering steps toward a market economy were not fully productive or efficient, but once people learn how to function in the new environment, they will resist any changes that reduce their power. After working as extensions of a machine for ten or twenty years, workers can be expected to take early missteps but should soon learn to handle their redefined roles.

This is not to suggest that every employee will make the transition successfully. Employees who have not been challenged in the past may have lost some of their knowledge or problem-solving ability. They may also have inadequate confidence to work effectively without direct supervision. Others may have such deep-seated hostility or distrust that it will always get in the way. But most can make the transition and will thrive in an environment where they feel they are making an important contribution to their work group's success.

An empowered workforce should be a more productive workforce. The potential for improvement is dramatic. The 30 to 40 percent increases found in the research may not be realized in every situation, but even 10 to 15 percent would significantly improve most bottom lines, and more than a few organizations have noted much greater increases in performance. The potential makes it difficult to justify the continuation of traditional work management practices.

Planning the Transition to a High-Performance Organization

The transition to this new world of work is not smooth or simple. Change is never easy to accept. Long-standing beliefs about appropriate behaviors in a work setting can be tough to overcome. These beliefs both influence our personal behavior and provide a framework for evaluating the behavior of others. Behavioral change requires a period of trial and error before an organization can expect to be fully effective. Employees and supervisors alike will have to reconsider their work habits and develop new work relationships with the people around them.

Organizations are extraordinarily complex, and major change initiatives must contend with a long list of "action levers" (defined in Chapter One as new policies, practices, or technology that can improve productivity, adopted singly or in combination and managed by the organization). That the results have failed to meet management's expectations in numerous situations warrants caution and detailed planning. Experience with total quality management suggests how difficult it is to transform an organization. TQM can be profoundly important to an organization's future, but it has become obvious that it is difficult to get everyone on the same bandwagon.

The list of action levers in Chapter One is a long one; most of them must be made to fit each organization's unique needs. This is not a shopping list of off-the-shelf alternatives. Our experience with TQM suggests clearly that narrowly focused change efforts in isolation have a limited chance of success. The levers are interrelated and should be applied in a systematic way. Figure 1.1 illustrates a model for considering the factors that affect workforce performance. No single lever by itself is an adequate answer.

Unfortunately, we do not fully understand how the action levers come together to create a high-performance organization. We can recognize one from the performance data, and the employees in that organization can ordinarily tell that something good is happening. But they may not be able to explain why they are performing at higher levels. The work unit has a history that precedes the success, and that history involves a number of changes and prior interventions intended to improve aspects of the operation. To understand how high performance got started, we would have to understand the circumstances that preceded the shift to high performance.

Experience suggests that the problems—and the failures—are often attributable to change efforts that are too narrowly focused. For example, the introduction of a local area network (LAN) can significantly increase productivity. But if that is the only change, there will always be employees who use the system only for sending E-mail messages. A LAN changes the way employees interact, making it significantly easier and faster for people in different parts of an organization to communicate directly. The implications of this technological change for the formal and informal interpersonal network created before E-mail need to be understood before it is rolled out. If the interpersonal impact is ignored, the technology could adversely affect established working relationships, or a lot of money could be spent with little or no impact.

Understanding the action levers is the starting point. Eventually, they have to be combined to create an operating system of people and technology. This is far more complicated than the job of an architect in linking together the operating systems—electrical, plumbing, heating, structural—to create a building. High-performing organizations cannot happen without the technical expertise behind the action levers. That expertise comes from a number of professional disciplines. Bringing these experts together is one of the objectives of this book. However, technical expertise alone cannot generate an action plan for becoming a high-performance organization.

Getting There from Here

The action levers mean very little until we assess the current situation, understand the factors that can be expected to impede the change initiative, and develop an integrated strategy for moving ahead. It is probably true that every organization can improve its operations. Some, however, will find that they have a long way to go to become high performers. The action levers are tools available to managers, but they cannot be used effectively until the problems have been fully understood.

Because performance is driven in part by cultural factors, an assessment of the culture is an important early step. This can be done by conducting focus groups or by using written or electronic survey questionnaires. The emphasis placed on performance and on reaching high performance levels is a key consideration that can be analyzed. It is particularly important to identify performance problems and to seek input on solutions from employees.

An element of the culture is the labor-management relationship. In some organizations, this may be the overriding constraint to changing the way work is organized and managed.

In every organization, employees work within the parameters of a so-called psychological contract. The contract is unwritten and largely unstated, but it implicitly recognizes what the company is going to do for the employee and what the employee is going to do for the company. It controls the level of effort the employee is willing and expected to make as well as the linkage between performance and organizational rewards. For example, if an employee is asked to work more hours than normal, as might be occur on a special project, it may be advantageous for the employer to grant extra time off when the project is completed or to recognize the extra effort with a bonus or other special reward—otherwise, the employee may be reluctant to put forth the same level of effort the next time.

We must appreciate that employee willingness to accept change—a clause in the psychological contract—has been adversely affected by the recent round of layoffs. Over the past few years, workers have lost all sense of job security, even in companies that have not experienced staff reductions. They are now leery of change and more reluctant than ever to believe that it is in their best interests to accept change.

A change initiative that requires different behavior from employees prompts a need to renegotiate the contract. The options for the employee are to seek other employment, to go along merely to placate management and to survive, or to work with management to influence the proposed changes so that both sides win. Most of the action levers represent a change in the work situation; either they involve the need to develop new social and working relationships, or they require the development of new work behaviors. These behavioral changes demand a redefinition of the contract. The situation will prompt a high level of discomfort until new and satisfactory work relationships are established. This makes the contract an important consideration in planning a change initiative.

It is also important to understand how technology can be augmented to improve performance. Productivity and quality are often constrained by technology, so any limits must be taken into account when assessing the potential for performance improvement.

Following the assessment, it should be possible to estimate the potential improvement. In most situations, it will be useful to estimate "stretch" performance improvement goals. People who are goal-oriented work most effectively when they have something to shoot for. If there are reasons to anticipate dramatic improvement, it may make sense to move incrementally toward the goal. If the goals appear to be too difficult, they could trigger labor-management friction. Because employees share a sense of the performance norms and expectations, it will be important for them to feel good about their achievements.

Alternatively, it may make sense to focus on a continuous improvement strategy. This is consistent with the TQM philosophy. Rather than working to achieve specific performance goals, employees are asked to produce incremental improvements over time.

The assessment should also establish a framework for a change strategy. The objective is to identify the work system parameters that need to be changed, the action levers that appear suited to the situation, and the schedule for the initiative.

A Champion to Lead the Way

High performance does not happen by itself. It must be carefully planned, and experience indicates that it needs a "champion" who provides leadership and organizational support. People do not feel comfortable with change; they tend to resist the unknown, and they are often reluctant to commit to a change initiative that has an uncertain future. The champion provides the leadership needed to get people on the bandwagon.

Championship sports teams always have one or more individuals who help provide the cohesion that brings individual players together into a smoothly functioning team. They also play a role in creating the work ethic and emotional commitment needed to outperform other teams. The leaders also help set and gain acceptance for group performance standards. Some teams are probably satisfied to be average; others expect to be champions. That starts with the team leader, who must make excellence a group goal.

The leader's role in setting performance expectations or standards is often overlooked. Someone has to decide and convince others that it is possible to be the best. It is not easy or in most cases reasonable to aspire to world-class standards. People like to be challenged, but they need to be convinced that the improbable is nevertheless possible.

From a different perspective, many of our human resource practices have focused on minimal performance standards. This has in part been imposed by equal employment opportunity laws, but by now it has become part of the group psychology in many work units: "Everyone was 'good enough' to be hired." It has also been perpetuated by our merit pay systems: "We need to keep our employees 'whole.' Everyone deserves some pay increase." The job of the leader is to make sure that all employees know that they have the capabilities to be the best. "Raising the bar," as this is sometimes called, is an essential role of a leader.

Within an organization, the champion must also play a role in gaining the support of other internal resources. People often view change skeptically, making it difficult for them to provide the support that may be needed. In fact, change initiatives are often resisted by support units if they alter individual work roles. For example, work teams often assume some degree of responsibility for quality, which diminishes the importance of separate quality departments. This may make quality staff members reluctant to provide the training needed for team members to understand quality management issues. The champion justifies and expedites the support needed by the team involved in the change initiative.

The role of the champion has to be filled by the right individuals. Corporate search committees spend months choosing a new CEO. In a number of recent top executive searches covered in the business press, the individual was selected more on softer abilities, such as the proven ability to change organizations, than on technical or industrial knowledge. As we move more toward teams, where the power to issue commands or direct orders is diminished, the softer leadership skills will become even more important.

To Benchmark or Not to Benchmark?

Benchmarking has gained wide acceptance as a simple process for understanding what works and what doesn't. The logic is simple: if we can find out how the best-performing companies do something, we can learn from them and replicate their success. Site visits are essential to benchmarking, and it is important to commit enough time to the process to understand the nuances that explain each organization's successes and failures.

There is no question that benchmarking may be useful. However, it involves a significant commitment of time and expense. The process cannot be planned as a couple of two-hour meetings. Learning what not to do is often easy; learning all the reasons why an organization is successful will take time. It is important to appreciate that each benchmarking discussion is a learning experience that provides new insights. Trying to develop adequate expertise to ensure success will require an extensive time investment.

An overriding consideration is the complexity of the problems in transforming work management systems. It may not be possible to understand all of the reasons why organizations are outstanding at something.

The flip side of this problem is how difficult it is to replicate another organization's success. Every organization and even every work group (unless it is a greenfield operation) has a track record of prior successes and failures and a history of interpersonal relations. This baggage will affect any current initiatives to change the group's functioning. If the group had no ongoing problems, it would not be necessary to change the work system. This reality makes it virtually impossible to rely on another organization's strategies or action plans to achieve success. Benchmarking may make it possible to identify and avoid the obvious potholes, but the magic of outstanding performance is situationally unique.

"You Get What You Measure"

Each organization's unique characteristics must be understood and considered in developing the change strategy. Following an evaluation of the potential for improvement and of the alternative action levers, the planning should start with the specification of management's goals and expectations. If there is a need for changed behavior at the management level, that must be addressed in the planning process. The plan should include the identification of measures to assess the impact of the initiative.

Some initiatives have an immediate payoff, but others represent an investment that are expected to pay off in the future. If the workforce is an asset, it makes sense to plan for future returns. From this perspective, it can be a sound strategy to make current investments in the organization, with the realization that it will take months or even longer until the changes begin to pay off.

The issue of measurement is an ongoing concern. We have to assess the impact of the change initiative and, because the primary focus is workforce performance, its impact on how workers perform. Exhibit 20.1 lists possible measures. It is a long list that encompasses both hard measures of operating performance and soft measures of employee attitudes and organizational effectiveness. If the change initiative affects the organization's performance, some combination of these measures will capture its impact and provide a basis for assessing and managing the initiative.

The measurement process serves both to keep senior managers abreast of results and to provide feedback to members of the work group, confirming their progress and highlighting areas where they need to improve. Ongoing communication and feedback are vital in any change process. Management must recognize that the performance data are important to workers and managers alike. Traditionally, managers have focused on financial performance data, particularly measures of profitability, but there is strong evidence that workers respond best to "line of sight" measures—those that are relevant to operations that the workers control or influence (such as scrap). These measures have meaning and provide direct, almost immediate feedback on their performance. The organization stands to benefit if workers can see and appreciate the importance of their efforts.

Exhibit 20.1. Common Work Redesign Measures.

Financial and Production Outcomes

Quantity
- Output or sales/raw scores
- Actual to budget/standard

Quality
- Rejects, repairs, defects
- Customer returns
- Redo, rework
- Yield
- Scrap, materials usage

Costs
- Repairs, errors, defects
- Downtime
- Labor costs, staffing ratios
- Overtime, subcontracted hours
- Recruitment costs
- Treatment of injuries
- Complaints or grievances
- Job stress, psychosomatic symptoms
- Skill or competency levels
- Work stoppages and strikes
- Suggestions

Work Team or Group Attitudes
- Goal clarity
- Cohesiveness
- Values
- Process effectiveness

Attitudes Toward the Work Itself
- Task responsibility
- Task significance, challenge, identity
- Task freedom and autonomy
- Knowledge of results
- Task effort
- Organization commitment
- Organization culture
- Skill, task variety
- Leadership, supervisory skills
- Leadership initiating structure

Individual Attitudes
- Job satisfaction
- Supervisor satisfaction
- Client or customer satisfaction
- Co-worker satisfaction
- Work motivation
- Job involvement and commitment
- Intrinsic rewards
- Extrinsic rewards
- Union receptivity
- Attitudes toward change

The line-of-sight concept is an important recent development. It is instructive to consider the concept in light of our experience with profit-sharing plans. These plans have been in use for decades, but concern about their effectiveness is widespread. First, many employers are reluctant to disclose true profitability data to workers, in part due to confidentiality considerations. More important, experience with profit-sharing plans has never confirmed the expectation that they can be effective motivators.

Despite the common logic that workers will work harder if they share in the profits, research has shown that workers do not fully accept, at the level needed for motivation, profitability as a measure of their performance. Few workers fully understand how net income is determined, and too many factors intervene between their performance and bottom-line profits. Their line of sight is clouded by such factors as accounting policies, demand for the product, and the price and availability of raw materials. Because workers do not see a clear link between their efforts and profits, profit-sharing plans have generally failed to live up to their purported promise.

This is not to suggest that there are no successful profit-sharing plans or that it is inappropriate to include a measure of profitability in new incentive plans. It is fundamentally important to select measures that are linked to profitability. At each level in the organization, the link between work group performance and financial success must be reflected in the design of incentive plans and communicated to employees. Even if profit sharing is not a strong motivator, it is important to reinforce the importance of remaining profitable and to limit payouts if profits go south.

Making the performance data available to work groups serves to reinforce their empowerment. As they begin to understand how their performance affects results, they may—with an effective strategy—accept responsibility for the results and reorient their behavior to produce improvements in the measures. One of the most important goals is to create a "business partnership" among workers, their unions, and the organization.

"What's in It for Me?"

The acceptance of responsibility is important to the success of a performance improvement initiative. For some workers, particularly independent professionals and owner-operators, we have an almost automatic expectation that they are committed to high performance standards and to the importance of meeting customer expectations. It is their business, and success rides on their performance. For other workers, we too often expect them to put forth a minimal effort or to be indifferent to the performance of their unit. The goal, of course, is to transform the latter attitude to the former.

Realistically, lackadaisical or indifferent workers developed their negative attitudes over a long period of time, events throughout their lives contributing to their outlook today. For many, their work experience has instilled a deep-seated distrust of management or hostility toward supervision. This is almost inevitable in an "us versus them" environment, and organizations have found it difficult to develop more positive working relationships. These relationships have evolved and been reinforced for too many years. The problems will continue to surface and adversely affect operations until we have a new generation of managers and workers.

Nevertheless, the belief is strong that people would like to do a good job, to be viewed by co-workers and supervisors as valuable contributors, and to have opportunities to develop and use their full capabilities. The more success they experience, the more they want. In contrast to the counterproductive performance of workers in some situations, this is a very optimistic view of human nature. Yet in most instances, workers demonstrate a strong commitment and acceptance of unusually high work standards. People are not born with an innate reluctance to be cooperative. Moreover, it is illogical to assume that only certainly types of workers (such as professionals) want to be successful. The problem was spawned by traditional work management philosophies.

Workers who are committed to high performance meet important personal needs at work. That is clearly true of professionals of all descriptions and others in a surprising assortment of occupations. Even workers in the most menial and repetitive jobs can exhibit the same sense of commitment that we expect in highly educated professionals. The underlying personal needs are driven by human nature, and the importance of meeting those needs has been confirmed in a variety of work settings (see Maslow, 1954).

Within this context, an employer can control and manage its reward system to help workers satisfy their needs. The North American culture places a heavy emphasis on financial rewards, but there is also an almost endless array of nonfinancial rewards. Nonfinancial rewards can take almost any form, but most satisfy individual needs for recognition and acknowledgment of personal worth. Every time a supervisor talks to an employee, it presents an opportunity to reward some aspect of the employee's importance and contribution to the work group. It is unfortunate that we too often fail to take advantage of these small opportunities to satisfy employee needs.

This is not to ignore or downplay financial rewards. Our economic system rides on the importance of monetary rewards for accomplishments and organizational success. This is deeply entrenched in our societal values and is an expected component of any contractual relationship: "If we're successful, we will all benefit from that success." This is part of the underlying logic for the early interest in profit sharing and, more recently, the gain-sharing or goal-sharing systems. In defining contracts between organizations, the negotiation of a mutually acceptable quid pro quo relationship is integral to contract agreement. Unfortunately, that logic is too often forgotten in dealing with employees.

Under our wage system, we are effectively buying an individual's time hour by hour, with the expectation of a minimal acceptable effort. An hourly wage system by itself does not buy commitment and certainly does not give an employer a reason to expect sustained, above-the-norm effort. Employers need to consider their performance standards and expectations in designing their reward systems. This needs to be covered when a psychological contract is defined. If high standards are not incorporated into the contract, higher standards can be introduced only by fear or by modifying the reward system to provide a quid pro quo for accepting the new work standards.

Reward systems can be disruptive and trigger counterproductive behavior (Kohn, 1993). That can happen just as easily at the management or professional level. People behave in the manner that they perceive to be in their best interest. For example, if we pay for the quantity produced (our traditional piece-rate system), it should not be surprising that there is little concern for quality or customer satisfaction. This does not mean that rewards are inherently a problem. Realistically, we cannot stop rewarding employees; that inevitably happens in one form or another. It means only that the system has to be redesigned to support organizational needs.

Rewards can also be used to lead an organizational change initiative. Too often, employees resist change because they continue to be rewarded for old work patterns. If we want them to change, their rewards must be realigned with new work patterns. For example, experience has shown that it is often difficult to make the transition to total quality management. TQM advocates contend that this will happen almost automatically when workers are empowered to control their work and have adequate organizational support. However, a large number of organizations have come to realize that it is not so simple. That realization has been one of the reasons why a growing number of organizations, including nonprofits such as hospitals, have elected to link cash rewards to such measures as indexes of customer or patient satisfaction.

For better or worse, our culture makes the question "What's in it for me?" a central consideration in designing work systems. We all want to believe that we will be rewarded for good performance and that we stand to benefit if we help our organization succeed. A simple hourly or weekly pay system along with a prevailing entitlement culture clearly fails to take advantage of the incentive potential of pay. There are many effective ways to reward employees (see Peters and Waterman, 1982), but it is probably safe to say that none can take the place of pay. If the rewards are not aligned with desired performance or commensurate with the level of effort and prospective benefits to the organization, the workforce may not be willing to accept and commit to management's plans. That will make it difficult for a change initiative to succeed.

Public Policy Considerations

The changing nature of work and of organizations has impact beyond the private sector. There has been much talk of "reinventing government," and much of that talk reflects actions being taken in private sector organizations. At the same time, government bodies can constrain or support the changes taking place in organizations today. Both legislation and regulation limit initiatives being taken to make work and the workplace more relevant to today's needs.

Labor relations law presents a stumbling block to realize the potential of worker participation. As described in Chapter Eighteen, the Electromation case and the attitudes of some labor advocates make much participation questionable from a legal perspective, unless it is done with the cooperation of a certified union representing the participating workers. Although the perception of participation as a union avoidance tactic could be a problem in some organizations, it seems clear that the whole area of employee relations legislation and regulation should be reexamined. It would be unfortunate if the legislation that was supposed to enhance worker rights to have an impact on the workplace acted to strangle developments providing greater worker voice than would have been imagined possible by scientific management experts or labor advocates a generation ago. Clearly, thought must be given to revising employee relations law to reflect new realities.

Compensation-related law is a second area that is proving troublesome to the development of the new workplace and the new work. The Fair Labor Standards Act, with its differentiation of exempt and nonexempt workers and its rigid definition of terms and conditions of work for nonexempt workers (such as the forty-hour workweek and overtime rates), protected workers of a generation ago from exploitation. It is more difficult to see how these laws relate to workers in the virtual organization. Does the employee who works out of a home office and literally chooses when to work and when to attend to other things have a forty-hour week? The law notes that employees are working even if the employer "allows, suffers or permits" them to be at the workplace, regardless of whether work is being done. When the home, the car, or the beach is the workplace, the employee may be argued to have a 168-hour week. When employees are members of an autonomous work group, how will we differentiate the exempt from the nonexempt? If all workers on a team have management authority, do they all become exempt? If management is by consensus, do they all become nonexempt? Again, the whole notion of the kinds of protection needed by workers and the way compensation programs should be regulated needs rethinking.

A third major area for rethinking is that of Fair Employment Practice law. Equal employment opportunity laws and regulations are based on the notion of job relevance. All human resource decisions must, under the terms of the legal uniform guidelines, be based on job-relevant criteria. Thus hiring decisions must be based on how potential employees measure up against job specifications generated by a job analysis. Job descriptions are the foundation of fair employment practice rulings. Yet organizations increasingly do not have job descriptions, at least not couched in terms that job analysts are used to seeing. If you ask a customer service team member what his or her duties are, the answer you are likely to get is, "Whatever it takes." This does not make for a traditional job description.

Trait measures have long been both unfashionable and legally risky. One organization uses criteria for hiring that include literacy, numeracy, interpersonal skills, and the ability to learn. Defending hiring decisions based on these criteria would not be pleasant for most organizations, and in fact, these criteria could serve as masks for discriminatory practices. Much thought should be given to how the rights of protected groups can continue to be safeguarded while allowing organizations to select employees who will add value and are capable of growing with the organization.

In these and other areas where federal, state, and local laws and regulations mediate the employment relationship, new initiatives are needed to determine how employee rights can continue to be protected within the context of new realities, new work designs, and new organizations.

References

Kohn, A. (1993). Why incentive plans cannot work. *Harvard Business Review*, *71*(5), 54–63.

Maslow, A. (1954). *Motivation and Personality*. New York: HarperCollins.

Peters, T. J., and Waterman, R. H. (1982). *In Search of Excellence*. New York: HarperCollins.

Thurow, L. C. (1992). *Head to Head: The Coming Economic Battle Among Japan, Europe, and America*. New York: Morrow.

Index